BRITISH MORALISTS

BRITISH MORALISTS

1650–1800

SELECTED AND EDITED
WITH COMPARATIVE NOTES AND
ANALYTICAL INDEX

BY

D. D. RAPHAEL

*Formerly Edward Caird Professor of
Political and Social Philosophy
in the University of Glasgow*

I

HOBBES–GAY

HACKETT PUBLISHING COMPANY, INC.
INDIANAPOLIS/CAMBRIDGE

Republication of this work was made possible
by the gracious support of Oxford University Press,
which first published it in 1969.

For further information, please contact
  Hackett Publishing Company, Inc.
  P.O. Box 44937
  Indianapolis, Indiana 46244-0937

Library of Congress Cataloging in Publication Data

British moralists, 1650–1800/selected and edited with comparative notes and an-
  alytic index by D. D. Raphael.
        p.   cm.
    Reprint. Originally published: Oxford: Clarendon Press, 1969.
    Includes bibliographical references and index.
    Contents: 1. Hobbes–Gay. 2. Hume–Bentham and index.
    ISBN 0-87220-118-X (v. 1: alk. paper),—ISBN 0-87220-119-8 (v. 2: alk.
    paper).—ISBN 0-87220-121-X (set: alk. paper).—ISBN 0-87220-116-3 (v.
    1: pbk.: alk. paper).—ISBN 0-87220-117-1 (v. 2: pbk. alk. paper).—ISBN
    0-87220-120-1 (set: pbk.: alk. paper).
      1. Ethics, Modern—17th century. 2. Ethics, Modern—18th century. 3.
    Ethics, British. I. Raphael, D. D. (David Daiches), 1916–   .
    BJ801.B75   1991
    170′.941′09032—dc20   90-85423
                                                                        CIP

PREFACE

SIR L. A. SELBY-BIGGE's *British Moralists*, first published by the Clarendon Press in 1897, is well known to many students of moral philosophy. The original edition has been out of print for a number of years, and the Delegates of the Press invited me to make a new selection. Readers may like to have a note of the main differences.

Selby-Bigge confined himself largely to writers of the eighteenth century (including Cudworth among them because his *Eternal and Immutable Morality* was published posthumously in 1731), but adding extracts from Hobbes and Locke 'for convenience of reference'. I felt that the new selection should start quite firmly with Hobbes, who gave the initial impetus to the lively controversies of the British Moralists. (The very title of the greatest work in British philosophy, Hume's *Treatise of Human Nature*, was suggested, I believe, by the use of the phrase in the body of Hobbes's brilliant little book, *Human Nature*.) Consequently the new selection is of British Moralists from 1650 to 1800.

The second major change was not made so readily. Selby-Bigge omitted Hume, presumably because he had already produced separate editions of Hume's *Treatise* and *Enquiries*. If I had followed a similar principle of excluding works now available in convenient modern editions, I should have had to leave out not only Hume but also Hobbes's *Leviathan*, Locke, Butler, Price, and Bentham. With these omissions the book would have lost its backbone as a representative selection of the thought of the period. On the other hand, I should have had a great deal more space for authors of lesser importance whose works cannot easily be consulted. It was hard to choose between the two alternatives, and I sought the advice of several scholars both in Britain and in the United States. All but one of them strongly supported my own inclination to include the writers I have named, with plenty of space for Hobbes, Butler, Hume, and Price, even though this meant reducing or omitting the contribution of others, given that the total size of the book had to be roughly the same as that of Selby-Bigge. The difficulty was of course increased by the overt extension of the period covered, and also by the clear need to add a substantial excerpt from Reid (unaccountably absent from Selby-Bigge). In consequence, some of Selby-Bigge's authors reappear only with the barest minimum of space, and three are omitted altogether. This is regrettable, but it seemed, both to my advisers and to myself, to be the lesser evil. In selecting authors, and in allotting space to them, I have been guided by the extent to which a thinker appears to us today to have been influential in the history of the subject. The writers represented here and not in Selby-Bigge are Cumberland, Hume, Hartley, and Reid; those included in Selby-Bigge and not in the new selection are John Clarke, John Brown, and Kames.

The third difference concerns the order in which the moralists are printed. Selby-Bigge placed writers of 'the sentimental school' in his first volume, and those of 'the intellectual school' (together with 'more or less independent critics') in the second. The dichotomy has only a limited application and is not necessarily more significant than two or three other possible methods of classification. It therefore seemed more sensible to use a straightforward chronological order, showing how the thought of the British Moralists developed and was modified by their criticism of each other. In fixing the chronological order I have (with one exception) taken as the determining date for each author the year of first publication of the earliest of his works reprinted here. The one exception is Cudworth, for whom I have used the probable date of completed composition instead of the much later date of posthumous publication.

Again with the exception of books first published posthumously, I have, wherever possible, reprinted from that edition of a work which was the last to appear during the author's lifetime or to have received his approval before his death. I have modernized spelling and have reduced the incidence of italics and initial capital letters, but (with a few exceptions) I have retained the original punctuation; this is mainly a matter of taste, and another editor might well have followed a different policy. Authors' footnotes are shown with the kind of indicators (asterisks, etc., or letters of the alphabet) used in the original texts; editor's footnotes are enclosed in square brackets and are indicated by numerals.

I have not followed Selby-Bigge's example of writing an introductory essay, since an editor's comments are liable to become outdated more quickly than the considerations which have guided his selection of excerpts, and I preferred to add the extra pages to those in which the British Moralists could speak for themselves. On the other hand I have not grudged the space for an analytical index even longer than Selby-Bigge's. In my experience of using his book over a period of thirty years, I have found his index invaluable. Both in the index and in the brief comparative notes, I have indicated a number of instances in which influence or direct criticism on particular points of interest seems quite clear. The bibliographical note does not pretend to be anything like complete.

I am of course enormously indebted to Selby-Bigge, especially for the form of the index and for a number of the names in the bibliographical note. I wish to record also my gratitude for assistance given personally by a number of people. Among the scholars on both sides of the Atlantic whom I consulted about the principle of selection, I would mention particularly the late Professor J. L. Austin, Professor W. K. Frankena, my colleague and friend Professor W. G. Maclagan, Professor Bernard Peach, and Sir David Ross. Mr. T. E. Kinsey, of the Department of Humanity at the University of Glasgow, checked my translation of Cumberland and suggested some revisions. Dr. W. von Leyden allowed me to reprint a part of his text and translation of Locke's *Essays on the Law of Nature*, and the late Professor J. Y. T. Greig allowed me to reprint two extracts from his edition of *The Letters of David Hume*. Most of the typing of my long and difficult manuscript was done, with meticulous care and a remarkable degree of accuracy, by the late Mrs. Chris McCulloch, who acted as my secretary from 1961 to January 1967, when she died of cancer, to the sorrow of all who knew her. The final parts of the book, including the analytical index, were typed with equal excellence by her successor, Miss Anne S. Hutton, who has the added advantage of acquaintance with the subject-matter of moral philosophy. I am further indebted to Miss Hutton, and also to Mr. R. S. Downie of the Department of Moral Philosophy at the University of Glasgow, for assistance in reading the proofs.

A final word of appreciation is due to two institutions. In 1959 the Leverhulme Trust awarded me a research grant to cover the expenses of visiting libraries and the costs of typing some of the early texts. I owe it to the University of Glasgow that there was no need for these facilities to be extended beyond one year, partly because I was then provided with the services of a secretary, and partly because so many of the texts in the original editions are to be found among the splendid resources of the Glasgow University Library. For this last benefit I am no doubt indebted to some of the British Moralists themselves, who occupied the Chair of Moral Philosophy in this University.

D. D. R.

Glasgow
1967

CONTENTS OF VOLUME I

§§

THOMAS HOBBES

1588–1679

I. HUMAN NATURE:
or the Fundamental Elements of Policy

[First printed, 1650. Second edition, corrected, 1651. Reprinted here from the second edition, with misprints corrected, spelling modified, and reduction of italics and initial capital letters]

II. LEVIATHAN:
or the Matter, Form, and Power of a Commonwealth, ecclesiastical and civil

[First printed, 1651. There are inferior reprints bearing the same date. Reprinted here from the original edition, with errors corrected, spelling modified, and reduction of italics and initial capital letters]

III. OF LIBERTY AND NECESSITY

[First printed, in an unauthorized edition, 1654. Corrected reprint (probably approved by Hobbes himself), 1654. Reprinted here from the corrected version of the first edition, with further correction of misprints and with reduction of italics and initial capital letters]

SUPPLEMENTARY EXTRACTS FROM

I. DE CIVE
(English title: Philosophical Rudiments concerning Government and Society)

[Privately printed, 1642. First public edition, 1647. English translation, 1651. Reprinted here from the first edition of the English version, 1651]

II. DE CORPORE POLITICO:
or the Elements of Law, moral and politic

[First printed, 1650. Reprinted here from the first edition, with misprints corrected]

THOMAS HOBBES

Human Nature

CHAP. I

1. The true and perspicuous explication of the elements of *laws* **1**
natural and *politic* (which is my present scope) dependeth upon the
knowledge of what is *human nature*, what is *body politic*, and what it
is we call a *law*; concerning which points, as the writings of men
from antiquity downwards have still increased, so also have the
doubts and controversies concerning the same: and seeing that true
knowledge begetteth not doubt nor controversy but knowledge, it
is manifest from the present controversies, that they which have
heretofore written thereof, have not well understood their own
subject.

★   ★   ★   ★

4. Man's *nature* is the sum of his natural faculties and powers,
as the faculties of nutrition, motion, generation, sense, reason,
etc. These powers we do unanimously call *natural*, and are contained in the definition of man, under these words, *animal* and
rational.

5. According to the two principal parts of man, I divide his
faculties into two sorts, faculties of the body, and faculties of the
mind.

6. Since the minute and distinct anatomy of the powers of the
body is nothing necessary to the present purpose, I will only sum
them up in these three heads, power nutritive, power motive, and
power generative.

7. Of the powers of the mind there be two sorts, cognitive,
imaginative, or conceptive—and motive; and first of cognitive.

★   ★   ★   ★

CHAP. VI

2   9. . . . And thus much of sense, imagination, discursion, ratiocination, and knowledge, which are the acts of our power *cognitive*, or *conceptive*. That power of the mind which we call *motive*, differeth from the power motive of the body: for the power motive of the body is that by which it moveth other bodies, and which we call *strength*; but the power motive of the mind, is that by which the mind giveth animal motion to that body wherein it existeth; the acts hereof are our affections and passions, of which I am to speak in general.

CHAP. VII

3   1. In the eighth section of the second chapter is showed, that conceptions and apparitions are nothing really, but motion in some internal substance of the head; which motion not stopping there, but proceeding to the heart, of necessity must there either help or hinder the motion which is called *vital*: when it helpeth, it is called *delight, contentment,* or *pleasure*, which is nothing really but motion about the heart, as conception is nothing but motion in the head; and the objects that cause it are called *pleasant* or *delightful*, or by some name equivalent. The Latins have *jucundum, a juvando,* from helping; and the same delight, with reference to the object, is called *love*: but when such motion weakeneth or hindereth the vital motion, then it is called *pain*; and in relation to that which causeth it, *hatred*, which the Latins express sometimes by *odium*, and sometimes by *taedium*.

2. This motion, in which consisteth pleasure or pain, is also a solicitation or provocation either to draw near to the thing that pleaseth, or to retire from the thing that displeaseth; and this solicitation is the endeavour or internal beginning of animal motion, which when the object delighteth, is called *appetite*; when it displeaseth, it is called *aversion*, in respect of the displeasure present; but in respect of the displeasure expected, *fear*. So that *pleasure, love,* and *appetite*, which is also called desire, are divers names, for divers considerations of the same thing.

4   3. Every man, for his own part, calleth that which pleaseth, and is delightful to himself, *good*; and that *evil* which displeaseth him:

insomuch that while every man differeth from other in constitution, they differ also from one another concerning the common distinction of good and evil. Nor is there any such thing as absolute goodness, considered without relation: for even the goodness which we apprehend in God Almighty, is his goodness to us. And as we call *good* and *evil* the things that please and displease; so call we *goodness* and *badness* the qualities or powers whereby they do it: and the signs of that goodness are called by the Latins in one word *pulchritudo*, and the signs of evil *turpitudo*; to which we have no words precisely answerable.

4. As all conceptions we have immediately by the sense, are, delight, or pain, or appetite, or fear; so are all the imaginations after sense. But as they are weaker imaginations, so are they also weaker pleasures, or weaker pain.

5. As appetite is the beginning of animal motions towards something that pleaseth us; so is the attaining thereof the *end* of that motion, which we also call the *scope*, and aim, and final cause of the same: and when we attain that end, the delight we have thereby is called the *fruition*: so that *bonum* and *finis* are different names, but for different considerations of the same thing.

6. And of ends, some of them are called *propinqui*, that is, near at hand; others *remoti*, far off: but when the ends that be nearer attaining, be compared with those that be further off, they are called not ends, but *means*, and the *way* to those. But for an *utmost* end, in which the ancient philosophers have placed *felicity*, and disputed much concerning the way thereto, there is no such thing in this world, nor way to it, more than to Utopia: for while we live, we have desires, and desire presupposeth a further end. Those things which please us, as the way or means to a further end, we call *profitable*; and the fruition of them, *use*; and those things that profit not, *vain*.

7. Seeing all delight is appetite; and presupposeth a further end, there can be no contentment but in proceeding; and therefore we are not to marvel, when we see, that as men attain to more riches, honour, or other power, so their appetite continually groweth more and more; and when they are come to the utmost degree of some kind of power, they pursue some other, as long as in any kind they think themselves behind any other: of those therefore that have attained to the highest degree of honour and riches, some have affected mastery in some art; as Nero in music and poetry,

Commodus in the art of a gladiator; and such as affect not some such thing, must find diversion and recreation of their thoughts in the contention either of play or business: and men justly complain of a great grief, that they know not what to do. *Felicity* therefore, by which we mean continual delight, consisteth not in *having* prospered, but in *prospering*.

8. There are few things in this world, but either have mixture of good and evil, or there is a chain of them so necessarily linked together, that the one cannot be taken without the other: as for example, the pleasures of sin, and the bitterness of punishment, are inseparable; as is also labour and honour, for the most part. Now when in the whole chain the greater part is good, the whole is called good; and when the evil over-weigheth, the whole is called evil.

9. There are two sorts of pleasure, whereof the one seemeth to affect the corporeal organ of the sense, and that I call *sensual*; the greatest part whereof, is that by which we are invited to give continuance to our species; and the next, by which a man is invited to meat, for the preservation of his individual person: the other sort of delight is not particular to any part of the body, and is called the delight of the mind, and is that which we call *joy*. Likewise of pains, some affect the body, and are therefore called the *pains* of the body; and some not, and those are called *grief*.

CHAP. IX

6   1. *Glory*, or internal gloriation or triumph of the mind, is the passion which proceedeth from the imagination or conception of our own power above the power of him that contendeth with us; the signs whereof, besides those in the countenance, and other gestures of the body which cannot be described, are, ostentation in words, and insolency in actions: and this passion, of them whom it displeaseth, is called *pride*; by them whom it pleaseth, it is termed a *just valuation* of himself. This imagination of our power or worth, may be from an assured and certain experience of our own actions; and then is that glory just, and well grounded, and begetteth an opinion of increasing the same by other actions to follow; in which consisteth the appetite which we call *aspiring*, or proceeding from one degree of power to another. The same passion may proceed not from any conscience of our own actions, but from fame and trust of others,

whereby one may think well of himself, and yet be deceived; and this is *false glory*, and the aspiring consequent thereto procureth ill success. Further, the fiction (which is also imagination) of actions done by ourselves, which never were done, is glorying; but because it begetteth no appetite nor endeavour to any further attempt, it is merely vain and unprofitable; as when a man imagineth himself to do the actions whereof he readeth in some romance, or to be like unto some other man whose acts he admireth: and this is called *vain glory*; and is exemplified in the fable, by the fly sitting on the axle-tree, and saying to himself, What a dust do I make rise! The expression of vain glory is that wish, which some of the School, mistaking for some appetite distinct from all the rest, have called *velleity*, making a new word, as they made a new passion which was not before. Signs of vain glory in the gesture, are, imitation of others, counterfeiting and usurping the signs of virtue they have not; affectation of fashions, captation of honour from their dreams, and other little stories of themselves, from their country, from their names, and from the like.

2. The passion contrary to glory, proceeding from apprehension of our own infirmity, is called *humility* by those by whom it is approved; by the rest, *dejection* and poorness: which conception may be well or ill grounded; if well, it produceth fear to attempt any thing rashly; if ill, it cows a man, that he neither dares speak publicly, nor expect good success in any action.

3. It happeneth sometimes, that he that hath a good opinion of himself, and upon good ground, may nevertheless, by reason of the frowardness which that passion begetteth, discover in himself some defect or infirmity, the remembrance whereof dejecteth him; and this passion is called *shame*; by which being cooled and checked in his forwardness, he is more wary for the time to come. This passion, as it is a sign of infirmity, which is dishonour; so also it is a sign of knowledge, which is honour. The sign of it is blushing, which appeareth less in men conscious of their own defect, because they less betray the infirmities they acknowledge.

4. *Courage*, in a large signification, is the absence of fear in the presence of any evil whatsoever: but in a strict and more common meaning, it is contempt of wounds and death, when they oppose a man in the way to his end.

5. *Anger* or sudden courage is nothing but the appetite or desire of

overcoming present opposition. It hath been defined commonly to be grief proceeding from an opinion of contempt; which is confuted by the often experience which we have of being moved to anger by things inanimate, and without sense, and consequently incapable of contemning us.

8   6. *Revengefulness* is that passion which ariseth from an expectation or imagination of making him that hath hurt us, find his own action hurtful to himself, and to acknowledge the same; and this is the height of revenge: for though it be not hard, by returning evil for evil, to make one's adversary displeased with his own fact; yet to make him acknowledge the same, is so difficult, that many a man had rather die than do it. Revenge aimeth not at the death, but at the captivity or subjection of an enemy; which was well expressed in the exclamation of Tiberius Caesar, concerning one, that, to frustrate his revenge, had killed himself in prison; *Hath he escaped me?* To kill, is the aim of them that hate, to rid themselves out of fear: revenge aimeth at triumph, which over the dead is not.

7. *Repentance* is the passion which proceedeth from opinion or knowledge that the action they have done is out of the way to the end they would attain: the effect whereof is, to pursue that way no longer, but, by the consideration of the end, to direct themselves into a better. The first motion therefore in this passion is grief; but the expectation or conception of returning again into the way, is joy; and consequently, the passion of repentance is compounded and alloyed of both: but the predominant is joy; else were the whole grief, which cannot be, forasmuch as he that proceedeth towards the end he conceiveth good, proceedeth with appetite; and appetite is joy, as hath been said, Chap. 7. Sect. 2.

9   8. *Hope* is expectation of good to come, as fear is the expectation of evil: but when there be causes, some that make us expect good, and some that make us expect evil, alternately working in our mind; if the causes that make us expect good, be greater than those that make us expect evil, the whole passion is hope; if contrarily, the whole is fear. Absolute privation of hope is *despair*; a degree whereof is *diffidence*.

9. *Trust* is a passion proceeding from the belief of him from whom we expect or hope for good, so free from doubt that upon the same we pursue no other way to attain the same good: as *distrust* or diffidence is doubt, that maketh him endeavour to provide himself by

other means. And that this is the meaning of the words trust and distrust, is manifest from this, that a man never provideth himself by a second way, but when he mistrusteth that the first will not hold.

10. *Pity* is imagination or fiction of future calamity to ourselves, **10** proceeding from the sense of another man's calamity. But when it lighteth on such as we think have not deserved the same, the compassion is greater, because then there appeareth more probability that the same may happen to us: for, the evil that happeneth to an innocent man, may happen to every man. But when we see a man suffer for great crimes, which we cannot easily think will fall upon ourselves, the pity is the less. And therefore men are apt to pity those whom they love: for, whom they love, they think worthy of good, and therefore not worthy of calamity. Thence it is also, that men pity the vices of some persons at the first sight only, out of love to their aspect. The contrary of pity is *hardness of heart*, proceeding either from slowness of imagination, or some extreme great opinion of their own exemption from the like calamity, or from hatred of all or most men.

11. *Indignation* is that grief which consisteth in the conception of good success happening to them whom they think unworthy thereof. Seeing therefore men think all those unworthy whom they hate, they think them not only unworthy of the good fortune they have, but also of their own virtues. And of all the passions of the mind, these two, indignation and pity, are most raised and increased by eloquence: for, the aggravation of the calamity, and extenuation of the fault, augmenteth pity; and the extenuation of the worth of the person, together with the magnifying of his success, which are the parts of an orator, are able to turn these two passions into fury.

12. *Emulation* is grief arising from seeing oneself exceeded or excelled by his concurrent, together with hope to equal or exceed him in time to come, by his own ability. But, *envy* is the same grief joined with pleasure conceived in the imagination of some ill fortune that may befall him.

13. There is a passion that hath no name; but the sign of it is that **11** distortion of the countenance which we call *laughter*, which is always joy: but what joy, what we think, and wherein we triumph when we laugh, is not hitherto declared by any. That it consisteth in wit, or, as they call it, in the jest, experience confuteth: for men laugh at mischances and indecencies, wherein there lieth no wit nor jest at all.

And forasmuch as the same thing is no more ridiculous when it groweth stale or usual, whatsoever it be that moveth laughter, it must be new and unexpected. Men laugh often (especially such as are greedy of applause from every thing they do well) at their own actions performed never so little beyond their own expectations; as also at their own jests: and in this case it is manifest, that the passion of laughter proceedeth from a sudden conception of some ability in himself that laugheth. Also men laugh at the infirmities of others, by comparison wherewith their own abilities are set off and illustrated. Also men laugh at jests, the wit whereof always consisteth in the elegant discovering and conveying to our minds some absurdity of another: and in this case also the passion of laughter proceedeth from the sudden imagination of our own odds and eminency: for what is else the recommending of ourselves to our own good opinion, by comparison with another man's infirmity or absurdity? For when a jest is broken upon ourselves, or friends of whose dishonour we participate, we never laugh thereat. I may therefore conclude, that the passion of laughter is nothing else but sudden glory arising from some sudden conception of some eminency in ourselves, by comparison with the infirmity of others, or with our own formerly: for men laugh at the follies of themselves past, when they come suddenly to remembrance, except they bring with them any present dishonour. It is no wonder therefore that men take heinously to be laughed at or derided, that is, triumphed over. Laughing without offence, must be at absurdities and infirmities abstracted from persons, and when all the company may laugh together: for, laughing to oneself putteth all the rest into jealousy, and examination of themselves. Besides, it is vainglory, and an argument of little worth, to think the infirmity of another, sufficient matter for his triumph.

14. The passion opposite hereunto, (whose signs are another distortion of the face with tears) called *weeping*, is the sudden falling out with ourselves, or sudden conception of defect; and therefore children weep often: for seeing they think that every thing ought to be given them which they desire, of necessity every repulse must be a check of their expectation, and puts them in mind of their too much weakness to make themselves masters of all they look for. For the same cause women are more apt to weep than men, as being not only more accustomed to have their wills, but also to measure their powers by the power and love of others that protect them. Men are apt

to weep that prosecute revenge, when the revenge is suddenly stopped or frustrated by the repentance of their adversary; and such are the tears of reconciliation. Also revengeful men are subject to this passion upon the beholding those men they pity, and suddenly remember they cannot help. Other weeping in men proceedeth for the most part from the same cause it proceedeth from in women and children.

15. The appetite which men call *lust*, and the fruition that apper- **12** taineth thereunto, is a sensual pleasure, but not only that; there is in it also a delight of the mind: for it consisteth of two appetites together, to please, and to be pleased; and the delight men take in delighting, is not sensual, but a pleasure or joy of the mind consisting in the imagination of the power they have so much to please. But the name *lust* is used where it is condemned; otherwise it is called by the general word *love*: for the passion is one and the same indefinite desire of different sex, as natural as hunger.

16. Of *love*, by which is understood the joy man taketh in the fruition of any present good, hath been already spoken of in the first Section, Chap. 7. under which is contained the love men bear to one another, or pleasure they take in one another's company, and by which men are said to be sociable by nature. But there is another kind of love, which the Greeks call ἔρως, and is that which we mean, when we say that a man is in love: forasmuch as this passion cannot be without diversity of sex, it cannot be denied but that it participateth of that indefinite love mentioned in the former section. But there is a great difference betwixt the desire of a man indefinite, and the same desire limited *ad hunc*; and this is that love which is the great theme of poets: but notwithstanding their praises, it must be defined by the word *need*: for it is a conception a man hath of his need of that one person desired. The cause of this passion is not always nor for the most part beauty, or other quality in the beloved, unless there be withal hope in the person that loveth: which may be gathered from this, that in great difference of persons, the greater have often fallen in love with the meaner; but not contrary. And from hence it is, that for the most part they have much better fortune in love, whose hopes are built upon something in their person, than those that trust to their expressions and service; and they that care less, than they that care more: which not perceiving, many men cast away their services, as one arrow after another, till, in the end, together with their hopes, they lose their wits.

13 17. There is yet another passion sometimes called *love*, but more properly *good will* or *charity*. There can be no greater argument to a man, of his own power, than to find himself able not only to accomplish his own desires, but also to assist other men in theirs: and this is that conception wherein consisteth charity. In which, first, is contained that natural affection of parents to their children, which the Greeks call στοργή, as also, that affection wherewith men seek to assist those that adhere unto them. But the affection wherewith men many times bestow their benefits on strangers, is not to be called charity, but either *contract*, whereby they seek to purchase friendship; or *fear*, which maketh them to purchase peace. The opinion of Plato concerning honourable love, delivered according to his custom in the person of Socrates, in the dialogue entitled *Convivium*, is this, that a man full and pregnant with wisdom and other virtues, naturally seeketh out some beautiful person, of age and capacity to conceive, in whom he may, without sensual respects, engender and produce the like. And this is the *Idea* of the then-noted love of Socrates wise and continent, to Alcibiades young and beautiful: in which love, is not sought the honour, but the issue of his knowledge; contrary to the common love, to which though issue sometimes follows, yet men seek not that, but to please, and to be pleased. It should be therefore this charity, or desire to assist and advance others. But why then should the wise seek the ignorant, or be more charitable to the beautiful than to others? There is something in it savouring of the use of that time: in which matter though Socrates be acknowledged for continent, yet the continent have the passion they contain, as much and more than they that satiate the appetite; which maketh me suspect this Platonic love for merely sensual; but with an honourable pretence for the old to haunt the company of the young and beautiful.

14 18. Forasmuch as all knowledge beginneth from experience, therefore also new experience is the beginning of new knowledge, and the increase of experience the beginning of the increase of knowledge. Whatsoever therefore happeneth new to a man, giveth him matter of hope of knowing somewhat that he knew not before. And this hope and expectation of future knowledge from any thing that happeneth new and strange, is that passion which we commonly call *admiration*; and the same considered as appetite, is called *curiosity*, which is appetite of knowledge. As in the discerning faculties, man leaveth all community with beasts at the faculty of imposing names; so also doth he surmount their nature at this passion of curiosity: for when a beast seeth any thing new and strange to him, he considereth it so far only as to discern whether it be likely to serve his turn or hurt him, and accordingly approacheth nearer to it, or fleeth from it: whereas man, who in most events remembereth in what manner they were caused and begun, looketh for the cause and beginning of every thing that ariseth new unto him. And from this passion of admiration and curiosity, have arisen not only the invention of names, but also supposition of such causes of all things as they thought might produce them. And from this beginning is derived all philosophy; as astronomy from the admiration of the course of heaven; natural philosophy from the strange effects of the elements and other bodies. And from the degrees of curiosity, proceed also the degrees of knowledge amongst men: for, to a man in the chase of riches or authority, (which in respect of knowledge are but sensuality) it is a diversity of little pleasure, whether it be the motion of the sun or the earth that maketh the day, or to enter into other contemplations of any strange accident, than whether it conduce or not to the end he pursueth. Because curiosity is delight, therefore also novelty is so, but especially that novelty from which a man conceiveth an opinion, true or false, of bettering his own estate: for, in such case, they stand affected with the hope that all gamesters have while the cards are shuffling.

19. Divers other passions there be, but they want names: whereof 15 some nevertheless have been by most men observed: for example; from what passion proceedeth it, that men take pleasure to behold from the shore the danger of them that are at sea in a tempest, or in fight, or from a safe castle to behold two armies charge one another in the field? It is certainly, in the whole sum, joy; else men would never flock to such a spectacle. Nevertheless there is in it both joy and grief: for as there is novelty and remembrance of our own security present, which is delight: so there is also pity, which is grief: but the delight is so far predominant, that men usually are content in such a case to be spectators of the misery of their friends.

20. *Magnanimity* is no more than glory, of the which I have spoken in the first section; but glory well grounded upon certain experience of a power sufficient to attain his end in open manner. And *pusillanimity* is the doubt of that. Whatsoever therefore is a sign of vain glory, the same is also a sign of pusillanimity: for sufficient power

maketh glory a spur to one's end. To be pleased or displeased with fame true or false, is a sign of that same, because he that relieth on fame, hath not his success in his own power. Likewise art and fallacy are signs of pusillanimity, because they depend not upon our own power, but the ignorance of others. Also proneness to anger, because it argueth difficulty of proceeding. Also ostentation of ancestors, because all men are more inclined to make show of their own power when they have it, than of another's. To be at enmity and contention with inferiors, is a sign of the same, because it proceedeth from want of power to end the war. To laugh at others, because it is an affectation of glory from other men's infirmities, and not from any ability of their own. Also irresolution, which proceedeth from want of power enough to contemn the little difficulties that make deliberations hard.

16   21. The comparison of the life of man to a race, though it hold not in every part, yet it holdeth so well for this our purpose, that we may thereby both see and remember almost all the passions before mentioned. But this race we must suppose to have no other goal, nor other garland, but being foremost; and in it:

To endeavour, is *appetite*.

To be remiss, is *sensuality*.

To consider them behind, is *glory*.

To consider them before, is *humility*.

To lose ground with looking back, *vain glory*.

To be holden, *hatred*.

To turn back, *repentance*.

To be in breath, *hope*.

To be weary, *despair*.

To endeavour to overtake the next, *emulation*.

To supplant or overthrow, *envy*.

To resolve to break through a stop foreseen, *courage*.

To break through a sudden stop, *anger*.

To break through with ease, *magnanimity*.

To lose ground by little hindrances, *pusillanimity*.

To fall on the sudden, is disposition to *weep*.

To see another fall, is disposition to *laugh*.

To see one out-gone whom we would not, is *pity*.

To see one out-go whom we would not, is *indignation*.

To hold fast by another, is to *love*.

To carry him on that so holdeth, is *charity*.
To hurt oneself for haste, is *shame*.
Continually to be out-gone, is *misery*.
Continually to out-go the next before, is *felicity*.
And to forsake the course, is to *die*.

CHAP. XII

1. It hath been declared already, how external objects cause **17**
conceptions, and conceptions appetite and fear, which are the first
unperceived beginnings of our actions: for either the actions immediately follow the first appetite, as when we do any thing upon a
sudden; or else to our first appetite there succeedeth some conception
of evil to happen to us by such actions, which is fear, and which
holdeth us from proceeding. And to that fear may succeed a new
appetite, and to that appetite another fear alternately, till the action
be either done, or some accident come between to make it impossible; and so this alternate appetite and fear ceaseth. This alternate
succession of appetite and fear during all the time the action is in our
power to do or not to do, is that we call *deliberation*; which name hath
been given it for that part of the definition wherein it is said that it
lasteth so long as the action whereof we deliberate is in our power:
for, so long we have liberty to do or not to do; and deliberation
signifieth a taking away of our own liberty.

2. Deliberation therefore requireth in the action deliberated two
conditions; one, that it be future; the other, that there be hope of
doing it, or possibility of not doing it: for, appetite and fear are
expectations of the future; and there is no expectation of good, without hope; or of evil, without possibility: of necessaries therefore
there is no deliberation. In deliberation, the last appetite, as also the
last fear, is called *will*; viz. the last appetite, will to do; the last fear,
will not to do, or will to omit. It is all one therefore to say *will*, and
last will: for, though a man express his present inclination and appetite concerning the disposing of his goods, by word or writing, yet
shall it not be accounted his will, because he hath still liberty to
dispose of them other ways: but when death taketh away that
liberty, then it is his will.

3. *Voluntary* actions and omissions are such as have beginning in **18**
the will; all other are *involuntary* or *mixed*: *voluntary*, such as a man

doth upon appetite or fear; *involuntary*, such as he doth by necessity of nature, as when he is pushed, or falleth, and thereby doth good or hurt to another: *mixed*, such as participate of both; as, when a man is carried to prison, ⟨he is pulled on against his will, and yet goeth upright voluntary, for fear of being trailed along the ground; insomuch that in going to prison,⟩[1] going is voluntary, to the prison is involuntary: the example of him that throweth his goods out of a ship into the sea, to save his person, is of an action altogether voluntary; for, there is nothing therein involuntary, but the hardness of the choice, which is not his action, but the action of the winds; what he himself doth, is no more against his will, than to flee from danger is against the will of him that seeth no other means to preserve himself.

4. Voluntary also are the actions that proceed from sudden anger, or other sudden appetite, in such men as can discern good or evil: for, in them the time precedent is to be judged deliberation; for then also he deliberateth in what cases it is good to strike, deride, or do any other action proceeding from anger or other such sudden passion.

5. Appetite, fear, hope, and the rest of the passions are not called voluntary; for they proceed *not from, but are the will*, and the will is not voluntary: for, a man can no more say he will will, than he will will will, and so make an infinite repetition of the word *will*; which is absurd, and insignificant.

6. Forasmuch as will to do is appetite, and will to omit, fear; the cause of appetite and fear is the cause also of our will: but the propounding of the benefits and of harms, that is to say, of reward and punishment, is the cause of our appetite, and of our fears, and therefore also of our wills, so far forth as we believe that such rewards and benefits as are propounded, shall arrive unto us; and consequently, our wills follow our opinions, as our actions follow our wills; in which sense they say truly and properly, that say the world is governed by opinion.

19   7. When the wills of many concur to one and the same action and effect, this concourse of their wills is called *consent*; by which we must not understand one will of many men (for every man hath his

---

[1 The passage in angle brackets, essential to the sense, is omitted, presumably in error, from the original editions. It is added here from the version edited by F. Tönnies from the manuscripts and entitled *The Elements of Law* (1889).]

several will) but many wills to the producing of one effect: but when the wills of two divers men produce such actions as are reciprocally resistant one to the other, this is called *contention*; and, being upon the persons one of another, *battle*: whereas actions proceeding from consent, are mutual *aid*.

8. When many wills are involved or included in the will of one or more consenting, (which how it may be, shall be hereafter declared) then is that involving of many wills in one or more, called *union*.

9. In deliberations interrupted, as they may be by diversion of other business, or by sleep, the last appetite of such part of the deliberation is called *intention*, or *purpose*.

CHAP. XIII

★   ★   ★   ★

5. The expression of those conceptions which cause in us the **20** expectation of good while we deliberate, as also of those which cause our expectation of evil, is that which we call *counselling*, and is the internal deliberation of the mind concerning what we ourselves are to do, or not to do. The consequences of our actions are our counsellors, by alternate succession in the mind. So in the counsel which a man taketh from other men, the counsellors alternately do make appear the consequences of the action, and do not any of them deliberate, but furnish, among them all, him that is counselled, with arguments whereupon to deliberate with himself.

6. Another use of speech is expression of appetite, intention, and will; as the appetite of knowledge by *interrogation*; appetite to have a thing done by another, as request, *prayer*, petition: expressions of our purpose or intention, as *promise*, which is the affirmation or negation of some action to be done in the future: *threatening*, which is the promise of evil; and *commanding*, which is that speech by which we signify to another our appetite or desire to have any thing done, or left undone, for reasons contained in the will itself: for it is not properly said, *Sic volo, sic jubeo*, without that other clause, *Stet pro ratione voluntas*: and when the command is a sufficient reason to move us to action, then is that command called a *law*.

★   ★   ★   ★

Leviathan

21 Nature (the art whereby God hath made and governs the world) is by the *art* of man, as in many other things, so in this also imitated, that it can make an artificial animal. For seeing life is but a motion of limbs, the beginning whereof is in some principal part within; why may we not say, that all *automata* (engines that move themselves by springs and wheels as doth a watch) have an artificial life? For what is the heart, but a spring; and the nerves, but so many strings; and the joints, but so many wheels, giving motion to the whole body, such as was intended by the artificer? *Art* goes yet further, imitating that rational and most excellent work of nature, *man*. For by art is created that great LEVIATHAN called a COMMONWEALTH, or STATE, (in Latin CIVITAS) which is but an artificial man; though of greater stature and strength than the natural, for whose protection and defence it was intended; and in which, the sovereignty is an artificial soul, as giving life and motion to the whole body; the magistrates, and other officers of judicature and execution, artificial joints; reward and punishment (by which fastened to the seat of the sovereignty, every joint and member is moved to perform his duty) are the nerves, that do the same in the body natural; the wealth and riches of all the particular members, are the strength; *salus populi* (the people's safety) its business; counsellors, by whom all things needful for it to know, are suggested unto it, are the memory; equity and laws, an artificial reason and will; concord, health; sedition, sickness; and civil war, death. Lastly, the pacts and covenants, by which the parts of this body politic were at first made, set together, and united, resemble that *fiat*, or the *Let us make man*, pronounced by God in the creation.

To describe the nature of this artificial man, I will consider

First, the *matter* thereof, and the *artificer*; both which is *man*.

Secondly, *how* and by what *covenants* it is made; what are the *rights* and just *power* or *authority* of a sovereign; and what it is that *preserveth* and *dissolveth* it.

Thirdly, what is a *Christian commonwealth*.
Lastly, what is the *kingdom of darkness*.

Concerning the first, there is a saying much usurped of late, that **22**
wisdom is acquired, not by reading of books, but of men. Consequently whereunto, those persons, that for the most part can give no
other proof of being wise, take great delight to show what they
think they have read in men, by uncharitable censures of one another
behind their backs. But there is another saying not of late understood, by which they might learn truly to read one another, if they
would take the pains; and that is, *Nosce teipsum*, *Read thyself*: which
was not meant, as it is now used, to countenance, either the bar-
barous state of men in power, towards their inferiors; or to encourage men of low degree, to a saucy behaviour towards their betters;
but to teach us, that for the similitude of the thoughts, and passions
of one man, to the thoughts and passions of another, whosoever
looketh into himself, and considereth what he doth, when he does
think, opine, reason, hope, fear, etc, and upon what grounds; he
shall thereby read and know, what are the thoughts, and passions of
all other men, upon the like occasions. I say the similitude of *passions*,
which are the same in all men, desire, fear, hope, etc; not the similitude of the *objects* of the passions, which are the things desired, feared,
hoped, etc: for these the constitution individual, and particular
education do so vary, and they are so easy to be kept from our
knowledge, that the characters of man's heart, blotted and confounded as they are, with dissembling, lying, counterfeiting, and
erroneous doctrines, are legible only to him that searcheth hearts.
And though by men's actions we do discover their design sometimes; yet to do it without comparing them with our own, and
distinguishing all circumstances, by which the case may come to
be altered, is to decipher without a key, and be for the most part
deceived, by too much trust, or by too much diffidence; as he that
reads, is himself a good or evil man.

But let one man read another by his actions never so perfectly, it
serves him only with his acquaintance, which are but few. He that is
to govern a whole nation, must read in himself, not this, or that
particular man; but mankind: which though it be hard to do, harder
than to learn any language, or science; yet, when I shall have set
down my own reading orderly, and perspicuously, the pains left

another, will be only to consider, if he also find not the same in himself. For this kind of doctrine, admitteth no other demonstration.

PART I—OF MAN

CHAP. VI—OF THE INTERIOR BEGINNINGS OF VOLUNTARY MOTIONS; COMMONLY CALLED THE PASSIONS. AND THE SPEECHES BY WHICH THEY ARE EXPRESSED[1]

23   There be in animals, two sorts of *motions* peculiar to them: one called *vital*; begun in generation, and continued without interruption through their whole life; such as are the course of the blood, the pulse, the breathing, the concoction, nutrition, excretion, etc; to which motions there needs no help of imagination: the other is *animal motion*, otherwise called *voluntary motion*; as to go, to speak, to move any of our limbs, in such manner as is first fancied in our minds. That sense, is motion in the organs and interior parts of man's body, caused by the action of the things we see, hear, etc; and that fancy is but the relics of the same motion, remaining after sense, has been already said in the first and second chapters. And because going, speaking, and the like voluntary motions, depend always upon a precedent thought of whither, which way, and what; it is evident, that the imagination is the first internal beginning of all voluntary motion. And although unstudied men, do not conceive any motion at all to be there, where the thing moved is invisible; or the space it is moved in, is (for the shortness of it) insensible; yet that doth not hinder, but that such motions are. For let a space be never so little, that which is moved over a greater space, whereof that little one is part, must first be moved over that. These small beginnings of motion, within the body of man, before they appear in walking, speaking, striking, and other visible actions, are commonly called ENDEAVOUR.

24   This endeavour, when it is toward something which causes it, is called APPETITE, or DESIRE; the latter, being the general name; and the other, often-times restrained to signify the desire of food, namely hunger and thirst. And when the endeavour is fromward something, is is generally called AVERSION. These words, *appetite*, and *aversion*,

[1 Cf. §§ 3–18.]

we have from the Latins; and they both of them signify the motions, one of approaching, the other of retiring. So also do the Greek words for the same, which are ὁρμή, and ἀφορμή. For nature itself does often press upon men those truths, which afterwards, when they look for somewhat beyond nature, they stumble at. For the Schools find in mere appetite to go, or move, no actual motion at all: but because some motion they must acknowledge, they call it metaphorical motion; which is but an absurd speech: for though words may be called metaphorical; bodies and motions cannot.

That which men desire, they are also said to LOVE: and to HATE those things, for which they have aversion. So that desire, and love, are the same thing; save that by desire, we always signify the absence of the object; by love, most commonly the presence of the same. So also by aversion, we signify the absence; and by hate, the presence of the object.

Of appetites, and aversions, some are born with men; as appetite of food, appetite of excretion, and exoneration, (which may also and more properly be called aversions, from somewhat they feel in their bodies;) and some other appetites, not many. The rest, which are appetites of particular things, proceed from experience, and trial of their effects upon themselves, or other men. For of things we know not at all, or believe not to be, we can have no further desire, than to taste and try. But aversion we have for things, not only which we know have hurt us, but also that we do not know whether they will hurt us, or not.

Those things which we neither desire, nor hate, we are said to *contemn*: CONTEMPT being nothing else but an immobility, or contumacy of the heart, in resisting the action of certain things; and proceeding from that the heart is already moved otherwise, by other more potent objects; or from want of experience of them.

And because the constitution of a man's body, is in continual mutation; it is impossible that all the same things should always cause in him the same appetites, and aversions: much less can all men consent, in the desire of almost any one and the same object.

But whatsoever is the object of any man's appetite or desire; that 25 is it which he for his part calleth *good*: and the object of his hate, and aversion, *evil*; and of his contempt, *vile* and *inconsiderable*. For these words of good, evil, and contemptible, are ever used with relation to the person that useth them: there being nothing simply and absolutely so; nor any common rule of good and evil, to be taken from the nature of the objects themselves; but from the person of the man (where there is no commonwealth;) or, (in a commonwealth,) from the person that representeth it; or from an arbitrator or judge, whom men disagreeing shall by consent set up, and make his sentence the rule thereof.

The Latin tongue has two words, whose significations approach to those of good and evil; but are not precisely the same; and those are *pulchrum* and *turpe*. Whereof the former signifies that, which by some apparent signs promiseth good; and the latter, that, which promiseth evil. But in our tongue we have not so general names to express them by. But for *pulchrum*, we say in some things, *fair*; in others, *beautiful*, or *handsome*, or *gallant*, or *honourable*, or *comely*, or *amiable*; and for *turpe*, *foul*, *deformed*, *ugly*, *base*, *nauseous*, and the like, as the subject shall require; all which words, in their proper places, signify nothing else, but the mien, or countenance, that promiseth good and evil. So that of good there be three kinds; good in the promise, that is *pulchrum*; good in effect, as the end desired, which is called *jucundum*, *delightful*; and good as the means, which is called *utile*, *profitable*; and as many of evil: for evil in promise, is that they call *turpe*; evil in effect, and end, is *molestum*, *unpleasant*, *troublesome*; and evil in the means, *inutile*, *unprofitable*, *hurtful*.

26   As, in sense, that which is really within us, is (as I have said before) only motion, caused by the action of external objects, but in appearance; to the sight, light and colour; to the ear, sound; to the nostril, odour, etc: so, when the action of the same object is continued from the eyes, ears, and other organs to the heart; the real effect there is nothing but motion, or endeavour; which consisteth in appetite, or aversion, to, or from the object moving. But the appearance, or sense of that motion, is that we either call DELIGHT, or TROUBLE OF MIND.

This motion, which is called appetite, and for the appearance of it *delight*, and *pleasure*, seemeth to be, a corroboration of vital motion, and a help thereunto; and therefore such things as caused delight, were not improperly called *jucunda* (*a juvando*,) from helping or fortifying; and the contrary, *molesta*, *offensive*, from hindering, and troubling the motion vital.

Pleasure therefore, (or *delight*,) is the appearance, or sense of good; and *molestation* or *displeasure*, the appearance, or sense of evil. And consequently all appetite, desire, and love, is accompanied with some delight more or less; and all hatred, and aversion, with more or less displeasure and offence.

Of pleasures, or delights, some arise from the sense of an object present; and those may be called *pleasures of sense*, (the word *sensual*, as it is used by those only that condemn them, having no place till there be laws.) Of this kind are all onerations and exonerations of the body; as also all that is pleasant, in the sight, hearing, smell, taste, or touch; others arise from the expectation, that proceeds from foresight of the end, or consequence of things; whether those things in the sense please or displease: and these are *pleasures of the mind* of him that draweth those consequences; and are generally called JOY. In the like manner, displeasures, are some in the sense, and called PAIN; others, in the expectation of consequences, and are called GRIEF.

These simple passions called *appetite, desire, love, aversion, hate, joy,* **27** and *grief,* have their names for divers considerations diversified. As first, when they one succeed another, they are diversely called from the opinion men have of the likelihood of attaining what they desire. Secondly, from the object loved or hated. Thirdly, from the consideration of many of them together. Fourthly, from the alteration or succession itself.

For *appetite*, with an opinion of attaining, is called HOPE. **28**

The same, without such opinion, DESPAIR.

Aversion, with opinion of *hurt* from the object, FEAR.

The same, with hope of avoiding that hurt by resistance, COURAGE.

Sudden *courage*, ANGER.

Constant *hope*, CONFIDENCE of ourselves.

Constant *despair*, DIFFIDENCE of ourselves.

Anger for great hurt done to another, when we conceive the same **29** to be done by injury, INDIGNATION.

Desire of good to another, BENEVOLENCE, GOOD WILL, CHARITY. If to man generally, GOOD NATURE.

Desire of riches, COVETOUSNESS: a name used always in signification of blame; because men contending for them, are displeased with one another's attaining them; though the desire in itself, be to be blamed, or allowed, according to the means by which those riches are sought.

Desire of office, or precedence, AMBITION: a name used also in the worse sense, for the reason before mentioned.

Desire of things that conduce but a little to our ends; and fear of things that are but of little hindrance, PUSILLANIMITY.

Contempt of little helps, and hindrances, MAGNANIMITY.

Magnanimity, in danger of death, or wounds, VALOUR, FORTITUDE.

Magnanimity, in the use of riches, LIBERALITY.

Pusillanimity, in the same, WRETCHEDNESS, MISERABLENESS; or PARSIMONY; as it is liked, or disliked.

Love of persons for society, KINDNESS.

Love of persons for pleasing the sense only, NATURAL LUST.

Love of the same, acquired from rumination, that is, imagination of pleasure past, LUXURY.

Love of one singularly, with desire to be singularly beloved, THE PASSION OF LOVE. The same, with fear that the love is not mutual, JEALOUSY.

Desire, by doing hurt to another, to make him condemn some fact of his own, REVENGEFULNESS.

30   *Desire*, to know why, and how, CURIOSITY; such as is in no living creature but man: so that man is distinguished, not only by his reason, but also by this singular passion from other animals; in whom the appetite of food, and other pleasures of sense, by predominance, take away the care of knowing causes; which is a lust of the mind, that by a perseverance of delight in the continual and indefatigable generation of knowledge, exceedeth the short vehemence of any carnal pleasure.

Fear of power invisible, feigned by the mind, or imagined from tales publicly allowed, RELIGION; not allowed, SUPERSTITION. And when the power imagined, is truly such as we imagine, TRUE RELIGION.

Fear, without the apprehension of why, or what, PANIC TERROR; called so from the fables, that make Pan the author of them; whereas in truth, there is always in him that so feareth, first, some apprehension of the cause, though the rest run away by example; every one supposing his fellow to know why. And therefore this passion happens to none but in a throng, or multitude of people.

Joy, from apprehension of novelty, ADMIRATION; proper to man, because it excites the appetite of knowing the cause.

31   *Joy*, arising from the imagination of a man's own power and ability, is that exultation of the mind which is called GLORYING: which if grounded upon the experience of his own former actions,

is the same with *confidence*: but if grounded on the flattery of others; or only supposed by himself, for delight in the consequences of it, is called VAIN-GLORY: which name is properly given; because a well grounded *confidence* begetteth attempt; whereas the supposing of power does not, and is therefore rightly called *vain*.

Grief, from opinion of want of power, is called DEJECTION of mind.

The *vain-glory* which consisteth in the feigning or supposing of abilities in ourselves, which we know are not, is most incident to young men, and nourished by the histories, or fictions of gallant persons; and is corrected oftentimes by age, and employment.

Sudden glory, is the passion which maketh those *grimaces* called LAUGHTER; and is caused either by some sudden act of their own, that pleaseth them; or by the apprehension of some deformed thing in another, by comparison whereof they suddenly applaud themselves. And it is incident most to them, that are conscious of the fewest abilities in themselves; who are forced to keep themselves in their own favour, by observing the imperfections of other men. And therefore much laughter at the defects of others, is a sign of pusillanimity. For of great minds, one of the proper works is, to help and free others from scorn; and compare themselves only with the most able.

On the contrary, *sudden dejection*, is the passion that causeth WEEPING; and is caused by such accidents, as suddenly take away some vehement hope, or some prop of their power: and they are most subject to it, that rely principally on helps external, such as are women, and children. Therefore some weep for the loss of friends; others for their unkindness; others for the sudden stop made to their thoughts of revenge, by reconciliation. But in all cases, both laughter, and weeping, are sudden motions; custom taking them both away. For no man laughs at old jests; or weeps for an old calamity.

Grief, for the discovery of some defect of ability, is SHAME, or the passion that discovereth itself in BLUSHING; and consisteth in the apprehension of some thing dishonourable; and in young men, is a sign of the love of good reputation, and commendable: in old men it is a sign of the same; but because it comes too late, not commendable.

The *contempt* of good reputation is called IMPUDENCE.

Grief, for the calamity of another, is PITY; and ariseth from the **32** imagination that the like calamity may befall himself; and therefore is called also COMPASSION, and in the phrase of this present time a

FELLOW-FEELING: and therefore for calamity arriving from great wickedness, the best men have the least pity; and for the same calamity, those have least pity, that think themselves least obnoxious to the same.

Contempt, or little sense of the calamity of others, is that which men call CRUELTY; proceeding from security of their own fortune. For, that any man should take pleasure in other men's great harms, without other end of his own, I do not conceive it possible.

Grief, for the success of a competitor in wealth, honour, or other good, if it be joined with endeavour to enforce our own abilities to equal or exceed him, is called EMULATION: but joined with endeavour to supplant, or hinder a competitor, ENVY.

33 When in the mind of man, appetites, and aversions, hopes, and fears, concerning one and the same thing, arise alternately; and divers good and evil consequences of the doing, or omitting the thing propounded, come successively into our thoughts; so that sometimes we have an appetite to it; sometimes an aversion from it; sometimes hope to be able to do it; sometimes despair, or fear to attempt it; the whole sum of desires, aversions, hopes and fears, continued till the thing be either done, or thought impossible, is that we call DELIBERATION.

Therefore of things past, there is no deliberation; because manifestly impossible to be changed: nor of things known to be impossible, or thought so; because men know, or think such deliberation vain. But of things impossible, which we think possible, we may deliberate; not knowing it is in vain. And it is called *deliberation*; because it is a putting an end to the *liberty* we had of doing, or omitting, according to our own appetite, or aversion.

This alternate succession of appetites, aversions, hopes and fears, is no less in other living creatures than in man: and therefore beasts also deliberate.

Every deliberation is then said to *end*, when that whereof they deliberate, is either done, or thought impossible; because till then we retain the liberty of doing, or omitting; according to our appetite, or aversion.

In deliberation, the last appetite, or aversion, immediately adhering to the action, or to the omission thereof, is that we call the WILL; the act, (not the faculty,) of *willing*. And beasts that have deliberation, must necessarily also have will. The definition of the will, given commonly by the Schools, that it is a *rational appetite*, is not good. For if it were, then could there be no voluntary act against reason. For a *voluntary act* is that, which proceedeth from the *will*, and no other. But if instead of a rational appetite, we shall say an appetite resulting from a precedent deliberation, then the definition is the same that I have given here. *Will* therefore *is the last appetite in deliberating*. And though we say in common discourse, a man had a will once to do a thing, that nevertheless he forbore to do; yet that is properly but an inclination, which makes no action voluntary; because the action depends not of it, but of the last inclination, or appetite. For if the intervenient appetites, make any action voluntary; then by the same reason all intervenient aversions, should make the same action involuntary; and so one and the same action, should be both voluntary and involuntary.

By this it is manifest, that not only actions that have their beginning from covetousness, ambition, lust, or other appetites to the thing propounded; but also those that have their beginning from aversion, or fear of those consequences that follow the omission, are *voluntary actions*.

The forms of speech by which the passions are expressed, are **35** partly the same, and partly different from those, by which we express our thoughts. And first generally all passions may be expressed *indicatively*; as *I love, I fear, I joy, I deliberate, I will, I command*: but some of them have particular expressions by themselves, which nevertheless are not affirmations, unless it be when they serve to make other inferences, besides that of the passion they proceed from. Deliberation is expressed *subjunctively*; which is a speech proper to signify suppositions, with their consequences; as, *If this be done, then this will follow*; and differs not from the language of reasoning, save that reasoning is in general words; but deliberation for the most part is of particulars. The language of desire, and aversion, is *imperative*; as *Do this, forbear that*; which when the party is obliged to do, or forbear, is *command*; otherwise *prayer*; or else *counsel*. The language of vain-glory, of indignation, pity and revengefulness, *optative*: but of the desire to know, there is a peculiar expression, called *interrogative*; as, *What is it, when shall it, how is it done*, and *why so?* other language of the passions I find none: for cursing, swearing, reviling, and the like, do not signify as speech; but as the actions of a tongue accustomed.

These forms of speech, I say, are expressions, or voluntary significations of our passions: but certain signs they be not; because they
may be used arbitrarily, whether they that use them, have such
passions or not. The best signs of passions present, are either in the
countenance, motions of the body, actions, and ends, or aims,
which we otherwise know the man to have.

36 And because in deliberation, the appetites, and aversions are raised
by foresight of the good and evil consequences, and sequels of the
action whereof we deliberate; the good or evil effect thereof dependeth on the foresight of a long chain of consequences, of which
very seldom any man is able to see to the end. But for so far as a man
seeth, if the good in those consequences, be greater than the evil, the
whole chain is that which writers call *apparent*, or *seeming good*. And
contrarily, when the evil exceedeth the good, the whole is *apparent*,
or *seeming evil*: so that he who hath by experience, or reason, the
greatest and surest prospect of consequences, deliberates best himself; and is able when he will, to give the best counsel unto others.

37 *Continual success* in obtaining those things which a man from time
to time desireth, that is to say, continual prospering, is that men call
FELICITY; I mean the felicity of this life. For there is no such thing as
perpetual tranquillity of mind, while we live here; because life itself
is but motion, and can never be without desire, nor without fear, no
more than without sense. What kind of felicity God hath ordained
to them that devoutly honour him, a man shall no sooner know,
than enjoy; being joys, that now are as incomprehensible, as the
word of Schoolmen *beatifical vision* is unintelligible.

The form of speech whereby men signify their opinion of the
goodness of any thing, is PRAISE. That whereby they signify the
power and greatness of any thing, is MAGNIFYING. And that whereby
they signify the opinion they have of a man's felicity, is by the
Greeks called μακαρισμός, for which we have no name in our tongue.
And thus much is sufficient for the present purpose, to have been
said of the PASSIONS.

CHAP. X—OF POWER, WORTH, DIGNITY, HONOUR, AND WORTHINESS

38 The POWER of a man, (to take it universally,) is his present means, to
obtain some future apparent good; and is either *original*, or *instrumental*.

Natural power, is the eminence of the faculties of body, or mind: as extraordinary strength, form, prudence, arts, eloquence, liberality, nobility. *Instrumental* are those powers, which acquired by these, or by fortune, are means and instruments to acquire more: as riches, reputation, friends, and the secret working of God, which men call good luck. For the nature of power, is in this point, like to fame, increasing as it proceeds; or like the motion of heavy bodies, which the further they go, make still the more haste.

The greatest of human powers, is that which is compounded of **39** the powers of most men, united by consent, in one person, natural, or civil, that has the use of all their powers depending on his will; such as is the power of a commonwealth: or depending on the wills of each particular; such as is the power of a faction, or of divers factions leagued. Therefore to have servants, is power; to have friends, is power: for they are strengths united.

Also riches joined with liberality, is power; because it procureth friends, and servants: without liberality, not so; because in this case they defend not; but expose men to envy, as a prey.

Reputation of power, is power; because it draweth with it the adherence of those that need protection.

So is reputation of love of a man's country, (called popularity,) for the same reason.

Also, what quality soever maketh a man beloved, or feared of many; or the reputation of such quality, is power; because it is a means to have the assistance, and service of many.

Good success is power; because it maketh reputation of wisdom, or good fortune; which makes men either fear him, or rely on him.

Affability of men already in power, is increase of power; because it gaineth love.

Reputation of prudence in the conduct of peace or war, is power; because to prudent men, we commit the government of ourselves, more willingly than to others.

Nobility is power, not in all places, but only in those commonwealths, where it has privileges: for in such privileges consisteth their power.

Eloquence is power; because it is seeming prudence.

Form is power; because being a promise of good, it recommendeth men to the favour of women and strangers.

The sciences, are small power; because not eminent; and therefore, not acknowledged in any man; nor are at all, but in a few; and in them, but of a few things. For science is of that nature, as none can understand it to be, but such as in a good measure have attained it.

Arts of public use, as fortification, making of engines, and other instruments of war; because they confer to defence, and victory, are power: and though the true mother of them, be science, namely the mathematics; yet, because they are brought into the light, by the hand of the artificer, they be esteemed (the midwife passing with the vulgar for the mother,) as his issue.

40   The *value*, or WORTH of a man, is as of all other things, his price; that is to say, so much as would be given for the use of his power: and therefore is not absolute; but a thing dependent on the need and judgement of another. An able conductor of soldiers, is of great price in time of war present, or imminent; but in peace not so. A learned and uncorrupt judge, is much worth in time of peace; but not so much in war. And as in other things, so in men, not the seller, but the buyer determines the price. For let a man (as most men do,) rate themselves at the highest value they can; yet their true value is no more than it is esteemed by others.

The manifestation of the value we set on one another, is that which is commonly called honouring, and dishonouring. To value a man at a high rate, is to *honour* him; at a low rate, is to *dishonour* him. But high, and low, in this case, is to be understood by comparison to the rate that each man setteth on himself.

The public worth of a man, which is the value set on him by the commonwealth, is that which men commonly call DIGNITY. And this value of him by the commonwealth, is understood, by offices of command, judicature, public employment; or by names and titles, introduced for distinction of such value.

41   To pray to another, for aid of any kind, is to HONOUR; because a sign we have an opinion he has power to help; and the more difficult the aid is, the more is the honour.

To obey, is to honour; because no man obeys them, whom they think have no power to help, or hurt them. And consequently to disobey, is to *dishonour.*

★   ★   ★   ★

Honourable is whatsoever possession, action, or quality, is an argument and sign of power.

And therefore to be honoured, loved, or feared of many, is honourable; as arguments of power. To be honoured of few or none, *dishonourable*.

Dominion, and victory is honourable; because acquired by power; and servitude, for need, or fear, is dishonourable.

Good fortune (if lasting,) honourable; as a sign of the favour of God. Ill fortune, and losses, dishonourable. Riches, are honourable; for they are power. Poverty, dishonourable. Magnanimity, liberality, hope, courage, confidence, are honourable; for they proceed from the conscience of power. Pusillanimity, parsimony, fear, diffidence, are dishonourable.

⋆   ⋆   ⋆   ⋆

Nor does it alter the case of honour, whether an action (so it be **42** great and difficult, and consequently a sign of much power,) be just or unjust: for honour consisteth only in the opinion of power. Therefore the ancient heathen did not think they dishonoured, but greatly honoured the gods, when they introduced them in their poems, committing rapes, thefts, and other great, but unjust, or unclean acts: in so much as nothing is so much celebrated in Jupiter, as his adulteries; nor in Mercury, as his frauds, and thefts: of whose praises, in a hymn of Homer, the greatest is this, that being born in the morning, he had invented music at noon, and before night, stolen away the cattle of Apollo, from his herdsmen.

Also amongst men, till there were constituted great common-wealths, it was thought no dishonour to be a pirate, or a highway thief; but rather a lawful trade, not only amongst the Greeks, but also amongst all other nations; as is manifest by the histories of ancient time. And at this day, in this part of the world, private duels are, and always will be honourable, though unlawful, till such time as there shall be honour ordained for them that refuse, and ignominy for them that make the challenge. For duels also are many times effects of courage; and the ground of courage is always strength or skill, which are power; though for the most part they be effects of rash speaking, and of the fear of dishonour, in one, or both the combatants; who engaged by rashness, are driven into the lists to avoid disgrace.

⋆   ⋆   ⋆   ⋆

43   WORTHINESS, is a thing different from the worth, or value of a man; and also from his merit, or desert; and consisteth in a particular power, or ability for that, whereof he is said to be worthy: which particular ability, is usually named FITNESS, or *aptitude*.

For he is worthiest to be a commander, to be a judge, or to have any other charge, that is best fitted, with the qualities required to the well discharging of it; and worthiest of riches, that has the qualities most requisite for the well using of them: any of which qualities being absent, one may nevertheless be a worthy man, and valuable for some thing else. Again, a man may be worthy of riches, office, and employment, that nevertheless, can plead no right to have it before another; and therefore cannot be said to merit or deserve it. For merit, presupposeth a right, and that the thing deserved is due by promise: of which I shall say more hereafter, when I shall speak of contracts.

CHAP XI—OF THE DIFFERENCE OF MANNERS

44   By MANNERS, I mean not here, decency of behaviour; as how one man should salute another, or how a man should wash his mouth, or pick his teeth before company, and such other points of the *small morals*; but those qualities of mankind, that concern their living together in peace, and unity. To which end we are to consider, that the felicity of this life, consisteth not in the repose of a mind satisfied. For there is no such *finis ultimus*, (utmost aim,) nor *summum bonum*, (greatest good,) as is spoken of in the books of the old moral philosophers. Nor can a man any more live, whose desires are at an end, than he, whose senses and imaginations are at a stand. Felicity is a continual progress of the desire, from one object to another; the attaining of the former, being still but the way to the latter. The cause whereof is, that the object of man's desire, is not to enjoy once only, and for one instant of time; but to assure for ever, the way of his future desire. And therefore the voluntary actions, and inclinations of all men, tend, not only to the procuring, but also to the assuring of a contented life; and differ only in the way: which ariseth partly from the diversity of passions, in divers men; and partly from the difference of the knowledge, or opinion each one has of the causes, which produce the effect desired.

So that in the first place, I put for a general inclination of all mankind, a perpetual and restless desire of power after power, that ceaseth only in death. And the cause of this, is not always that a man hopes for a more intensive delight, than he has already attained to; or that he cannot be content with a moderate power: but because he cannot assure the power and means to live well, which he hath present, without the acquisition of more. And from hence it is, that kings, whose power is greatest, turn their endeavours to the assuring it at home by laws, or abroad by wars: and when that is done, there succeedeth a new desire; in some, of fame from new conquest; in others, of ease and sensual pleasure; in others, of admiration, or being flattered for excellence in some art, or other ability of the mind.

Competition of riches, honour, command, or other power, **45** inclineth to contention, enmity, and war: because the way of one competitor, to the attaining of his desire, is to kill, subdue, supplant, or repel the other. Particularly, competition of praise, inclineth to a reverence of antiquity. For men contend with the living, not with the dead; to these ascribing more than due, that they may obscure the glory of the other.

Desire of ease, and sensual delight, disposeth men to obey a common power: because by such desires, a man doth abandon the protection might be hoped for from his own industry, and labour. Fear of death, and wounds, disposeth to the same; and for the same reason. On the contrary, needy men, and hardy, not contented with their present condition; as also, all men that are ambitious of military command, are inclined to continue the causes of war; and to stir up trouble and sedition: for there is no honour military but by war; nor any such hope to mend an ill game, as by causing a new shuffle.

Desire of knowledge, and arts of peace, inclineth men to obey a common power: for such desire, containeth a desire of leisure; and consequently protection from some other power than their own.

Desire of praise, disposeth to laudable actions, such as please them whose judgement they value; for of those men whom we contemn, we contemn also the praises. Desire of fame after death does the same. And though after death, there be no sense of the praise given us on earth, as being joys, that are either swallowed up in the unspeakable joys of heaven, or extinguished in the extreme torments of hell: yet is not such fame vain; because men have a present delight therein, from the foresight of it, and of the benefit that may redound thereby to their posterity: which though they now see not, yet they imagine; and any thing that is pleasure in the sense, the same also is pleasure in the imagination.

46 To have received from one, to whom we think ourselves equal, greater benefits than there is hope to requite, disposeth to counterfeit love; but really secret hatred; and puts a man into the estate of a desperate debtor, that in declining the sight of his creditor, tacitly wishes him there, where he might never see him more. For benefits oblige; and obligation is thraldom; and unrequitable obligation, perpetual thraldom; which is to one's equal, hateful. But to have received benefits from one, whom we acknowledge for superior, inclines to love; because the obligation is no new depression: and cheerful acceptation, (which men call *gratitude*,) is such an honour done to the obliger, as is taken generally for retribution. Also to receive benefits, though from an equal, or inferior, as long as there is hope of requital, disposeth to love: for in the intention of the receiver, the obligation is of aid, and service mutual; from whence proceedeth an emulation of who shall exceed in benefiting; the most noble and profitable contention possible; wherein the victor is pleased with his victory, and the other revenged by confessing it.

To have done more hurt to a man, than he can, or is willing to expiate, inclineth the doer to hate the sufferer. For he must expect revenge, or forgiveness; both which are hateful.

Fear of oppression, disposeth a man to anticipate, or to seek aid by society: for there is no other way by which a man can secure his life and liberty.

★　　　★　　　★　　　★

CHAP. XIII—OF THE NATURAL CONDITION OF MANKIND, AS CONCERNING THEIR FELICITY, AND MISERY

47 Nature hath made men so equal, in the faculties of body, and mind; as that though there be found one man sometimes manifestly stronger in body, or of quicker mind than another; yet when all is reckoned together, the difference between man, and man, is not so considerable, as that one man can thereupon claim to himself any benefit, to which another may not pretend, as well as he. For as to the strength of body, the weakest has strength enough to kill the strongest, either by secret machination, or by confederacy with others, that are in the same danger with himself.

And as to the faculties of the mind, (setting aside the arts grounded upon words, and especially that skill of proceeding upon general, and infallible rules, called science; which very few have, and but in few things; as being not a native faculty, born with us; nor attained, (as prudence,) while we look after somewhat else,) I find yet a greater equality amongst men, than that of strength. For prudence, is but experience; which equal time, equally bestows on all men, in those things they equally apply themselves unto. That which may perhaps make such equality incredible, is but a vain conceit of one's own wisdom, which almost all men think they have in a greater degree, than the vulgar; that is, than all men but themselves, and a few others, whom by fame, or for concurring with themselves, they approve. For such is the nature of men, that howsoever they may acknowledge many others to be more witty, or more eloquent, or more learned; yet they will hardly believe there be many so wise as themselves: for they see their own wit at hand, and other men's at a distance. But this proveth rather that men are in that point equal, than unequal. For there is not ordinarily a greater sign of the equal distribution of any thing, than that every man is contented with his share.

From this equality of ability, ariseth equality of hope in the attain- **48** ing of our ends. And therefore if any two men desire the same thing, which nevertheless they cannot both enjoy, they become enemies; and in the way to their end, (which is principally their own conservation, and sometimes their delectation only,) endeavour to destroy, or subdue one another. And from hence it comes to pass, that where an invader hath no more to fear, than another man's single power; if one plant, sow, build, or possess a convenient seat, others may probably be expected to come prepared with forces united, to dispossess, and deprive him, not only of the fruit of his labour, but also of his life, or liberty. And the invader again is in the like danger of another.

And from this diffidence of one another, there is no way for any man to secure himself, so reasonable, as anticipation; that is, by force, or wiles, to master the persons of all men he can, so long, till he see no other power great enough to endanger him: and this is no more than his own conservation requireth, and is generally allowed. Also because there be some, that taking pleasure in contemplating their own power in the acts of conquest, which they pursue farther than their security requires; if others, that otherwise would be glad to be at ease within modest bounds, should not by invasion increase their power, they would not be able, long time, by standing only on their defence, to subsist. And by consequence, such augmentation of dominion over men, being necessary to a man's conservation, it ought to be allowed him.

Again, men have no pleasure, (but on the contrary a great deal of grief) in keeping company, where there is no power able to over-awe them all. For every man looketh that his companion should value him, at the same rate he sets upon himself: and upon all signs of contempt, or undervaluing, naturally endeavours, as far as he dares (which amongst them that have no common power to keep them in quiet, is far enough to make them destroy each other,) to extort a greater value from his contemners, by damage; and from others, by the example.

49   So that in the nature of man, we find three principal causes of quarrel. First, competition; secondly, diffidence; thirdly, glory.

The first, maketh men invade for gain; the second, for safety; and the third, for reputation. The first use violence, to make themselves masters of other men's persons, wives, children, and cattle; the second, to defend them; the third, for trifles, as a word, a smile, a different opinion, and any other sign of undervalue, either direct in their persons, or by reflection in their kindred, their friends, their nation, their profession, or their name.

50   Hereby it is manifest, that during the time men live without a common power to keep them all in awe, they are in that condition which is called war; and such a war, as is of every man, against every man. For WAR, consisteth not in battle only, or the act of fighting; but in a tract of time, wherein the will to contend by battle is sufficiently known: and therefore the notion of *time*, is to be considered in the nature of war; as it is in the nature of weather. For as the nature of foul weather, lieth not in a shower or two of rain; but in an inclination thereto of many days together: so the nature of war, consisteth not in actual fighting; but in the known disposition thereto, during all the time there is no assurance to the contrary. All other time is PEACE.

Whatsoever therefore is consequent to a time of war, where every man is enemy to every man; the same is consequent to the time, wherein men live without other security, than what their own strength, and their own invention shall furnish them withal. In such condition, there is no place for industry; because the fruit thereof is uncertain: and consequently no culture of the earth; no navigation, nor use of the commodities that may be imported by sea; no commodious building; no instruments of moving, and removing such things as require much force; no knowledge of the face of the earth; no account of time; no arts; no letters; no society; and which is worst of all, continual fear, and danger of violent death; and the life of man, solitary, poor, nasty, brutish, and short.

It may seem strange to some man, that has not well weighed these **51** things; that nature should thus dissociate, and render men apt to invade, and destroy one another: and he may therefore, not trusting to this inference, made from the passions, desire perhaps to have the same confirmed by experience. Let him therefore consider with himself, when taking a journey, he arms himself, and seeks to go well accompanied; when going to sleep, he locks his doors; when even in his house he locks his chests; and this when he knows there be laws, and public officers, armed, to revenge all injuries shall be done him; what opinion he has of his fellow subjects, when he rides armed; of his fellow citizens, when he locks his doors; and of his children, and servants, when he locks his chests. Does he not there as much accuse mankind by his actions, as I do by my words? But neither of us accuse man's nature in it. The desires, and other passions of man, are in themselves no sin. No more are the actions, that proceed from those passions, till they know a law that forbids them: which till laws be made they cannot know: nor can any law be made, till they have agreed upon the person that shall make it.

It may peradventure be thought, there was never such a time, nor **52** condition of war as this; and I believe it was never generally so, over all the world: but there are many places, where they live, so now. For the savage people in many places of America, except the government of small families, the concord whereof dependeth on natural lust, have no government at all; and live at this day in that brutish manner, as I said before. Howsoever, it may be perceived what manner of life there would be, where there were no common power to fear; by the manner of life, which men that have formerly lived under a peaceful government, use to degenerate into, in a civil war.

But though there had never been any time, wherein particular men were in a condition of war one against another; yet in all times, kings, and persons of sovereign authority, because of their independency, are in continual jealousies, and in the state and posture of gladiators; having their weapons pointing, and their eyes fixed on one another; that is, their forts, garrisons, and guns upon the frontiers of their kingdoms; and continual spies upon their neighbours; which is a posture of war. But because they uphold thereby, the industry of their subjects; there does not follow from it, that misery, which accompanies the liberty of particular men.

53   To this war of every man against every man, this also is consequent; that nothing can be unjust. The notions of right and wrong, justice and injustice have there no place. Where there is no common power, there is no law: where no law, no injustice. Force, and fraud, are in war the two cardinal virtues. Justice, and injustice are none of the faculties neither of the body, nor mind. If they were, they might be in a man that were alone in the world, as well as his senses, and passions. They are qualities, that relate to men in society, not in solitude. It is consequent also to the same condition, that there be no propriety,[1] no dominion, no *mine* and *thine* distinct; but only that to be every man's, that he can get; and for so long, as he can keep it. And thus much for the ill condition, which man by mere nature is actually placed in; though with a possibility to come out of it, consisting partly in the passions, partly in his reason.

54   The passions that incline men to peace, are fear of death; desire of such things as are necessary to commodious living; and a hope by their industry to obtain them. And reason suggesteth convenient articles of peace, upon which men may be drawn to agreement. These articles, are they, which otherwise are called the laws of nature: whereof I shall speak more particularly, in the two following chapters.

CHAP. XIV—OF THE FIRST AND SECOND NATURAL LAWS, AND OF CONTRACTS

55   The RIGHT OF NATURE, which writers commonly call *jus naturale*, is the liberty each man hath, to use his own power, as he will himself, for the preservation of his own nature; that is to say, of his own life; and consequently, of doing any thing, which in his own judgement, and reason, he shall conceive to be the aptest means thereunto.

[1 i.e. property.]

By LIBERTY, is understood, according to the proper signification of the word, the absence of external impediments: which impediments, may oft take away part of a man's power to do what he would; but cannot hinder him from using the power left him, according as his judgement, and reason shall dictate to him.

A LAW OF NATURE, (*lex naturalis,*) is a precept, or general rule, **56** found out by reason, by which a man is forbidden to do, that, which is destructive of his life, or taketh away the means of preserving the same; and to omit, that, by which he thinketh it may be best preserved. For though they that speak of this subject, use to confound *jus,* and *lex,* *right* and *law*; yet they ought to be distinguished; because RIGHT, consisteth in liberty to do, or to forbear; whereas LAW, determineth, and bindeth to one of them: so that law, and right, differ as much, as obligation, and liberty; which in one and the same matter are inconsistent.

And because the condition of man, (as hath been declared in the **57** precedent chapter) is a condition of war of every one against every one; in which case every one is governed by his own reason; and there is nothing he can make use of, that may not be a help unto him, in preserving his life against his enemies; it followeth, that in such a condition, every man has a right to every thing; even to one another's body. And therefore, as long as this natural right of every man to every thing endureth, there can be no security to any man, (how strong or wise soever he be,) of living out the time, which nature ordinarily alloweth men to live. And consequently it is a precept, or general rule of reason, *That every man, ought to endeavour peace, as far as he has hope of obtaining it; and when he cannot obtain it, that he may seek, and use, all helps, and advantages of war.* The first branch of which rule, containeth the first, and fundamental law of nature; which is, *to seek peace, and follow it.* The second, the sum of the right of nature; which is, *By all means we can, to defend ourselves.*

From this fundamental law of nature, by which men are com- **58** manded to endeavour peace, is derived this second law; *That a man be willing, when others are so too, as far-forth, as for peace, and defence of himself he shall think it necessary, to lay down this right to all things; and be contented with so much liberty against other men, as he would allow other men against himself.* For as long as every man holdeth this right, of doing any thing he liketh; so long are all men in the condition of war. But if other men will not lay down their right, as well as he;

then there is no reason for any one, to divest himself of his: for that were to expose himself to prey, (which no man is bound to) rather than to dispose himself to peace. This is that law of the Gospel; *Whatsoever you require that others should do to you, that do ye to them*. And that law of all men, *Quod tibi fieri non vis, alteri ne feceris*.

59   To *lay down* a man's *right* to any thing, is to *divest* himself of the *liberty*, of hindering another of the benefit of his own right to the same. For he that renounceth, or passeth away his right, giveth not to any other man a right which he had not before; because there is nothing to which every man had not right by nature: but only standeth out of his way, that he may enjoy his own original right, without hindrance from him; not without hindrance from another. So that the effect which redoundeth to one man, by another man's defect of right, is but so much diminution of impediments to the use of his own right original.

Right is laid aside, either by simply renouncing it; or by transferring it to another. By *simply* RENOUNCING; when he cares not to whom the benefit thereof redoundeth. By TRANSFERRING; when he intendeth the benefit thereof to some certain person, or persons. And when a man hath in either manner abandoned, or granted away his right; then is he said to be OBLIGED, or BOUND, not to hinder those, to whom such right is granted, or abandoned, from the benefit of it: and that he *ought*, and it is his DUTY, not to make void that voluntary act of his own: and that such hindrance is INJUSTICE, and INJURY, as being *sine jure*; the right being before renounced, or transferred. So that *injury*, or *injustice*, in the controversies of the world, is somewhat like to that, which in the disputations of scholars is called *absurdity*. For as it is there called an absurdity, to contradict what one maintained in the beginning: so in the world, it is called injustice, and injury, voluntarily to undo that, which from the beginning he had voluntarily done.[1] The way by which a man either simply renounceth, or transferreth his right, is a declaration, or signification, by some voluntary and sufficient sign, or signs, that he doth so renounce, or transfer; or hath so renounced, or transferred the same, to him that accepteth it. And these signs are either words only, or actions only; or (as it happeneth most often) both words, and actions. And the same are the BONDS, by which men are bound, and obliged: bonds, that have their strength, not from their own

[1 See also § 102.]

nature, (for nothing is more easily broken than a man's word,) but from fear of some evil consequence upon the rupture.

Whensoever a man transferreth his right, or renounceth it; it is **60** either in consideration of some right reciprocally transferred to himself; or for some other good he hopeth for thereby. For it is a voluntary act: and of the voluntary acts of every man, the object is some *good to himself*. And therefore there be some rights, which no man can be understood by any words, or other signs, to have abandoned, or transferred. As first a man cannot lay down the right of resisting them, that assault him by force, to take away his life; because he cannot be understood to aim thereby, at any good to himself. The same may be said of wounds, and chains, and imprisonment; both because there is no benefit consequent to such patience; as there is to the patience of suffering another to be wounded, or imprisoned: as also because a man cannot tell, when he seeth men proceed against him by violence, whether they intend his death or not. And lastly the motive, and end for which this renouncing, and transferring of right is introduced, is nothing else but the security of a man's person, in his life, and in the means of so preserving life, as not to be weary of it. And therefore if a man by words, or other signs, seem to despoil himself of the end, for which those signs were intended; he is not to be understood as if he meant it, or that it was his will; but that he was ignorant of how such words and actions were to be interpreted.

The mutual transferring of right, is that which men call CONTRACT. **61**

There is difference, between transferring of right to the thing; and transferring, or tradition, that is, delivery of the thing itself. For the thing may be delivered together with the translation of the right; as in buying and selling with ready money; or exchange of goods, or lands: and it may be delivered some time after.

Again, one of the contractors, may deliver the thing contracted for on his part, and leave the other to perform his part at some determinate time after, and in the mean time be trusted; and then the contract on his part, is called PACT, or COVENANT: or both parts may contract now, to perform hereafter: in which cases, he that is to perform in time to come, being trusted, his performance is called *keeping of promise*, or faith; and the failing of performance (if it be voluntary) *violation of faith*.

When the transferring of right, is not mutual; but one of the parties transferreth, in hope to gain thereby friendship, or service from another, or from his friends; or in hope to gain the reputation of charity, or magnanimity; or to deliver his mind from the pain of compassion; or in hope of reward in heaven; this is not contract, but GIFT, FREE-GIFT, GRACE: which words signify one and the same thing.

62   Signs of contract, are either *express*, or *by inference*. Express, are words spoken with understanding of what they signify: and such words are either of the time present, or past; as, *I give, I grant, I have given, I have granted, I will that this be yours*: or of the future; as, *I will give, I will grant*: which words of the future, are called PROMISE.

Signs by inference, are sometimes the consequence of words; sometimes the consequence of silence; sometimes the consequence of actions; sometimes the consequence of forbearing an action: and generally a sign by inference, of any contract, is whatsoever sufficiently argues the will of the contractor.

Words alone, if they be of the time to come, and contain a bare promise, are an insufficient sign of a free-gift and therefore not obligatory. For if they be of the time to come, as, *To-morrow I will give*, they are a sign I have not given yet, and consequently that my right is not transferred, but remaineth till I transfer it by some other act. But if the words be of the time present, or past, as, *I have given, or do give to be delivered to-morrow*, then is my to-morrow's right given away to-day; and that by the virtue of the words, though there were no other argument of my will. And there is a great difference in the signification of these words, *Volo hoc tuum esse cras*, and *Cras dabo*; that is, between *I will that this be thine to-morrow*, and, *I will give it thee to-morrow*: for the word *I will*, in the former manner of speech, signifies an act of the will present; but in the latter, it signifies a promise of an act of the will to come: and therefore the former words, being of the present, transfer a future right; the latter, that be of the future, transfer nothing. But if there be other signs of the will to transfer a right, besides words; then, though the gift be free, yet may the right be understood to pass by words of the future: as if a man propound a prize to him that comes first to the end of a race, the gift is free; and though the words be of the future, yet the right passeth: for if he would not have his words so be understood, he should not have let them run.

In contracts, the right passeth, not only where the words are of the time present, or past; but also where they are of the future:

because all contract is mutual translation, or change of right; and therefore he that promiseth only, because he hath already received the benefit for which he promiseth, is to be understood as if he intended the right should pass: for unless he had been content to have his words so understood, the other would not have performed his part first. And for that cause, in buying, and selling, and other acts of contract, a promise is equivalent to a covenant; and therefore obligatory.

He that performeth first in the case of a contract, is said to MERIT **63** that which he is to receive by the performance of the other; and he hath it as *due*. Also when a prize is propounded to many, which is to be given to him only that winneth; or money is thrown amongst many, to be enjoyed by them that catch it; though this be a free gift; yet so to win, or so to catch, is to *merit*, and to have it as DUE. For the right is transferred in the propounding of the prize, and in throwing down the money; though it be not determined to whom, but by the event of the contention. But there is between these two sorts of merit, this difference, that in contract, I merit by virtue of my own power, and the contractor's need; but in this case of free gift, I am enabled to merit only by the benignity of the giver: in contract, I merit at the contractor's hand that he should depart with his right; in this case of gift, I merit not that the giver should part with his right; but that when he has parted with it, it should be mine, rather than another's.

★ ★ ★ ★

If a covenant be made, wherein neither of the parties perform **64** presently, but trust one another; in the condition of mere nature, (which is a condition of war of every man against every man,) upon any reasonable suspicion, it is void: but if there be a common power set over them both, with right and force sufficient to compel performance; it is not void. For he that performeth first, has no assurance the other will perform after; because the bonds of words are too weak to bridle men's ambition, avarice, anger, and other passions, without the fear of some coercive power; which in the condition of mere nature, where all men are equal, and judges of the justness of their own fears, cannot possibly be supposed. And therefore he which performeth first, does but betray himself to his enemy; contrary to the right (he can never abandon) of defending his life, and means of living.

But in a civil estate, where there is a power set up to constrain those that would otherwise violate their faith, that fear is no more reasonable; and for that cause, he which by the covenant is to perform first, is obliged so to do.

The cause of fear, which maketh such a covenant invalid, must be always something arising after the covenant made; as some new fact, or other sign of the will not to perform: else it cannot make the covenant void. For that which could not hinder a man from promising, ought not to be admitted as a hindrance of performing.

★   ★   ★   ★

65   The matter, or subject of a covenant, is always something that falleth under deliberation; (for to covenant, is an act of the will; that is to say an act, and the last act, of deliberation;) and is therefore always understood to be something to come; and which is judged possible for him that covenanteth, to perform.

And therefore, to promise that which is known to be impossible, is no covenant. But if that prove impossible afterwards, which before was thought possible, the covenant is valid, and bindeth, (though not to the thing itself,) yet to the value; or, if that also be impossible, to the unfeigned endeavour of performing as much as is possible: for to more no man can be obliged.

Men are freed of their covenants two ways; by performing; or by being forgiven. For performance, is the natural end of obligation; and forgiveness, the restitution of liberty; as being a re-transferring of that right, in which the obligation consisted.

Covenants entered into by fear, in the condition of mere nature, are obligatory. For example, if I covenant to pay a ransom, or service for my life, to an enemy; I am bound by it. For it is a contract, wherein one receiveth the benefit of life; the other is to receive money, or service for it; and consequently, where no other law (as in the condition of mere nature) forbiddeth the performance, the covenant is valid. Therefore prisoners of war, if trusted with the payment of their ransom, are obliged to pay it: and if a weaker prince, make a disadvantageous peace with a stronger, for fear; he is bound to keep it; unless (as hath been said before) there ariseth some new, and just cause of fear, to renew the war. And even in commonwealths, if I be forced to redeem myself from a thief by promising him money, I am bound to pay it, till the civil law discharge me. For whatsoever I may lawfully do without obligation, the same I may lawfully covenant to do through fear: and what I lawfully covenant, I cannot lawfully break.

* * * *

The force of words, being (as I have formerly noted) too weak to **66** hold men to the performance of their covenants; there are in man's nature, but two imaginable helps to strengthen it. And those are either a fear of the consequence of breaking their word; or a glory, or pride in appearing not to need to break it. This latter is a generosity too rarely found to be presumed on, especially in the pursuers of wealth, command, or sensual pleasure; which are the greatest part of mankind. The passion to be reckoned upon, is fear; whereof there be two very general objects: one, the power of spirits invisible; the other, the power of those men they shall therein offend. Of these two, though the former be the greater power, yet the fear of the latter is commonly the greater fear. The fear of the former is in every man, his own religion: which hath place in the nature of man before civil society. The latter hath not so; at least not place enough, to keep men to their promises; because in the condition of mere nature, the inequality of power is not discerned, but by the event of battle. So that before the time of civil society, or in the interruption thereof by war, there is nothing can strengthen a covenant of peace agreed on, against the temptations of avarice, ambition, lust, or other strong desire, but the fear of that invisible power, which they every one worship as God; and fear as a revenger of their perfidy. All therefore that can be done between two men not subject to civil power, is to put one another to swear by the God he feareth: which *swearing*, or OATH, is a form of speech, added to a promise; by which he that promiseth, signifieth, that unless he perform, he renounceth the mercy of his God, or calleth to him for vengeance on himself. Such was the heathen form, *Let Jupiter kill me else, as I kill this beast.* So is our form, *I shall do thus, and thus, so help me God.* And this, with the rites and ceremonies, which every one useth in his own religion, that the fear of breaking faith might be the greater.

* * * *

It appears also, that the oath adds nothing to the obligation. For a covenant, if lawful, binds in the sight of God, without the oath, as much as with it: if unlawful, bindeth not at all; though it be confirmed with an oath.

CHAP. XV—OF OTHER LAWS OF NATURE

67 From that law of nature, by which we are obliged to transfer to another, such rights, as being retained, hinder the peace of mankind, there followeth a third; which is this, *That men perform their covenants made*: without which, covenants are in vain, and but empty words; and the right of all men to all things remaining, we are still in the condition of war.

And in this law of nature, consisteth the fountain and original of JUSTICE. For where no covenant hath preceded, there hath no right been transferred, and every man has right to every thing; and consequently, no action can be unjust. But when a covenant is made, then to break it is *unjust*: and the definition of INJUSTICE, is no other than *the not performance of covenant*. And whatsoever is not unjust, is *just*.

But because covenants of mutual trust, where there is a fear of not performance on either part, (as hath been said in the former chapter,) are invalid; though the original of justice be the making of covenants; yet injustice actually there can be none, till the cause of such fear be taken away; which while men are in the natural condition of war, cannot be done. Therefore before the names of just, and unjust can have place, there must be some coercive power, to compel men equally to the performance of their covenants, by the terror of some punishment, greater than the benefit they expect by the breach of their covenant; and to make good that propriety, which by mutual contract men acquire, in recompense of the universal right they abandon: and such power there is none before the erection of a commonwealth. And this is also to be gathered out of the ordinary definition of justice in the Schools: for they say, that *Justice is the constant will of giving to every man his own*. And therefore where there is no *own*, that is no propriety, there is no injustice; and where there is no coercive power erected, that is, where there is no commonwealth, there is no propriety; all men having right to all things: therefore where there is no commonwealth, there nothing is unjust. So that the nature of justice, consisteth in keeping of valid covenants: but the validity of covenants begins not but with the constitution of a civil power, sufficient to compel men to keep them: and then it is also that propriety begins.

★ ★ ★ ★

As justice dependeth on antecedent covenant; so does GRATITUDE **68** depend on antecedent grace; that is to say, antecedent free-gift: and is the fourth law of nature; which may be conceived in this form, *That a man which receiveth benefit from another of mere grace, endeavour that he which giveth it, have no reasonable cause to repent him of his good will.* For no man giveth, but with intention of good to himself; because gift is voluntary; and of all voluntary acts, the object is to every man his own good; of which if men see they shall be frustrated, there will be no beginning of benevolence, or trust; nor consequently of mutual help; nor of reconciliation of one man to another; and therefore they are to remain still in the condition of war; which is contrary to the first and fundamental law of nature, which commandeth men to seek peace. The breach of this law, is called *ingratitude*; and hath the same relation to grace, that injustice hath to obligation by covenant.

A fifth law of nature is COMPLAISANCE; that is to say, *That every* **69** *man strive to accommodate himself to the rest.* For the understanding whereof, we may consider, that there is in men's aptness to society, a diversity of nature, rising from their diversity of affections; not unlike to that we see in stones brought together for building of an edifice. For as that stone which by the asperity, and irregularity of figure, takes more room from others, than itself fills; and for the hardness, cannot be easily made plain, and thereby hindereth the building, is by the builders cast away as unprofitable, and troublesome: so also, a man that by asperity of nature, will strive to retain those things which to himself are superfluous, and to others necessary; and for the stubbornness of his passions, cannot be corrected, is to be left, or cast out of society, as cumbersome thereunto. For seeing every man, not only by right, but also by necessity of nature, is supposed to endeavour all he can, to obtain that which is necessary for his conservation; he that shall oppose himself against it, for things superfluous, is guilty of the war that thereupon is to follow; and therefore doth that, which is contrary to the fundamental law of nature, which commandeth to seek peace. The observers of this law, may be called SOCIABLE, (the Latins call them *commodi*;) the contrary, *stubborn, insociable, froward, intractable.*

A sixth law of nature, is this, *That upon caution of the future time,* **70** *a man ought to pardon the offences past of them that repenting, desire it.* For PARDON, is nothing but granting of peace; which though granted to them that persevere in their hostility, be not peace, but fear; yet not granted to them that give caution of the future time, is sign of an aversion to peace; and therefore contrary to the law of nature.

71   A seventh is, *That in revenges,* (that is, retribution of evil for evil,) *men look not at the greatness of the evil past, but the greatness of the good to follow.* Whereby we are forbidden to inflict punishment with any other design, than for correction of the offender, or direction of others. For this law is consequent to the next before it, that commandeth pardon, upon security of the future time. Besides, revenge without respect to the example, and profit to come, is a triumph, or glorying in the hurt of another, tending to no end; (for the end is always somewhat to come;) and glorying to no end, is vain-glory, and contrary to reason; and to hurt without reason, tendeth to the introduction of war; which is against the law of nature; and is commonly styled by the name of *cruelty.*

72   And because all signs of hatred, or contempt, provoke to fight; insomuch as most men choose rather to hazard their life, than not to be revenged; we may in the eighth place, for a law of nature, set down this precept, *That no man by deed, word, countenance, or gesture, declare hatred, or contempt of another.* The breach of which law, is commonly called *contumely.*

73   The question who is the better man, has no place in the condition of mere nature; where, (as has been shown before,) all men are equal. The inequality that now is, has been introduced by the laws civil. I know that Aristotle in the first book of his *Politics,* for a foundation of his doctrine, maketh men by nature, some more worthy to command, meaning the wiser sort (such as he thought himself to be for his philosophy;) others to serve, (meaning those that had strong bodies, but were not philosophers as he;) as if master and servant were not introduced by consent of men, but by difference of wit: which is not only against reason; but also against experience. For there are very few so foolish, that had not rather govern themselves, than be governed by others: nor when the wise in their own conceit, contend by force, with them who distrust their own wisdom, do they always, or often, or almost at any time, get the victory. If nature therefore have made men equal, that equality is to be acknowledged: or if nature have made men unequal; yet because men that think themselves equal, will not enter into conditions of peace, but upon equal terms, such equality must be admitted. And therefore for the ninth law of nature, I put this, *That every man acknowledge another for his equal by nature.* The breach of this precept is *pride.*

On this law, dependeth another, *That at the entrance into conditions of peace, no man require to reserve to himself any right, which he is not content should be reserved to every one of the rest.* As it is necessary for all men that seek peace, to lay down certain rights of nature; that is to say, not to have liberty to do all they list: so is it necessary for man's life, to retain some; as right to govern their own bodies; enjoy air, water, motion, ways to go from place to place; and all things else, without which a man cannot live, or not live well. If in this case, at the making of peace, men require for themselves, that which they would not have granted to others, they do contrary to the precedent law, that commandeth the acknowledgement of natural equality, and therefore also against the law of nature. The observers of this law, are those we call *modest,* and the breakers *arrogant* men. The Greeks call the violation of this law πλεονεξία; that is, a desire of more than their share.

Also if *a man be trusted to judge between man and man,* it is a precept **74** of the law of nature, *that he deal equally between them.* For without that, the controversies of men cannot be determined but by war. He therefore that is partial in judgement, doth what in him lies, to deter men from the use of judges, and arbitrators; and consequently, (against the fundamental law of nature) is the cause of war.

The observance of this law, from the equal distribution to each man, of that which in reason belongeth to him, is called EQUITY, and (as I have said before) distributive justice: the violation, *acception of persons,* προσωποληψία.

*   *   *   *

These are the laws of nature, dictating peace, for a means of the **75** conservation of men in multitudes; and which only concern the doctrine of civil society. There be other things tending to the destruction of particular men; as drunkenness, and all other parts of intemperance; which may therefore also be reckoned amongst those things which the law of nature hath forbidden; but are not necessary to be mentioned, nor are pertinent enough to this place.

And though this may seem too subtle a deduction of the laws of nature, to be taken notice of by all men; whereof the most part are too busy in getting food, and the rest too negligent to understand;

yet to leave all men inexcusable, they have been contracted into one easy sum, intelligible even to the meanest capacity; and that is, *Do not that to another, which thou wouldest not have done to thyself*; which showeth him, that he has no more to do in learning the laws of nature, but, when weighing the actions of other men with his own, they seem too heavy, to put them into the other part of the balance, and his own into their place, that his own passions, and self-love, may add nothing to the weight; and then there is none of these laws of nature that will not appear unto him very reasonable

76 The laws of nature oblige *in foro interno*; that is to say, they bind to a desire they should take place: but *in foro externo*; that is, to the putting them in act, not always. For he that should be modest, and tractable, and perform all he promises, in such time, and place, where no man else should do so, should but make himself a prey to others, and procure his own certain ruin, contrary to the ground of all laws of nature, which tend to nature's preservation. And again, he that having sufficient security, that others shall observe the same laws towards him, observes them not himself, seeketh not peace, but war; and consequently the destruction of his nature by violence.

And whatsoever laws bind *in foro interno*, may be broken, not only by a fact contrary to the law, but also by a fact according to it, in case a man think it contrary. For though his action in this case, be according to the law; yet his purpose was against the law, which, where the obligation is *in foro interno*, is a breach.

77 The laws of nature are immutable and eternal; for injustice, ingratitude, arrogance, pride, iniquity, acception of persons, and the rest, can never be made lawful. For it can never be that war shall preserve life, and peace destroy it.

The same laws, because they oblige only to a desire, and endeavour, I mean an unfeigned and constant endeavour, are easy to be observed. For in that they require nothing but endeavour; he that endeavoureth their performance, fulfilleth them; and he that fulfilleth the law, is just.

And the science of them, is the true and only moral philosophy. For moral philosophy is nothing else but the science of what is good, and evil, in the conversation, and society of mankind. *Good*, and *evil*, are names that signify our appetites, and aversions; which in different tempers, customs, and doctrines of men, are different: and divers men, differ not only in their judgement, on the senses of what is pleasant, and unpleasant to the taste, smell, hearing, touch, and sight; but also of what is comformable, or disagreeable to reason, in the actions of common life. Nay, the same man, in divers times, differs from himself; and one time praiseth, that is, calleth good, what another time he dispraiseth, and calleth evil: from whence arise disputes, controversies, and at last war. And therefore so long a man is in the condition of mere nature, (which is a condition of war,) as private appetite is the measure of good, and evil: and consequently all men agree on this, that peace is good, and therefore also the way, or means of peace, which (as I have showed before) are justice, gratitude, modesty, equity, mercy, and the rest of the laws of nature, are good; that is to say; *moral virtues*; and their contrary *vices*, evil. Now the science of virtue and vice, is moral philosophy; and therefore the true doctrine of the laws of nature, is the true moral philosophy. But the writers of moral philosophy, though they acknowledge the same virtues and vices; yet not seeing wherein consisted their goodness; nor that they come to be praised, as the means of peaceable, sociable, and comfortable living; place them in a mediocrity of passions: as if not the cause, but the degree of daring, made fortitude; or not the cause, but the quantity of a gift, made liberality.

These dictates of reason, men use to call by the name of laws; but improperly: for they are but conclusions, or theorems concerning what conduceth to the conservation and defence of themselves; whereas law, properly, is the word of him, that by right hath command over others. But yet if we consider the same theorems, as delivered in the word of God, that by right commandeth all things; then are they properly called laws.

CHAP. XVI—OF PERSONS, AUTHORS, AND THINGS PERSONATED

A PERSON, is he, whose words or actions are considered, either as **78** his own, or as representing the words or actions of another man, or of any other thing, to whom they are attributed, whether truly or by fiction.

When they are considered as his own, then is he called a *natural person*: and when they are considered as representing the words and actions of another, then is he a *feigned* or *artificial person*.

*   *   *   *

Of persons artificial, some have their words and actions *owned* by those whom they represent. And then the person is the *actor*; and he that owneth his words and actions, is the AUTHOR: in which case the actor acteth by authority. For that which in speaking of goods and possessions, is called an owner, and in Latin *dominus*, in Greek κύριος; speaking of actions, is called author. And as the right of possession, is called dominion; so the right of doing any action, is called AUTHORITY. So that by authority, is always understood a right of doing any act; and *done by authority*, done by commission, or licence from him whose right it is.

★   ★   ★   ★

PART II—OF COMMONWEALTH

CHAP. XVII—OF THE CAUSES, GENERATION, AND DEFINITION OF A COMMONWEALTH

79   The final cause, end, or design of men, (who naturally love liberty, and dominion over others,) in the introduction of that restraint upon themselves, (in which we see them live in commonwealths,) is the foresight of their own preservation, and of a more contented life thereby; that is to say, of getting themselves out from that miserable condition of war, which is necessarily consequent (as hath been shown) to the natural passions of men, when there is no visible power to keep them in awe, and tie them by fear of punishment to the performance of their covenants, and observation of those laws of nature set down in the fourteenth and fifteenth chapters.

For the laws of nature (as justice, equity, modesty, mercy, and (in sum) doing to others, as we would be done to,) of themselves, without the terror of some power, to cause them to be observed, are contrary to our natural passions, that carry us to partiality, pride, revenge, and the like. And covenants, without the sword, are but words, and of no strength to secure a man at all. Therefore notwithstanding the laws of nature, (which every one hath then kept, when he has the will to keep them, when he can do it safely,) if there be no power erected, or not great enough for our security; every man will, and may lawfully rely on his own strength and art, for caution against all other men. And in all places, where men have lived by small families, to rob and spoil one another, has been a trade, and so far from being reputed against the law of nature, that the greater spoils they gained, the greater was their honour; and men observed no other laws therein, but the laws of honour; that is, to abstain from cruelty, leaving to men their lives, and instruments of husbandry. And as small families did then; so now do cities and kingdoms which are but greater families (for their own security) enlarge their dominions, upon all pretences of danger, and fear of invasion, or assistance that may be given to invaders, endeavour as much as they can, to subdue, or weaken their neighbours, by open force, and secret arts, for want of other caution, justly; and are remembered for it in after ages with honour.

★　　　★　　　★　　　★

It is true, that certain living creatures, as bees, and ants, live sociably one with another, (which are therefore by Aristotle numbered amongst political creatures;) and yet have no other direction, than their particular judgements and appetites; nor speech, whereby one of them can signify to another, what he thinks expedient for the common benefit: and therefore some man may perhaps desire to know, why mankind cannot do the same. To which I answer,

First, that men are continually in competition for honour and dignity, which these creatures are not; and consequently amongst men there ariseth on that ground, envy and hatred, and finally war; but amongst these not so.

Secondly, that amongst these creatures, the common good differeth not from the private; and being by nature inclined to their private, they procure thereby the common benefit. But man, whose joy consisteth in comparing himself with other men, can relish nothing but what is eminent.

★　　　★　　　★　　　★

Lastly, the agreement of these creatures is natural; that of men, is by covenant only, which is artificial: and therefore it is no wonder if there be somewhat else required (besides covenant) to make their agreement constant and lasting; which is a common power, to keep them in awe, and to direct their actions to the common benefit.

The only way to erect such a common power, as may be able to 81 defend them from the invasion of foreigners, and the injuries of one another, and thereby to secure them in such sort, as that by their own industry, and by the fruits of the earth, they may nourish themselves and live contentedly; is, to confer all their power and strength upon one man, or upon one assembly of men, that may reduce all their wills, by plurality of voices, unto one will: which is as much as to say, to appoint one man, or assembly of men, to bear their person; and every one to own, and acknowledge himself to be author of whatsoever he that so beareth their person, shall act, or cause to be acted, in those things which concern the common peace and safety; and therein to submit their wills, every one to his will, and their judgements, to his judgement. This is more than consent, or concord; it is a real unity of them all, in one and the same person, made by covenant of every man with every man, in such manner, as if every man should say to every man, *I authorize and give up my right of governing myself, to this man, or to this assembly of men, on this condition, that thou give up thy right to him, and authorize all his actions in like manner.* This done, the multitude so united in one person, is called a COMMONWEALTH, in Latin CIVITAS. This is the generation of that great LEVIATHAN, or rather (to speak more reverently) of that *mortal god,* to which we owe under the *immortal God,* our peace and defence. For by this authority, given him by every particular man in the commonwealth, he hath the use of so much power and strength conferred on him, that by terror thereof, he is enabled to form the wills of them all, to peace at home, and mutual aid against their enemies abroad. And in him consisteth the essence of the commonwealth; which (to define it,) is one person, of whose acts a great multitude, by mutual covenants one with another, have made themselves every one the author, to the end he may use the strength and means of them all, as he shall think expedient, for their peace and common defence.

And he that carrieth this person, is called SOVEREIGN, and said to have *sovereign power;* and every one besides, his SUBJECT.

The attaining to this sovereign power, is by two ways. One, by natural force; as when a man maketh his children, to submit themselves, and their children to his government, as being able to destroy them if they refuse; or by war subdueth his enemies to his will, giving them their lives on that condition. The other, is when men agree amongst themselves, to submit to some man, or assembly of men, voluntarily, on confidence to be protected by him against all others. This latter, may be called a political commonwealth, or commonwealth by *institution;* and the former, a commonwealth by *acquisition.* And first, I shall speak of a commonwealth by institution.

CHAP. XXI—OF THE LIBERTY OF SUBJECTS

LIBERTY, or FREEDOM, signifieth (properly) the absence of opposi- **82** tion; (by opposition, I mean external impediments of motion;) and may be applied no less to irrational, and inanimate creatures, than to rational. For whatsoever is so tied, or environed, as it cannot move, but within a certain space, which space is determined by the opposition of some external body, we say it hath not liberty to go further. And so of all living creatures, whilst they are imprisoned, or restrained, with walls, or chains; and of the water whilst it is kept in by banks, or vessels, that otherwise would spread itself into a larger space, we use to say, they are not at liberty, to move in such manner, as without those external impediments they would. But when the impediment of motion, is in the constitution of the thing itself, we use not to say, it wants the liberty; but the power to move; as when a stone lieth still, or a man is fastened to his bed by sickness.

And according to this proper, and generally received meaning of the word, a FREE-MAN, is he, that in those things, which by his strength and wit he is able to do, is not hindered to do what he has a will to. But when the words *free*, and *liberty*, are applied to any thing but bodies, they are abused; for that which is not subject to motion, is not subject to impediment: and therefore, when it is said (for example) the way is free, no liberty of the way is signified, but of those that walk in it without stop. And when we say a gift is free, there is not meant any liberty of the gift, but of the giver, that was not bound by any law, or covenant to give it. So when we *speak freely*, it is not the liberty of voice, or pronunciation, but of the man, whom no law hath obliged to speak otherwise than he did. Lastly, from the use of the word *free will*, no liberty can be inferred of the will, desire, or inclination, but the liberty of the man; which consisteth in this, that he finds no stop, in doing what he has the will, desire, or inclination to do.

Fear and liberty are consistent; as when a man throweth his goods **83** into the sea for fear the ship should sink, he doth it nevertheless very willingly, and may refuse to do it if he will: it is therefore the action, of one that was free: so a man sometimes pays his debt, only for fear of imprisonment, which because no body hindered him from detaining, was the action of a man at liberty. And generally all actions which men do in commonwealths, for fear of the law, are actions, which the doers had liberty to omit.

Liberty and *necessity* are consistent: as in the water, that hath not only liberty, but a necessity of descending by the channel; so likewise in the actions which men voluntarily do; which (because they proceed from their will) proceed from liberty; and yet, because every act of man's will, and every desire, and inclination proceedeth from some cause, and that from another cause, in a continual chain, (whose first link is in the hand of God the first of all causes,) proceed from necessity. So that to him that could see the connection of those causes, the necessity of all men's voluntary actions, would appear manifest. And therefore God, that seeth, and disposeth all things, seeth also that the liberty of man in doing what he will, is accompanied with the necessity of doing that which God will, and no more, nor less. For though men may do many things, which God does not command, nor is therefore author of them; yet they can have no passion, nor appetite to any thing, of which appetite God's will is not the cause. And did not his will assure the necessity of man's will, and consequently of all that on man's will dependeth, the liberty of men would be a contradiction, and impediment to the omnipotence and liberty of God. And this shall suffice, (as to the matter in hand) of that natural liberty, which only is properly called *liberty*.[1]

84   But as men, for the attaining of peace, and conservation of themselves thereby, have made an artificial man, which we call a commonwealth; so also have they made artificial chains, called *civil laws*, which they themselves, by mutual covenants, have fastened at one end, to the lips of that man, or assembly, to whom they have given the sovereign power; and at the other end to their own ears. These bonds, in their own nature but weak, may nevertheless be made to hold, by the danger, though not by the difficulty of breaking them.

In relation to these bonds only it is, that I am to speak now, of the *liberty* of *subjects*. For seeing there is no commonwealth in the world, wherein there be rules enough set down, for the regulating of all the actions, and words of men, (as being a thing impossible:) it followeth necessarily, that in all kinds of actions, by the laws praetermitted, men have the liberty, of doing what their own reasons shall suggest, for the most profitable to themselves.

     ★   ★   ★   ★

[1 See also §§ 90–9.]

CHAP. XXV—OF COUNSEL[1]

How fallacious it is to judge of the nature of things by the 85 ordinary and inconstant use of words, appeareth in nothing more, than in the confusion of counsels, and commands, arising from the imperative manner of speaking in them both, and in many other occasions besides. For the words *Do this*, are the words not only of him that commandeth; but also of him that giveth counsel; and of him that exhorteth; and yet there are but few, that see not, that these are very different things; or that cannot distinguish between them, when they perceive who it is that speaketh, and to whom the speech is directed, and upon what occasion. But finding those phrases in men's writings, and being not able, or not willing to enter into a consideration of the circumstances, they mistake sometimes the precepts of counsellors, for the precepts of them that command; and sometimes the contrary; according as it best agreeth with the conclusions they would infer, or the actions they approve. To avoid which mistakes, and render to those terms of commanding, counselling, and exhorting, their proper and distinct significations, I define them thus.

COMMAND, is where a man saith, *Do this*, or *Do not this*, without expecting other reason than the will of him that says it. From this it followeth manifestly, that he that commandeth, pretendeth thereby his own benefit: for the reason of his command is his own will only, and the proper object of every man's will, is some good to himself.

COUNSEL, is where a man saith, *Do*, or *Do not this*, and deduceth his reasons from the benefit that arriveth by it to him to whom he saith it. And from this it is evident, that he that giveth counsel, pretendeth only (whatsoever he intendeth) the good of him, to whom he giveth it.

Therefore between counsel and command, one great difference is, that command is directed to a man's own benefit; and counsel to the benefit of another man. And from this ariseth another difference, that a man may be obliged to do what he is commanded; as when he hath covenanted to obey: but he cannot be obliged to do as he is counselled, because the hurt of not following it, is his own; or if he should covenant to follow it, then is the counsel turned into the nature of a command.

★   ★   ★   ★

[1 See also §§ 20, 100, 103.]

CHAP. XXVIII—OF PUNISHMENTS, AND REWARDS

86   A PUNISHMENT, is an evil inflicted by public authority, on him that hath done, or omitted that which is judged by the same authority to be a transgression of the law; to the end that the will of men may thereby the better be disposed to obedience.

Before I infer any thing from this definition, there is a question to be answered, of much importance; which is, by what door the right, or authority of punishing in any case, came in. For by that which has been said before, no man is supposed bound by covenant, not to resist violence; and consequently it cannot be intended, that he gave any right to another to lay violent hands upon his person. In the making of a commonwealth, every man giveth away the right of defending another; but not of defending himself. Also he obligeth himself, to assist him that hath the sovereignty, in the punishing of another; but of himself not. But to covenant to assist the sovereign, in doing hurt to another, unless he that so covenanteth have a right to do it himself, is not to give him a right to punish. It is manifest therefore that the right which the commonwealth (that is, he, or they that represent it) hath to punish, is not grounded on any concession, or gift of the subjects. But I have also showed formerly, that before the institution of commonwealth, every man had a right to every thing, and to do whatsoever he thought necessary to his own preservation; subduing, hurting, or killing any man in order thereunto. And this is the foundation of that right of punishing, which is exercised in every commonwealth. For the subjects did not give the sovereign that right; but only in laying down theirs, strengthened him to use his own, as he should think fit, for the preservation of them all: so that it was not given, but left to him, and to him only; and (excepting the limits set him by natural law) as entire, as in the condition of mere nature, and of war of every one against his neighbour.

87   From the definition of punishment, I infer, first, that neither private revenges, nor injuries of private men, can properly be styled punishment; because they proceed not from public authority.

*   *   *   *

Fifthly, that all evil which is inflicted without intention, or possibility of disposing the delinquent, or (by his example) other men, to obey the laws, is not punishment; but an act of hostility; because without such an end, no hurt done is contained under that name.

★   ★   ★   ★

All punishments of innocent subjects, be they great or little, are against the law of nature: for punishment is only for transgression of the law, and therefore there can be no punishment of the innocent. It is therefore a violation, first, of that law of nature, which forbiddeth all men, in their revenges, to look at any thing but some future good: for there can arrive no good to the commonwealth, by punishing the innocent. Secondly, of that, which forbiddeth ingratitude: for seeing all sovereign power, is originally given by the consent of every one of the subjects, to the end they should as long as they are obedient, be protected thereby; the punishment of the innocent, is a rendering of evil for good. And thirdly, of the law that commandeth equity; that is to say, an equal distribution of justice; which in punishing the innocent is not observed.

★   ★   ★   ★

Hitherto I have set forth the nature of man, (whose pride and **88** other passions have compelled him to submit himself to government;) together with the great power of his governor, whom I compared to Leviathan, taking that comparison out of the two last verses of the one and fortieth of *Job*; where God having set forth the great power of Leviathan, calleth him king of the proud. *There is nothing*, saith he, *on earth, to be compared with him. He is made so as not to be afraid. He seeth every high thing below him*; *and is king of all the children of pride.*

★   ★   ★   ★

CHAP. XXXI—OF THE KINGDOM OF GOD BY NATURE[1]

The right of nature, whereby God reigneth over men, and punish- **89** eth those that break his laws, is to be derived, not from his creating them, as if he required obedience, as of gratitude for his benefits; but from his *irresistible power*. I have formerly shown, how the sovereign right ariseth from pact: to show how the same right may arise from nature, requires no more, but to show in what case it is never taken

[1 See also § 101.]

away. Seeing all men by nature had right to all things, they had right every one to reign over all the rest. But because this right could not be obtained by force, it concerned the safety of every one, laying by that right, to set up men (with sovereign authority) by common consent, to rule and defend them: whereas if there had been any man of power irresistible; there had been no reason, why he should not by that power have ruled, and defended both himself, and them, according to his own discretion. To those therefore whose power is irresistible, the dominion of all men adhereth naturally by their excellence of power; and consequently it is from that power, that the kingdom over men, and the right of afflicting men at his pleasure, belongeth naturally to God Almighty; not as creator, and gracious; but as omnipotent. And though punishment be due for sin only, because by that word is understood affliction for sin; yet the right of afflicting, is not always derived from men's sin, but from God's power.

★   ★   ★   ★

Of Liberty and Necessity

Dedicated to the Lord Marquess of NEWCASTLE

Right Honourable

I had once resolved to answer my Lord Bishop's[1] objections to my **90**
book *De* CIVE in the first place, as that which concerns me most,
and afterwards to examine his Discourse of LIBERTY and NECESSITY,
which (because I had never uttered my opinion of it) concerned me
the less. But seeing it was your Lordship's and my Lord Bishop's
desire that I should begin with the latter, I was contented so to do,
and here I present and submit it to your Lordship's judgement.

And first I assure your Lordship, I find in it no new argument,
neither from Scripture nor from Reason, that I have not often heard
before, which is as much as to say, I am not surprised.

The preface is a handsome one, but it appeareth even in that, that
he hath mistaken the question. For whereas he says thus, *If I be free to
write this discourse, I have obtained the cause*, I deny that to be true, for
it is enough to his freedom of writing, that he had not written it
unless he would himself. If he will obtain the cause, he must prove
that before he writ it, it was not necessary he should write it afterward.
It may be his Lordship thinks it all one to say; *I was free* to write it,
and *It was not necessary* I should write it, but I think otherwise; for
he is *free* to do a thing, that may do it, if he have the will to do it,
and may forbear, if he have the will to forbear. And yet if there be a
necessity that he shall have the will to do it, the action is necessarily
to follow; and if there be a *necessity* that he shall have the will to
forbear, the forbearing also will be necessary. The question therefore
is not whether a man be a free agent, that is to say, whether he can
write, or forbear, speak, or be silent, according to his will, but,
whether the will to write, and the will to forbear, come upon him
according to his will, or according to any thing else in his own
power. I acknowledge this liberty, that I can do if I will, but to say,

[1 Dr. Bramhall, Bishop of Londonderry.]

I can will if I will, I take to be an absurd speech, wherefore I cannot grant my Lord the cause upon his preface.

★   ★   ★   ★

To the Arguments from Reason

91   Of the arguments from Reason, the first is that which his Lordship saith is drawn from Zeno's beating of his man, which is therefore called *argumentum baculinum*, that is to say, a wooden argument. The story is this: Zeno held that all actions were necessary; his man therefore, being for some fault beaten, excused himself upon the necessity of it; to avoid this excuse, his master pleaded likewise the necessity of beating him. So that not he that maintained, but he that derided the necessity, was beaten, contrary to that his Lordship would infer. And the argument was rather withdrawn than drawn from the story.

92   The second argument is taken from certain inconveniences, which his Lordship thinks would follow such an opinion. It is true that ill use might be made of it, and therefore your Lordship and my Lord Bishop, ought at my request to keep private what I say here of it. But the inconveniences are indeed none, and what use soever be made of truth, yet truth is truth, and now the question is not, what is fit to be preached, but, what is true.

The first inconvenience he says is this. *That the laws, which prohibit any action, will be unjust.*

2. That all consultations are vain.

3. That admonitions to men of understanding, are of no more use, than to children, fools, and madmen.

4. That praise, dispraise, reward and punishment are in vain.

5, 6. That counsels, arts, arms, books, instruments, study, tutors, medicines, are in vain.

To which arguments his Lordship expecting I should answer, by saying, the ignorance of the event were enough to make us use the means, adds (as it were a reply to my answer foreseen) these words. *Alas! how should our not knowing the event be a sufficient motive to make us use the means?* Wherein his Lordship says right, but my answer is not that which he expecteth; I answer:

93   First, that the necessity of an action doth not make the laws that prohibit it unjust. To let pass that not the necessity, but the will to break the law, maketh the action unjust, because the law regardeth the will and no other precedent causes of action. And to let pass, that no law can possibly be unjust, in as much as every man maketh (by his consent) the law he is bound to keep, and which consequently must be just, unless a man can be unjust to himself. I say, what necessary cause soever precede an action, yet if the action be forbidden, he that doth it willingly, may justly be punished. For instance, suppose the law on pain of death prohibit stealing, and that there be a man, who by the strength of temptation is necessitated to steal, and is thereupon put to death, does not this punishment deter others from theft? Is it not a cause that others steal not? Doth it not frame and make their wills to justice?

To make the law, is therefore to make a *cause* of *justice*, and to *necessitate* justice, and consequently it is no injustice to make such a law.

The intention of the law is not to grieve the delinquent for that which is past, and not to be undone, but to make him and others just, that else would not be so, and respecteth not the evil act *past*, but the *good to come*, in so much as without the good intention for the future, no past act of a delinquent could justify his killing in the sight of God. But you will say, how is it just to kill one man to amend another, if what were done were *necessary*? To this I answer, that men are justly killed, not for that their actions are not *necessitated*, but because they are *noxious*; and they are spared and preserved whose actions are not noxious. For where there is no law, there no killing, nor any thing else can be unjust, and by the right of nature, we destroy (without being unjust) all that is noxious, both beasts and men, and for beasts we kill them justly when we do it in order to our own preservation, and yet my Lord himself confesseth, that their actions, as being only *spontaneous*, and not *free*, are all *necessitated* and determined to that one thing they shall do. For men, when we make societies or commonwealths, we lay [not][1] down our right to kill, excepting in certain cases, as murder, theft or other offensive action; so that the right, which the commonwealth hath to put a man to death for crimes, is not created by the *law*, but remains from the first right of *nature*, which every man hath to preserve himself, for that the law

---

[1] The word 'not' appears in the original editions, but the passage makes better sense if it is omitted. It is probably a misprint. Cf. the excellent edition (of the two treatises, *Human Nature* and *Liberty and Necessity*) by Philip Mallet (1812).

doth not take the right away in the case of criminals, who were by the law excepted. Men are not therefore put to death, or punished, for that their theft proceedeth from *election*, but because it was *noxious*, and contrary to men's preservation, and the punishment conducing to the preservation of the rest, in as much as to punish those that do voluntary hurt, and none else, frameth and maketh men's wills such as men would have them. And thus it is plain, that from the necessity of a voluntary action, cannot be inferred the injustice of the law that forbiddeth it, or the magistrate that punisheth it.

94 Secondly, I deny that it maketh consultations to be in vain; it is the consultation that *causeth* a man, and *necessitateth* him to *choose* to do one thing rather than another, so that unless a man say that that cause is in vain, which necessitateth the effect, he cannot infer the superfluousness of consultation out of the necessity of the election proceeding from it. But it seemeth his Lordship reasons thus:—If I must do this rather than that, I shall do this rather than that, though I consult not at all;—which is a false proposition, and a false consequence, and no better than this: If I shall live till to-morrow, I shall live till to-morrow, though I run myself through with a sword to-day. If there be a necessity that an action shall be done, or that any effect shall be brought to pass, it does not therefore follow, that there is nothing necessarily requisite as a means to bring it to pass; and therefore when it is determined, that one thing shall be chosen before another, it is determined also for what *cause* it shall so be chosen, which cause, for the most part, is deliberation or consultation; and therefore consultation is not in vain, and indeed the less in vain, by how much the election is more necessitated; if *more* and *less* had any place in *necessity*.

The same answer is to be given to the third supposed inconvenience, namely, that admonitions are in vain; for the admonitions are parts of consultation, the admonitor being a counsellor for the time, to him that is admonished.

The fourth pretended inconvenience is, that praise, dispraise, reward and punishment will be in vain. To which I answer, that for praise and dispraise, they depend not at all on the *necessity* of the action praised or dispraised. For what is it else to *praise*, but to say a thing is good? Good, I say, for me, or for some body else, or for the state and commonwealth. And what is it to say an action is good, but to say it is as I would wish? Or as another would have it, or according to the will of the state? that is to say, according to the law. Does my Lord think that no action can please me, or him, or the commonwealth, that should proceed from necessity? Things may be therefore necessary, and yet praise-worthy, as also necessary, and yet dispraised, and neither of them both in vain, because praise and dispraise, and likewise reward and punishment, do by example make and conform the will to good and evil. It was a very great praise in my opinion, that Velleius Paterculus gives Cato, where he says that he was good by *nature, Et quia aliter esse non potuit.*

To the fifth and sixth inconveniences, that counsels, arts, arms, instruments, books, study, medicines, and the like, would be superfluous, the same answer serves as to the former, that is to say, that this consequence, *If the effect shall necessarily come to pass, then it shall come to pass without its causes,* is a false one, and those things named counsels, arts, arms, etc. are the causes of these effects.

★   ★   ★   ★

The fourth argument from reason is this: The order, beauty and **95** perfection of the world requireth that in the universe should be agents of all sorts; some necessary, some free, some contingent. He that shall make all things necessary, or all things free, or all things contingent, doth overthrow the beauty and perfection of the world.

In which argument I observe first a contradiction, for seeing he that *maketh* any thing, in that he maketh it, maketh it to be *necessary,* it followeth that he that maketh all things, maketh all things necessarily to be; as, if a workman make a garment, the garment must necessarily be, so, if God make every thing, every thing must necessarily be. Perhaps the beauty of the world requireth (though we know it not) that some agents should work without deliberation (which his Lordship calls *necessary* agents), and some agents with deliberation (and those both he and I call *free* agents), and that some agents should work, and we not know how (and their effects we both call *contingents*); but this hinders not, but that he that electeth may have his *election* necessarily determined to *one* by *former* causes, and that which is *contingent* and imputed to fortune, be nevertheless *necessary* and depend on *precedent* necessary causes. For by *contingent,* men do not mean that which hath *no* cause, but that which hath not for cause any thing that we perceive; as for example, when a traveller meets with a shower, the journey had a cause, and the rain had a cause sufficient to produce it, but because the journey caused not the rain, nor the rain the journey, we say they were contingent one to another. And thus you see, that though there be three sorts of events, *necessary, contingent, and free,* yet they may be *all* necessary, without destruction of the beauty or perfection of the universe.

★   ★   ★   ★

My Opinion about Liberty and Necessity

96   First I conceive, that when it cometh into a man's mind to do, or not to do some certain action, if he have no time to deliberate, the doing it, or abstaining *necessarily* follow the present thought he hath of the good or evil consequence thereof to himself. As for example, in sudden anger, the action shall follow the thought of revenge; in sudden fear, the thought of escape. Also when a man hath time to deliberate, but deliberates not, because never any thing appeared that could make him doubt of the consequence, the action follows his opinion of the goodness or harm of it. These actions I call VOLUN-TARY: my Lord, if I understand him aright, calls them SPONTANEOUS. I call them *voluntary,* because those actions, that follow immediately the *last* appetite, are voluntary, and here where is one only appetite, that one is the last. Besides, I see it is reasonable to punish a *rash* action, which could not be justly done by man to man, unless the same were *voluntary.* For no action of a man can be said to be without deliberation, though never so sudden, because it is supposed he had time to deliberate all the precedent time of his life, whether he should do that kind of action or not. And hence it is, that he that killeth in a sudden passion of anger, shall nevertheless be justly put to death, because all the time, wherein he was able to consider, whether to kill were good or evil, shall be held for one continual deliberation, and consequently the killing shall be judged to proceed from election.

Secondly, I conceive when a man deliberates, whether he shall do a thing or not do it, that he does nothing else but consider whether it be better for himself to do it, or not to do it. And to *consider* an action, is to imagine the consequences of it, both good and evil. From whence is to be inferred, that deliberation is nothing else but alternate imagination of the good and evil sequels of an action, or (which is the same thing) alternate hope and fear, or alternate appetite to do or quit the action of which he deliberateth.

Thirdly, I conceive that in all deliberations, that is to say, in an alternate succession of contrary appetites, the last is that which we call the WILL, and is immediately next before the doing of the action, or next before the doing of it become impossible. All other appetites to do, and to quit, that come upon a man during his deliberations, are called *intentions*, and *inclinations*, but not *wills*, there being but *one* will, which also in this case may be called the *last* will, though the *intentions* change often.

Fourthly, I conceive that those actions, which a man is said to do upon deliberation, are said to be voluntary, and done upon choice and election, so that *voluntary* action, and action proceeding from *election*, is the same thing, and that of a voluntary agent, it is all one to say, he is *free*, and to say, he hath not made an end of *deliberating*.

Fifthly, I conceive *liberty* to be rightly defined in this manner; *liberty is the absence of all the impediments to action that are not contained in the nature and intrinsical quality of the agent.* As for example, the water is said to descend *freely*, or to have *liberty* to descend by the channel of the river, because there is no impediment that way; but not across, because the banks are impediments. And though the water cannot ascend, yet men never say it wants the *liberty* to ascend, but the *faculty* or power, because the impediment is in the nature of the water, and intrinsical. So also we say, he that is tied wants the *liberty* to go, because the impediment is not in him, but in his bands, whereas we say not so of him that is sick or lame, because the impediment is in himself.

Sixthly, I conceive that nothing taketh beginning from itself, but **97** from the action of some other immediate agent without itself. And that therefore, when first a man hath an appetite or will to something, to which immediately before he had no appetite nor will, the *cause* of his will, is not the will itself, but something else not in his own disposing. So that whereas it is out of controversy, that of voluntary actions the *will* is the *necessary* cause, and by this which is said, the will is also *caused* by other things whereof it disposeth not, it followeth, that voluntary actions have all of them *necessary* causes, and therefore are *necessitated*.

Seventhly, I hold that to be a *sufficient cause*, to which nothing is wanting that is needful to the producing of the *effect*. The same also is a *necessary* cause. For if it be possible that a *sufficient* cause shall not bring forth the *effect*, then there wanteth somewhat which was needful to the producing of it, and so the *cause* was not *sufficient*: but if it be impossible that a *sufficient* cause should not produce the *effect*, then is a *sufficient* cause a *necessary* cause (for that is said to produce an effect *necessarily* that cannot but produce it.) Hence it is manifest, that whatsoever is produced, is produced *necessarily*, for whatsoever is produced hath had a *sufficient* cause to produce it, or else it had not been, and therefore also *voluntary* actions are *necessitated*.

Lastly, I hold, that the ordinary definition of a *free agent*, namely, *that a* free agent *is that, which, when all things are present, which are needful to produce the* effect, *can nevertheless not produce it*, implies a contradiction, and is nonsense, being as much as to say, the cause may be *sufficient*, that is to say, *necessary*, and yet the effect shall not follow.

My Reasons

98   For the first five points, wherein it is explicated: 1. what *spontaneity* is: 2. what *deliberation* is: 3. what *will*, *propension* and *appetite* is: 4. what a *free agent* is: 5. what *liberty* is: there can no other proof be offered but every man's own experience, by reflection on himself, and remembering what he useth to have in his mind, that is, what he himself meaneth when he saith—an action is *spontaneous*,— a man *deliberates*,—such is his *will*,—that *agent* or that *action* is *free*. Now he that reflecteth so on himself, cannot but be satisfied, that *deliberation* is the consideration of the good and evil sequels of an action to come; that by *spontaneity* is meant inconsiderate action (or else nothing is meant by it;) that *will* is the last act of our deliberation; that a *free agent* is he that can do if he will, and forbear if he will; and that *liberty* is the absence of external impediments. But, to those that out of custom speak not what they conceive, but what they hear, and are not able, or will not take the pains to consider what they think when they hear such words, no argument can be sufficient, because *experience* and *matter of fact* is not verified by other men's arguments, but by every man's own *sense* and *memory*. For example, how can it be proved, that to *love* a thing and to think it *good* is all one, to a man that doth not mark his own meaning by those words? Or how can it be proved that *eternity* is not *nunc stans* to a man that says those words by custom, and never considers how he can conceive the thing in his mind?

Also the sixth point, that a man cannot imagine anything to begin **99**
without a cause, can no other way be made known, but by trying
how he can imagine it, but if he try, he shall find as much reason (if
there be no cause of the thing) to conceive it should begin at one
time as another, that is, he hath equal reason to think it should begin
at all times, which is impossible, and therefore he must think there
was some special cause why it began then, rather than sooner or
later; or else that it began never, but was eternal.

For the seventh point, which is that all *events* have *necessary*
causes, it is there proved in that they have *sufficient* causes. Further
let us in this place also suppose any event never so casual, as the
throwing (for example) *ames ace* upon a pair of dice, and see, if it
must not have been *necessary* before it was thrown. For seeing it was
thrown, it had a beginning, and consequently a *sufficient* cause to
produce it, consisting partly in the dice, partly in outward things, as
the posture of the parts of the hand, the measure of force applied by
the caster, the posture of the parts of the table, and the like. In sum
there was nothing wanting which was necessarily requisite to the
producing of that particular cast, and consequently the cast was
necessarily thrown, for if it had not been thrown, there had wanted
somewhat requisite to the throwing of it, and so the cause had not
been *sufficient*. In the like manner it may be proved that every other
accident, how *contingent* soever it seem, or how *voluntary* soever it be,
is produced *necessarily*, which is that that my L. Bishop disputes
against. The same may be proved also in this manner. Let the case
be put, for example, of the weather. *It is necessary that to-morrow it
shall rain or not rain.* If therefore it be not *necessary* it shall rain, it is
necessary it shall not rain; otherwise there is no necessity that the
proposition, *It shall rain or not rain*, should be true. I know there be
some that say, it may necessarily be true that one of the two shall
come to pass, but not, singly that it shall rain, or that it shall not rain;
which is as much as to say, *one* of them is *necessary*, yet *neither* of
them is *necessary*; and therefore to seem to avoid that absurdity, they
make a distinction, that neither of them is true *determinatè*, but *indeter-
minatè*; which distinction either signifies no more but this, One of
them is true, but we know not which, and so the necessity remains,
though we know it not; or if the meaning of the distinction be not
that, it hath no meaning, and they might as well have said, One of
them is true *Titirice*, but neither of them *Tu patulice*.

The last thing in which also consisteth the whole controversy, namely that there is no such thing as an agent, which when all things requisite to action are present, can nevertheless forbear to produce it, or (which is all one) that there is no such thing as *freedom from necessity*, is easily inferred from that which hath been before alleged. For if it be an *agent* it can *work*, and if it *work* there is nothing wanting of what is requisite to produce the *action*, and consequently the cause of the action is *sufficient*, and if *sufficient*, then also *necessary*, as hath been proved before.

★　　　★　　　★　　　★

De Cive

CHAP. XIV—OF LAWS AND TRESPASSES[1]

I. They who less seriously consider the force of words, do some- **100** times confound *law* with *counsel*, sometimes with *covenant*, sometimes with *right*. They confound *law* with *counsel*, who think, that it is the duty of monarchs not only to give ear to their counsellors, but also to obey them, as though it were in vain to take counsel, unless it were also followed. We must fetch the distinction between *counsel*, and *law*, from the difference between *counsel*, and *command*. Now COUNSEL is a precept in which the reason of my obeying it, is taken from the thing itself which is advised; but COMMAND is a precept in which the cause of my obedience depends on the will of the commander. For it is not properly said, *Thus I will*, and *thus I command*, except the will stand for a reason; now when obedience is yielded to the laws, not for the thing itself, but by reason of the adviser's will, the law is not a counsel, but a command, and is defined thus, LAW is the *command of that person (whether man, or court) whose precept contains in it the reason of obedience*; as the precepts of God in regard of men, of magistrates in respect of their subjects, and universally of all the powerful in respect of them who cannot resist, may be termed their laws; *law* and *counsel* therefore differ many ways; law belongs to him who hath power over them whom he adviseth, counsel to them who have no power. To follow what is prescribed by law, is duty, what by counsel, is free-will. Counsel is directed to his end that receives it, law, to his that gives it. Counsel is given to none but the willing, law even to the unwilling. To conclude, the right of the counsellor is made void by the will of him to whom he gives counsel, the right of the law-giver is not abrogated at the pleasure of him who hath a law imposed.

II. They confound *law*, and *covenant*, who conceive the laws to be

[1 Cf. §§ 20, 85, 103.]

nothing else but certain ὁμολογήματα, or forms of living, determined by the common consent of men. . . . For *contract is a promise, law a command.* In contracts we say, *I will do this*; in laws, *Do this.* *Contracts oblige us, laws tie us fast, being obliged. A contract obligeth of itself, the law holds the party obliged by virtue of the universal contract of yielding obedience; therefore in contract it is first determined what is to be done, before we are obliged to do it; but in law we are first obliged to perform, and what is to be done, is determined afterwards.

★   ★   ★   ★

CHAP. XV—OF THE KINGDOM OF GOD BY NATURE[1]

★   ★   ★   ★

101   VII. Now if God have the right of sovereignty from his power, it is manifest, that the *obligation* of yielding him obedience lies on men by reason of their †weakness; for that *obligation* which rises from contract, of which we have spoken in the second chapter, can have no place here, where the right of ruling (no covenant passing between) rises only from nature. But there are two species of *natural obligation*, one when liberty is taken away by corporal impediments, according to which we say that heaven and earth, and all creatures, do obey the common laws of their creation: the other when it is taken away by hope, or fear, according to which the weaker, despairing of his own power to resist, cannot but yield to the stronger.

★ *Contracts oblige us*] *To be obliged,* and *to be tied being obliged,* seems to some men to be one, and the same thing, and that therefore here seems to be some distinction in words, but none indeed. More clearly therefore, I say thus, that a man is obliged by his contracts, that is, that he ought to perform for his promise sake; but that the law ties him being obliged, that is to say, it compels him to make good his promise, for fear of the punishment appointed by the law.

† *By reason of their weakness*] If this shall seem hard to any man, I desire him with a silent thought to consider, if there were two omnipotents, whether were bound to obey; I believe he will confess that neither is bound: if this be true, then it is also true what I have set down, that men are subject unto God because they are not omnipotent. And truly our Saviour admonishing Paul (who at that time was an enemy to the Church) that he should not kick against the pricks, seems to require obedience from him for this cause, because he had not power enough to resist.

[1 Cf. § 89.]

From this last kind of obligation, that is to say from fear, or conscience of our own weakness (in respect of the divine power), it comes to pass, that we are obliged to obey God in his natural kingdom; reason dictating to all, acknowledging the divine power and providence, *that there is no kicking against the pricks.*

★ ★ ★ ★

De Corpore Politico

★ ★ ★ ★

102 2. The breach or violation of covenant, is that which men call *injury*, consisting in some action or omission, which is therefore called *unjust*. For it is action or omission without *jus*, or right, which was transferred or relinquished before. There is a great similitude between that we call *injury*, or *injustice* in the actions and conversations of men in the world, and that which is called *absurd* in the arguments and disputations of the Schools. For as he which is driven to contradict an assertion by him before maintained, is said to be reduced to an absurdity; so he that through passion doth, or omitteth that which before by covenant he promised not to do, or not to omit, is said to commit injustice, and there is in every breach of covenant a contradiction properly so called. For he that covenanteth, willeth to do, or omit, in the time to come. And he that doth any action, willeth it in that present, which is part of the future time contained in the covenant. And therefore he that violateth a covenant, willeth the doing and the not doing of the same thing, at the same time, which is a plain contradiction. And so *injury* is an *absurdity* of conversation, as absurdity is a kind of injustice in disputation.

★ ★ ★ ★

PART II—CHAP. X[2]

103 1. Thus far concerning the nature of man, and the constitution and properties of a body politic. There remaineth only for the last chapter, to speak of the nature and sorts of law. And first it is manifest, that all laws are declarations of the mind, concerning some action future to be done, or omitted. And all declarations and expressions of the mind concerning future actions and omissions, are either *promissive*, as *I will do, or not do*; or *provisive*, as for example,

[1 Cf. § 59.]   [2 Cf. §§ 20, 85, 100.]

If this be done or not done, this will follow; or *imperative*, as *Do this, or do it not*. In the first sort of these expressions, consisteth the nature of a covenant; in the second, consisteth counsel; in the third, command.

2. It is evident, when a man doth, or forbeareth to do any action, if he be moved thereto by this only consideration, that the same is good or evil in itself; and that there be no reason why the will or pleasure of another, should be of any weight in his deliberation, that then neither to do nor omit the action deliberated is any breach of law. And consequently, whatsoever is a law to a man, respecteth the will of another, and the declaration thereof. But a covenant is a declaration of a man's own will. And therefore a law and a covenant differ: and though they be both obligatory, and a law obligeth no otherwise than by virtue of some covenant made by him who is subject thereunto, yet they oblige by several sorts of promises. For a covenant obligeth by promise of an action, or omission, especially named and limited; but a law bindeth by a promise of obedience in general, whereby the action to be done, or left undone, is referred to the determination of him, to whom the covenant is made. So that the difference between a covenant and a law, standeth thus: in simple covenant, the action to be done, or not done, is first limited and made known, and then followeth the promise to do or not do; but in a law, the obligation to do or not to do, precedeth, and the declaration what is to be done, or not done, followeth after.

3. And from this may be deduced, that which to some may seem a paradox, that the command of him, whose command is a law in one thing, is a law in every thing. For seeing a man is obliged to obedience before what he is to do be known, he is obliged to obey in general, that is to say, in every thing.

4. That the counsel of a man is no law to him that is counselled, and that he who alloweth another to give him counsel, doth not thereby oblige himself to follow the same, is manifest enough. And yet men usually call counselling, by the name of governing, not that they are not able to distinguish between them, but because they envy many times those men that are called to counsel, and are therefore angry with them that are counselled. But if to counsellors there should be given a right to have their counsel followed, then are they no more counsellors, but masters of them whom they counsel; and their counsels no more counsels, but laws. For the difference between a law and a counsel being no more but this, that in counsel the

expression is *Do, because it is best*; in a law, *Do, because I have a right to compel you*; or *Do, because I say Do*; when counsel, ⟨which⟩ should give the reason of the action it adviseth to, becometh the reason thereof itself, ⟨it⟩ is no more counsel, but a law.[1]

★   ★   ★   ★

[1 In the final part of this sentence, the original editions omit the words 'which' and 'it', here placed in angle brackets, and read 'because' for 'becometh'. The amendments here are taken from the version of F. Tönnies (in *The Elements of Law*), edited from the manuscripts. The version in the original printed editions, presumably owing to a printer's error, does not make sense.]

RICHARD CUMBERLAND

1631–1718

DE LEGIBUS NATURAE
Disquisitio Philosophica

[First printed, 1672. Reprinted here from the first edition, with reduction of initial capital letters. An English translation by the present editor is added]

RICHARD CUMBERLAND

De Legibus Naturae

CAP. I—DE NATURA
RERUM

CHAP. I—ON THE NATURE OF
THINGS

104 I. Quamquam nonnulli, Sceptici scilicet, et Epicuraei, leges naturales existere negarunt olim, et etiamnum pernegant, convenit tamen inter nos atque illos quid hoc nomine significare velimus utrinque. Enimvero utrobique intelligimus propositiones quasdam immutabilis veritatis quae actiones voluntarias circa bonorum electionem, malorumque fugam dirigunt, ac obligationem ad actus externos inducunt: etiam citra leges civiles, et seposita consideratione pactorum regimen constituentium. Hujusmodi aliquot veritates a rerum, hominumque natura mentibus humanis necessario suggeri, ab iis percipi, et memoria (dum valent) retineri, adeoque ibidem existere; hoc est quod a nobis affirmatur, hoc idem a dictis adversariis non minus diserte denegatur.

Quocirca ut harum proposi-

I. Although some people, such as the Sceptics and Epicureans, used to deny, and still continue to deny, that there are natural laws, nevertheless both they and we are agreed on the meaning of this term. We both understand by it certain propositions of immutable truth, which guide voluntary actions about the choice of good and the avoidance of evil, and which impose an obligation to outward acts, even without regard to civil laws and laying aside consideration of the compacts that set up government. What we assert, and what our said adversaries no less clearly deny, is that some truths of this kind are necessarily supplied to the human mind by the nature of things and of men, that they are perceived and remembered by the mind so long as it remains sound, and therefore that they exist there. **104**

In order that the essential

tionum essentia, ac forma melius innotescat, necesse est ut primo rerum universim, deinde hominum, denique boni naturam, quatenus ad hanc quaestionem spectant, inspiciamus: postea vero ut ostendamus quales propositiones praxin humanam dirigant ac legum vim, seu obligationem naturaliter secum ferant, utpote indicantes praxin ad finem necessario quaesitum necessariam. Tandem earum existentia ex causarum illas generantium existentia, ac determinato influxu satis evincetur.

105   II. Nec mirum cuiquam videri debet quod primo rerum hujus universi naturam respiciendam dixerim; quippe haud aliter hominum amplissimae facultates rerum plurimarum indigae, et ab omnibus ad operandum excitatae intelligi possunt. Ecquis enim intelligere valeat quid humanae menti aut corpori maxime conveniat, quidve iisdem noceat, nisi consideret omnes (quoad possit) causas tam remotas, quam proximas quae hominem constituerunt ac jam conservant, quaeque eundem in posterum tueri, aut corrumpere possunt? Immo nec satis intelligitur quid optimum sit quod

character and the form of these propositions may become more evident, we must consider, so far as is relevant to this inquiry, first the nature of things universally, then the nature of man, and finally the nature of the good. Afterwards we must show what sort of propositions direct human conduct and naturally carry with them the force or obligation of laws, in that they indicate the conduct necessary for securing a necessarily sought end. Lastly, their existence will be sufficiently proved from the existence and determinate influence of the causes that produce them.

II. It should not seem strange **105** to anyone that I have said we ought first to consider the nature of things in the universe; for we cannot otherwise understand the very extensive faculties of man, which stand in need of very many things and are stirred into operation by all things. Could anyone understand what is most suitable for the human mind or body, or what harms them, if he did not consider, as far as possible, all the causes, remote as well as immediate, which have formed man and now keep him in being, and which can in the future preserve or destroy him? Again, we cannot adequately understand what is the best thing

in dato casu quispiam facere possit, nisi effecta tam remota quam proxima, quae ab ipso in omni circumstantiarum varietate proveniant, prospiciantur, et inter se comparentur.

Cogitatio autem tam causarum a quibus homines pendent, quam effectorum quae ab eorum viribus aliquantisper concurrentibus produci possint, mentem cujusque necessario perducet tum ad considerandos alios homines ubicunque sparsos, seipsum autem velut exiguam humani generis partem, tum etiam ad perpendendam totam hanc rerum compagem, primumque ejus conditorem regemque Deum. His tandem pro virili expensis, generalia quaedam dictamina proferre poterit animus noster, quibus pronunciet quales actus humani ad commune bonum entium, praesertim rationalium, (quo propria foelicitas cujusque continetur) maxime conducant. In hujusmodi autem dictaminibus, si modo vera fuerint et necessaria, legem naturae contineri postea videbimus.

106 III. Nihilominus instituti nostri ratio non postulat ut rerum omnium genera quae sint ostendamus. . . . Sufficiet nobis in opusculi hujus initio lectorem monuisse, totam moralis

that anyone can do on a given occasion, unless we foresee and compare with each other the effects, remote as well as immediate, that he may give rise to in all different kinds of circumstances.

But thought of the causes on which men depend, and of the effects which may be produced for a time by the concurrence of their powers, will necessarily lead each man not only to consider other men, wherever dispersed, and himself as being a mere tiny part of the human race; it will also lead him to reflect upon the whole framework of things, and upon God, its original founder and its ruler. Having duly pondered on these matters to the best of our ability, our minds will be able to bring forth certain general precepts for deciding what sort of human actions may best promote the common good of all beings, and especially of rational beings, in which the proper happiness of each is contained. In such precepts, provided they be true and necessary, is the law of nature contained, as we shall see later.

III. Nevertheless the purpose **106** of our undertaking does not require a survey of the different kinds of all things. . . . It is enough for us to have warned the reader, at the beginning of

philosophiae, legumque naturalium doctrinam in observationes naturales omnium experientia notas, aut in conclusiones a vera physiologia agnitas, et stabilitas ultimo resolvi. Physiologiam autem tam lato hic sumo sensu, ut ea non tantum omnia quae experimur corporum naturalium phaenomena complectatur; sed et praeterea animorum nostrorum naturam ex observatis eorum actibus, perfectionibusque propriis investiget; tandemque ex ordine causarum naturalium ad Primi Motoris notitiam homines deducat, eumque effectuum omnium necessariorum causam esse agnoscat. Enimvero natura tam creata, quam Creatoris notiones illas omnes, adeoque materiam e qua leges naturales conflantur, ut propositionum practicarum veritatem suggerit; Creatoris autem agnitio iisdem plenam insuper praestat authoritatem. Atque haec quidem hoc loco paulo uberius veniunt illustranda.

107 IV. Quamquam autem innumera sint quae e cognitione universi desumi possint in materiam particularium dictaminum ad mores formandos dirigentium, visum est tamen

this little work, that the whole of what is to be learned of moral philosophy and of natural laws is ultimately resolved into observations of nature that are known by the experience of all, or into conclusions acknowledged and established by true natural science. I here take the term 'natural science' in a wide sense, such that it not only embraces all experiential phenomena of natural bodies, but investigates in addition the nature of our minds from observation of their workings and proper perfections, and eventually leads men from the order of natural causes to a knowledge of the First Mover and acknowledges him to be the cause of all necessary effects. For the nature of the creation, as well as of the Creator, supplies all those notions and therefore the material of which natural laws are composed, just as it supplies the truth of practical propositions; but the acknowledgement of the Creator adds to them complete authority. These things must here be explained a little more fully.

IV. But although there are **107** countless things that could be picked out from a knowledge of the universe for the material of particular precepts directing the formation of morals, I have thought it best to select only a

pauca tantum, eaque generalissima seligere, quae generalem, quam initio proposui, legum naturae descriptionem aliquatenus explicent, et in unico dictamine, omnium legum naturalium parente, paulo apertius continentur. Illud autem ita se habet. 'Benevolentia maxima singulorum agentium rationalium erga omnes statum constituit singulorum, omniumque benevolorum, quantum fieri ab ipsis potest, foelicissimum; et ad statum eorum, quem possunt assequi, foelicissimum necessario requiritur; ac proinde, commune bonum erit suprema lex.' Sensus hujus propositionis (1) recte explicandus est. (2) Ostendendum est quomodo ea e rerum natura discatur; tandem ex iis quae in sequente libello continentur eam vim habere legis, immo et omnia naturae praecepta inde profluere liquido uti spero constabit. Sciant itaque lectores me nusquam benevolentiae nomine intelligere languidam illam et emortuam eorum volitionem, quae nihil efficiat eorum quae dicuntur velle, sed illam solum cujus vi quamprimum et quantum possumus exequimur quae animitus volumus. Liceat interim hoc nomine complecti affectum

few, and those the most general, which may explain to some extent the general description of the laws of nature which I gave at the beginning. They are a little more clearly contained in a single precept, the fount of all natural laws. It runs thus: 'The greatest benevolence of each rational agent towards all forms the happiest state of each and of all benevolent persons, so far as it can be produced by them themselves; and it is necessarily required for the happiest state that they can attain; and therefore the common good will be the supreme law.' First, the meaning of this proposition must be rightly explained. Secondly, I must show how it may be learned from the nature of things. Finally, it will, I hope, be plain from what follows in this book that the proposition has the force of a law, and further that all the precepts of nature clearly flow from it. Now I would have the reader know that I nowhere understand by the term 'benevolence' that languid, lifeless volition of people which effects nothing of what they are said to desire, but only that one by whose force we carry out, as soon and as far as we can, what we heartily desire. The term may, however, be allowed to cover also that

etiam illum, quo superioribus grata volumus, qui pietatis in Deum, patriam, parentes, nomine speciatim insignitur. Atque ideo hoc verbo uti placeat potius quam [amor] quoniam vi suae compositionis actum voluntatis nostrae cum objecto suo generalissimo conjunctum innuit, et in malum sensum non usurpatur, quod amori contigit. Maximam autem benevolentiam hic sumpsimus ut idonea causa summae foelicitatis poneretur. Alibi indicabimus quomodo scrupuli qui inde oriuntur, facile eximantur. Verbo [omnes] totum illud innuo quod constituitur e singulis simul consideratis, in ordine ad unum finem quem status foelicissimi nomine ibidem indigitamus. Deum autem hominesque rationalium nomine complecti liceat; idque Cicerone praeeunte, feci, quem in usu verbi Latini tuto mihi videor ducem sequi. Is enim I. *de Legibus*, rationem Deo, hominibusque communem agnoscit, et sapientiam (quam omnes Deo tribuunt) nihil aliud esse docuit praeter rationem adultam. Usus sum verbo [constituit] ut innuerem benevolentiam illam et

disposition whereby we desire what is pleasing to superiors, and which is specifically marked by the name of 'piety' towards God, country, or parents. I preferred to use this word rather than 'love', because the components of the word 'benevolence' indicate an act of the will joined with its most general object, and because it is not misused in a bad sense, as has befallen the word 'love'. I have spoken of 'the greatest benevolence' in order to posit an adequate cause of the highest happiness. I shall show elsewhere how the doubts that arise because of this may be easily removed. By the word 'all' I mean that whole which is made up of the individual persons when they are considered together, each in his place, in relation to a single end, which in the same place I call 'the happiest state'. Under the term 'rational' agents we may include God and men. Here I have followed the precedent of Cicero, who is, I think, a safe guide on the usage of a Latin word. In *De Legibus*, Book I, he acknowledges that reason is common to God and men, and he has held that wisdom (which all ascribe to God) is nothing other than reason in its fully developed state. I have used the word 'forms' to indicate that the aforesaid benevo-

causam esse intrinsecam praesentis, et efficientem futurae foelicitatis, et utriusque respectu necessario requisitam. Addidi autem [quantum ab ipsis fieri potest] ut innuerem rerum externarum adjumenta in nostra saepe non esse potestate, quamquam illa ad vitae animalis foelicitatem requirantur; et a legibus naturae moralisque philosophiae non alia expectanda esse vitae beatae auxilia, quam praecepta circa actiones, et ea actionum objecta quae in nostra sunt potestate. Et quanquam contingat ut diversi homines pro diversis animorum, et corporum viribus, immo ut iidem in diversis circumstantiis positi, nunc plus nunc minus possint ad commune bonum: lex tamen naturalis satis observatur, et finis ejus obtinetur, si quantum quisque in datis circumstantiis valeat, praestetur. Verum latior hujus sententiae explicatio in sequentibus occurret.

lence is both the intrinsic cause of present happiness and the efficient cause of future happiness, and is necessarily required in respect of both. But I have added 'so far as it can be produced by them themselves' to indicate that the advantages of external things are often not within our power although they are required for the happiness of animal life; and to indicate also that no other means of assistance towards a life of bliss are to be looked for from the laws of nature and of moral philosophy than precepts about action and those objects of action that are within our power. Although it so happens that different men, owing to differences in their mental or bodily powers, or indeed the same men when placed in different circumstances, are not always able to promote the common good to the same extent, nevertheless natural law is sufficiently observed, and its end attained, if it is fulfilled as far as each person is able in given circumstances. But a fuller explanation of this maxim will be given later.

★   ★   ★   ★

108 VI. Quod attinet ad nexum terminorum hujus propositionis in quo necessario ejus veritas consistit, is mihi videtur

VI. As regards the connection **108** between the terms of this proposition, constituting its necessary truth, that seems to me quite

admodum evidens. Idem enim significat ac si diceretur. Ea volitio, seu prosecutio bonorum omnium in nostra potestate sitorum, quae maxime efficax est ad nostrum aliorumque rationalium fruitionem, maximum est quod homines efficere possunt, ut ipsi, aliique iis foelicissime perfruantur. Seu nulla vis in hominibus major est, qua sibi, aliisque omnium bonorum complexionem comparent, quam voluntas suam cujusque foelicitatem, simul cum foelicitate aliorum prosequendi: in quibus verbis illud primo patet, nullam esse in hominibus majorem vim quicquam efficiendi quam sit voluntas ad ultimum virium suarum determinata. Deinde et illud liquido constat foelicitatem singulorum *v.g.* Socratis et Platonis et caeterorum individuorum (de qua praedicatum loquitur) sigillatim non posse separari a foelicitate omnium (cujus causa in subjecto continetur) quippe totum a partibus simul sumptis non differt. Intelligenda autem est haec propositio universalis de omnium benevolentia pronuncians, hactenus cum legibus convenire,

plain. For its meaning is the same as if this were said: 'That volition or pursuit of all good things placed within our power, which is most effective for the enjoyment of them by ourselves and other rational beings, is the best means available to men for the happiest enjoyment of those goods by themselves and by others.' Or alternatively: 'There is no greater power in men, whereby they may procure for themselves and others a combination of all good things, than the will of each man to pursue his own happiness together with the happiness of others.' In these words, what stands out most clearly first, is that there is no greater power in men of effecting anything than a will determined to the utmost extent of its powers. Secondly, it is also perfectly plain that the happiness of each person, e.g. of Socrates, Plato, and all the other individuals, (which is referred to in the predicate), cannot be severally separated from the happiness of all (the cause of which is comprised in the subject), because the whole is no different from the parts taken together. Now this universal proposition, which makes a pronouncement about the benevolence of all, must be understood to be like laws to this extent: it does not

quod indicet, non quid unus quispiam aut pauci faciant ad suam sejunctam ab aliorum cura foelicitatem, sed quid et omnes simul facere possunt ut sint beati, et quid singuli absque ulla inter se repugnantia (quippe quae cum ratione, cujus omnes participes sunt, non consistit) faciant, ut communem omnium foelicitatem assequantur, in qua maxima singulis possibilis continetur, et efficacissime promovetur. Prius et plenius notum est in genere, utpote e communibus et essentialibus humanae naturae attributis fluens, quid omnes facere possint, aut non possint ad communem finem conducens, quam quid singulari alicui in determinatis circumstantiis possibile est; hae enim infinitae sunt, et ideo nemini cognoscibiles. Ut productis pluribus in campum exercitibus, notius est non posse omnes pugnando vincere, quam quis exercitus vincet.

109 Tertio denique singularis cujuspiam, aut paucorum foelicitatis cura exuitur de praesenti, et nulla probabili ratione sperari potest in posterum, dum quaeritur per oppugnatam, aut posthabitam aliorum omnium ra-

tell us what any one or a few persons should do for their own happiness dissociated from a concern for others; it tells us what all together can do to be happy, and what individuals, without any clash with each other (since that is contrary to reason, which is shared by all), should do in order to attain the common happiness of all, in which the greatest possible happiness for each is contained and is most effectively promoted. One knows sooner and more fully in general, as flowing from the common essential attributes of human nature, what all can or cannot do to serve a common end, than one knows what is possible for any one person in determinate circumstances; for these are infinite, and therefore no one can know them. Just as, when several armies have been brought into the field, one has a better knowledge that they cannot all win the battle, than one has of which army will win.

In the third and last place, the 109 cultivation of the happiness of any one person, or of a few, is put out of court so far as the present is concerned, and cannot have any probable grounds of hope for the future, so long as it is sought by opposing or neglecting the happiness of all other

tionalium beatitudinem. Quippe et animo ita affecto pars quaedam essentialis suae perfectionis deest; nempe pax interna ex uniformi sapientia secum semper consentiente. Repugnat enim sibi quum aliter circa se agendum esse statuit, aliter circa alios ejusdem naturae participes. Deest etiam magna illa laetitia quae in animo benevolo ex alienae foelicitatis sensu nascitur: ne quid nunc dicam de invidia, superbia caeterisque omnibus vitiis quorum legiones omnes malevolum obsident, et necessario miserum constituunt, utpote pessimis animi morbis laborantem.

Praeterea vero non est cur quis merito speret se foelicem fore, siquidem causas externas caeteras rationales (Deum nempe et homines a quorum auxilio spes illa necessario dependet) negligit, immo in suam perniciem lacessit. Non alia ergo est via quae quemlibet ad suam ducat foelicitatem, quam quae omnes ducat ad communem. Sufficiat haec hoc loco breviter indicasse, quod eo tantum consilio feci ut ostendam ex hujusmodi obser-

rational beings. For indeed the mind that is so disposed lacks a certain element essential to its perfection, namely the internal peace that comes from a uniform, continually self-consistent wisdom. For it is in conflict with itself when it decides that it should act in one way concerning itself and in another way concerning others who share the same nature. There is also lacking that great joy which arises in a benevolent mind from the perception of the happiness of others; to say nothing at present of envy, pride, and all the other vices which besiege the malevolent man in all their legions and necessarily render him unhappy in that he labours under the worst diseases of the mind.

Furthermore, there are no just grounds for anyone to hope to be happy if he neglects, or rather I should say provokes to his own ruin, all other rational causes outside himself, namely God and men, on whose help that hope of his necessarily depends. There is therefore no path leading anyone to his own happiness, other than the path which leads all to the common happiness. Let it suffice to have pointed this out briefly here, my sole purpose having been to show, from observations of this kind that are perfectly familiar

vatis, vulgari experientia notissimis, veritatem praedictae propositionis admodum luculenter constare. Haec autem latius postea deducemus.

110   VII. Agnosco interim hanc propositionem non prius efficacem esse posse ad cujusvis mores formandos, quam ille effectum, de quo hic pronunciatur, nempe foelicitatem suam cum aliorum foelicitate conjunctam in finem sibi proposuerit, et varios, quos benevolentia in se continet, actus pro mediis sumpserit. Veritas tamen illius necessaria prius innotescere potest, et earum omnium propositionum quae exinde justa consequentia deduci possunt; quales sunt illae minus generales, quae pronunciant de vi fidei, gratitudinis, στοργῆς, et caeterarum virtutum particularium, ad partem aliquam humanae foelicitatis obtinendam. Tota enim tam generalis illius propositionis, quam earum quae inde sequuntur veritas dependet a naturali, et necessaria vi talium actuum, velut causarum, ad tales effectus producendos. Abstrahunt autem ab existentia ejusmodi actuum, quae quidem a liberis pendet causis. Interim sufficit ad eandem veritatem

in common experience, that the truth of the aforesaid proposition is completely evident. But I shall demonstrate this more fully later.

VII. I acknowledge, however, **110** that this proposition cannot be effective for the forming of anyone's morals until he has placed before himself as his end the effect that is here laid down, namely his own happiness joined with the happiness of others, and until he has chosen as means the various actions that benevolence comprises. Nevertheless one can clearly see beforehand the necessary truth of that proposition and of all those other propositions which can be deduced as properly following from it; I mean such things as those less general propositions which make pronouncements about the force of keeping faith, of gratitude, of affection, and of the other particular virtues, for the purpose of obtaining some part of human happiness. For the whole truth of that general proposition, as well as of those that follow from it, depends on the natural and necessary force of such actions, as causes, for producing such effects. But the propositions abstract from the existence of such actions, which indeed depend on free causes. However, it is sufficient evidence of the same truth

quod quandocunque tales causae existent, effectus ejusmodi inde enascentur. In confesso res est in solutione omnigenorum problematum mathematicorum. De qua tamen quin vera detur scientia, nemo dubitat. Norunt omnes actus ducendi lineas, easque inter se conferendi in calculatione geometrica a libero hominum arbitrio produci. Libere addimus, subtrahimus, etc. interim necessario quisquis secundum regulas operatur, verum reperit summam, quae aequatur partibus inter se additis. Similia de differentia, facto, orto, radice dicantur: et generatim in omni quaestione cujus solutio possibilis est e datis, necessario ex his operationibus rite peractis quaesitum invenitur. Certus est nexus inter effectum desideratum, ejusque causas ab hac scientia indicatas. Ad hoc exemplar comformandae sunt aliae disciplinae practicae, idque in principiis morum emendandorum tradendis, conati sumus assequi; reducendo ad unum generale nomen [benevolentia] actus voluntarios a morali philosophia dirigendos: ejus species

to point out that whenever such causes exist, effects of that kind will arise from them. Everyone acknowledges this in the solution of all kinds of mathematical problems, yet no one doubts that true science results from that. All know that the actions of drawing and joining lines in geometrical reasoning are produced by the free will of men. We add, subtract, etc., freely; yet it is a matter of necessity that anyone who operates according to the rules, undoubtedly finds the total, which is equal to the parts added together. The same may be said of the remainder in subtraction, the product in multiplication, the quotient in division, and the root in extraction; and generally in every question whose solution is possible from what is given, the answer is found necessarily from these operations duly performed. The connection between the desired effect and its causes as shown by this science, is certain. Other studies relating to practice ought to follow this model, and that is what I have tried to achieve in propounding the principles of moral improvement. I have proceeded by reducing to one general term, 'benevolence', the voluntary acts that fall under the direction of moral philosophy; by inquiring

quaerendo, nexum denique ostendendo hujus actus cum effectu expetito.

*   *   *   *

111 X. Hic illud solum adjiciam, veritatem hanc, ut et caeteras pariter evidentes, praecipue vero quae hinc derivantur necessario, a Deo provenire, et annexum habere ejus observationi praemium, transgressioni poenam; talesque esse ut dirigendis nostris moribus aptae sint natura sua. His praestitis non video quid desit ut legis habeat vigorem. Addam tamen in calce hujus operis in ea contineri et in Deum pietatem, et in homines charitatem: in quibus utriusque tabulae legis divinae Mosaicae, et Evangelicae summa continetur. Eadem opera ostendam hinc omnes moralis philosophiae virtutes desumi posse; ac jura gentium tam quae pacem, quam quae bellum spectant. Quod autem a Deo authore evidens adeo veritas imprimatur, brevissime ostenditur ex illa physiologia, quae impressiones omnes in sensus nostros fieri ostendit, juxta leges (uti vocantur) motus

into the species of this genus; and finally by showing the connection between this action and the desired effect.

X. Here I shall only add that **111** this truth, as also the others that are equally evident, but especially those that are necessarily derived from this one, comes from God, and has reward annexed to its observance and punishment to its transgression, these being such as are fitted by their nature to direct our conduct. This being assured, I do not see what is lacking for the proposition to have the force of a law. However, I shall add at the end of this work that the proposition comprises both piety towards God and charity towards men; and these comprise the sum of both tables of the divine law, that of Moses and that of the Gospels. By the same means I shall show that there can be derived from it all the virtues of moral philosophy and the international law both of peace and of war. That the impression of a truth so evident has God as its author is very quickly shown from that natural science which shows that all impressions upon our senses are made in accordance with the natural laws (as they are called) of motion,

naturales; motum autem et primitus a Deo systemati huic corporeo fuisse impressum, et immutatum ab eo conservari. Hac methodo, quae mihi videtur certissima, totaque demonstrationibus nititur, citissime fit resolutio effectuum omnium necessariorum in primum motorem. Impressio autem terminorum hujus propositionis (quatenus saltem provenit a materia mota) est effectus naturalis; et perceptio identitatis sive cohaerentiae terminorum istorum prout in imaginatione existunt, nihil aliud est quam perceptio quod uterque terminus est impressio quaedam ab eadem causa in nos facta. Ipsa autem mentis perceptio qua vel terminos in imaginatione positos apprehendit, et qua eorum nexum perspicit, et vires suas, actionesque persentiscit, adeo naturaliter et necessario sequitur praesentiam eorum in imaginatione, et propensionem mentis intrinsecam, naturalem et inculpabilem ad observanda ea quae coram posita sunt, ut mentis causae efficienti, id est, Deo, non possint non ascribi, ab illo qui Deum Creatorem rerum omnium Primumve Motorem agnoscit. Aliae autem omnes methodi naturam explicandi

and that motion both was at first impressed by God upon this corporeal system and is conserved by him unchanged. By this method, which seems to me most certain and rests wholly on demonstration, all necessary effects are very quickly resolved into the first mover. Now the impression of the terms of our proposition (at least so far as the impression is produced by matter in motion) is a natural effect; and the perception of the identity or coherence of those terms, as they exist in the imagination, is nothing else than the perception that both terms are certain impressions made upon us by the same cause. But the very perception of the mind, by which it even apprehends the terms placed in the imagination, perceives their connection, and is aware of its own powers and activities, follows naturally and necessarily upon their presence in the imagination and upon the intrinsic, natural, faultless inclination of the mind towards observing the things that are placed before it; so much so that they are bound to be ascribed to the efficient cause of the mind, that is, to God, by those who acknowledge God to be the Creator or First Mover of all things. But then all other methods of explaining nature,

quantumcunque aut ab hac, aut inter se dissentiant, in hoc conveniunt, quod necessariorum hujusmodi effectuum causam primam Deum esse concedant: quanquam plurimi non videntur hoc satis observasse, et terminorum simplicium apprehensionem, et eorundem cum evidenter coincidant, compositionem (unde necessaria gignitur propositio) numerandas esse inter effectus necessarios (*i.e.*) tales qui non possint non fieri, positis impressionibus motuum naturalibus, et posita natura intelligente cui clare ac distincte proponuntur: quod tamen ad rem nostram facit plurimum, quoniam necessariis veritatibus practicis (quae scilicet actus ad finem necessarium necessarios indicant) ab agnito authore Deo legum asserit authoritatem.

however much they may differ from this one or among themselves, agree in allowing that God is the first cause of such necessary effects: though very many people do not seem to have given sufficient attention to the fact that apprehending simple terms, and putting them together when they obviously coincide (thus making a necessary proposition), are to be reckoned among necessary effects, that is, among such effects as are bound to occur, given the natural impressions of motion, and given an intelligent nature before which they are clearly and distinctly placed. Now this contributes a great deal to our purpose, since it claims for necessary practical truths (which of course point out the actions that are necessary means to a necessary end) the authority of laws from their acknowledged author, God.

*   *   *   *

CAP. V—DE LEGE NATURAE EJUSQUE OBLIGATIONE

CHAP. V—ON THE LAW OF NATURE AND ITS OBLIGATION

112 I. Munita jam via ad ea quae sequuntur omnia, caput hoc auspicabimur a definitione legis naturalis. *Lex naturae est propositio a natura rerum ex voluntate*

I. Having now prepared the **112** way for all that follows, I shall begin this chapter with a definition of natural law. *A law of nature is a proposition quite clearly presented to, or impressed upon, the mind by the nature of things from*

Primae Causae menti satis aperte oblata vel impressa, actionem indicans bono rationalium communi deservientem, quam si praestetur praemia, sin negligatur, poenae sufficientes ex natura rationalium sequuntur. Hujus definitionis pars prior praeceptum, posterior sanctionem continet: et utraque a natura rerum imprimitur. Illa autem *praemia poenaeque sufficiunt,* quae tanta sunt, et tam certo distribuuntur, ut manifesto magis conducat ad integram singulorum foelicitatem (quam per naturam universi obtinere possunt, et necessario expetunt) si publico bono perpetuo serviant, quam si quicquam in contrarium attentarent. Contrariae huic fini actiones et omissiones iisque annexa mala hoc modo videntur pariter et indicari et prohiberi, siquidem privationes ex oppositis suis optime intelliguntur.

the will of the First Cause, pointing out an action, of service to the common good of rational beings, the performance of which is followed, owing to the nature of rational beings, by adequate reward, while its neglect is followed by adequate punishment. The former part of this definition covers the precept, the latter the sanction; and both are impressed upon the mind by the nature of things. Now *adequate rewards and punishments* are those whose amount is so great and distribution so certain that individuals will obviously contribute more to the complete happiness of themselves if they are constantly devoted to the public good than if they attempt anything to the contrary. (In speaking of the complete happiness of individuals, I mean that which they can attain, the nature of the universe being what it is, and which they necessarily desire.) Actions and omissions which are contrary to this end, and the evils annexed to them, are evidently likewise made known and forbidden by this means, since negatives are best understood from their opposites.

★   ★   ★   ★

113

IV. . . . Quoniam autem et nomina finis et mediorum am-

113

IV. . . . 'End' and 'means' are terms whose very names have

biguae admodum sunt significationis, et liberam agentis rationalis intentionem, variis modis mutabilem, et incerto cognitam connotant, adeoque materiam demonstrationibus minus idoneam cogitationibus nostris ingenerant; visum est mihi, re, quae prae manibus est, non mutata, sub alia notione eam considerare. Scilicet quoniam magis conspicuus est nexus, planeque insolubilis inter causas efficientes et effectus inde oriundos; perpetuaque experientia, et observatio frequens quales effectus datas causas sequantur apertius edoceat; ideoque bonum publicum tanquam effectum, actiones autem viresque nostras a quibus aliquid ejusmodi speratur tanquam causas effectrices, in definitione protulimus. Hoc enim pacto quaestiones morales et politicae de fine et mediis, in terminos vertuntur philosophis naturalibus usitatos, An hae causae efficientes hunc effectum producere valeant, necne? Hujusmodi autem quaestionibus responsum detur demonstrabile ex olim observata humanorum actuum efficacia, spectatorum tum per se, tum in concursu cum

a highly ambiguous meaning. They also connote a rational agent's free intention, which can be changed in various ways, and which is not known for certain. They therefore provide our thought with material that is not so suitable for demonstration. Consequently I have thought it best to use another concept [cause and effect] for considering, though without changing, the matter in hand. For, of course, the connection between efficient causes and the effects arising from them is more obvious and plainly indissoluble, while constant experience and frequent observation would show us pretty clearly what sort of effects follow given causes; and for this reason I have, in the definition, treated the public good as an effect, and our actions and powers, whereby we hope to achieve anything of that kind, as efficient causes. For in this way questions of morals and politics about end and means are converted into the terms commonly used by scientists, 'Are these efficient causes able to produce this effect or not?' And to questions of this kind an answer may be given which can be demonstrated from the formerly observed efficacy of human actions, considered now by themselves and now in conjunction

114 aliis causis, iis, quae nunc ponuntur, non absimilibus. Quamvis enim, dum deliberamus, liberi merito dicamur,[1] et effectus postmodum e nostris actibus futuri, respectu illius libertatis, omni jure dicantur contingentes; postquam tamen nos determinavimus ad agendum, nexus inter actus nostros, et effectus omnes inde pendentes necessarius est, ac plane naturalis, adeoque demonstrationi subjectus; quod videre licet in effectionibus geometricis, quae non minus libere fiunt, quam aliae quaevis actiones humanae. Ideoque quemadmodum longa series consequentiarum ultra spem imperitorum, de ratione linearum, aut angulorum inter se deduci potest demonstrative, ex eo quod quis paucas lineas duxerit juxta praxes in geometria praescriptas: ita e principiis physiologiae demonstrari possunt multa consecutura actum humanum motum imprementem notum corpori intra notum systema aliorum corporum; adeoque saepe quid hominis vitae, membrorum sanitati, inte-

with other causes not unlike those at present posited. For although, while we deliberate, we may justly be called free,[1] and the immediate future effects of our action may, in respect of that freedom, quite properly be called contingent, yet after we have set ourselves upon action, the connection between our acts and all the effects depending on them is necessary and plainly natural, and therefore susceptible of demonstration. This may be seen in geometrical operations, which are carried out no less freely than any other human actions. Just as a long series of consequences, going beyond the expectations of those unversed in geometry, about the mutual relations of lines and angles can be demonstratively deduced from the fact that someone has drawn a few lines in accordance with prescribed geometrical practice, so from the principles of natural science we can demonstrate many future consequences of a human action impressing a known motion upon a body within a known system of other bodies. Thus we can often demonstrate what will cause harm to the life of man, to the health of his body, to the soundness of his mind and to the capacity of self-movement

[1 Cf. Hobbes, § 96 (and § 17).]

gritati et locomotivae facultati (in cujus usu libertas incarcerationi opposita cernitur) aut etiam bonis quae quis possidet noxam afferet; quidve contra in cujuspiam, aut plurium cedet emolumentum. Evicit autem (si quid ego judico) praestantior physiologia mutationes omnes corporum omnium, etiam humanorum, quae ab extra veniunt (nam excipiendae sunt determinationes ab interna voluntatis libertate) sive in melius, sive deterius fieri secundum ea de motu theoremata, quae per analysin geometricam inveniuntur, et demonstrantur. Pauca fateor sunt, licet magni momenti, quae adhuc ea de re fuerint exhibita; ostensa tamen est methodus motus, quantumvis implicatos, calculo geometrico subjiciendi, et theoremata de lineis, figuris, motusque determinationibus inde ortis quotcunque adinveniendi, atque adeo (cum tota natura corporea in ejus extensionem, figuras, motusque varie implicatos resolvenda sit) generalis monstrata est via effecta ejus omnia sub

(in the use of which is shown our liberty, as opposed to constraint), or, likewise, to the goods which anyone possesses; or on the other hand we can demonstrate what will result to the advantage of any one or more persons. Now advances in natural science have established (if I am not quite mistaken) that all changes in all bodies, including those of human beings, which are due to an external cause (for we must except determinations by the internal freedom of the will), whether they are for the better or for the worse, take place according to those theorems about motion which are discovered and demonstrated by geometrical analysis. I admit that the things which have so far been proved concerning this matter are few in number, though of great importance. However, there has been pointed out a method of subjecting motions, however complicated, to geometrical calculation, and of finding out any number of theorems about lines, figures, and the determinations of motion that arise from them; and so, since the whole nature of body is to be resolved into its extension, figure, and motion, related together in different ways, there has been shown a general way of bringing all its

demonstratione reducendi. Haec autem a me ideo tantum dicta sunt obiter, ut ostendam qua methodo insistendum sit ut ea perfecte, e necessaria cohaerentia terminorum, habeamus demonstrata, quae ex communi observatione, perpetuaque experientia satis sunt comperta existere in natura rerum, atque ab invicem pendere, ut causas et effecta, quaeque alii aliis e principiis physicis conantur deducere. Qualia sunt actus illi quibus homines alii aliorum vitas, libertates, fortunasque eripere, aut e contra conservare solent.

effects under demonstration. I have mentioned these things by the way, only in order to point out what method we must pursue if we are to have perfectly demonstrated, from the necessary connection of terms, those things which are sufficiently well known, from common observation and constant experience, to exist in nature and to be mutually dependent on each other as causes and effects, and which different people try to deduce from different principles of science. Among these things are those acts whereby men are wont to take away, or on the other hand to defend, the lives, liberty, and fortunes of one another.

* * * *

115 XVI. Quoniam autem multa quae dicturus sum de moribus hinc pendent, alia adjiciam eodem facientia. Cum certum sit e natura voluntatis, actionisve voluntariae, maximi boni effectionem esse finem maximum a ratione praescriptum, illud erit vel maximum bonum commune (quo refero quicquid cum eo consistit) vel maximum quod possibile videtur cuivis singulari,

XVI. Because much of what **115** I am about to say concerning morals depends on what I have just stated, I shall add something else serving the same purpose. Since it is certain, from the nature of the will and of voluntary action, that the production of the greatest good is the greatest end prescribed by reason, that good will be either the greatest common good (I mean whatever is consistent with that), or else the good that seems the greatest possible for any indi-

ut suum quisque finem, maxima nempe quae sibi cupere possit commoda, prosequatur, omniaque huic subordinare conetur.[1] Nam familiae alicujus, vel civitatis bonum, vel nondum supponitur spectari, vel si spectetur iisdem fere consequentiis urgetur, quibus prosecutio privati alicujus boni. Non permittit ratio ut cujusvis singularis bonum maximum quod cupere possit vel imaginari, pro ultimo fine statuatur. Quippe cum bona certissime sit actio quae ad finem vere ultimum recta, seu maximo compendio perducet, positis diversis finibus ultimis quorum causae sint oppositae, oppositae sibi invicem erunt actiones vere bonae; quod est impossibile. *v.g.* Si recta ratio Titium doceat ejus foelicitatem possibilem, finemque quaerendum consistere in fruitione pleni dominii in fundos, quos occuparunt Seius et Sempronius, eorumque personas, atque aliorum omnium fundos: non potest vera ratio Seio et Sempronio dictare eorum foelicitatem quaerendam posi-

vidual, with the result that each pursues his own end, namely the greatest advantage that he can seek for himself, and tries to subordinate everything to this. (For the good of a man's family, or state, either is not yet supposed to be considered, or, if it be considered, is urged upon him through much the same consequences as is the pursuit of a man's private good.) Reason does not allow that the good of any one individual, be it as great as he can desire or imagine, should be appointed as an ultimate end. For an action which leads directly, or by the shortest possible way, to a truly ultimate end is most certainly good; and if there be posited different ultimate ends, whose causes are opposed to each other, then there will be truly good actions likewise opposed to each other; which is impossible. For example, suppose right reason tells Titius that the happiness possible for him, and the end he should pursue, consist in the enjoyment of complete dominion over the land occupied by Seius and Sempronius, and over their persons, and over the land of all others; then true reason cannot dictate to Seius and Sempronius that their happiness, which they are to seek, lies in the enjoyment

[1 The original reads *conatur*.]

tam esse in fruitione pleni dominii in fundos, et personam Titii, aliorumque pariter omnium. Haec enim apertam includunt contradictionem, adeoque alterum tantum dictamen verum supponi potest. At cum nulla sit causa cur unius horum foelicitas ipsi sit ultimus finis magis quam alteri sua, colligere licet rationem dictare nemini, ut suam tantum foelicitatem sibi ut finem maximum proponat, verum unicuique suam potius cum aliorum foelicitate conjunctam; atque hoc est quod quaerendum contendimus commune bonum. Nempe illud solum est unus ille *finis* cum summa possibili singulorum foelicitate consistens, eamque maxime promovens; in quem et naturae impetus suum, et ratio commune bonum spectans conspirent.

* * * *

116 XXXVI. Exposita jam qua potui brevitate, summa sententiae nostrae de obligationis naturalis essentia, et origine, necessarium duxi scrupulos

of complete dominion over the land and person of Titius and likewise of all others. For these precepts involve an obvious contradiction, so that only one of the two can be supposed true. But since there is no reason why the happiness of one of these parties should be the ultimate end for him, rather than that the other party's happiness should be so for them, we may infer that reason dictates to no one that he should propose to himself his own happiness alone as his greatest end; but rather that reason dictates to everyone as the end his own happiness joined with the happiness of others; and this is the common good which I maintain is to be pursued. Plainly that alone is the one *end* which is consistent with, and which best promotes, the highest possible happiness of each individual. Towards it natural impulse and reason conspire together, the former looking to its own good, the latter to the common good.

XXXVI. Having now expounded, as briefly as I could, the gist of my opinion about the essential character and the origin of natural obligation, I have thought it necessary to remove two doubts which might disturb **116**

duos eximere qui melioris notae mentes inquietare possint. (1) Quod incertae videntur vitiorum poenae, nec satis certo cognita virtutis praemia, ut indicia sint sufficientia obligationis naturalis, et voluntatis primae causae. (2) Quod ex hac sententia videri possit commune bonum cujusque privatae foelicitati postponi et subordinari. Neutrum autem horum vere in nostram sententiam objici posse ostendemus.

* *

117 XLV. Pergamus itaque ad solvendam eam objectionem qua suggeritur, nostra methodo investigandi obligationem legum naturalium effici, ut commune bonum, adeoque Dei honos, et omnium aliorum hominum foelicitas privati cujusque foelicitati postponatur, et ei inserviat, velut fini supremo. Absit autem ut ego tale quicquam docerem: immo vero id hic stabilire conor, quod ejusmodi sententiam funditus subvertit, quippe nemini jus ad vitam, aut necessaria ad vitam conservandam competere monui, nisi in quantum cujusque vita boni communis aut pars est, aut causa, aut cum eo saltem

minds of the better stamp: (1) that the punishments for vice seem to be uncertain, and that the rewards for virtue are not known with sufficient certainty to be adequate signs of natural obligation and of the will of the first cause; (2) that from this opinion the common good might seem to be ranked lower than, and subordinated to, the private happiness of each. But I shall show that neither of these objections can properly be levelled against my opinion.

* *

XLV. Let me now proceed **117** to solve the difficulty whereby it is suggested that my method of tracing out the obligation of natural laws has the effect of ranking the common good, and so the honour of God and the happiness of all other men, below the private happiness of each, and of making the common good serve private good as the supreme end. Far be it from me to teach any such thing. On the contrary, what I am here trying to establish entirely overthrows such an opinion, since I have pointed out that the right to life, or the necessary means of preserving life, is due to no man except in so far as the life of each is part or cause of the common good, or at least is consistent

consistit. Verum distincte ostendemus quomodo haec inter se
cohaereant.

with it. But I shall show distinctly how these things fit together.

★ ★ ★ ★

118 XLVI. . . . Id autem hic
praecipue observatum velim
quod quanquam nostrae foelicitatis cura ad causarum rationalium naturam considerandam
nos deduxerit; ipsis tamen omnibus intrinseca ratio, ac voluntas,
naturaliter ad foelicitatem sibi
possibilem determinata, omnis-
que ea, quam agnovimus in
ipsis, perfectio bonitasque ad
statum universi relata efficit ut
et possint communem hunc
finem sibi proponere, et necessarium sit ut reipsa eum prosequi
statuant, si quid cum recta
ratione de praxi sua statuere
velint. Quippe unicus est finis
in quo prosequendo omnes con-
sentire possint; et certissimum
est, nihil secundum rectam
rationem statui posse, in quod
omnes non possint consentirei
Ideoque a communi rational.
natura oritur necessitas ut quisque universalem exercendo
benevolentiam, commune semper quaerat bonum, suumque
tantum ut ejus partem, eique
adeo subordinatum, quae legis
naturalis summa est.

XLVI. . . . I should particu- **118**
larly wish this to be noted here:
although the concern for our
happiness has led us to consider
the nature of rational causes, yet
reason, intrinsic to all rational
causes themselves, and desire,
naturally directed towards the
happiness possible for them, and
all that perfection and goodness
which we see in them, bring it
about, when related to the state
of the universe, both that they
can propose this common end
to themselves, and that they
must in fact decide to pursue it if
they wish to make any decision
about their conduct with right
reason. For there is only one end
in the pursuit of which all can
agree; and it is most certain that
no decision can be in accordance
with right reason unless all can
agree on it. Therefore there
arises from our common rational
nature a necessity that each, by exercising universal benevolence,
should always seek the common
good, and should seek his own
as only a part of that and consequently subordinated to it; and
this is the sum of natural law.

★ ★ ★ ★

RALPH CUDWORTH

1617–1688

I. *A TREATISE CONCERNING ETERNAL AND IMMUTABLE MORALITY*

[Written before 1688. First printed, 1731. Reprinted here from the first edition, with spelling modified, initial capital letters and italics reduced, and footnotes (giving quotations or technical terms in Greek or Latin) omitted]

II. *A TREATISE OF FREEWILL*

[Written before 1688. First printed, 1838, edited by John Allen. Reprinted here from that edition, with errors corrected, spelling slightly modified, and the editor's footnotes omitted]

RALPH CUDWORTH

A Treatise concerning Eternal and Immutable Morality

BOOK I

CHAP. I

1. As the vulgar generally look no higher for the original of moral **119** good and evil, just and unjust, than the codes and pandects, the tables and laws of their country and religion; so there have not wanted pretended philosophers in all ages who have asserted nothing to be good and evil, just and unjust, naturally and immutably; but that all these things were positive, arbitrary and factitious only.

★   ★   ★   ★

5. But whatsoever was the true meaning of these philosophers, that affirm justice and injustice to be only by law and not by nature (of which I shall discourse afterwards,) certain it is, that divers modern theologers do not only seriously, but zealously contend in like manner, that there is nothing absolutely, intrinsically and naturally good and evil, just and unjust, antecedently to any positive command or prohibition of God; but that the arbitrary will and pleasure of God, (that is, an omnipotent being devoid of all essential and natural justice) by its commands and prohibitions, is the first and only rule and measure thereof. Whence it follows unavoidably, that nothing can be imagined so grossly wicked, or so foully unjust or dishonest, but if it were supposed to be commanded by this omnipotent Deity, must needs upon that hypothesis forthwith become holy, just and righteous.

★   ★   ★   ★

Wherefore since there are so many, both philosophers and theologers, that seemingly and verbally acknowledge such things as moral good and evil, just and unjust, that contend notwithstanding that these are not by nature, but institution, and that there is nothing naturally or immutably just or unjust; I shall from hence fetch the rise of this ethical discourse or inquiry concerning things good and evil, just and unjust, laudable and shameful: (for so I find these words frequently used as synonymous in Plato, and other ancient authors,) demonstrating in the first place, that if there be any thing at all good or evil, just or unjust, there must of necessity be something naturally and immutably good and just. And from thence I shall proceed afterward to show what this natural, immutable, and eternal justice is, with the branches and species of it.

CHAP. II

120 1. Wherefore in the first place, it is a thing which we shall very easily demonstrate, that moral good and evil, just and unjust, honest and dishonest, (if they be not mere names without any signification, or names for nothing else but willed and commanded, but have a reality in respect of the persons obliged to do and avoid them) cannot possibly be arbitrary things, made by will without nature; because it is universally true, that things are what they are, not by will but by nature. As for example, things are white by whiteness, and black by blackness, triangular by triangularity, and round by rotundity, like by likeness, and equal by equality, that is, by such certain natures of their own. Neither can omnipotence itself (to speak with reverence) by mere will make a thing white or black without whiteness or blackness; that is, without such certain natures, whether we consider them as qualities in the objects without us according to the peripatetical philosophy, or as certain dispositions of parts in respect of magnitude, figure, site and motion, which beget those sensations or phantasms of white and black in us. Or, to instance in geometrical figures, omnipotence itself cannot by mere will make a body triangular, without having the nature and properties of a triangle in it; that is, without having three angles equal to two right ones, nor circular without the nature of a circle; that is, without having a circumference equidistant every where from the centre or middle point. Or lastly, to instance in things relative only; omnipotent will cannot make things like or equal one to another, without the natures of likeness and equality. The reason whereof is plain, because all these things imply a manifest contradiction; that things should be what they are not. And this is a truth fundamentally necessary to all knowledge, that contradictories cannot be true: for otherwise, nothing would be certainly true or false. Now things may as well be made white or black by mere will, without whiteness or blackness, equal and unequal, without equality and inequality, as morally good and evil, just and unjust, honest and dishonest, *debita* and *illicita*, by mere will, without any nature of goodness, justice, honesty. For though the will of God be the supreme efficient cause of all things, and can produce into being or existence, or reduce into nothing what it pleaseth, yet it is not the formal cause of any thing besides itself, as the Schoolmen have determined, in these words, *that God himself cannot supply the place of a formal cause*: and therefore it cannot supply the formal cause, or nature, of justice or injustice, honesty or dishonesty. Now all that we have hitherto said amounts to no more than this, that it is impossible any thing should be by will only, that is, without a nature or entity, or that the nature and essence of any thing should be arbitrary.

2. And since a thing cannot be made any thing by mere will without a being or nature, every thing must be necessarily and immutably determined by its own nature, and the nature of things be that which it is, and nothing else. For though the will and power of God **121** have an absolute, infinite and unlimited command upon the existences of all created things to make them to be, or not to be, at pleasure; yet when things exist, they are what they are, this or that, absolutely or relatively, not by will or arbitrary command, but by the necessity of their own nature. There is no such thing as an arbitrarious essence, mode or relation, that may be made indifferently any thing at pleasure: for an arbitrarious essence is a being without a nature, a contradiction, and therefore a non-entity. Wherefore the natures of justice and injustice cannot be arbitrarious things, that may be applicable by will indifferently to any actions or dispositions whatsoever. For the modes of all subsistent beings, and the relation of things to one another, are immutably and necessarily what they are, and not arbitrary, being not by will but by nature.

3. Now the necessary consequence of that which we have hitherto **122** said is this, that it is so far from being true, that all moral good and

evil, just and unjust, are mere arbitrary and factitious things, that are
created wholly by will; that (if we would speak properly) we must
needs say that nothing is morally good or evil, just or unjust, by mere
will without nature, because every thing is what it is by nature, and
not by will. For though it will be objected here, that when God, or
civil powers, command a thing to be done, that was not before
obligatory or unlawful, the thing willed or commanded doth forthwith become obligatory; that which ought to be done by creatures
and subjects respectively; in which the nature of moral good or evil
is commonly conceived to consist. And therefore if all good and evil,
just and unjust, be not the creatures of mere will (as many assert),
yet at least positive things must needs owe all their morality, their
good and evil, to mere will without nature: yet notwithstanding, if
we well consider it, we shall find that even in positive commands
themselves, mere will doth not make the thing commanded just or
obligatory, or beget and create any obligation to obedience; but that
it is natural justice or equity, which gives to one the right or authority of commanding, and begets in another duty and obligation to
obedience. Therefore it is observable, that laws and commands do
not run thus, to will that this or that thing shall become just or
unjust, obligatory or unlawful; or that men shall be obliged or
bound to obey; but only to require that something be done or not
done, or otherwise to menace punishment to the transgressors
thereof. For it was never heard of, that any one founded all his
authority of commanding others, and others' obligation or duty to
obey his commands, in a law of his own making, that men should
be required, obliged, or bound to obey him. Wherefore since the
thing willed in all laws is not that men should be bound or obliged
to obey; this thing cannot be the product of the mere will of the
commander, but it must proceed from something else; namely, the
right or authority of the commander, which is founded in natural
justice and equity, and an antecedent obligation to obedience in the
subjects; which things are not made by laws, but presupposed before
all laws to make them valid: and if it should be imagined, that any
one should make a positive law to require that others should be
obliged, or bound, to obey him, every one would think such a law
ridiculous and absurd; for if they were obliged before, then this law
would be in vain, and to no purpose; and if they were not before
obliged, then they could not be obliged by any positive law, because

they were not previously bound to obey such a person's commands: so that obligation to obey all positive laws is older than all laws, and previous or antecedent to them. Neither is it a thing that is arbitrarily made by will, or can be the object of command, but that which either is or is not by nature. And if this were not morally good and just in its own nature before any positive command of God, *that God should be obeyed by his creatures*, the bare will of God himself could not beget an obligation upon any to do what he willed and commanded, because the natures of things do not depend upon will, being not things that are arbitrarily made, but things that are. To conclude therefore, even in positive laws and commands it is not mere will that obligeth, but the natures of good and evil, just and unjust, really existing in the world.

4. Wherefore that common distinction betwixt things, *things* **123** *naturally and positively good and evil*, or (as others express it) betwixt things that are therefore commanded because they are good and just, and things that are therefore good and just because they are commanded, stands in need of a right explication, that we be not led into a mistake thereby, as if the obligation to do those thetical and positive things did arise wholly from will without nature: whereas it is not the mere will and pleasure of him that commandeth, that obligeth to do positive things commanded, but the intellectual nature of him that is commanded. Wherefore the difference of these things lies wholly in this, that there are some things which the intellectual nature obligeth to of itself, and directly, absolutely and perpetually, and these things are called naturally good and evil; other things there are which the same intellectual nature obligeth to by accident only, and hypothetically, upon condition of some voluntary action either of our own or some other persons, by means whereof those things which were in their own nature indifferent, falling under something that is absolutely good or evil, and thereby acquiring a new relation to the intellectual nature, do for the time become such things as ought to be done or omitted, being made such not by will but by nature. As for example, *to keep faith and perform covenants*, is that which natural justice obligeth to absolutely; therefore upon the supposition that any one maketh a promise, which is a voluntary act of his own, to do something which he was not before obliged to by natural justice, upon the intervention of this voluntary act of his own, that indifferent thing promised falling now under something

absolutely good, and becoming the matter of promise and covenant, standeth for the present in a new relation to the rational nature of the promiser, and becometh for the time a thing which ought to be done by him, or which he is obliged to do. Not as if the mere will or words and breath of him that covenanteth had any power to change the moral natures of things, or any ethical virtue of obliging; but because natural justice and equity obligeth to keep faith and perform covenants. In like manner natural justice, that is, the rational or intellectual nature, obligeth not only to obey God, but also civil powers, that have lawful authority of commanding, and to observe political order amongst men; and therefore if God or civil powers command any thing to be done that is not unlawful in itself; upon the intervention of this voluntary act of theirs, those things that were before indifferent, become by accident for the time obligatory, such things as ought to be done by us, not for their own sakes, but for the sake of that which natural justice absolutely obligeth to.

124   And these are the things that are commonly called positively good and evil, just or unjust, such as though they are adiaphorous or indifferent in themselves, yet natural justice obligeth to accidentally, on supposition of the voluntary action of some other person rightly qualified in commanding, whereby they fall into something absolutely good. Which things are not made good or due by the mere will or pleasure of the commander, but by that natural justice which gives him right and authority of commanding, and obligeth others to obey him; without which natural justice, neither covenants nor commands could possibly oblige any one. For the will of another doth no more oblige in commands, than our own will in promises and covenants. To conclude therefore, things called naturally good and due are such things as the intellectual nature obliges to immediately, absolutely and perpetually, and upon no condition of any voluntary action that may be done or omitted intervening; but those things that are called positively good and due, are such as natural justice or the intellectual nature obligeth to accidentally and hypothetically, upon condition of some voluntary act of another person invested with lawful authority in commanding.

And that it is not the mere will of the commander, that makes these positive things to oblige or become due, but the nature of things; appears evidently from hence, because it is not the volition of every one that obligeth, but of a person rightly qualified and

invested with lawful authority; and because the liberty of commanding is circumscribed within certain bounds and limits, so that if any
commander go beyond the sphere and bounds that nature sets him,
which are indifferent things, his commands will not at all oblige.

5. But if we would speak yet more accurately and precisely, we **125**
might rather say, that no positive commands whatsoever do make
any thing morally good and evil, just and unjust, which nature had
not made such before. For indifferent things commanded, considered
materially in themselves, remain still what they were before in their
own nature, that is, indifferent, because (as Aristotle speaks) *will cannot change nature.* And those things that are by nature indifferent,
must needs be as immutably so, as those things that are by nature just
or unjust, honest or shameful. But all the moral goodness, justice and
virtue that is exercised in obeying positive commands, and doing
such things as are positive only, and to be done for no other cause
but because they are commanded, or in respect to political order,
consisteth not in the materiality of the actions themselves, but in that
formality of yielding obedience to the commands of lawful authority in them. Just as when a man covenanteth or promiseth to do an
indifferent thing which by natural justice he was not bound to do,
the virtue of doing it consisteth not in the materiality of the action
promised, but in the formality of keeping faith and performing
covenants. Wherefore in positive commands, the will of the commander doth not create any new moral entity, but only diversely
modifies and determines that general duty or obligation of natural
justice to obey lawful authority and keep oaths and covenants, as our
own will in promising doth but produce several modifications of
keeping faith. And therefore there are no new things just or due
made by either of them, besides what was alway by nature such, to
keep our own promises, and obey the lawful commands of others.

6. We see then that it is so far from being true, that all moral good **126**
and evil, just and unjust, (if they be any thing) are made by mere
will and arbitrary commands (as many conceive), that it is not possible that any command of God or man should oblige otherwise than
by virtue of that which is naturally just. And though particular
promises and commands be made by will, yet it is not will but nature
that obligeth to the doing of things promised and commanded, or
makes them such things as ought to be done. For mere will cannot
change the moral nature of actions, nor the nature of intellectual

beings. And therefore if there were no natural justice, that is, if the rational or intellectual nature in itself were indetermined and unobliged to any thing, and so destitute of all morality, it were not possible that any thing should be made morally good or evil, obligatory or unlawful, or that any moral obligation should be begotten by any will or command whatsoever.

CHAP. III

127   1. But some there are that will still contend, that though it should be granted that moral good and evil, just and unjust, do not depend upon any created will, yet notwithstanding they must needs depend upon the arbitrary will of God, because the natures and essences of all things, and consequently all verities and falsities, depend upon the same. For if the natures and essences of things should not depend upon the will of God, it would follow from hence, that something that was not God was independent upon God.

*   *   *   *

6. Now it is certain, that if the natures and essences of all things, as to their being such or such, do depend upon a will of God that is essentially arbitrary, there can be no such thing as science or demonstration, nor the truth of any mathematical or metaphysical proposition be known any otherwise, than by some revelation of the will of God concerning it, and by a certain enthusiastic or fanatic faith and persuasion thereupon, that God would have such a thing to be true or false at such a time, or for so long. And so nothing would be true or false naturally, but positively only, all truth and science being mere arbitrarious things. Truth and falsehood would be only names. Neither would there be any more certainty in the knowledge of God himself, since it must wholly depend upon the mutability of a will in him essentially indifferent and undetermined; and if we would speak properly according to this hypothesis, God himself would not know or be wise by knowledge or by wisdom, but by will.

128   7. Wherefore as for that argument, that unless the essences of things and all verities and falsities depend upon the arbitrary will of God, there would be something that was not God, independent upon

God; if it be well considered, it will prove a mere bugbear, and nothing so terrible and formidable as Cartesius seemed to think it. For there is no other genuine consequence deducible from this assertion, *that the essences and verities of things are independent upon the will of God*, but that there is an eternal and immutable wisdom in the mind of God, and thence participated by created beings independent upon the will of God. Now the wisdom of God is as much God as the will of God; and whether of these two things in God, that is, will or wisdom, should depend upon the other, will be best determined from the several natures of them. For wisdom in itself hath the nature of a rule and measure, it being a most determinate and inflexible thing; but will being not only a blind and dark thing, as considered in itself, but also indefinite and indeterminate, hath therefore the nature of a thing regulable and measurable. Wherefore it is the perfection of will, as such, to be guided and determined by wisdom and truth; but to make wisdom, knowledge and truth, to be arbitrarily determined by will, and to be regulated by such a plumbean and flexible rule as that is, is quite to destroy the nature of it; for science or knowledge is the comprehension of that which necessarily is, and there can be nothing more contradictious than truth and falsehood arbitrary. Now all the knowledge and wisdom that is in creatures, whether angels or men, is nothing else but a participation of that one eternal, immutable and uncreated wisdom of God, or several signatures of that one archetypal seal, or like so many multiplied reflections of one and the same face, made in several glasses, whereof some are clearer, some obscurer, some standing nearer, some further off.

8. Moreover, it was the opinion of the wisest of the philosophers, **129** (as we shall show afterward) that there is also in the scale of being a nature of goodness superior to wisdom, which therefore measures and determines the wisdom of God, as his wisdom measures and determines his will, and which the ancient Cabalists were wont to call כתר, a crown, as being the top or crown of the Deity, of which more afterward. Wherefore although some novelists make a contracted idea of God, consisting of nothing else but will and power; yet his nature is better expressed by some in this mystical or enigmatical representation of an infinite circle, whose inmost centre is simple goodness, the rays and expanded plate thereof, all comprehending and immutable wisdom, the exterior periphery or

interminate circumference, omnipotent will or activity, by which every thing without God is brought forth into existence. Wherefore the will and power of God have no command inwardly either upon the wisdom and knowledge of God, or upon the ethical and moral disposition of his nature, which is his essential goodness; but the sphere of its activity is without God, where it hath an absolute command upon the existences of things; and it is always free, though not always indifferent, since it is its greatest perfection to be determined by infinite wisdom and infinite goodness. But this is to anticipate what according to the laws of method should follow afterward in another place.

BOOK II

CHAP. I

130 1. Now the demonstrative strength of our cause lying plainly in this, that it is not possible that any thing should be without a nature, and the natures or essences of all things being immutable, therefore upon supposition that there is any thing really just or unjust, due or unlawful, there must of necessity be something so both naturally and immutably, which no law, decree, will, nor custom can alter. There have not wanted some among the old philosophers, that rather than they would acknowledge any thing immutably just or unjust, would not stick to shake the very foundations of all things, and to deny that there was any immutable nature or essence of any thing, and by consequence any absolute certainty of truth or knowledge; maintaining this strange paradox, that both all being and knowledge was fantastical and relative only, and therefore that nothing was good or evil, just or unjust, true or false, white or black, absolutely and immutably, but relatively to every private person's humour or opinion.

2. The principal assertor of this extravagant opinion was Protagoras the Abderite, who, as Plato instructs us in his *Theaetetus*, held, *that nothing was any thing in itself absolutely, but was always made so to something else, and essence or being was to be removed from every thing.*

* * * * *

CHAP. VI

1. Again, as this scepticism or fantasticism of Protagoras is most **131** absurd and contradictious in itself, so there is not any foundation for it at all in the old atomical philosophy, but contrariwise, nothing doth more effectually and demonstratively overthrow both these assertions, *that knowledge is sense*, and that all truth and knowledge is but fantastical and relative, than this atomical philosophy doth.

For first, since no sense can judge of itself, or its own appearances, much less make any judgement of the appearances belonging to another sense, for those things which are perceived by one of our powers, it is impossible to perceive them by another, as the objects of hearing by sight, or the objects of sight by hearing, and the like.

The sight cannot judge of sounds, which belong to the hearing, nor the hearing of light and colours; wherefore that which judges of all the senses and their several objects, cannot be itself any sense, but something of a superior nature.

2. Moreover, that which judges that the appearances of all the senses have something fantastical in them, cannot possibly be itself fantastical, but it must be something which hath a power of judging what really and absolutely is or is not. This being not a relative, but an absolute truth, that sensible appearances have something fantastical in them. Neither could Protagoras ever have arrived to the knowledge of this truth, if he had not had some faculty in him superior to sense, that judgeth of what is and is not absolutely.

*   *   *   *

BOOK III

CHAP. III

1. For, first, sense only suffering and receiving from without, and **132** having no active principle of its own, to take acquaintance with what it receives, it must needs be a stranger to that which is altogether adventitious to it, and therefore cannot know or understand it. For to know or understand a thing, is nothing else but by some inward anticipation of the mind, that is native and domestic, and so familiar to it, to take acquaintance with it; of which I shall speak more afterward.

2. Sense is but the offering or presenting of some object to the mind, to give it an occasion to exercise its own inward activity upon. Which two things being many times nearly conjoined together in time, though they be very different in nature from one another, yet they are vulgarly mistaken for one and the same thing, as if it were all nothing but mere sensation or passion from the body. Whereas sense itself is but the passive perception of some individual material forms, but to know or understand, is actively to comprehend a thing by some abstract, free and universal reasonings, from whence the mind, as it were looking down (as Boethius expresseth it) upon the individuals below it, views and understands them. But sense which lies flat and grovelling in the individuals, and is stupidly fixed in the material form, is not able to rise up or ascend to an abstract universal notion; for which cause it never affirms or denies any thing of its object, because (as Aristotle observes) in all affirmation, and negation at least, the predicate is always universal. The eye which is placed in a level with the sea, and touches the surface of it, cannot take any large prospect upon the sea, much less see the whole amplitude of it. But an eye elevated to a higher station, and from thence looking down, may comprehensively view the whole sea at once, or at least so much of it as is within our horizon. The abstract universal reasons are that higher station of the mind, from whence looking down upon individual things, it hath a commanding view of them, and as it were *a priori* comprehends or knows them.

But sense, which either lies in the same level with that particular material object which it perceives, or rather under it and beneath it, cannot emerge to any knowledge or truth concerning it.

*   *   *   *

BOOK IV

CHAP. VI

133   1. We have now abundantly confuted the Protagorean philosophy, which, that it might be sure to destroy the immutable natures of just and unjust, would destroy all science or knowledge, and make it relative and fantastical. Having showed that this tenet is not only most absurd and contradictious in itself, but also manifestly repugnant to that very atomical physiology, on which Protagoras endeavoured to found it, and, than which nothing can more effectually confute and destroy it: and also largely demonstrated, that though sense be indeed a mere relative and fantastical perception, as Protagoras thus far rightly supposed; yet notwithstanding there is a superior power of intellection and knowledge of a different nature from sense, which is not terminated in mere seeming and appearance only, but in the truth and reality of things, and reaches to the comprehension of that which really and absolutely is, whose objects are the eternal and immutable essences and natures of things, and their unchangeable relations to one another.

2. To prevent all mistake, I shall again remember, what I have before intimated, that where it is affirmed that the essences of all things are eternal and immutable; which doctrine the theological Schools have constantly avouched, this is only to be understood of the intelligible essences and *rationes* of things, as they are the objects of the mind: and that there neither is nor can be any other meaning of it, than this, that there is an eternal knowledge and wisdom, or an eternal mind or intellect, which comprehends within itself the steady and immutable *rationes* of all things and their verities, from which all particular intellects are derived, and on which they do depend. But not that the constitutive essences of all individual created things were eternal and uncreated, as if God in creating of the world, did nothing else, but as some sarcastically express it, *sartoris instar rerum essentias vestire existentia*, only clothed the eternal, uncreated, and antecedent essences of things with a new outside garment of existence, and not created the whole of them: and as if the constitutive essences of things could exist apart separately from the things themselves, which absurd conceit Aristotle frequently, and no less deservedly chastises.

3. Wherefore the result of all that we have hitherto said is this, that **134** the intelligible natures and essences of things are neither arbitrary nor fantastical, that is, neither alterable by any will whatsoever, nor changeable by opinion; and therefore every thing is necessarily and immutably to science and knowledge what it is, whether absolutely, or relatively, to all minds and intellects in the world. So that if moral good and evil, just and unjust, signify any reality, either absolute or relative, in the things so denominated, as they must have some certain natures, which are the actions or souls of men, they are neither alterable by mere will nor opinion.

Upon which ground that wise philosopher Plato, in his *Minos*, determines that νόμος, a law, is not δόγμα πόλεως, any arbitrary decree of a city or supreme governors; because there may be unjust decrees, which therefore are no laws; but the invention[1] of that which IS, or what is absolutely or immutably just, in its own nature. Though it be very true also, that the arbitrary constitutions of those that have lawful authority of commanding, when they are not materially unjust, are laws also in a secondary sense, by virtue of that natural and immutable justice or law that requires political order to be observed.

135   4. But I have not taken all this pains only to confute scepticism or fantasticism, or merely to defend and corroborate our argument for the immutable natures of just and unjust; but also for some other weighty purposes that are very much conducing to the business that we have in hand. And first of all, that the soul is not a mere *rasa tabula*, a naked and passive thing, which had no innate furniture or activity of its own, nor any thing at all in it, but what was impressed upon it without; for if it were so, then there could not possibly be any such thing as moral good and evil, just and unjust; forasmuch as these differences do not arise merely from the outward objects, or from the impresses which they make upon us by sense, there being no such thing in them; in which sense it is truly affirmed by the author of the *Leviathan*, page 24,[2] *that there is no common rule of good and evil to be taken from the nature of the objects themselves*, that is, either considered absolutely in themselves, or relatively to external sense only, but according to some other interior analogy which things have to a certain inward determination in the soul itself, from whence the foundation of all this difference must needs arise, as I shall show afterwards; not that the anticipations of morality spring merely from intellectual forms and notional ideas of the mind, or from certain rules or propositions, arbitrarily printed upon the soul as upon a book, but from some other more inward, and vital principle, in intellectual beings, as such, whereby they have a natural determination in them to do some things, and to avoid others, which could not be, if they were mere naked passive things. Wherefore since the nature of morality cannot be understood, without some

[1 In the old sense of 'finding', 'discovery'. The Greek, quoted in Cudworth's own footnote, is τοῦ ὄντος ἐξεύρεσις.]

[2 Cf. Hobbes, § 25.]

knowledge of the nature of the soul, I thought it seasonable and requisite here to take this occasion offered, and to prepare the way to our following discourse, by showing in general, that the soul is not a mere passive and receptive thing, which hath no innate active principle of its own, because upon this hypothesis there could be no such thing as morality.

*   *   *   *

A Treatise of Freewill

136   I. We seem clearly to be led by the *instincts of nature* to think that there is something ἐφ' ἡμῖν, *in nostra potestate, in our own power* (though dependently upon God Almighty), and that we are not altogether passive in our actings, nor determined by inevitable necessity in whatsoever we do. Because we praise and dispraise, commend and blame men for their actings, much otherwise than we do inanimate beings or brute animals. When we blame or commend a clock or automaton, we do it so as not imputing to that automaton its being the cause of its own moving well or ill, agreeably or disagreeably to the end it was designed for, this being ascribed by us only to the artificer; but when we blame a man for any wicked actions, as for taking away another man's life, either by perjury or by wilful murder; we blame him not only as doing otherwise than ought to have been done, but also than he might have done, and that it was possible for him to have avoided it, so that he was himself the cause of the evil thereof. We do not impute the evil of all men's wicked actions to God the creator and *maker* of them, after the same manner as we do the faults of a clock or watch wholly to the watchmaker. All men's words at least free God from the blame of wicked actions, pronouncing ὁ Θεὸς ἀναίτιος, God is causeless and guiltless of them, and we cast the blame of them wholly on the men themselves, as principles of action and the true causes of the moral defects of them. So also do we blame men's acting viciously and immorally in another sense than we blame a halting or a stumbling horse; or than we blame the natural and necessary infirmities of men themselves when uncontracted by vice. For in this case we so blame the infirmities as to pity the men themselves, looking upon them as unfortunate but not as faulty. But we blame men's vices, with a displeasure against the persons themselves.

137   The same sense of nature's instincts appears yet more plainly from men's blaming, accusing, and condemning themselves for their own actions, when done either rashly, inconsiderately, and imprudently, to their own private disadvantage, or else immorally and viciously, and against the dictate of honesty. In which latter case men have an inward sense of *guilt* (besides *shame*), remorse of conscience, with horror, confusion, and astonishment; and they *repent* of those their actions afterward with a kind of self-detestation, and sometimes not without exercising revenge upon themselves as being a piece of justice due. No man accuses or condemns himself, nor looks upon himself as guilty for having had a fever, the stone, or the gout, when uncontracted by vice; and if all human actions were necessary, men would be said no more to *repent* of them than of diseases, or that they were not born princes, or heirs to a thousand pounds a year.

Lastly, we have also a sense of retributive, punitive, vindictive 138 justice, as not mere fancy, but a thing really existing in nature, when punishments are inflicted upon malefactors for their unjust and illegal actions past, by civil magistrates in particular commonwealths. For though it be true that these civil punishments do in part look forward to prevent the like for the future, by terrifying others from doing the same, or to hinder these malefactors themselves from doing the like mischief again by cutting them off by death, as we kill noxious animals,[1] wolves, and vipers, and serpents, and mad dogs, yet it is not true that this is all the meaning of them, and that they have no retrospect to the actions past; as being satisfaction to the equitable nature of rational beings, when they see wicked men who have both abused and debased themselves, and also acted injuriously to others, to have disgrace and pain for their reward.

*   *   *   *

II. Notwithstanding which, there have not wanted some in all 139 ages who have contended that there is no such thing as *liberum arbitrium*, nothing in our own power, no contingent liberty in human actions, but whatsoever is done by men was absolutely and unavoidably necessary.

And this upon two different grounds, first, because according to some, this contingent liberty is πρᾶγμα ἀνύπαρκτον or ἀνυπόστατον, a thing both unintelligible and impossible to exist in nature. Secondly, because though there be such a thing possible, and actually existing, yet is the exercise thereof peculiar only to God Almighty —so that he is the only self-determining being, and the actions of all creatures were by his decrees from all eternity made necessary.

The reasons alleged why there should be no such thing in nature

[1 Cf. Hobbes, § 93.]

existing anywhere, as a contingent liberty or freewill, are chiefly such as these—First, because nothing can move itself, but *quicquid movetur movetur ab alio*; therefore whatsoever is moved is moved by something else which moveth necessarily. Secondly, because though it should be granted that there is something self-active, or moving from itself, yet nothing can change itself, or act upon itself, or determine its own action. Since the same thing cannot be both agent and patient at once.

Thirdly, because οὐδὲν ἀναίτιον, nothing can come to pass without a cause; or whatsoever is done or produced had a sufficient cause antecedent; and, as Hobbes adds, *every sufficient cause is a necessary cause.*[1] Fourthly, because all volition is determined by the reason of good, or the appearance of the greater good; now the appearances and reasons of good are in the understanding, and therefore not arbitrary but necessary, wherefore all volitions must be necessary. Fifthly, because that which is indifferent in itself can never to eternity determine itself, but will stand indifferent for ever, without motion, volition, or action, either way. Lastly, Hobbes sophistically argues the necessity of every disjunctive proposition.[2]

$$\star \qquad \star \qquad \star \qquad \star$$

140   IV. Now that this is not true, *quod cuncta necesse intestinum habeant*, or that nothing *in rerum natura* can possibly act otherwise than it suffers or is acted upon; but that, on the contrary, there is some contingent liberty in nature, and that men, and other rational creatures, can add or cast in something of their own to turn the scales when even, may, I think, sufficiently appear from hence. Because it cannot be denied but that there are, and may be, many cases in which several objects propounded to our choice at the same time, are so equal, or exactly alike, as that there cannot possibly be any reason or motive in the understanding necessarily to determine the choice to one of them rather than to another of them. As for example, suppose one man should offer to another, out of twenty guinea pieces of gold, or golden balls, or silver globulites, so exactly alike in bigness, figure, colour, and weight, as that he could discern no manner of difference between them, to make his choice of one and no more; add, also, that these guineas or golden balls may be so placed circularly as to be equidistant from the chooser's hand. Now it cannot be

[1 Cf. Hobbes, §§ 97, 99.]   [2 Cf. Hobbes, § 99.]

doubted but that, in this case, any man would certainly choose one, and not stand in suspense or demur because he could not tell which to prefer or choose before another. But if being necessitated by no motive or reason antecedent to choose this rather than that, he must determine himself contingently, or fortuitously, or causelessly, it being all one to him which he took, nor could there be any knowledge *ex causis* beforehand which of these twenty would certainly be taken. But if you will say there was some hidden, necessarily determining in this case, then if the trial should be made an hundred times over and over again, or by a hundred several persons, there is no reason why we must not allow that all of them must needs take the same guinea every time, that is either the first, or second, or third, etc., of them, as they lie in order from the right or left hand.

From hence, alone, it appears that rational beings, or human souls, can extend themselves further than necessary natures, or can act further than they suffer, that they can actively change themselves and determine themselves contingently or fortuitously, when they are not necessarily determined by causes antecedent. Here is, therefore, a great difference between corporeal and incorporeal things; bodies that cannot move themselves, can never act further than they suffer, and, therefore, if causes of motions or impulsions made upon them be of equal force or strength, they cannot move at all, neither one way nor the other. If two equal scales in a balance have equal weights put into them, they will rest to eternity, and neither of them be able to move up or down. But rational beings and human souls standing in equipoise as to motive reasons, and having the scales equiponderant, from the weight of the objects themselves without them, will not perpetually of necessity always thus hang in suspense, but may themselves add or cast in some grains into one scale rather than the other, to make that preponderant, so that the determination here will be contingent or loose, and not necessarily linked with what went before. Here, therefore, is a sufficient cause which is not necessary, here is something changing itself, or acting upon itself, a thing which, though indifferent as to reason, yet can determine itself and take away that passive indifference.

★   ★   ★   ★

V. But this contingent liberty of self-determination, which we **141** have hitherto spoken of, (called by some of the Greek philosophers epeleustic liberty), when there is a perfect equality in objects and a mere fortuitous self-determination, is not that αὐτεξούσιον, that *liberum arbitrium*, which is the foundation of praise or dispraise, commendation or blame. For when two objects, perfectly equal and exactly alike, are propounded to a man's choice, as two eggs, or two guineas, or two golden balls, of equal bigness, and weight, and value, he cannot be justly blamed by any other or himself, for choosing one of them rather than another.

And the case must needs be the same in all other objects of choice, that have a perfect equality of good in them, or are means equally tending and conducing to the same end. There can be no just blame or dispraise, but only where the objects, being in themselves really unequal, the one better, the other worse, a man refuseth the better and chooseth the worse. As in the difference between the dictate of honesty or conscience, and the suggestion of the lower appetites, inclining either to sensual pleasure or private utility; he that resisting these lower and worser inclinations, firmly adhereth to the better principle or dictate of honesty and virtue, hath in all ages and places in the world been accounted ἐπαινετός, praiseworthy, as being κρείττων ἑαυτῷ, superior to himself, or a self-conqueror. But he that yieldeth up himself as vanquished or succumbeth under the lower affections, called the law of the members, in opposition to that superior dictate of honesty, or law of the mind, is accounted blameworthy as being ἥσσων ἑαυτῷ, inferior to himself, or conquered by his worser part. Now that there is such an αὐτεξούσιον as this too, such a liberty of will (where there is an inequality in the objects) of determining oneself better or worse, and so of deserving commendation or blame (though it be not rightly taken by some for an absolute perfection as will be showed elsewhere,) is undeniably evident, both from the common notions of mankind, and from the sense of conscience in all men, accusing or excusing them.

142   Nevertheless, it must be granted that there is no small difficulty in the explaining of this phenomenon rightly, so as clearly to make out and vindicate the same from all exceptions made against it, especially since the vulgar psychology, or the now generally received way of philosophizing concerning the soul, doth either quite baffle and betray this liberty of will, or else render it absurd, ridiculous, or monstrous.

For the vulgarly received psychology runs thus, that in the rational soul there are two faculties, understanding and will, which understanding hath nothing of will in it, and will nothing of understanding in it. And to these two faculties are attributed the actions of intellection and volition; the understanding, say they, understandeth, and the will willeth. But then follows a *bivium*, wherein these philosophers are divided: for, first, many of them suppose this understanding to be the beginner and first mover of all actions. For this reason, because *ignoti nulla cupido*, there can be no desire nor no will of that which is unknown. And, secondly, they conclude that the understanding acteth necessarily upon its several objects, without anything of will to determine either its exercise or specification of them, (which necessity some call a train of thoughts); because the will being blind, therefore cannot determine the understanding, either to exercise or specification of objects. Thirdly, that the understanding judgeth necessarily of all things, not only as to the truth or falsehood of speculative things, but also as to eligibility of practicals, what is to be done or not done. Lastly, that the blind faculty of will always necessarily follows the last practical judgement of the necessary understanding.

But others there are, who, in order to the salving of this phenomenon of liberty of will, think it necessary to suppose, that first of all, the will, though blind, yet determines the understanding both to exercise, and specification of object. And though the understanding, being necessary in its judgements, doth only propound to the blind will what he thinks ought to be done, or his last practical judgement in the case, and no more, only to allure and invite the will thereunto; but that this sovereign queen, or empress of the soul, the blind will, still remaineth as free, and indifferent to do or not to do this or that, as if the understanding had given no judgement at all in the case, and doth at last fortuitously determine itself without respect to the same either way. Which is the meaning of that definition of liberty of will commonly given, that *voluntas, positis omnibus ad agendum requisitis, potest agere, vel non agere*, that the will after all things put, the last dictate or judgement of the understanding itself therein included, is yet free and absolutely indifferent, both as to exercise and to specification, and doth determine itself to do or not, to this or that, fortuitously. There being no other way, as these men conceive, to salve the liberty of the will but this only.

143   VI. But, I say, if this psychology be true, then either can there be
no liberty at all, no freedom from necessity, or else no other than
such as is absurd and ridiculous or monstrous. For, first, if the blind
will do alway necessarily follow a necessary dictate of the understanding antecedent, then must all volitions and actions needs be
necessary. That pretence which some here make to salve liberty of
will, notwithstanding it, from *the amplitude of the understanding*, as
having a larger scope and prospect before it; these fancies and
hormae, each whereof is determined to one, signifying nothing at all,
so long as the understanding in its approbations and judgements
concerning the difference of those objects, acts altogether necessarily.
But whereas some others of those philosophers, who contend that
the will must, therefore, of necessity follow the last dictate or practical judgement of the necessary understanding, because it is in itself
a blind faculty, do nevertheless, in order to maintain liberty, assert
that this blind faculty of will doth first of all move and determine
the understanding, both as to its exercise and objects. This is a manifest contradiction in itself. Besides, they are here forced to run round
in an endless circle. They maintaining that the will can will nothing,
but as represented to it first by the understanding, (since otherwise
it must will it know not what), and again that the understanding
cannot act about this or that but as it is moved and determined thereunto by the will, so that there must be both an action of the understanding going before every act of the will, and also an act of the
will going before every act of the understanding, which is further
contradictious and impossible.

144   But if the blind will does not only at first fortuitously determine
the understanding both to exercise and object, but also after all is
done remains indifferent to follow the last dictate of it or not, and
doth fortuitously determine itself either in compliance with the
same or otherwise, then will liberty of will be mere irrationality,
and madness itself acting or determining all human actions. Nor is
this all, but that which willeth in every man will perpetually will not
only it knows not why, but also it knows not what. Then is all
consideration and deliberation of the mind, all counsel and advice
from others, all exhortation and persuasion, nay the faculty of reason
and understanding itself, in a man, altogether useless, and to no purpose at all. Then can there be no habits either of virtue or vice, that
fluttering uncertainty and fortuitous indifference, which is supposed

to be essential to this blind will, being utterly incapable of either. Nor, after all, could this hypothesis salve the phenomena of commendation and blame, reward and punishment, praise and dispraise; for no praise, commendation, or blame, could belong to men for their freewilled actions neither. Since when they did well they acted but fortuitously and temerariously and by chance, and when they did ill their wills did but *uti jure suo*, use their own natural right and essential privilege, or property of acting ὁπότερον τυγχάνει, as it happeneth, or any way, without reason.

Lastly, as for this scholastic definition of freewill, viz. that it is, after all things put besides the volition itself, even the last practical judgement in the soul too, an indifferency of not doing or of doing this or that. This is an upstart thing, which the ancient peripatetics, as Alexander and others, were unacquainted with, their account thereof being this, that αὐτοῖς περιεστῶσι, the same things being circumstant, the same impressions being made upon men from without, all that they are passive to being the same, yet they may, notwithstanding, act differently. The last practical judgement also, as according to these, being that which as men are not merely passive to, so is it really the same thing with the βούλησις, the will, or volition.

VII. But this scholastic philosophy is manifestly absurd, and mere 145 scholastic jargon; for to attribute the act of intellection and perception to the faculty of understanding, and acts of volition to the faculty of will, or to say that it is the understanding that understandeth, and the will that willeth. This is all one as if one should say that the faculty of walking walketh, and the faculty of speaking speaketh, or that the musical faculty playeth a lesson upon the lute, or sings this or that tune.

Moreover, since it is generally agreed upon by all philosophers, that *actiones sunt suppositorum*, whatsoever acts is a subsistent thing. Therefore by this kind of language are these two faculties of understanding and will made to be two *supposita*, two subsistent things, two agents, and two persons, in the soul. Agreeable to which are these forms of speech commonly used by scholastics, that the understanding, propounds to the will, represents to the will, allures and invites the will, and the will either follows the understanding, or else refuses to comply with its dictates, exercising its own liberty. Whence is that inextricable confusion and unintelligible nonsense, of the will's both first moving the understanding, and also the understanding first moving the will, and this in an infinite and endless circuit. So that this faculty of will must needs be supposed to move understandingly, or knowingly of what it doth, and the faculty of understanding to move willingly, or not without will; whereas to intellect as such, or as a faculty, belongs nothing but mere intellection or perception, without anything of will; and to will as such, or as a faculty, nothing but mere volition, without anything of intellection. But all this while it is really the man or the soul that understands, and the man or the soul that wills, as it is the man that walks, and the man that speaks or talks, and the musician that plays a lesson on the lute. So that it is one and the same subsistent thing, one and the same soul that both understandeth and willeth, and the same agent only that acteth diversely. And thus may it well be conceived that one and the same reasonable soul in us may both will understandingly or knowingly of what it wills; and understand or think of this or that object willingly.

It is not denied but that the rational soul is πολυδύναμος, hath many powers or faculties in it; that is, that it can and doth display itself in several kind of energies as the same air or breath in an organ, passing through several pipes, makes several notes. But there is a certain order or method that may be conceived wherein the soul puts itself forth in these its several operations and affections, of which I shall proceed to treat in the next place.

146   VIII. It is a very material question which Aristotle starteth, τί τὸ πρώτως κινοῦν; What is that that first moveth in the soul and setteth all the other wheels on work? that is, What is that vital power and energy which the soul first displayeth itself in, and which in order of nature precedes all its other powers, it implying them, or setting them on work? First, therefore, I say the outward observations of corporeal sense are not the only beginning and first movers or causes of all cogitations in us, as the Epicureans, Hobbians, and Atheists suppose. Who, indeed, make all cogitation to be nothing but local motions in the brain, these being only occasionally intercurrent, raising a variety of cogitations. But there is a thread of life always spinning out, and a living spring or fountain of cogitation in the soul itself. Now divers of the scholastics, as we said before, tell us that it is no other than an indifferent or blind will which first moveth the understanding and causeth deliberation, and yet after this, itself blindly chooseth and determineth all human actions. Whereas, if the first mover be perfectly blind, then must it move to it knows not what, and it knows not why. Moreover it is not conceivable that mere indetermination and indifferency should be the first mover of all actions; besides which, necessary nature must be the beginner and spring of all action; whereas, if there were any such faculty of the soul as a blind will (which is impossible) knowledge must of necessity go before it, to represent things to it, and to hold a torch to light it and show it its way, and this must come after it, it must follow it as its guide; therefore knowledge and understanding, counsel and reason, and deliberation, seem to bid the fairest for the first mover in the soul, and that which leads the vanguard. Nevertheless it is certain that neither the speculative nor deliberative understanding doth alway act in us necessarily of itself and uninterruptedly, but we are sensible that our minds are employed and set at work by something else, that we apply them both in contemplation and deliberation to this or that object, and continue or call them off at pleasure, as much as we open and shut our eyes, and by moving our eyes determine our sight to this or that object of sight. Were our souls in a constant gaze or study, always spinning out a necessary thread or series of uninterrupted concatenate thoughts; then could we never have any presence of mind, no attention to passing occasional occurrences, always thinking of something else, or having our wits running out a wool-gathering, and so be totally inapt for action; or, could we do nothing at all, but after studied deliberation, then should we be often in a puzzle, at a stand, demur, and fumble a long time before we could act or will any thing. Aristotle himself determines that βουλή, counsel, cannot be the first moving principle in the soul, because then we must *consider*, to *consider*, to *consider* infinitely. Again, the principle of all actions, and therefore intellection itself is ends and good; every thing acting for the sake of some end and good. And concerning ends, the same Aristotle hath rightly observed, that they are οὐκ αὐθαίρετα ἀλλὰ φῦναι δεῖ, that they are not chosen, studied out, or devised by us, but exist in nature, and preventively obtrude themselves upon us.

Wherefore, we conclude that the τὸ πρώτως κινοῦν, that which **147** first moveth in us, and is the spring and principle of all deliberative action, can be no other than a constant, restless, uninterrupted desire, or love of good as such, and happiness. This is an ever bubbling fountain in the centre of the soul, an elater or spring of motion, both a *primum* and *perpetuum mobile* in us, the first wheel that sets all the other wheels in motion, and an everlasting and incessant mover. God an absolutely perfect being is not this love of indigent desire, but a love of overflowing fulness and redundancy, communicating itself. But imperfect beings, as human souls, especially lapsed, by reason of the *penia* which is in them, are in continual inquest, restless desire, and search, always pursuing a scent of good before them and hunting after it. There are several things which have a face and mien, or alluring show, and promising aspect of good to us. As pleasure, joy, and ease, in opposition to pain, and sorrow, and disquiet, and labour, and turmoil. Abundance, plenty, and sufficiency of all things, in opposition to poverty, straitness, scantiness, and penury. Power, not only as it can remove want, and command plenty, and supply pleasures, but also in the sense of the thing itself. Honour, worship, and veneration, in opposition to the evils of disgrace, contempt, and scorn. Praise, commendation, and applause, in opposition to the censure of others, ignominy, and infamy. Clarity, and celebrity, in opposition to private obscurity, and living in corners. Precellency over others, superiority, victory, and success, in opposition to being worsted or foiled, left behind, outdone, and disappointed. Security, in opposition to anxiety, and fear of losing the prize. Pulchritude, in opposition to ugliness, and deformity. Liberty, in opposition to restraint, bondage, servility, to be subject to commands and prohibitions. Knowledge, and truth, in opposition to the evils of ignorance, folly, and error, since no man would willingly be foolish, no man would err or be mistaken.

But above all these, and such like things, the soul of man hath in it μάντευμά τι, a certain vaticination, presage, scent, and odour of one *summum bonum*, one supreme highest good transcending all others, without which they will be all ineffectual as to complete happiness, and signify nothing, a certain philosophers' stone that can turn all into gold.

Now this love and desire of good, as good, in general, and of happiness, traversing the soul continually, and actuating and provoking it continually, is not a mere passion or *horme*, but a settled resolved principle, and the very source, and fountain, and centre of life. It is necessary nature in us, which is immutable, and always continues the same, in equal quantity. As Cartesius supposes the same quantity of motion to be perpetually conserved in the universe, but not alike in all the same bodies, but transferred, and passing from one to other; so, more or less, here and there, is there the same stock of love and desire of good always alive, working in the soul by necessity of nature, and agitating it, though by men's will and choice, it may be diversely dispensed out, and placed upon different objects, more and less.

But there are many other powers and energies of the soul, that are **148** necessary and natural in us too, besides that lowest of the plastic life, subject to no command of the will. Its vital sympathy with the body displaying itself in the perceptions of the outward sense and of bodily pleasure and pain, the sentiments whereof the soul, as willing, hath no *imperium* over, though it have a despotic and undisputed power locomotive in the members of the body. Then fancy or imagination, sudden passions and *hormae*, and commotions called concupiscible and irascible, whose first assaults prevent our will, intended by nature as spurs to action, and the quickeners of life, which else without them would grow dull and languish, and sometimes, as it were, fall asleep; these are natural too, come upon us unawares, invade us, and surprise us with their sudden force, and we have no absolute, despotic, easy, undisputed power over them; notwithstanding which the hegemonic of the soul may, by conatives and endeavours, acquire more and more power over them. Above all these is the dictate of honesty, commonly called the dictate of conscience, which often majestically controls them, and clashes with the former; this is necessary nature too, being here the hegemonic, sometimes joining its assistance to the better one, and sometimes taking part with the worser against it. Lastly, the understanding, both speculative understanding, or the soul, as considering about the truth and falsehood of things, and the practical, considering their good and evil, or what is to be done and not done; both of them inferring consequences from premises in way of discursive reason. The perceptions of which, are all natural and necessary, subject to no command of will, though both the exercise, and their specification of objects, be determinable by ourselves.

IX. The next grand inquiry is, what is τὸ ἡγεμονικόν, the ruling, **149** governing, commanding, determining principle in us. For here, or nowhere else, is to be found the τὸ ἐφ' ἡμῖν and the τὸ αὐτεξούσιον, *sui potestas*, self-power, or such a liberty of will as whereby men deserve praise or dispraise, commendation or blame.

*   *   *   *

150   X. I say, therefore, that the τὸ ἡγεμονικόν in every man, and indeed that which is properly, we ourselves, (we rather having those other things of necessary nature than being them), is the soul as comprehending itself, all its concerns and interests, its abilities and capacities, and holding itself, as it were, in its own hand, as it were redoubled upon itself, having a power of intending or exerting itself more or less, in consideration and deliberation, in resisting the lower appetites that oppose it, both of utility, reason, and honesty; in self-recollection and attention, and vigilant circumspection, or standing upon our guard, in purposes and resolutions, in diligence in carrying on steady designs and active endeavours, in order to self-improvement and the self-promoting of its own good, the fixing and conserving itself in the same. Though by accident and by abuse, it often proves a self-impairing power, the original of sin, vice, and wickedness; whereby men become to themselves the causes of their own evil, blame, punishment, and misery. Wherefore this hegemonicon always determines the passive capability of men's nature one way or other, either for better or for worse; and has a self-forming and self-framing power by which every man is self-made into what he is, and accordingly deserves either praise or dispraise, reward or punishment.

Now I say, in the first place, that a man's soul as hegemonical over itself, having a power of intending and exerting itself more or less in consideration and deliberation, when different objects, or ends, or mediums, are propounded to his choice, that are in themselves really better and worse, may, upon slight considerations and immature deliberations, (he attending to some appearance of good in one of them without taking notice of the evils attending it), choose and prefer that which is really worse before the better, so as to deserve blame thereby. But this not because it had by nature an equal indifferency and freedom to a greater or lesser good, which is absurd, or because it had a natural liberty of will either to follow or not follow its own last practical judgement, which is all one as to say a liberty to follow or not follow its own volition. For upon both these suppositions there would have been no such thing as fault or blame. But here also the person being supposed to follow the greater apparent good at this time, and not altogether to clash with his last practical judgement neither. But because he might have made a better judgement than now he did, had he more intensely considered, and more maturely deliberated, which, that he did not, was his own fault. Now to say that a man hath not this power over himself to consider and deliberate more or less, is to contradict common experience and inward sense. And to deny that a man is blameworthy for inward temerity, in acting in any thing of moment without due and full deliberation, and so choosing the worser is absurd. But if a man have this power over himself to consider and deliberate more or less; then is he not always determined thereunto by any antecedent necessary causes. These two things being inconsistent and contradictious, and consequently there was something of contingency in the choice.

*　　*　　*　　*

XVIII. I now proceed to answer all the arguments or objections **151** made against this faculty of the τὸ ἐφ' ἡμῖν or αὐτεξούσιον, the *sui potestas*, or power over ourselves, which infers contingency or non-necessity, and is commonly called *arbitrium* and *liberum arbitrium*—the foundation of praise and dispraise, of retributive justice rewarding and punishing. And this as the matter hath been now already explained by us will be very easy for us to do.

*　　*　　*　　*

XXII. Another argument for the natural necessity of all actions **152** much used by the Stoics was this, that οὐδὲν ἀναίτιον, nothing can be without a cause, and whatsoever hath a cause must of necessity come to pass. Mr. Hobbes[1] thinks to improve this argument into a demonstration after this manner. Nothing can come to pass without a sufficient cause, and a sufficient cause is that to which nothing is needful to produce the effect, wherefore every sufficient cause must needs be a necessary cause, or produce the effect necessarily.

To which childish argumentation the reply is easy, that a thing may have sufficient power, or want nothing of power necessary to enable it to produce an effect, which yet may have power also or

[¹ Cf. Hobbes, §§ 97, 99.]

freedom not to produce it. Nothing is produced without an efficient cause, and such an efficient cause as had sufficiency of power to enable it to produce it. But yet that person, who had sufficient power to produce an effect, might notwithstanding will not to produce it. So that there are two kinds of sufficient causes, one is such as acteth necessarily and can neither suspend nor determine its own action, another such as acteth contingently or arbitrarily, and hath a power over its own action, either to suspend it or determine it as it pleaseth.

153   I shall subjoin to this another argument, which Mr. Hobbes[1] glories of, as being the sole inventor of. From the necessity of a disjunctive proposition, nothing can be so contingent but that it was necessarily true of it beforehand that it will either come to pass or not come to pass. Therefore, says he, if there be a necessity in the disjunction, there must be a necessity in one or other of the two parts thereof alone by itself; if there be no necessity that it shall come to pass, then must it be necessary that it shall not come to pass, as if there could not be no[2] necessity in the disjunction, though both the members of it were contingent, and neither of them necessary. This is a most shameful ignorance in logic, especially for one who pretends so much to geometrical demonstration.

   And yet this childish and ridiculous nonsense and sophistry of his was stolen from the Stoics too, who played the fools in logic after the same manner. Every proposition, said they, concerning a supposed future contingent, that it will come to pass, was either true or false beforehand and from eternity. If it were true then it must of necessity come to pass, if false then was it necessary that it should not come to pass. And yet this ridiculous sophistry puzzled not only Cicero but also Aristotle himself, so much as to make them hold that propositions concerning future contingents were neither true nor false.

★   ★   ★   ★

[1 Cf. Hobbes, § 99.]
[2 The second negative here is presumably pleonastic, repeating, instead of cancelling, the force of the preceding 'not'. Cf. 'nor no will', § 142. The 'as if' clause gives Cudworth's reply to Hobbes.]

JOHN LOCKE

1632–1704

AN ESSAY CONCERNING HUMAN UNDERSTANDING

[First printed, 1690. Reprinted here from the fourth edition, 1700, with misprints corrected, spelling modified, and reduction of italics and initial capital letters]

SUPPLEMENTARY EXTRACT FROM

ESSAYS ON THE LAW OF NATURE

[Written shortly after 1660. First printed, 1954, edited and translated by W. von Leyden. Latin text and English translation reprinted here from the corrected reprint, 1958, by kind permission of Dr. von Leyden and the Delegates of the Clarendon Press]

JOHN LOCKE

An Essay concerning Human Understanding

BOOK I

CHAP. III—NO INNATE PRACTICAL PRINCIPLES

1. If those speculative maxims, whereof we discoursed in the fore- **154**
going chapter, have not an actual universal assent from all mankind,
as we there proved, it is much more visible concerning practical
principles, that they come short of an universal reception: and I
think it will be hard to instance any one moral rule, which can
pretend to so general and ready an assent as, *What is, is,* or to be so
manifest a truth as this, *That it is impossible for the same thing to be, and
not to be.* Whereby it is evident, that they are farther removed from
a title to be innate; and the doubt of their being native impressions
on the mind, is stronger against these moral principles than the other.
Not that it brings their truth at all in question. They are equally true,
though not equally evident. Those speculative maxims carry their
own evidence with them: but moral principles require reasoning and
discourse, and some exercise of the mind, to discover the certainty
of their truth. They lie not open as natural characters engraven on
the mind; which if any such were, they must needs be visible by
themselves, and by their own light be certain and known to every
body. But this is no derogation to their truth and certainty, no more
than it is to the truth or certainty, of the three angles of a triangle
being equal to two right ones, because it is not so evident, as *The
whole is bigger than a part*; nor so apt to be assented to at first hearing.
It may suffice, that these moral rules are capable of demonstration:
and therefore it is our own faults, if we come not to a certain knowledge of them. But the ignorance wherein many men are of them,
and the slowness of assent, wherewith others receive them, are manifest proofs, that they are not innate, and such as offer themselves to
their view without searching.

155   2. Whether there be any such moral principles, wherein all men do agree, I appeal to any, who have been but moderately conversant in the history of mankind, and looked abroad beyond the smoke of their own chimneys. Where is that practical truth, that is universally received without doubt or question, as it must be if innate? *Justice,* and keeping of contracts, is that which most men seem to agree in. This is a principle, which is thought to extend itself to the dens of thieves, and the confederacies of the greatest villains; and they who have gone farthest towards the putting off of humanity itself, keep faith and rules of justice one with another. I grant that outlaws themselves do this one amongst another: but it is without receiving these as the innate laws of nature. They practise them as rules of convenience within their own communities: but it is impossible to conceive, that he embraces justice as a practical principle, who acts fairly with his fellow highwaymen, and at the same time plunders, or kills the next honest man he meets with. Justice and truth are the common ties of society; and therefore, even outlaws and robbers, who break with all the world besides, must keep faith and rules of equity amongst themselves, or else they cannot hold together. But will any one say, that those that live by fraud and rapine, have innate principles of truth and justice which they allow and assent to?

156   3. Perhaps it will be urged, that the tacit assent of their minds agrees to what their practice contradicts. I answer, first, I have always thought the actions of men the best interpreters of their thoughts. But since it is certain, that most men's practice, and some men's open professions, have either questioned or denied these principles, it is impossible to establish an universal consent (though we should look for it only amongst grown men) without which, it is impossible to conclude them innate. Secondly, it is very strange and unreasonable, to suppose innate practical principles, that terminate only in contemplation. Practical principles derived from nature, are there for operation, and must produce conformity of action, not barely speculative assent to their truth, or else they are in vain distinguished from speculative maxims. Nature, I confess, has put into man a desire of happiness, and an aversion to misery: these indeed are innate practical principles, which (as practical principles ought) do continue constantly to operate and influence all our actions, without ceasing: these may be observed in all persons and all ages, steady and universal; but these are inclinations of the appetite to good, not impressions of truth on the understanding. I deny not, that there are natural tendencies imprinted on the minds of men; and that, from the very first instances of sense and perception, there are some things, that are grateful, and others unwelcome to them; some things that they incline to, and others that they fly: but this makes nothing for innate characters on the mind, which are to be the principles of knowledge, regulating our practice. Such natural impressions on the understanding, are so far from being confirmed hereby, that this is an argument against them; since if there were certain characters, imprinted by nature on the understanding, as the principles of knowledge, we could not but perceive them constantly operate in us, and influence our knowledge, as we do those others on the will and appetite; which never cease to be the constant springs and motives of all our actions, to which we perpetually feel them strongly impelling us.

4. Another reason that makes me doubt of any innate practical **157** principles, is, that I think, there cannot any one moral rule be proposed, whereof a man may not justly demand a reason: which would be perfectly ridiculous and absurd, if they were innate, or so much as self-evident; which every innate principle must needs be, and not need any proof to ascertain its truth, nor want any reason to gain it approbation. He would be thought void of common sense, who asked on the one side, or on the other side went about to give a reason, *Why it is impossible for the same thing to be, and not to be*. It carries its own light and evidence with it, and needs no other proof: he that understands the terms, assents to it for its own sake, or else nothing will ever be able to prevail with him to do it. But should that most unshaken rule of morality, and foundation of all social virtue, *That one should do as he would be done unto*, be proposed to one, who never heard it before, but yet is of capacity to understand its meaning; might he not without any absurdity ask a reason why? And were not he that proposed it, bound to make out the truth and reasonableness of it to him? Which plainly shows it not to be innate; for if it were, it could neither want nor receive any proof: but must needs (at least, as soon as heard and understood) be received and assented to, as an unquestionable truth, which a man can by no means doubt of. So that the truth of all these moral rules, plainly depends upon some other antecedent to them, and from which they must be deduced,

which could not be, if either they were innate, or so much as self-evident.

*　　　*　　　*　　　*

158　6. Hence naturally flows the great variety of opinions, concerning moral rules, which are to be found amongst men, according to the different sorts of happiness, they have a prospect of, or propose to themselves: which could not be, if practical principles were innate, and imprinted in our minds immediately by the hand of God. I grant the existence of God, is so many ways manifest, and the obedience we owe him, so congruous to the light of reason, that a great part of mankind give testimony to the law of nature: but yet I think it must be allowed, that several moral rules, may receive, from mankind, a very general approbation, without either knowing, or admitting the true ground of morality; which can only be the will and law of a God, who sees men in the dark, has in his hand rewards and punishments, and power enough to call to account the proudest offender. For God, having, by an inseparable connection, joined *virtue* and public happiness together; and made the practice thereof, necessary to the preservation of society, and visibly *beneficial* to all, with whom the virtuous man has to do; it is no wonder, that every one should, not only allow, but recommend, and magnify those rules to others, from whose observance of them, he is sure to reap advantage to himself. He may, out of interest, as well as conviction, cry up that for sacred; which if once trampled on, and profaned, he himself cannot be safe nor secure. This, though it takes nothing from the moral and eternal obligation, which these rules evidently have; yet it shows, that the outward acknowledgement men pay to them in their words, proves not that they are innate principles: nay, it proves not so much, as, that men assent to them inwardly in their own minds, as the inviolable rules of their own practice: since we find that self-interest and the conveniences of this life, make many men, own an outward profession and approbation of them, whose actions sufficiently prove, that they very little consider the law-giver, that prescribed these rules; nor the hell he has ordained for the punishment of those that transgress them.

*　　　*　　　*　　　*

159　13. . . . . I would not be here mistaken, as if, because I deny an innate law, I thought there were none but positive laws. There is a great deal of difference between an innate law, and a law of nature; between something imprinted on our minds in their very original, and something that we being ignorant of may attain to the knowledge of, by the use and due application of our natural faculties. And I think they equally forsake the truth, who running into the contrary extremes, either affirm an innate law, or deny that there is a law, knowable by the light of nature; i.e. without the help of positive revelation.

★　　★　　★　　★

BOOK II

CHAP. XX—OF MODES OF PLEASURE AND PAIN

1. Amongst the simple ideas, which we receive both from *sensa-* **160** *tion* and *reflection, pain* and *pleasure* are two very considerable ones. For as in the body, there is sensation barely in itself, or accompanied with pain or pleasure; so the thought, or perception of the mind is simply so, or else accompanied also with pleasure or pain, delight or trouble, call it how you please. These like other simple ideas cannot be described, nor their names defined; the way of knowing them is, as of the simple ideas of the senses, only by experience. For to define them by the presence of good or evil, is no otherwise to make them known to us, than by making us reflect on what we feel in ourselves, upon the several and various operations of good and evil upon our minds, as they are differently applied to, or considered by us.

2. Things then are good or evil, only in reference to pleasure or pain. That we call *good*, which is apt to cause or increase pleasure, or diminish pain in us; or else to procure, or preserve us the possession of any other good, or absence of any evil. And on the contrary we name that *evil*, which is apt to produce or increase any pain, or diminish any pleasure in us; or else to procure us any evil, or deprive us of any good. By pleasure and pain, I must be understood to mean of body or mind, as they are commonly distinguished; though in truth, they be only different constitutions of the mind, sometimes occasioned by disorder in the body, sometimes by thoughts of the mind.

3. Pleasure and pain, and that which causes them, good and evil, are the hinges on which our *passions* turn: and if we reflect on

ourselves, and observe how these, under various considerations, operate in us; what modifications or tempers of mind, what internal sensations, (if I may so call them,) they produce in us, we may thence form to ourselves the ideas of our passions.

★ ★ ★ ★

161 6. The uneasiness a man finds in himself upon the absence of any thing, whose present enjoyment carries the idea of delight with it, is that we call *desire*, which is greater or less, as that uneasiness is more or less vehement. Where by the by it may perhaps be of some use to remark, that the chief if not only spur to human industry and action is uneasiness. For whatever good is proposed, if its absence carries no displeasure nor pain with it; if a man be easy and content without it, there is no desire of it, nor endeavour after it; there is no more but a bare *velleity*, the term used to signify the lowest degree of desire, and that which is next to none at all, when there is so little uneasiness in the absence of any thing, that it carries a man no farther than some faint wishes for it, without any more effectual or vigorous use of the means to attain it. Desire also is stopped or abated by the opinion of the impossibility or unattainableness of the good proposed, as far as the uneasiness is cured or allayed by that consideration. This might carry our thoughts farther were it seasonable in this place.

★ ★ ★ ★

CHAP. XXI—OF POWER

★ ★ ★ ★

162 5. This at least I think evident, that we find in ourselves a *power* to begin or forbear, continue or end several actions of our minds, and motions of our bodies, barely by a thought or preference of the mind ordering, or as it were commanding the doing or not doing such or such a particular action. This power which the mind has, thus to order the consideration of any idea, or the forbearing to consider it; or to prefer the motion of any part of the body to its rest, and *vice versa* in any particular instance is that which we call the *will*. The actual exercise of that power, by directing any particular action, or its forbearance is that which we call *volition* or *willing*. The forbearance or performance of that action, consequent to such order or command of the mind is called *voluntary*. And whatsoever action is performed without such a thought of the mind is called *involuntary*. The power of perception is that which we call the *understanding*. Perception, which we make the act of the understanding, is of three sorts: 1. The perception of ideas in our minds. 2. The perception of the signification of signs. 3. The perception of the connection or repugnancy, agreement or disagreement, that there is between any of our ideas. All these are attributed to the understanding, or perceptive power, though it be the two latter only that use allows us to say we understand.

6. These powers of the mind, viz. of *perceiving*, and of *preferring*, **163** are usually called by another name: and the ordinary way of speaking is, that the *understanding* and *will* are two *faculties* of the mind; a word proper enough, if it be used as all words should be, so as not to breed any confusion in men's thoughts, by being supposed (as I suspect it has been) to stand for some real beings in the soul, that performed those actions of understanding and volition.[1] For when we say the *will* is the commanding and superior faculty of the soul; that it is, or is not free; that it determines the inferior faculties; that it follows the dictates of the *understanding*, etc.; though these, and the like expressions, by those that carefully attend to their own ideas, and conduct their thoughts more by the evidence of things, than the sound of words, may be understood in a clear and distinct sense: yet I suspect, I say, that this way of speaking of *faculties*, has misled many into a confused notion of so many distinct agents in us, which had their several provinces and authorities, and did command, obey, and perform several actions, as so many distinct beings; which has been no small occasion of wrangling, obscurity, and uncertainty in questions relating to them.

7. Every one, I think, finds in himself a *power* to begin or forbear, **164** continue or put an end to several actions in himself. From the consideration of the extent of the power of the mind over the actions of the man, which every one finds in himself, arise the ideas of *liberty* and *necessity*.

8. All the actions, that we have any idea of, reducing themselves, as has been said, to these two, viz. thinking and motion, so far as a

[1 Cf. Cudworth, § 145. Locke probably had some knowledge of Cudworth's unpublished works through his connection with Cudworth's daughter, Lady Masham. Cf. also § 168, below.]

man has a power to think, or not to think; to move, or not to move, according to the preference or direction of his own mind, so far is a man *free*. Wherever any performance or forbearance are not equally in a man's power; wherever doing or not doing, will not equally follow upon the preference of his mind, there he is not *free*, though perhaps the action may be voluntary. So that the idea of *liberty*, is the idea of a power in any agent to do or forbear any action, according to the determination or thought of the mind, whereby either of them is preferred to the other; where either of them is not in the power of the agent to be produced by him according to his volition, there he is not at *liberty*, that agent is under *necessity*. So that liberty cannot be, where there is no thought, no volition, no will; but there may be thought, there may be will, there may be volition, where there is no liberty. A little consideration of an obvious instance or two may make this clear.

165   9. A tennis-ball, whether in motion, by the stroke of a racket, or lying still at rest, is not by any one taken to be a free agent. If we inquire into the reason, we shall find it is, because we conceive not a tennis-ball to think, and consequently not to have any volition, or preference of motion to rest, or *vice versa*; and therefore has not liberty, is not a free agent; but all its both motion and rest, come under our idea of necessary, and are so called. Likewise a man falling into the water, (a bridge breaking under him,) has not herein liberty, is not a free agent. For though he has volition, though he prefers his not falling to falling; yet the forbearance of that motion not being in his power, the stop or cessation of that motion follows not upon his volition; and therefore therein he is not free. So a man striking himself, or his friend, by a convulsive motion of his arm, which it is not in his power, by volition or the direction of his mind to stop, or forbear; no body thinks he has, in this, liberty; every one pities him, as acting by necessity and constraint.

10. Again, suppose a man be carried, whilst fast asleep, into a room, where is a person he longs to see and speak with; and be there locked fast in, beyond his power to get out: he awakes, and is glad to find himself in so desirable company, which he stays willingly in, i.e. prefers his stay to going away. I ask, Is not this stay voluntary? I think, no body will doubt it: and yet being locked fast in, it is evident he is not at liberty not to stay, he has not freedom to be gone. So that liberty is not an idea belonging to volition, or prefer-

ring; but to the person having the power of doing, or forbearing to do, according as the mind shall choose or direct. Our idea of liberty reaches as far as that power, and no farther. For wherever restraint comes to check that power, or compulsion takes away that indifferency to act, or not to act, there liberty, and our notion of it, presently ceases.

11. . . . *Voluntary* then is not opposed to *necessary*; but to *involun-* **166** *tary*. For a man may prefer what he can do, to what he cannot do; the state he is in, to its absence or change, though necessity has made it in itself unalterable.

★   ★   ★   ★

13. Wherever thought is wholly wanting, or the power to act or forbear according to the direction of thought, there *necessity* takes place. This in an agent capable of volition, when the beginning or continuation of any action is contrary to that preference of his mind, is called *compulsion*; when the hindering or stopping any action is contrary to his volition, it is called *restraint*. Agents that have no thought, no volition at all, are in every thing necessary agents.

14. If this be so, (as I imagine it is,) I leave it to be considered, **167** whether it may not help to put an end to that long agitated, and, I think, unreasonable, because unintelligible, question, viz. *Whether man's will be free, or no*. For if I mistake not, it follows, from what I have said, that the question itself is altogether improper; and it is as insignificant to ask, whether man's *will* be free, as to ask, whether his sleep be swift, or his virtue square: *liberty* being as little applicable to the *will*, as swiftness of motion is to sleep, or squareness to virtue. Every one would laugh at the absurdity of such a question, as either of these: because it is obvious, that the modifications of motion belong not to sleep, nor the difference of figure to virtue: and when any one well considers it, I think he will as plainly perceive, that liberty, which is but a power, belongs only to agents, and cannot be an attribute or modification of the will,[1] which is also but a power.

15. Such is the difficulty of explaining, and giving clear notions of internal actions by sounds, that I must here warn my reader that *ordering, directing, choosing, preferring*, etc. which I have made use of, will not distinctly enough express *volition*, unless he will reflect on

[1 Cf. Hobbes, § 82.]

what he himself does, when he *wills*. For example, *preferring*, which seems perhaps best to express the act of *volition*, does it not precisely. For though a man would prefer flying to walking, yet who can say he ever *wills* it? Volition, it is plain, is an act of the mind knowingly exerting that dominion it takes itself to have over any part of the man, by employing it in, or withholding it from any particular action. And what is the will, but the faculty to do this? And is that faculty any thing more in effect, than a power, the power of the mind to determine its thought, to the producing, continuing, or stopping any action, as far as it depends on us? For can it be denied, that whatever agent has a power to think on its own actions, and to prefer their doing or omission either to other, has that faculty called *will*? Will then is nothing but such a power. Liberty, on the other side, is the power a man has to do or forbear doing any particular action, according as its doing or forbearance has the actual preference in the mind, which is the same thing as to say, according as he himself wills it.

168   16. It is plain then, that the *will* is nothing but one power or ability, and *freedom* another power or ability: so that to ask, whether the *will has freedom*, is to ask, whether one power has another power, one ability another ability; a question at first sight too grossly absurd to make a dispute, or need an answer. For who is it that sees not, that powers belong only to agents, and are attributes only of substances, and not of powers themselves? So that this way of putting the question, viz. whether the *will be free*, is in effect to ask, whether the will be a substance, an agent, or at least to suppose it, since freedom can properly be attributed to nothing else. If freedom can with any propriety of speech be applied to power, it may be attributed to the power, that is in a man, to produce, or forbear producing motion in parts of his body, by choice or preference; which is that which denominates him free, and is freedom itself. But if any one should ask, whether freedom were free, he would be suspected, not to understand well what he said; and he would be thought to deserve Midas's ears, who knowing that *rich* was a denomination from the possession of riches, should demand whether riches themselves were rich.

    17. However the name *faculty*, which men have given to this power called the *will*, and whereby they have been led into a way of talking of the will as acting, may, by an appropriation that disguises

its true sense, serve a little to palliate the absurdity; yet the *will* in truth, signifies nothing but a power, or ability, to prefer or choose: and when the will, under the name of a *faculty*, is considered, as it is, barely as an ability to do something, the absurdity, in saying it is free, or not free, will easily discover itself. For if it be reasonable to suppose and talk of faculties, as distinct beings, that can act, (as we do, when we say the will orders, and the will is free,) it is fit that we should make a speaking faculty, and a walking faculty, and a dancing faculty, by which those actions are produced, which are but several modes of motion; as well as we make the will and understanding to be faculties, by which the actions of choosing and perceiving are produced, which are but several modes of thinking: and we may as properly say, that it is the singing faculty sings, and the dancing faculty dances; as that the will chooses, or that the understanding conceives;[1] or, as is usual, that the will directs the understanding, or the understanding obeys, or obeys not the will: it being altogether as proper and intelligible to say, that the power of speaking directs the power of singing, or the power of singing obeys òr disobeys the power of speaking.

*   *   *   *

21. To return then to the inquiry about liberty, I think *the question* **169** *is not proper, whether the will be free, but whether a man be free.*[2] Thus, I think,

1. That so far as any one can, by the direction or choice of his mind, preferring the existence of any action, to the non-existence of that action, and, *vice versa*, make it to exist, or not exist, so far he is free. For if I can, by a thought, directing the motion of my finger, make it move, when it was at rest, or *vice versa*, it is evident, that in respect of that, I am free: and if I can, by a like thought of my mind, preferring one to the other, produce either words, or silence, I am at liberty to speak, or hold my peace: and as far as this power reaches, of acting, or not acting, by the determination of his own thought preferring either, so far is a man free. For how can we think any one freer than to have the power to do what he will? And so far as any one can, by preferring any action to its not being, or rest to any action, produce that action or rest, so far can he do what

[1 Cf. Cudworth, § 145, and footnote to § 163, above.]
[2 Cf. § 167, and Hobbes, § 82.]

he will. For such a preferring of action to its absence, is the *willing* of it: and we can scarce tell how to imagine any being freer, than to be able to do what he wills. So that in respect of actions, within the reach of such a power in him, a man seems as free, as it is possible for freedom to make him.

170 22. But the inquisitive mind of man, willing to shift off from himself, as far as he can, all thoughts of guilt, though it be by putting himself into a worse state, than that of fatal necessity, is not content with this: freedom, unless it reaches farther than this, will not serve the turn: and it passes for a good plea, that a man is not free at all, if he be not as free to will, as he is to act, what he wills. Concerning a man's liberty there yet therefore is raised this farther question, *Whether a man be free to will*; which, I think, is what is meant, when it is disputed, Whether the will be free. And as to that I imagine,

23. 2. That willing, or choosing, being an action, and freedom consisting in a power of acting, or not acting, a man in respect of willing any action in his power, once proposed to his thoughts, cannot be free. The reason whereof is very manifest: for it being unavoidable that the action depending on his will, should exist, or not exist; and its existence, or not existence, following perfectly the determination, and preference of his will, he cannot avoid willing the existence, or not existence, of that action; it is absolutely necessary that he *will* the one, or the other, i.e. *prefer* the one to the other: since one of them must necessarily follow; and that which does follow, follows by the choice and determination of his mind, that is, by his willing it: for if he did not will it, it would not be. So that in respect of the act of willing, a man is not free: liberty consisting in a power to act, or not to act, which, in regard of volition, a man has not. For it is unavoidably necessary to prefer the doing, or forbearance, of an action in a man's power, which is once so proposed to his thoughts; a man must necessarily will the one, or the other of them, upon which preference, or volition, the action, or its forbearance, certainly follows, and is truly voluntary: but the act of volition, or preferring one of the two, being that which he cannot avoid, a man in respect of that action is under a necessity, and so cannot be free; unless necessity and freedom can consist together, and a man can be free and bound at once.

★　　　★　　　★　　　★

25. Since then it is plain, a man is not at liberty, whether he will **171**
will, or no; (for when an action in his power is proposed to his
thoughts, he cannot forbear volition, he must determine one way
or other;) the next thing to be demanded is, *Whether a man be at
liberty to will which of the two he pleases, motion or rest.* This question
carries the absurdity of it so manifestly in itself, that one might
thereby sufficiently be convinced, that liberty concerns not the will
in any case. For to ask, whether a man be at liberty to will either
motion, or rest; speaking, or silence; which he pleases; is to ask,
whether a man can will, what he wills; or be pleased with what he
is pleased with. A question, which, I think, needs no answer: and
they, who can make a question of it, must suppose one will to determine the acts of another, and another to determine that; and so on
in infinitum, an absurdity before taken notice of.

★   ★   ★   ★

29. Thirdly, the will being nothing but a power in the mind to **172**
direct the operative faculties of a man to motion or rest, as far as they
depend on such direction. To the question, What is it determines the
will? The true and proper answer is, The mind. For that which
determines the general power of directing, to this or that particular
direction, is nothing but the agent itself exercising the power it has,
that particular way. If this answer satisfies not, it is plain the meaning
of the question, *What determines the will?* is this, What moves the
mind, in every particular instance, to determine its general power of
directing, to this or that particular motion or rest? And to this I
answer, The motive, for continuing in the same state or action, is
only the present satisfaction in it; the motive to change, is always
some uneasiness: nothing setting us upon the change of state, or upon
any new action, but some uneasiness. This is the great motive that
works on the mind to put it upon action, which for shortness sake
we will call *determining of the will*, which I shall more at large explain.

30. But in the way to it, it will be necessary to premise, that though **173**
I have above endeavoured to express the act of *volition*, by *choosing*,
preferring, and the like terms, that signify *desire* as well as *volition*,
for want of other words to mark that act of the mind, whose proper
name is *willing* or *volition*; yet it being a very simple act, whosoever
desires to understand what it is, will better find it by reflecting on
his own mind, and observing what it does, when it wills, than by

any variety of articulate sounds whatsoever. This caution of being careful not to be misled by expressions, that do not enough keep up the difference between the *will*, and several acts of the mind, that are quite distinct from it, I think the more necessary: because I find the will often confounded with several of the affections, especially *desire*; and one put for the other, and that by men, who would not willingly be thought, not to have had very distinct notions of things, and not to have writ very clearly about them. This, I imagine, has been no small occasion of obscurity and mistake in this matter; and therefore is, as much as may be, to be avoided. For he, that shall turn his thoughts inwards upon what passes in his mind, when he wills, shall see, that the will or power of volition is conversant about nothing, but our own actions; terminates there; and reaches no farther; and that volition is nothing, but that particular determination of the mind, whereby, barely by a thought, the mind endeavours to give rise, continuation, or stop to any action, which it takes to be in its power. This well considered plainly shows, that the will is perfectly distinguished from desire, which in the very same action may have a quite contrary tendency from that which our will sets us upon. A man, whom I cannot deny, may oblige me to use persuasions to another, which at the same time I am speaking, I may wish may not prevail on him. In this case, it is plain the will and desire run counter. I will the action, that tends one way, whilst my desire tends another, and that the direct contrary. A man, who by a violent fit of the gout in his limbs, finds a doziness in his head, or a want of appetite in his stomach removed, desires to be eased too of the pain of his feet or hands (for wherever there is pain there is a desire to be rid of it) though yet, whilst he apprehends, that the removal of the pain may translate the noxious humour to a more vital part, his will is never determined to any one action, that may serve to remove this pain. Whence it is evident, that desiring and willing are two distinct acts of the mind; and consequently that the will, which is but the power of volition, is much more distinct from desire.

174   31. To return then to the inquiry, *What is it that determines the will in regard to our actions.* And that upon second thoughts I am apt to imagine is not, as is generally supposed, the greater good in view: but some (and for the most part the most pressing) *uneasiness* a man is at present under. This is that which successively determines the will, and sets us upon those actions, we perform. This uneasiness we may call, as it is, *desire*; which is an uneasiness of the mind for want of some absent good.

★   ★   ★   ★

35. It seems so established and settled a maxim by the general con- **175** sent of all mankind, that good, the greater good, determines the will, that I do not at all wonder, that when I first published my thoughts on this subject, I took it for granted; and I imagine, that by a great many I shall be thought more excusable, for having then done so, than that now I have ventured to recede from so received an opinion. But yet upon a stricter inquiry, I am forced to conclude, that good, the greater good, though apprehended and acknowledged to be so, does not determine the will, until our desire, raised proportionably to it, makes us uneasy in the want of it. Convince a man never so much, that plenty has its advantages over poverty; make him see and own, that the handsome conveniences of life are better than nasty penury: yet as long as he is content with the latter, and finds no uneasiness in it, he moves not; his will never is determined to any action, that shall bring him out of it. Let a man be never so well persuaded of the advantages of virtue, that it is as necessary to a man, who has any great aims in this world, or hopes in the next, as food to life: yet till he *hungers and thirsts after righteousness*; till he feels an uneasiness in the want of it, his will will not be determined to any action in pursuit of this confessed greater good; but any other uneasiness he feels in himself, shall take place, and carry his will to other actions. On the other side, let a drunkard see, that his health decays, his estate wastes; discredit and diseases, and the want of all things, even of his beloved drink, attends him in the course he follows: yet the returns of uneasiness to miss his companions; the habitual thirst after his cups, at the usual time, drives him to the tavern, though he has in his view the loss of health and plenty, and perhaps of the joys of another life: the least of which is no inconsiderable good, but such as he confesses, is far greater, than the tickling of his palate with a glass of wine, or the idle chat of a soaking club. It is not for want of viewing the greater good: for he sees, and acknowledges it, and in the intervals of his drinking hours, will take resolutions to pursue the greater good; but when the uneasiness to miss his accustomed delight returns, the greater acknowledged good

loses its hold, and the present uneasiness determines the will to the accustomed action; which thereby gets stronger footing to prevail against the next occasion, though he at the same time makes secret promises to himself, that he will do so no more; this is the last time he will act against the attainment of those greater goods. And thus he is, from time to time, in the state of that unhappy complainer, *Video meliora proboque, deteriora sequor*: which sentence, allowed for true, and made good by constant experience, may this, and possibly no other, way be easily made intelligible.

★   ★   ★   ★

176   41. If it be farther asked, what it is moves desire? I answer happiness and that alone. *Happiness* and *misery* are the names of two extremes, the utmost bounds whereof we know not; it is what *eye hath not seen, ear hath not heard, nor hath it entered into the heart of man to conceive*. But of some degrees of both, we have very lively impressions, made by several instances of delight and joy on the one side; and torment and sorrow on the other; which, for shortness sake, I shall comprehend under the names of pleasure and pain, there being pleasure and pain of the mind, as well as the body: *With him is fulness of joy, and pleasure for evermore*: or to speak truly, they are all of the mind; though some have their rise in the mind from thought, others in the body from certain modifications of motion.

177   42. *Happiness* then in its full extent is the utmost pleasure we are capable of, and *misery* the utmost pain: and the lowest degree of what can be called *happiness*, is so much ease from all pain, and so much present pleasure, as without which any one cannot be content. Now because pleasure and pain are produced in us, by the operation of certain objects, either on our minds or our bodies; and in different degrees: therefore what has an aptness to produce pleasure in us, is that we call *good*, and what is apt to produce pain in us, we call *evil*, for no other reason, but for its aptness to produce pleasure and pain in us, wherein consists our happiness and misery. Farther, though what is apt to produce any degree of pleasure, be in itself good; and what is apt to produce any degree of pain, be evil; yet it often happens, that we do not call it so, when it comes in competition with a greater of its sort; because when they come in competition the degrees also of pleasure and pain have justly a preference. So that if we will rightly estimate what we call *good* and *evil*, we shall find it lies much in comparison: for the cause of every less degree of pain, as well as every greater degree of pleasure, has the nature of good, and *vice versa*.

43. Though this be that, which is called *good* and *evil*; and all good **178** be the proper object of desire in general; yet all good, even seen, and confessed to be so, does not necessarily move every particular man's desire; but only that part, or so much of it, as is considered, and taken to make a necessary part of his happiness.... Thus, how much soever men are in earnest, and constant in pursuit of happiness; yet they may have a clear view of good, great and confessed good, without being concerned for it, or moved by it, if they think they can make up their happiness without it. Though, as to pain, that they are always concerned for; they can feel no uneasiness without being moved. And therefore being uneasy in the want of whatever is judged necessary to their happiness, as soon as any good appears to make a part of their portion of happiness, they begin to desire it.

★   ★   ★   ★

47. There being in us a great many uneasinesses always soliciting, **179** and ready to determine the will, it is natural, as I have said, that the greatest, and most pressing should determine the will to the next action; and so it does for the most part, but not always. For the mind having in most cases, as is evident in experience, a power to *suspend* the execution and satisfaction of any of its desires, and so all, one after another, is at liberty to consider the objects of them, examine them on all sides, and weigh them with others. In this lies the liberty man has; and from the not using of it right comes all that variety of mistakes, errors, and faults which we run into, in the conduct of our lives, and our endeavours after happiness; whilst we precipitate the determination of our wills, and engage too soon before due examination. To prevent this we have a power to suspend the prosecution of this or that desire, as every one daily may experiment in himself. This seems to me the source of all liberty; in this seems to consist that, which is (as I think improperly) called *free will*. For during this suspension of any desire, before the will be determined to action, and the action (which follows that determination) done, we have opportunity to examine, view, and judge of the good or evil of what we are going to do; and when, upon due examination, we have judged, we have done our duty, all that we can, or ought to do, in pursuit of

our happiness; and it is not a fault, but a perfection of our nature to desire, will, and act according to the last result of a fair examination.

180 48. This is so far from being a restraint or diminution of freedom, that it is the very improvement and benefit of it; it is not an abridgement, it is the end and use of our liberty; and the farther we are removed from such a determination, the nearer we are to misery and slavery. A perfect indifferency in the mind, not determinable by its last judgement of the good or evil, that is thought to attend its choice, would be so far from being an advantage and excellency of any intellectual nature, that it would be as great an imperfection, as the want of indifferency to act, or not to act, till determined by the will, would be an imperfection on the other side. A man is at liberty to lift up his hand to his head, or let it rest quiet: he is perfectly indifferent in either; and it would be an imperfection in him, if he wanted that power, if he were deprived of that indifferency. But it would be as great an imperfection, if he had the same indifferency whether he would prefer the lifting up his hand, or its remaining in rest, when it would save his head or eyes from a blow he sees coming: it is as much a perfection, that desire or the power of preferring should be determined by good, as that the power of acting should be determined by the will, and the certainer such determination is, the greater is the perfection. Nay were we determined by any thing but the last result of our own minds, judging of the good or evil of any action, we were not free.

*   *   *   *

181 50. But to give a right view of this mistaken part of liberty let me ask, Would any one be a changeling, because he is less determined by wise considerations, than a wise man? Is it worth the name of *freedom* to be at liberty to play the fool, and draw shame and misery upon a man's self? If to break loose from the conduct of reason, and to want that restraint of examination and judgement, which keeps us from choosing or doing the worse, be liberty, true liberty, mad men and fools are the only freemen: but yet, I think, no body would choose to be mad for the sake of such liberty, but he that is mad already. The constant desire of happiness, and the constraint it puts upon us to act for it, no body, I think, accounts an abridgement of liberty, or at least an abridgement of liberty to be complained of.

*   *   *   *

51. As therefore the highest perfection of intellectual nature, lies **182**
in a careful and constant pursuit of true and solid happiness; so the
care of ourselves, that we mistake not imaginary for real happiness,
is the necessary foundation of our liberty. The stronger ties, we have,
to an unalterable pursuit of happiness in general, which is our greatest
good, and which as such our desires always follow, the more are we
free from any necessary determination of our will to any particular
action, and from a necessary compliance with our desire, set upon
any particular, and then appearing greater good, till we have duly
examined, whether it has a tendency to, or be inconsistent with our
real happiness; and till we are as much informed upon this inquiry, as
the weight of the matter, and the nature of the case demands, we are
by the necessity of preferring and pursuing true happiness as our
greatest good, obliged to suspend the satisfaction of our desire in
particular cases.

★   ★   ★   ★

CHAP. XXVIII—OF OTHER RELATIONS

★   ★   ★   ★

4. Fourthly, there is another sort of relation, which is the con- **183**
formity, or disagreement, men's voluntary actions have to a rule, to
which they are referred, and by which they are judged of: which, I
think, may be called *moral relation*; as being that, which denominates
our moral actions, and deserves well to be examined, there being no
part of knowledge wherein we should be more careful to get determined ideas, and avoid, as much as may be, obscurity and confusion.
Human actions, when with their various ends, objects, manners, and
circumstances, they are framed into distinct complex ideas, are, as
has been shown, so many mixed modes, a great part whereof have
names annexed to them. Thus supposing gratitude to be a readiness
to acknowledge and return kindness received; polygamy to be the
having more wives than one at once: when we frame these notions
thus in our minds, we have there so many determined ideas of mixed
modes. But this is not all that concerns our actions; it is not enough
to have determined ideas of them, and to know what names belong
to such and such combinations of ideas. We have a farther and
greater concernment, and that is, to know whether such actions so
made up, are morally good, or bad.

5. Good and evil, as hath been shown, B. II. Ch. XX. § 2.[1] and Ch. XXI. § 42.[2] are nothing but pleasure or pain, or that which occasions, or procures pleasure or pain in us. *Morally good and evil* then, is only the conformity or disagreement of our voluntary actions to some law, whereby good and evil is drawn on us, from the will and power of the law-maker; which good and evil, pleasure or pain, attending our observance, or breach of the law, by the decree of the law-maker, is that we call *reward* and *punishment*.

184 6. Of these *moral rules*, or laws, to which men generally refer, and by which they judge of the rectitude or pravity of their actions, there seem to me to be *three sorts*, with their three different enforcements, or rewards and punishments. For since it would be utterly in vain, to suppose a rule set to the free actions of man, without annexing to it some enforcement of good and evil, to determine his will, we must, wherever we suppose a law, suppose also some reward or punishment annexed to that law. It would be in vain for one intelligent being, to set a rule to the actions of another, if he had it not in his power, to reward the compliance with, and punish deviation from his rule, by some good and evil, that is not the natural product and consequence of the action itself. For that being a natural convenience, or inconvenience, would operate of itself without a law. This, if I mistake not, is the true nature of all *law*, properly so called.

7. The *laws* that men generally refer their actions to, to judge of their rectitude, or obliquity, seem to me to be these three. 1. The *divine* law. 2. The *civil* law. 3. The law of *opinion* or *reputation*, if I may so call it. By the relation they bear to the first of these, men judge whether their actions are sins, or duties; by the second, whether they be criminal, or innocent; and by the third, whether they be virtues or vices.

185 8. First, the *divine* law, whereby I mean, that law which God has set to the actions of men, whether promulgated to them by the light of nature, or the voice of revelation. That God has given a rule whereby men should govern themselves, I think there is no body so brutish as to deny. He has a right to do it, we are his creatures: he has goodness and wisdom to direct our actions to that which is best: and he has power to enforce it by rewards and punishments, of infinite weight and duration, in another life: for no body can take us out of

[1 § 160, above.]   [2 § 177, above.]

his hands. This is the only true touchstone of *moral rectitude*; and by comparing them to this law, it is that men judge of the most considerable *moral good* or *evil* of their actions; that is, whether as *duties*, or *sins*, they are like to procure them happiness, or misery, from the hands of the ALMIGHTY.

9. Secondly, the *civil* law, the rule set by the commonwealth to the **186** actions of those, who belong to it, is another rule, to which men refer their actions, to judge whether they be *criminal*, or no. This law no body overlooks: the rewards and punishments, that enforce it, being ready at hand, and suitable to the power that makes it: which is the force of the commonwealth, engaged to protect the lives, liberties, and possessions, of those who live according to its laws, and has power to take away life, liberty, or goods, from him, who disobeys; which is the punishment of offences committed against this law.

10. Thirdly, the law of *opinion* or *reputation*. Virtue and vice are **187** names pretended, and supposed every where to stand for actions in their own nature right and wrong: and as far as they really are so applied, they so far are coincident with the divine law above-mentioned. But yet, whatever is pretended, this is visible, that these names, *virtue* and *vice*, in the particular instances of their application, through the several nations and societies of men in the world, are constantly attributed only to such actions, as in each country and society are in reputation or discredit. Nor is it to be thought strange, that men every where should give the name of *virtue* to those actions, which amongst them are called praise worthy; and call that *vice*, which they account blameable: since otherwise they would condemn themselves, if they should think any thing *right*, to which they allowed not commendation; any thing *wrong*, which they let pass without blame. Thus the measure of what is every where called and esteemed *virtue* and *vice* is this approbation or dislike, praise or blame, which by a secret and tacit consent establishes itself in the several societies, tribes, and clubs of men in the world: whereby several actions come to find credit or disgrace amongst them, according to the judgement, maxims, or fashions of that place. For though men uniting into politic societies, have resigned up to the public the disposing of all their force, so that they cannot employ it against any fellow-citizen, any farther than the law of the country directs: yet they retain still the power of thinking well or ill; approving or disapproving of the actions of those whom they live amongst, and

converse with: and by this approbation and dislike they establish amongst themselves, what they will call *virtue* and *vice*.

⋆　　⋆　　⋆　　⋆

188　12. If any one shall imagine, that I have forgot my own notion of a law, when I make the law, whereby men judge of virtue and vice, to be nothing else, but the consent of private men, who have not authority enough to make a law: especially wanting that, which is so necessary, and essential to a law, a power to enforce it: I think, I may say, that he, who imagines commendation and disgrace, not to be strong motives on men, to accommodate themselves to the opinions and rules of those, with whom they converse, seems little skilled in the nature, or history of mankind: the greatest part whereof he shall find to govern themselves chiefly, if not solely, by this law of fashion; and so they do that, which keeps them in reputation with their company, little regard the laws of God, or the magistrate. The penalties that attend the breach of God's laws, some, nay, perhaps, most men seldom seriously reflect on: and amongst those that do, many, whilst they break the law, entertain thoughts of future reconciliation, and making their peace for such breaches. And as to the punishments, due from the laws of the commonwealth, they frequently flatter themselves with the hopes of impunity. But no man escapes the punishment of their censure and dislike, who offends against the fashion and opinion of the company he keeps, and would recommend himself to. Nor is there one of ten thousand, who is stiff and insensible enough to bear up under the constant dislike, and condemnation of his own club. He must be of a strange, and unusual constitution, who can content himself, to live in constant disgrace and disrepute with his own particular society. Solitude many men have sought, and been reconciled to: but no body, that has the least thought, or sense of a man about him, can live in society, under the constant dislike, and ill opinion of his familiars, and those he converses with. This is a burden too heavy for human sufferance: and he must be made up of irreconcilable contradictions, who can take pleasure in company, and yet be insensible of contempt and disgrace from his companions.

13. These three then, first, the law of God; secondly, the law of politic societies; thirdly, the law of fashion, or private censure, are those, to which men variously compare their actions: and it is by

their conformity to one of these laws, that they take their measures, when they would judge of their moral rectitude, and denominate their actions good or bad.

★　　　★　　　★　　　★

BOOK IV

CHAP. III—OF THE EXTENT OF HUMAN KNOWLEDGE

★　　　★　　　★　　　★

18. . . . . The idea of a supreme being, infinite in power, goodness, **189** and wisdom, whose workmanship we are, and on whom we depend; and the idea of ourselves, as understanding, rational creatures, being such as are clear in us, would, I suppose, if duly considered, and pursued, afford such foundations of our duty and rules of action, as might place *morality amongst the sciences capable of demonstration*: wherein I doubt not, but from self-evident propositions, by necessary consequences, as incontestable as those in mathematics, the measures of right and wrong might be made out, to any one that will apply himself with the same indifferency and attention to the one, as he does to the other of these sciences. The relation of other modes may certainly be perceived, as well as those of number and extension: and I cannot see, why they should not also be capable of demonstration, if due methods were thought on to examine, or pursue their agreement or disagreement. *Where there is no property, there is no injustice*, is a proposition as certain as any demonstration in Euclid: for the idea of *property* being a right to any thing; and the idea to which the name *injustice* is given, being the invasion or violation of that right; it is evident, that these ideas being thus established, and these names annexed to them, I can as certainly know this proposition to be true, as that a triangle has three angles equal to two right ones. Again, *No government allows absolute liberty*: the idea of government being the establishment of society upon certain rules or laws, which require conformity to them; and the idea of absolute liberty being for any one to do whatever he pleases; I am as capable of being certain of the truth of this proposition, as of any in mathematics.

★　　　★　　　★　　　★

Essays on the Law of Nature

IV—AN RATIO PER RES A SENSIBUS
HAUSTAS PERVENIRE POTEST IN
COGNITIONEM LEGIS NATURAE?
AFFIRMATUR

IV.—CAN REASON ATTAIN TO THE
KNOWLEDGE OF NATURAL LAW
THROUGH SENSE-EXPERIENCE? YES

190 Legem naturae lumine naturae esse cognoscibilem supra probavimus. . . . Quandoquidem vero lumen hoc naturae (ut alibi ostensum est) nec traditio sit nec internum aliquod practicum principium mentibus nostris a natura inscriptum, nihil remanet quod lumen naturae dici possit praeter rationem et sensum, quae solum duae facultates hominum mentes instruere et erudire videntur et id praestare quod luminis proprium est, scilicet ut res aliter ignotae prorsus et in tenebris latentes animo obversentur et cognosci et quasi conspici possint. . . . Ut vero cognoscatur quomodo sensus et ratio dum sibi mutuo opitulentur nos deducere possunt in

We have proved above that **190** natural law can be known by the light of nature. . . . But since, as has been shown elsewhere, this light of nature is neither tradition nor some inward moral principle written in our minds by nature, there remains nothing by which it can be defined but reason and sense-perception. For only these two faculties appear to teach and educate the minds of men and to provide what is characteristic of the light of nature, namely that things otherwise wholly unknown and hidden in darkness should be able to come before the mind and be known and as it were looked into. . . . But in order that we may know how sense-experience and reason, as long as they assist one another mutually, can lead us to the knowledge of natural

[1 This brief extract from Locke's early work (not published by him) is included here in order to show what sort of proof of morality he was prepared to give in his younger days. It also indicates the relation between his early thoughts on morality and the main theme of the *Essay concerning Human Understanding*.]

cognitionem legis naturae, prae-
mittenda sunt aliqua quae ad
legis cujusvis cognitionem necessario supponuntur. Primo igitur,
ut se lege teneri quisquam co-
gnoscat, scire prius oportet esse
legislatorem, superiorem scilicet
aliquam potestatem cui jure
subjicitur. Secundo scire etiam
oportet esse aliquam superioris
illius potestatis voluntatem circa
res a nobis agendas, hoc est
legislatorem illum, quicunque
is demum fuerit, velle nos hoc
agere illud vero omittere, et
exigere a nobis ut vitae nostrae
mores suae voluntati sint con-
formes; ut vero haec duo supposita ad legis naturae cognitionem necessaria nobis innote-
scant, quid sensus confert quid
ratio in sequentibus patebit.

191   Primo igitur dicimus patere
ex sensu esse in rerum natura res
sensibiles, hoc est revera existere
corpora et eorum affectiones,
scilicet levitatem, gravitatem,
calorem, frigus, colores, et caeteras qualitates sensui obvias,
quae omnes aliquo modo ad
motum referri possint; esse
mundum hunc visibilem mira

law, certain facts must first be
set forth, because they are necessarily presupposed in the knowledge of any and every law.
First, in order that anyone may
understand that he is bound by a
law, he must know beforehand
that there is a law-maker, i.e.
some superior power to which
he is rightly subject. Secondly,
it is also necessary to know that
there is some will on the part of
that superior power with respect
to the things to be done by us,
that is to say, that the law-maker,
whoever he may prove to be,
wishes that we do this but leave
off that, and demands of us that
the conduct of our life should be
in accordance with his will. In
what follows it will become clear
what sense-experience contributes and what reason does, in
order that these two presuppo-
sitions, which are required for
knowledge of the law of nature,
may become known to us.

In the first place, then, we say **191**
it is evident from sense-experience that in the natural world
there are perceptible objects, i.e.
that there really exist solid bodies
and their conditions, namely
lightness and heaviness, warmth
and coldness, colours and the
rest of the qualities presented to
the senses, which can all in some
way be traced back to motion;
that this visible world is

arte et ordine constructum, cujus etiam pars nos sumus genus humanum; videmus enim perpetuo certoque cursu circum rotari sidera, volvi in mare flumina, et se certo ordine sequi anni et tempestatum vicissitudines. Haec et infinita pene plura nos docet sensus.

constructed with wonderful art and regularity, and of this world we, the human race, are also a part. We certainly see the stars turning round in an unbroken and fixed course, rivers rolling along into the sea, and the years and changes of the seasons following one another in a definite order. This and almost infinitely more we learn from the senses.

192 Secundo, dicimus, cum mens acceptam hujus mundi machinam secum accuratius perpenderit et rerum sensibilium speciem, ordinem, ornatum, et motum contemplaverit, inde progreditur ad eorum originem inquirendam, quae causa, quis author fuerit tam egregii operis, cum certo constet id casu et fortuito in tam justam tam undique perfectam affabreque factam compagem coalescere non potuisse: unde certe colligitur oportere esse potentem sapientemque harum rerum omnium opificem qui totum hunc fecit fabricavitque mundum et nos homines, non infimam in eo partem. . . . His ita positis necessario sequitur alium esse praeter nos potentiorem et sapientiorem authorem qui pro libitu suo nos producere,

Secondly, we say that the **192** mind, after more carefully considering in itself the fabric of this world perceived by the senses and after contemplating the beauty of the objects to be observed, their order, array, and motion, thence proceeds to an inquiry into their origin, to find out what was the cause, and who the maker, of such an excellent work, for it is surely undisputed that this could not have come together casually and by chance into so regular and in every respect so perfect and ingeniously prepared a structure. Hence it is undoubtedly inferred that there must be a powerful and wise creator of all these things, who has made and built this whole universe and us mortals who are not the lowest part of it. . . . After the case has been put thus it necessarily follows that above ourselves there exists another more powerful and wiser agent who at his will can

conservare, ac tollere potest. His ita a sensuum testimonio deductis dictat ratio aliquam esse superiorem potestatem cui merito subjicimur, Deus scilicet qui in nos justum habet et ineluctabile imperium, qui prout sibi visum fuerit nos erigere potest vel prosternere, eodem nutu faelices vel miseros reddere; qui cum animam ipse creavit corpusque mira arte contexuit, utriusque facultates, vires, et secretam fabricam naturamque probe perspectam habet, illam aerumnis vel gaudio, hoc dolore vel voluptate implere et exagitare potest et utrumque simul ad summam beatitudinem tollere vel miseriam poenamque detrudere. Unde liquido apparet rationem sensu monstrante viam nos deducere posse in cognitionem legislatoris sive superioris alicujus potestatis cui necessario subjicimur, quod primum erat requisitum ad cognitionem alicujus legis.

bring us into the world, maintain us, and take us away. Hence, having inferred this on the evidence of the senses, reason lays down that there must be some superior power to which we are rightly subject, namely God who has a just and inevitable command over us and at His pleasure can raise us up or throw us down, and make us by the same commanding power happy or miserable. And since He has Himself created the soul and constructed the body with wonderful art, and has thoroughly explored the faculties and powers of each, as well as their hidden constitution and nature, He can fill and stir the one with sorrow or delight, the other with pain or pleasure; He also can lift both together to a condition of the utmost happiness or thrust them down to a state of misery and torment. Hence it appears clearly that, with sense-perception showing the way, reason can lead us to the knowledge of a law-maker or of some superior power to which we are necessarily subject. And this was the first thing needed for the knowledge of any law.

* * * *

193 Secundo igitur, cum ex sensuum testimonio concludendum sit esse aliquem harum rerum

In the second place, then, **193** since on the evidence of the senses it must be concluded that

omnium opificem quem non solum potentem sed sapientem agnoscere necesse sit, sequitur inde illum non frustra et temere fecisse hunc mundum; repugnat enim tantae sapientiae nullo destinato fine operari, neque enim credere potest homo, cum se sentiat mentem habere agilem, capacem, ad omnia promptam et versatilem, ratione et cognitione ornatam, corpus insuper agile et pro animae imperio huc illuc mobile, haec omnia ad agendum parata sibi a sapientissimo authore dari ut nihil agat, his se facultatibus omnibus instrui ut eo splendidius otietur et torpescat: unde liquido constat Deum velle illum aliquid agere, quod secundum erat requisitum ad legis cujusvis cognitionem, scilicet voluntas superioris potestatis circa res a nobis agendas, hoc est velle illum nos aliquid agere.

194 Quid vero illud sit quod nobis agendum est partim ex fine rerum omnium, quae cum a beneplacito divino suam mutu-

there is some maker of all these things, whom it is necessary to recognize as not only powerful but also wise, it follows from this that he has not created this world for nothing and without purpose. For it is contrary to such great wisdom to work with no fixed aim; nor indeed can man believe, since he perceives that he has an agile, capable mind, versatile and ready for anything, furnished with reason and knowledge, and a body besides which is quick and easy to be moved hither and thither by virtue of the soul's authority, that all this equipment for action is bestowed on him by a most wise creator in order that he may do nothing, and that he is fitted out with all these faculties in order that he may thereby be more splendidly idle and sluggish. Hence it is quite evident that God intends man to do something, and this was the second of the two things required for the knowledge of any and every law, namely, the will on the part of a superior power with respect to the things to be done by us; that is, God wills that we do something. But what it is that is to be done **194** by us can be partly gathered from the end in view for all things. For since these derive their origin from a gracious

entur originem et opera sint authoris summe perfecti et sapientis non videntur ab eo ad alium destinari finem quam ad sui ipsius gloriam ad quam omnia referri debent, partim etiam officii nostri rationem certamque regulam colligere possumus ex hominis ipsius constitutione et facultatum humanarum apparatu; cum enim nec temere factus sit homo nec in nihilum his donatus facultatibus quae exerceri et possunt et debent, id videtur opus hominis ad quod naturaliter agendum instructus est, id est cum in se sensus et rationem reperit pronum se et paratum sentit ad Dei opera ejusque in iis sapientiam potentiamque contemplandam et laudem deinde honorem et gloriam tanto tamque benefico authore dignissimam tribuendam reddendamque; deinde ad vitae conjunctionem cum aliis hominibus conciliandam et conservandam non solum vitae usu et necessitate impelli, sed ad societatem ineundam propensione quadam naturae incitari eamque tuendam sermonis beneficio et linguae commercio instrui, quantum vero ad se ipsum conservandum

divine purpose and are the work of a most perfect and wise maker, they appear to be intended by Him for no other end than His own glory, and to this all things must be related. Partly also we can infer the principle and a definite rule of our duty from man's own constitution and the faculties with which he is equipped. For since man is neither made without design nor endowed to no purpose with these faculties which both can and must be employed, his function appears to be that which nature has prepared him to perform. That is to say, when he in himself finds sense-experience and reason, he feels himself disposed and ready to contemplate God's works and that wisdom and power of His which they display, and thereupon to assign and render praise, honour, and glory most worthy of so great and so beneficent a creator. Further, he feels himself not only to be impelled by life's experience and pressing needs to procure and preserve a life in society with other men, but also to be urged to enter into society by a certain propensity of nature, and to be prepared for the maintenance of society by the gift of speech and through the intercourse of language, in fact as much as he is obliged to

obligetur. Cum ad eam officii partem interno instinctu nimium quam impellatur, nemoque repertus sit qui se negligit, se ipsum abdicet, et in hanc rem omnes forte magis attenti sint quam oportet, non opus est ut hic moneam; sed de his tribus quae omne hominum erga Deum, vicinum, et se ipsum complectuntur officium alibi forte sigillatim disserendi erit locus.

preserve himself. But since man is very much urged on to this part of his duty by an inward instinct, and nobody can be found who does not care for himself or who disowns himself, and all direct perhaps more attention to this point than is necessary, there is no need for me here to admonish. But there will be room perhaps elsewhere to discuss one by one these three subjects which embrace all that men owe to God, their neighbour, and themselves.

ANTHONY ASHLEY COOPER
THIRD EARL OF SHAFTESBURY

1671–1713

AN INQUIRY CONCERNING VIRTUE, OR MERIT

[First printed, in an unauthorized edition, 1699. Corrected version included in *Characteristics of Men, Manners, Opinions, Times*, vol. ii, 1711; second edition, further corrected, 1714. Reprinted here from the second edition, with modified spelling, reduction of initial capital letters and italics, and omission of footnote references to other parts of the work]

LORD SHAFTESBURY

An Inquiry concerning Virtue, or Merit

BOOK I PART II

SECT. I

When we reflect on any ordinary frame or constitution either of **195**
art or nature; and consider how hard it is to give the least account of
a particular part, without a competent knowledge of the whole: we
need not wonder to find ourselves at a loss in many things relating
to the constitution and frame of nature herself. For to what end in
nature many things, even whole species of creatures, refer; or to
what purpose they serve; will be hard for any one justly to determine: but to what end the many proportions and various shapes of
parts in many creatures actually serve; we are able, by the help of
study and observation, to demonstrate, with great exactness.

We know that every creature has a private good and interest of
his own; which nature has compelled him to seek, by all the advantages afforded him, within the compass of his make. We know that
there is in reality a right and a wrong state of every creature; and that
his right one is by nature forwarded, and by himself affectionately
sought. There being therefore in every creature a certain *interest* or
good; there must be also a certain END to which every thing in his
constitution must *naturally* refer. To this END if any thing, either in
his appetites, passions, or affections, be not conducing, but the contrary; we must of necessity own it *ill* to him. And in this manner he
is ill, with respect to himself; as he certainly is, with respect to
others of his kind, when any such appetites or passions make him
any way injurious to them. Now, if by the natural constitution of
any rational creature, the same irregularities of appetite which make
him ill to others, make him ill also to himself; and if the same
regularity of affections, which causes him to be good in one sense,

causes him to be good also in the other; then is that goodness by which he is thus useful to others, a real good and advantage to himself. And thus *virtue* and *interest* may be found at last to agree.

196   Of this we shall consider particularly in the latter part of our *Inquiry*. Our first design is, to see if we can clearly determine what that quality is to which we give the name of *goodness*, or VIRTUE.

Should a historian or traveller describe to us a certain creature of a more solitary disposition than ever was yet heard of; one who had neither mate nor fellow of any kind; nothing of his own likeness, towards which he stood well-affected or inclined; nor any thing without, or beyond himself, for which he had the least passion or concern: we might be apt to say perhaps, without much hesitation, 'that this was doubtless a very melancholy creature, and that in this unsociable and sullen state he was like to have a very disconsolate kind of life.' But if we were assured, that notwithstanding all appearances, the creature enjoyed himself extremely, had a great relish of life, and was in nothing wanting to his own good; we might acknowledge perhaps, 'that the creature was no monster, nor absurdly constituted as to himself.' But we should hardly, after all, be induced to say of him, 'that he was a good creature.' However, should it be urged against us, 'that such as he was, the creature was still perfect in himself, and therefore to be esteemed good: for what had he to do with others?' In this sense, indeed, we might be forced to acknowledge, 'that he was a good creature; if he could be understood to be absolute and complete in himself; without any real relation to any thing in the universe besides.' For should there be any where in nature a system, of which this living creature was to be considered as a part; then could he no-wise be allowed good; whilst he plainly appeared to be such a part, as made rather to the harm than good of that system or whole in which he was included.

197   If therefore, in the structure of this or any other animal, there be any thing which points beyond himself, and by which he is plainly discovered to have relation to some other being or nature besides his own; then will this animal undoubtedly be esteemed a part of some other system. For instance, if an animal has the proportions of a male, it shows he has relation to a female. And the respective proportions both of the male and female will be allowed, doubtless, to have a joint relation to another existence and order of things beyond themselves. So that the creatures are both of them to be considered as parts of another system: which is that of a particular race or species of living creatures, who have some one common nature, or are provided for, by some one order or constitution of things subsisting together, and co-operating towards their conservation and support.

In the same manner, if a whole species of animals contribute to the existence or well-being of some other; then is that whole species, in general, a part only of some other system.

★   ★   ★   ★

Now, if the whole system of animals, together with that of vegetables, and all other things in this inferior world, be properly comprehended in one system of a globe or earth: and if, again, this globe or earth itself appears to have a real dependence on something still beyond; as, for example, either on its sun, the galaxy, or its fellow-planets: then is it in reality a PART only of some other system. And if it be allowed, that there is in like manner a SYSTEM *of all things, and a universal nature*; there can be no particular being or system which is not either good or ill in that general one of the universe: for if it be insignificant and of no use, it is a fault or imperfection, and consequently ill in the general system.

Therefore if any being be *wholly* and *really* ILL, it must be ill with **198** respect to the universal system; and then the system of the universe is ill, or imperfect. But if the ill of one private system be the good of others; if it makes still to the good of the general system (as when one creature lives by the destruction of another; one thing is generated from the corruption of another; or one planetary system or vortex may swallow up another) then is the ill of that private system no real ill in itself; any more than the pain of breeding teeth is ill, in a system or body which is so constituted, that without this occasion of pain, it would suffer worse, by being defective.

So that we cannot say of any being, that it is wholly and absolutely ill, unless we can positively show and ascertain, that what we call ILL is no where GOOD besides, in any other system, or with respect to any other order or economy whatsoever.

But were there in the world any entire species of animals destructive to every other, it may be justly called an ill species; as being ill in the animal system. And if in any species of animals (as in men, for example) one man is of a nature pernicious to the rest, he is in this respect justly styled an ill man.

199   We do not however say of any one, that he is an ill man, because he has the plague-spots upon him, or because he has convulsive fits which make him strike and wound such as approach him. Nor do we say on the other side, that he is a good man, when having his hands tied up, he is hindered from doing the mischief he designs; or (which is in a manner the same) when he abstains from executing his ill purpose, through a fear of some impending punishment, or through the allurement of some exterior reward.

So that in a sensible creature, that which is not done through any affection at all, makes neither good nor ill in the nature of that creature; who then only is supposed good, when the good or ill of the system to which he has relation, is the immediate object of some passion or affection moving him.

Since it is therefore by affection merely that a creature is esteemed good or ill, *natural* or *unnatural*; our business will be, to examine which are the *good* and *natural*, and which the *ill* and *unnatural* affections.

SECT. III

200   But to proceed from what is esteemed mere *goodness*, and lies within the reach and capacity of all sensible creatures, to that which is called VIRTUE or MERIT, and is allowed to man only.

In a creature capable of forming general notions of things, not only the outward beings which offer themselves to the sense, are the objects of the affection; but the very *actions* themselves, and the *affections* of pity, kindness, gratitude, and their contraries, being brought into the mind by reflection, become objects. So that, by means of this reflected sense, there arises another kind of affection towards those very affections themselves, which have been already felt, and are now become the subject of a new liking or dislike.

201   The case is the same in the mental or moral subjects, as in the ordinary bodies, or common objects of sense. The shapes, motions, colours, and proportions of these latter being presented to our eye; there necessarily results a beauty or deformity, according to the different measure, arrangement and disposition of their several parts. So in behaviour and actions, when presented to our understanding, there must be found, of necessity, an apparent difference, according to the regularity or irregularity of the subjects.

The MIND, which is spectator or auditor of other minds, cannot be without its eye and ear; so as to discern proportion, distinguish sound, and scan each sentiment or thought which comes before it. It can let nothing escape its censure. It feels the soft and harsh, the agreeable and disagreeable, in the affections; and finds a *foul* and *fair*, a *harmonious* and a *dissonant*, as really and truly here, as in any musical numbers, or in the outward forms or representations of sensible things. Nor can it withhold its *admiration* and *ecstasy*, its *aversion* and *scorn*, any more in what relates to one than to the other of these subjects. So that to deny the common and natural sense of a SUBLIME and BEAUTIFUL in things, will appear an affectation merely, to any one who considers duly of this affair.

Now as in the sensible kind of objects, the species or images of bodies, colours, and sounds, are perpetually moving before our eyes, and acting on our senses, even when we sleep; so in the moral and intellectual kind, the forms and images of things are no less active and incumbent on the mind, at all seasons, and even when the real objects themselves are absent.

In these vagrant characters or pictures of manners, which the mind of necessity figures to itself, and carries still about with it, the heart cannot possibly remain neutral; but constantly takes part one way or other. However false or corrupt it be within itself, it finds the difference, as to beauty and comeliness, between one heart and another, one turn of affection, one behaviour, one sentiment and another; and accordingly, in all disinterested cases, must approve in some measure of what is natural and honest, and disapprove what is dishonest and corrupt.

Thus the several motions, inclinations, passions, dispositions, and **202** consequent carriage and behaviour of creatures in the various parts of life, being in several views or perspectives represented to the mind, which readily discerns the good and ill towards the species or public; there arises a new trial or exercise of the heart: which must either rightly and soundly affect what is just and right, and disaffect what is contrary; or, corruptly affect what is ill, and disaffect what is worthy and good.

And in this case alone it is we call any creature *worthy* or *virtuous*, when it can have the notion of a public interest, and can attain the speculation or science of what is morally good or ill, admirable or blameable, right or wrong. For though we may vulgarly call an ill horse vicious, yet we never say of a good one, nor of any mere beast, idiot, or changeling, though ever so good-natured, that he is worthy or virtuous.

So that if a creature be generous, kind, constant, compassionate; yet if he cannot reflect on what he himself does, or sees others do, so as to take notice of what is *worthy* or *honest*; and make that notice or conception of *worth* and *honesty* to be an object of his affection; he has not the character of being *virtuous*: for thus, and no otherwise, he is capable of having a *sense of right or wrong*; a sentiment or judgement of what is done, through just, equal, and good affection, or the contrary.

★   ★   ★   ★

BOOK I PART III

SECT. I

★   ★   ★   ★

203 It is impossible to suppose a mere sensible creature originally so ill-constituted, and unnatural, as that from the moment he comes to be tried by sensible objects, he should have no one good passion towards his kind, no foundation either of pity, love, kindness, or social affection. It is full as impossible to conceive, that a rational creature coming first to be tried by rational objects, and receiving into his mind the images or representations of justice, generosity, gratitude, or other virtue, should have no *liking* of these, or *dislike* of their contraries; but be found absolutely indifferent towards whatsoever is presented to him of this sort. A soul, indeed, may as well be without sense, as without admiration in the things of which it has any knowledge. Coming therefore to a capacity of seeing and admiring in this new way, it must needs find a beauty and a deformity as well in actions, minds, and tempers, as in figures, sounds, or colours. If there be no *real* amiableness or deformity in moral acts, there is at least *an imaginary one* of full force. Though perhaps the thing itself should not be allowed in nature, the imagination or fancy of it must be allowed to be from nature alone. Nor can any thing besides art and strong endeavour, with long practice and meditation, overcome such a natural prevention, or prepossession of the mind, in favour of this moral distinction.

★   ★   ★   ★

SECT. III

*   *   *   *

Let us suppose a creature, who wanting reason, and being unable **204** to reflect, has, notwithstanding, many good qualities and affections; as love to his kind, courage, gratitude, or pity. It is certain that if you give to this creature a reflecting faculty, it will at the same instant approve of gratitude, kindness, and pity; be taken with any show or representation of the social passion, and think nothing more amiable than this, or more odious than the contrary. And this is *to be capable of* VIRTUE, and *to have a sense of* RIGHT *and* WRONG.

*   *   *   *

BOOK II PART I

SECT. I

We have considered *what* VIRTUE *is*, and to whom the character **205** belongs. It remains to inquire, *what obligation* there is *to* VIRTUE; or *what reason* to embrace it.

We have found, that to deserve the name of *good* or *virtuous*, a creature must have all his inclinations and affections, his dispositions of mind and temper, suitable, and agreeing with the good of his *kind*, or of that *system* in which he is included, and of which he constitutes a PART. To stand thus well affected, and to have one's affections *right* and *entire*, not only in respect of oneself, but of society and the public: this is *rectitude*, *integrity*, or VIRTUE. And to be wanting in any of these, or to have their contraries, is *depravity*, *corruption*, and VICE.

It has been already shown, that in the passions and affections of particular creatures, there is a constant relation to the interest of *a species*, or *common nature*. This has been demonstrated in the case of *natural affection*, parental kindness, zeal for posterity, concern for the propagation and nurture of the young, love of fellowship and company, compassion, mutual succour, and the rest of this kind. Nor will any one deny that this affection of a creature towards the good of the species or common nature, is as *proper* and *natural* to him, as it is to any organ, part or member of an animal body, or mere vegetable, to work its known course, and regular way of growth. It is not more natural for the stomach to digest, the lungs to breathe, the glands to separate juices, or other entrails to perform their several offices; however they may by particular impediments be sometimes disordered or obstructed in their operations.

206 There being allowed therefore in a creature such affections as these towards *the common nature*, or *system of the kind*, together with those other which regard *the private nature*, or *self-system*; it will appear that in following the first of these affections, the creature must on many occasions contradict and go against the latter. How else should the species be preserved? Or what would signify that implanted *natural affection*, by which a creature through so many difficulties and hazards preserves its offspring, and supports its kind?

It may therefore be imagined, perhaps, that there is a plain and absolute opposition between these two habits or affections. It may be presumed, that the pursuing the common interest or public good through the affections of one kind, must be a hindrance to the attainment of private good through the affections of another. For it being taken for granted, that hazards and hardships, of whatever sort, are naturally the *ill* of the private state; and it being certainly the nature of those public affections to lead often to the greatest hardships and hazards of every kind; it is presently inferred, 'that it is the creature's interest to be without any public affection whatsoever.'

This we know for certain; that all social love, friendship, gratitude, or whatever else is of this generous kind, does by its nature take place of the self-interesting passions, draws us out of ourselves, and makes us disregardful of our own convenience and safety. So that according to a known way of reasoning on *self-interest*, that which is of a social kind in us, should of right be abolished. Thus kindness of every sort, indulgence, tenderness, compassion, and in short, all natural affection should be industriously suppressed, and, as mere folly, and weakness of nature, be resisted and overcome; that, by this means, there might be nothing remaining in us, which was contrary to a direct *self-end*; nothing which might stand in opposition to a steady and deliberate pursuit of the most narrowly confined *self-interest*.

207 According to this extraordinary hypothesis, it must be taken for granted, 'that in the system of a kind or species, the interest of the private nature is directly opposite to that of the common one; the

interest of particulars directly opposite to that of the public in general.'—A strange constitution! in which it must be confessed there is much disorder and untowardness; unlike to what we observe elsewhere in nature. As if in any vegetable or animal body, the *part* or member could be supposed in a good and prosperous state as to itself, when under a contrary disposition, and in an unnatural growth or habit as to its WHOLE.

Now that this is in reality quite otherwise, we shall endeavour to demonstrate; so as to make appear, 'that what men represent as an ill order and constitution in the universe, by making moral rectitude appear *the ill*, and depravity *the good* or advantage of a creature, is in nature just the contrary. That to be well affected towards the *public interest* and *one's own*, is not only consistent, but inseparable: and that moral rectitude, or *virtue*, must accordingly be the advantage, and *vice* the injury and disadvantage of every creature.'

SECT. II

*   *   *   *

The parts and proportions of the mind, their mutual relation and **208** dependency, the connection and frame of those passions which constitute the soul or temper, may easily be understood by any one who thinks it worth his while to study this inward anatomy. It is certain that the order or symmetry of this inward part is, in itself, no less real and exact, than that of the body. However, it is apparent that few of us endeavour to become anatomists of this sort. Nor is any one ashamed of the deepest ignorance in such a subject. For though the greatest misery and ill is generally owned to be from disposition, and temper; though it is allowed that temper may often change, and that it actually varies on many occasions, much to our disadvantage; yet how this matter is brought about, we inquire not. We never trouble ourselves to consider thoroughly by what means or methods our inward constitution comes at any time to be impaired or injured. The *solutio continui*, which bodily surgeons talk of, is never applied in this case, by surgeons of another sort. The notion of *a whole* and *parts* is not apprehended in this science. We know not what the effect is, of straining any affection, indulging any wrong passion, or relaxing any proper and natural habit, or good inclination. Nor can we conceive how a particular action should have such a sudden influence on the whole mind, as to make the person an immediate sufferer. We suppose rather that a man may violate his faith, commit any wickedness unfamiliar to him before, engage in any vice or villainy, without the least prejudice to *himself*, or any misery *naturally* following from the ill action.

★　　　★　　　★　　　★

SECT. III

209　It has been shown before, that no animal can be said properly *to act*, otherwise than through affections or passions, such as are proper to an animal. For in convulsive fits, where a creature strikes either himself or others, it is a simple mechanism, an engine, or piece of clockwork, which acts, and not the animal.

Whatsoever therefore is done or acted by any animal as such, is done only through some affection or passion, as of fear, love, or hatred moving him.

And as it is impossible that a weaker affection should overcome a stronger, so it is impossible but that where the affections or passions are strongest in the main, and form in general the most considerable party, either by their force or number; thither the animal must incline: and according to this balance he must be governed, and led to action.

210　The affections or passions which must influence and govern the animal, are either,

1. The *natural affections*, which lead to the good of THE PUBLIC.

2. Or the *self-affections*, which lead only to the good of THE PRIVATE.

3. Or such as are neither of these; nor tending either to any good of THE PUBLIC or PRIVATE; but contrariwise: and which may therefore be justly styled *unnatural affections*.

So that according as these affections stand, a creature must be virtuous or vicious, good or ill.

The latter sort of these affections, it is evident, are wholly vicious. The two former may be vicious or virtuous, according to their degree.

211　It may seem strange, perhaps, to speak of natural affections as too strong, or of self-affections as too weak. But to clear this difficulty, we must call to mind what has been already explained, 'that natural affection may, in particular cases, be excessive, and in an unnatural degree:' as when pity is so overcoming as to destroy its own end, and prevent the succour and relief required; or as when love to the offspring proves such a fondness as destroys the parent, and consequently the offspring itself. And notwithstanding it may seem harsh to call that unnatural and vicious, which is only an extreme of some natural and kind affection; yet it is most certain, that wherever any single good affection of this sort is over-great, it must be injurious to the rest, and detract in some measure from their force and natural operation. For a creature possessed with such an immoderate degree of passion, must of necessity allow too much to that one, and too little to others of the same character, and equally natural and useful as to their end. And this must necessarily be the occasion of partiality and injustice, whilst only one duty or natural part is earnestly followed, and other parts or duties neglected, which should accompany it, and perhaps take place and be preferred.

      ★   ★   ★   ★

Now as in particular cases, public affection, on the one hand, may 212 be too high; so private affection may, on the other hand, be too weak. For if a creature be self-neglectful, and insensible of danger; or if he want such a degree of passion in any kind, as is useful to preserve, sustain, or defend himself; this must certainly be esteemed vicious, in regard of the design and end of Nature. She herself discovers this in her known method and stated rule of operation. It is certain, that her provisionary care and concern for the whole animal, must at least be equal to her concern for a single part or member. Now to the several parts she has given, we see, proper affections, suitable to their interest and security; so that even without our consciousness, they act in their own defence, and for their own benefit and preservation. Thus an eye, in its natural state, fails not to shut together, of its own accord, unknowingly to us, by a peculiar caution and timidity; which if it wanted, however we might intend the preservation of our eye, we should not in effect be able to preserve it, by any observation or forecast of our own. To be wanting therefore in those principal affections, which respect the good of the whole constitution, must be a vice and imperfection, as great surely in the principal part (the soul or temper) as it is in any of those inferior and subordinate parts to want the self-preserving affections which are proper to them.

And thus the affections towards private good become necessary and essential to goodness. For though no creature can be called good, or virtuous, merely for possessing these affections; yet since it is impossible that the public good, or good of the system, can be preserved without them; it follows that a creature really wanting in them, is in reality wanting in some degree to goodness and natural rectitude; and may thus be esteemed vicious and defective.

★   ★   ★   ★

213   But having shown what is meant by a passion's being in too high, or in too low a degree; and that, 'to have any natural affection too high, or any self-affection too low,' though it be often approved as virtue, is yet, strictly speaking, a vice and imperfection: we come now to the plainer and more essential part of VICE, and which alone deserves to be considered as such: that is to say,

1. 'When either the public affections are weak or deficient.'

2. 'Or the private and self-affections too strong.'

3. 'Or that such affections arise as are neither of these, nor in any degree tending to the support either of the public or private system.'

Otherwise than thus, it is impossible any creature can be such as we call ILL or VICIOUS. So that if once we prove that it is really not the creature's interest to be thus viciously affected, but contrariwise, we shall then have proved, 'that it is his interest to be wholly GOOD and VIRTUOUS:' since in a wholesome and sound state of his affections, such as we have described, he cannot possibly be other than sound, good, and virtuous, in his action and behaviour.

214   Our business, therefore, will be, to prove;

I. 'That to have the NATURAL, KINDLY, or GENEROUS AFFECTIONS strong and powerful towards the good of the public, is to have the chief means and power of self-enjoyment.' And 'that to want them, is certain misery and ill.'

II. 'That to have the PRIVATE or SELF-AFFECTIONS too strong, or beyond their degree of subordinacy to the kindly and natural, is also miserable.'

III. And, 'that to have the UNNATURAL AFFECTIONS (viz. such as are neither founded on the interest of the kind, or public; nor of the private person, or creature himself) is to be miserable in the highest degree.'

BOOK II PART II

SECT. I

To begin therefore with this proof, 'THAT TO HAVE THE NATURAL **215** AFFECTIONS (such as are founded in love, complacency, good-will, and in a sympathy with the kind or species) IS TO HAVE THE CHIEF MEANS AND POWER OF SELF-ENJOYMENT: and THAT TO WANT THEM IS CERTAIN MISERY AND ILL.'

We may inquire, first, what those are, which we call pleasures or satisfactions; from whence happiness is generally computed. They are (according to the common distinction) either satisfactions and pleasures of the body, or of the mind.

That the latter of these satisfactions are the greatest, is allowed by most people, and may be proved by this: that whenever the mind, having conceived a high opinion of the worth of any action or behaviour, has received the strongest impression of this sort, and is wrought up to the highest pitch or degree of passion towards the subject; at such time it sets itself above all bodily pain as well as pleasure, and can be no way diverted from its purpose by flattery or terror of any kind. Thus we see Indians, barbarians, malefactors, and even the most execrable villains, for the sake of a particular gang or society, or through some cherished notion or principle of honour or gallantry, revenge, or gratitude, embrace any manner of hardship, and defy torments and death. Whereas, on the other hand, a person being placed in all the happy circumstances of outward enjoyment, surrounded with every thing which can allure or charm the sense, and being then actually in the very moment of such a pleasing indulgence; yet no sooner is there any thing amiss *within*, no sooner has he conceived any *internal* ail or disorder, anything *inwardly* vexatious or distempered, than instantly his enjoyment ceases, the pleasure of sense is at an end; and every means of that sort becomes ineffectual, and is rejected as uneasy and subject to give distaste.

The pleasures of the mind being allowed, therefore, superior to **216** those of the body, it follows, 'that whatever can create in any intelligent being a constant flowing series or train of mental enjoyments, or pleasures of the mind, is more considerable to his happiness, than that which can create to him a like constant course or train of sensual enjoyments, or pleasures of the body.'

Now the mental enjoyments are either actually the very natural affections themselves in their immediate operation: or they wholly in a manner proceed from them, and are no other than their effects.

If so; it follows, that the natural affections duly established in a rational creature, being the only means which can procure him a constant series or succession of the mental enjoyments, they are the only means which can procure him a certain and solid *happiness*.

217   Now, in the first place, to explain, 'how much the natural affections are in themselves the highest pleasures and enjoyments:' there should methinks be little need of proving this to any one of human kind, who has ever known the condition of the mind under a lively affection of love, gratitude, bounty, generosity, pity, succour, or whatever else is of a social or friendly sort. He who has ever so little knowledge of human nature, is sensible what pleasure the mind perceives when it is touched in this generous way. The difference we find between solitude and company, between a common company and that of friends; the reference of almost all our pleasures to mutual converse, and the dependence they have on society either present or imagined; all these are sufficient proofs in our behalf.

How much the social pleasures are superior to any other, may be known by visible tokens and effects. The very outward features, the marks and signs which attend this sort of joy, are expressive of a more intense, clear, and undisturbed pleasure, than those which attend the satisfaction of thirst, hunger, and other ardent appetites. But more particularly still may this superiority be known, from the actual prevalence and ascendency of this sort of affection over all besides. Wherever it presents itself with any advantage, it silences and appeases every other motion of pleasure. No joy, merely of sense, can be a match for it. Whoever is judge of both the pleasures, will ever give the preference to the former. But to be able to judge of both, it is necessary to have a sense of each. The honest man indeed can judge of sensual pleasure, and knows its utmost force. For neither is his taste, or sense, the duller; but, on the contrary, the more intense and clear, on the account of his temperance, and a moderate use of appetite. But the immoral and profligate man can by no means be allowed a good judge of social pleasure, to which he is so mere a stranger by his nature.

Nor is it any objection here: that in many natures the good affection, though really present, is found to be of insufficient force. For where it is not *in its natural degree*, it is the same indeed as if it *were not*, or had *never been*. The less there is of this good affection in any untoward creature, the greater the wonder is, that it should at any time prevail; as in the very worst of creatures it sometimes will. And if it prevails but for once, in any single instance; it shows evidently, that if the affection were thoroughly experienced or known, it would prevail in all.

Thus the CHARM of kind affection is superior to all other pleasure: since it has the power of drawing from every other appetite or inclination. And thus in the case of love to the offspring, and a thousand other instances, the charm is found to operate so strongly on the temper, as, in the midst of other temptations, to render it susceptible of this passion alone; which remains as the master-pleasure and conqueror of the rest.

★   ★   ★   ★

We may observe that in the passion of love between the sexes, **218** where, together with the affection of a vulgar sort, there is a mixture of the kind and friendly, the sense or feeling of this latter is in reality superior to the former; since often through this affection, and for the sake of the person beloved, the greatest hardships in the world have been submitted to, and even death itself voluntarily embraced, without any expected compensation. For where should the ground of such an expectation lie? Not here, in this world, surely; for death puts an end to all. Nor yet hereafter, in any other; for who has ever thought of providing a heaven or future recompense for the suffering virtue of lovers?

We may observe, withal, in favour of the natural affections, that it is not only when joy and sprightliness are mixed with them that they carry a real enjoyment above that of the sensual kind. The very disturbances which belong to natural affection, though they may be thought wholly contrary to pleasure, yield still a contentment and satisfaction greater than the pleasures of indulged sense. And where a series or continued succession of the tender and kind affections can be carried on, even through fears, horrors, sorrows, griefs; the emotion of the soul is still agreeable. We continue pleased even with this melancholy aspect or sense of virtue. Her beauty supports itself under a cloud, and in the midst of surrounding calamities. For thus, when by mere illusion, as in a tragedy, the passions of this kind are skilfully excited in us; we prefer the entertainment to any other of equal duration. We find by ourselves, that the moving our passions in this mournful way, the engaging them in behalf of merit and worth, and the exerting whatever we have of social affection, and human sympathy, is of the highest delight, and affords a greater enjoyment in the way of thought and sentiment, than any thing besides can do in a way of sense and common appetite. And after this manner it appears, 'how much the mental enjoyments are actually the very natural affections themselves.'

219   Now, in the next place, to explain, 'how they proceed from them, as their natural effects:' we may consider first, that the EFFECTS of love or kind affection, in a way of mental pleasure, are, 'an enjoyment of good by communication. A receiving it, as it were, by reflection, or by way of participation in the good of others.' And 'a pleasing consciousness of the actual love, merited esteem or approbation of others.'

How considerable a part of happiness arises from the former of these effects, will be easily apprehended by one who is not exceedingly ill-natured. It will be considered how many the pleasures are, of sharing contentment and delight with others; of receiving it in fellowship and company; and gathering it, in a manner, from the pleased and happy states of those around us, from accounts and relations of such happiness, from the very countenances, gestures, voices and sounds, even of creatures foreign to our kind, whose signs of joy and contentment we can any way discern. So insinuating are these pleasures of sympathy, and so widely diffused through our whole lives, that there is hardly such a thing as satisfaction or contentment, of which they make not an essential part.

As for that other effect of social love, viz. the consciousness of merited kindness or esteem; it is not difficult to perceive how much this avails in mental pleasure, and constitutes the chief enjoyment and happiness of those who are, in the narrowest sense, voluptuous. How natural is it for the most selfish among us, to be continually drawing some sort of satisfaction from a character, and pleasing ourselves in the fancy of deserved admiration and esteem? For though it be mere fancy, we endeavour still to believe it truth, and flatter ourselves, all we can, with the thought of *merit* of some kind, and the persuasion of our deserving well from some few at least, with whom we happen to have a more intimate and familiar commerce.

What tyrant is there, what robber, or open violator of the laws of society, who has not a companion, or some particular set, either of his own kindred, or such as he calls friends; with whom he gladly shares his good; in whose welfare he delights; and whose joy and satisfaction he makes his own? What person in the world is there, who receives not some impressions from the flattery or kindness of such as are familiar with him? It is to this soothing hope and expectation of friendship, that almost all our actions have some reference. It is this which goes through our whole lives, and mixes itself even with most of our vices. Of this, *vanity*, *ambition*, and *luxury*, have a share; and many other disorders of our life partake. Even the unchastest *love* borrows largely from this source. So that were pleasure to be computed in the same way as other things commonly are; it might properly be said, that out of these two branches (viz. community or participation in the pleasures of others, and belief of meriting well from others) would arise more than nine tenths of whatever is enjoyed in life. And thus in the main sum of happiness, there is scarce a single article, but what derives itself from social love, and depends immediately on the natural and kind affections.

Now such as CAUSES are, such must be their EFFECTS. And therefore as *natural affection* or *social love* is perfect, or imperfect; so must be *the content* and *happiness* depending on it.

⋆   ⋆   ⋆   ⋆

There are TWO things, which to a rational creature must be **220** horridly offensive and grievous; viz. 'to have the reflection in his mind of any *unjust* action or behaviour, which he knows to be naturally *odious* and *ill-deserving*;' 'or, of any foolish action or behaviour, which he knows to be prejudicial to his own *interest* or *happiness.*'

The former of these is alone properly called CONSCIENCE; whether in a moral, or religious sense. For to have awe and terror of the Deity, does not, of itself, imply conscience. No one is esteemed the more conscientious for the fear of evil spirits, conjurations, enchantments, or whatever may proceed from any unjust, capricious, or devilish nature. Now to fear GOD any otherwise than as in consequence of some justly blameable and imputable act, is to fear a devilish nature; not a divine one. Nor does the fear of hell, or a thousand terrors of the DEITY imply conscience; unless where there is an apprehension of what is wrong, odious, morally deformed, and ill-deserving. And where this is the case, there conscience must have effect, and punishment of necessity be apprehended; even though it be not expressly threatened.

And thus *religious conscience* supposes *moral* or *natural conscience*. And though the former be understood to carry with it the fear of divine punishment; it has its force however from the apprehended moral deformity and odiousness of any act, with respect purely to the divine presence, and the natural veneration due to such a supposed being. For in such a presence, the shame of villainy or vice must have its force, independently on that further apprehension of the magisterial capacity of such a being, and his dispensation of particular rewards or punishments in a future state.

★　　★　　★　　★

CONCLUSION

221 Thus have we endeavoured to prove what was proposed in the beginning. And since in the common and known sense of vice and illness, no-one can be vicious or ill, except either,

1. By the deficiency or weakness of natural affections;

Or, 2. by the violence of the selfish;

Or, 3. by such as are plainly unnatural:

It must follow, that if each of these are pernicious and destructive to the creature, insomuch that his completest state of misery is made from hence; TO BE WICKED OR VICIOUS, IS TO BE MISERABLE AND UNHAPPY.

And since every vicious action must in proportion, more or less, help towards this mischief, and self-ill; it must follow, that EVERY VICIOUS ACTION MUST BE SELF-INJURIOUS AND ILL.

On the other side; the happiness and good of VIRTUE has been proved from the contrary effect of other affections, such as are according to nature, and the economy of the species or kind. We have cast up all those particulars, from whence (as by way of addition and subtraction) the main sum or general account of happiness, is either augmented or diminished. And if there be no article exceptionable in this scheme of moral arithmetic; the subject treated may be said to have an evidence as great as that which is found in numbers, or mathematics. For let us carry scepticism ever so far; let us doubt, if we can, of every thing about us; we cannot doubt of what passes *within ourselves*. Our passions and affections are known to us. *They* are certain, whatever the *objects* may be, on which they are employed. Nor is it of any concern to our argument, how these exterior objects stand; whether they are realities, or mere illusions; whether we wake or dream. For ill dreams will be equally disturbing: and a good dream (if life be nothing else) will be easily and happily passed. In this dream of life, therefore, our demonstrations have the same force; our balance and economy hold good, and our obligation to VIRTUE is in every respect the same.

Upon the whole: there is not, I presume, the least degree of **222** certainty wanting, in what has been said concerning the preferableness of the mental pleasures to the sensual; and even of the sensual, accompanied with good affection, and under a temperate and right use, to those which are no ways restrained, nor supported by any thing social or affectionate.

Nor is there less evidence in what has been said, of the united structure and fabric of the mind, and of those passions which constitute the temper, or soul; and on which its happiness or misery so immediately depend. It has been shown, that in this constitution, the impairing of any one part must instantly tend to the disorder and ruin of other parts, and of the whole itself; through the necessary connection and balance of the affections: that those very passions through which men are vicious, are of themselves a torment and disease; and that whatsoever is done which is knowingly ill, must be of ill consciousness; and in proportion, as the act is ill, must impair and corrupt social enjoyment, and destroy both the capacity of kind affection, and the consciousness of meriting any such. So that neither can we participate thus in joy or happiness with others, or receive satisfaction from the mutual kindness or imagined love of others: on which, however, the greatest of all our pleasures are founded.

If this be the case of moral delinquency; and if the state which is consequent to this defection from nature, be of all other the most horrid, oppressive, and miserable; it will appear, 'that to yield or consent to any thing ill or immoral, is a breach of interest, and leads to the greatest ills:' and, 'that, on the other side, every thing which is an improvement of virtue, or an establishment of right affection and integrity, is an advancement of interest, and leads to the greatest and most solid happiness and enjoyment.'

223 Thus the wisdom of what rules, and is FIRST and CHIEF *in nature*, has made it to be according to the *private interest* and *good* of every one, to work towards the *general good*, which if a creature ceases to promote, he is actually so far wanting to himself, and ceases to promote his own happiness and welfare. He is, on this account, directly his own enemy: nor can he any otherwise be good or useful to himself, than as he continues good to society, and to that *whole* of which he is himself a *part*. So that VIRTUE, which of all excellencies and beauties is the chief, and most amiable; that which is the prop and ornament of human affairs; which upholds communities, maintains union, friendship, and correspondence amongst men; that by which countries, as well as private families, flourish and are happy; and for want of which, every thing comely, conspicuous, great and worthy, must perish, and go to ruin; that single quality, thus beneficial to all society, and to mankind in general, is found equally a happiness and good to each creature in particular; and is that by which alone man can be happy, and without which he must be miserable.

And, thus, VIRTUE is *the good*, and VICE *the ill* of every one.

SAMUEL CLARKE

1675–1729

*A DISCOURSE concerning the Unchangeable Obliga-
tions of NATURAL RELIGION, and the Truth
and Certainty of the CHRISTIAN REVELATION*

[The Boyle Lectures, 1705 (following upon *A Demonstration of the Being and Attributes of God*, the Boyle
Lectures, 1704). First printed, 1706. Reprinted here
from the seventh edition, corrected, 1728, with modified spelling, reduction of initial capital letters and
italics, and omission of nearly all footnotes. The footnotes are mostly quotations from classical authors,
Hobbes, and Cumberland]

SAMUEL CLARKE

A Discourse of Natural Religion

Having in a former discourse endeavoured to lay firmly the first 224
foundations of religion, in the certainty of the existence and of the
attributes of God. . . .

    ★   ★   ★   ★

It remains now, in order to complete my design of proving and
establishing the truth and excellency of the whole superstructure of
our most holy religion; that I proceed upon this foundation of
the certainty of the *Being and Attributes of God*, to demonstrate in the
next place the *unalterable Obligations of Natural Religion*, and the
certainty of *Divine Revelation*; in opposition to the vain arguings of
certain vicious and profane men, who, merely upon account of their
incredulity, would be thought to be strict adherers to reason, and
sincere and diligent inquirers into truth; when indeed on the contrary there is but too much cause to fear, that they are not at all
sincerely and really desirous to be satisfied in the true state of things,
but only seek, under the pretence and cover of infidelity, to excuse
their vices and debaucheries; which they are so strongly enslaved to,
that they cannot prevail with themselves upon any account to forsake them: and yet a rational submitting to such truths, as just
evidence and unanswerable reason would induce them to believe,
must necessarily make them uneasy under those vices, and self-
condemned in the practice of them. It remains therefore (I say) in
order to finish the design I proposed to myself, of establishing the
truth and excellency of our holy religion, in opposition to all such
vain pretenders to reason as these; that I proceed at this time, by a
continuation of the same method of arguing, by which I before
demonstrated the being and attributes of God, to prove distinctly
the following propositions.

    ★   ★   ★   ★

225   I. The same necessary and eternal *different relations*, that different things bear one to another; and the same consequent *fitness* or *unfitness* of the application of different things or different relations one to another; with regard to which, the will of God always and necessarily *does* determine itself, to choose to act only what is agreeable to justice, equity, goodness and truth, in order to the welfare of the whole universe; *ought* likewise constantly to determine the wills of all subordinate rational beings, to govern all their actions by the same rules, for the good of the public, in their respective stations. That is; these eternal and necessary differences of things make it *fit and reasonable* for creatures so to act; they cause it to be their *duty*, or lay an *obligation* upon them, so to do; even separate from the consideration of these rules being the *positive will* or *command of God*; and also antecedent to any respect or regard, expectation or apprehension, of any *particular private and personal advantage or disadvantage, reward or punishment*, either present or future; annexed either by natural consequence, or by positive appointment, to the practising or neglecting of those rules.

The several parts of this proposition, may be proved distinctly, in the following manner.

226   1. That there are differences of things; and different relations, respects or proportions, of some things towards others; is as evident and undeniable, as that one magnitude or number, is greater, equal to, or smaller than another. That from these different relations of different things, there necessarily arises an agreement or disagreement of some things with others, or a fitness or unfitness of the application of different things or different relations one to another; is likewise as plain, as that there is any such thing as proportion or disproportion in geometry and arithmetic, or uniformity or difformity in comparing together the respective figures of bodies. Further, that there is a fitness or suitableness of certain circumstances to certain persons, and an unsuitableness of others; founded in the nature of things and the qualifications of persons, antecedent to all positive appointment whatsoever; also that from the different relations of different persons one to another, there necessarily arises a fitness or unfitness of certain manners of behaviour of some persons towards others: is as manifest, as that the properties which flow from the essences of different mathematical figures, have different congruities or incongruities between themselves; or that, in mechanics, certain

weights or powers have very different forces, and different effects
one upon another, according to their different distances, or different
positions and situations in respect of each other. For instance: that
God is infinitely superior to men; is as clear, as that infinity is larger
than a point, or eternity longer than a moment. And it is as certainly
fit, that men should honour and worship, obey and imitate God,
rather than on the contrary in all their actions endeavour to dishonour and disobey him; as it is certainly true, that they have an
entire dependence on him, and he on the contrary can in no respect
receive any advantage from them; and not only so, but also that his
will is as certainly and unalterably just and equitable in giving his
commands, as his power is irresistible in requiring submission to it.
Again; it is a thing absolutely and necessarily fitter in itself, that the
supreme author and creator of the universe, should govern, order,
and direct all things to certain constant and regular ends; than that
every thing should be permitted to go on at adventures, and produce
uncertain effects merely by chance and in the utmost confusion,
without any determinate view or design at all. It is a thing manifestly fitter in itself, that the all-powerful governor of the world,
should do always what is best in the whole, and what tends most
to the universal good of the whole creation; than that he should
make the whole continually miserable; or that, to satisfy the unreasonable desires of any particular depraved natures, he should at
any time suffer the order of the whole to be altered and perverted.
Lastly, it is a thing evidently and infinitely more fit, that any one
particular innocent and good being, should by the supreme ruler and
disposer of all things, be placed and preserved in an easy and happy
estate; than that, without any fault or demerit of its own, it should
be made extremely, remedilessly, and endlessly miserable. In like
manner; in men's dealing and conversing one with another; it is
undeniably more fit, absolutely and in the nature of the thing itself,
that all men should endeavour to promote the universal good and
welfare of all; than that all men should be continually contriving the
ruin and destruction of all. It is evidently more fit, even before all
positive bargains and compacts, that men should deal one with
another according to the known rules of justice and equity; than that
every man for his own present advantage, should without scruple
disappoint the most reasonable and equitable expectations of his
neighbours, and cheat and defraud, or spoil by violence, all others

without restraint. Lastly, it is without dispute more fit and reasonable in itself, that I should preserve the life of an innocent man, that happens at any time to be in my power; or deliver him from any imminent danger, though I have never made any promise so to do; than that I should suffer him to perish, or take away his life, without any reason or provocation at all.

227 These things are so notoriously plain and self-evident, that nothing but the extremest stupidity of mind, corruption of manners, or perverseness of spirit, can possibly make any man entertain the least doubt concerning them. For a man endued with reason, to deny the truth of these things; is the very same thing, as if a man that has the use of his sight, should at the same time that he beholds the sun, deny that there is any such thing as light in the world; or as if a man that understands geometry or arithmetic, should deny the most obvious and known proportions of lines or numbers, and perversely contend that the whole is not equal to all its parts, or that a square is not double to a triangle of equal base and height. Any man of ordinary capacity, and unbiassed judgement, plainness and simplicity; who had never read, and had never been told, that there were men and philosophers, who had in earnest asserted and attempted to prove, that there is no natural and unalterable difference between good and evil; would at the first hearing be as hardly persuaded to believe, that it could ever really enter into the heart of any intelligent man, to deny all natural difference between right and wrong; as he would be to believe, that ever there could be any geometer who would seriously and in good earnest lay it down as a first principle, that a crooked line is as straight as a right one. So that indeed it might justly seem altogether a needless undertaking, to attempt to prove and establish the eternal difference of good and evil; had there not appeared certain men, as Mr Hobbes and some few others, who have presumed, contrary to the plainest and most obvious reason of mankind, to assert, and not without some subtlety endeavoured to prove, that there is no such real difference originally, necessarily, and absolutely in the nature of things; but that all obligation of *duty to God*, arises merely from his absolute *irresistible power*; and all *duty towards men*, merely from *positive compact*:[1] and have founded their whole scheme of politics upon that opinion. Wherein as they have contradicted the judgement of all the wisest and soberest part of mankind, so they have not

[1 See Hobbes, §§ 89, 101.]

been able to avoid contradicting themselves also. For (not to mention now, that they have no way to show how compacts themselves come to be obligatory, but by inconsistently owning an eternal original fitness in the thing itself, which I shall have occasion to observe hereafter: besides this, I say,) if there be naturally and absolutely in things themselves, no difference between good and evil, just and unjust; then in the state of nature, before any compact be made, it is equally as good, just and reasonable, for one man to destroy the life of another, not only when it is necessary for his own preservation, but also arbitrarily and without any provocation at all, or any appearance of advantage to himself; as to preserve or save another man's life, when he may do it without any hazard of his own. The consequence of which, is; that not only the first and most obvious way for every particular man to secure himself effectually, would be (as Mr Hobbes teaches) to endeavour to prevent and cut off all others; but also that men might destroy one another upon every foolish and peevish or arbitrary humour, even when they did not think any such thing necessary for their own preservation. And the effect of this practice must needs be, that it would terminate in the destruction of all mankind. Which being undeniably a great and insufferable evil; Mr Hobbes himself confesses it reasonable, that, to prevent this evil, men should enter into certain compacts to preserve one another. Now if the destruction of mankind by each other's hands, be such an evil, that, to prevent it, it was fit and reasonable that men should enter into compacts to preserve each other; then, before any such compacts, it was manifestly a thing unfit and unreasonable in itself, that mankind should all destroy one another. And if so, then for the same reason it was also unfit and unreasonable, antecedent to all compacts, that any one man should destroy another arbitrarily and without any provocation, or at any time when it was not absolutely and immediately necessary for the preservation of himself. Which is directly contradictory to Mr Hobbes's first supposition, of there being no natural and absolute difference between good and evil, just and unjust, antecedent to positive compact.[1] And in like manner all others, who upon any **228** pretence whatsoever, teach that good and evil depend originally on the constitution of positive laws, whether divine or human; must unavoidably run into the same absurdity. For if there be no such

[1 See Hobbes, §§ 53, 67.]

thing as good and evil in the nature of things, antecedent to all laws; then neither can any one law be better than another; nor any one thing whatever, be more justly established, and enforced by laws, than the contrary; nor can any reason be given, why any laws should ever be made at all: but all laws equally, will be either arbitrary and tyrannical, or frivolous and needless; because the contrary might with equal reason have been established, if, before the making of the laws, all things had been alike indifferent in their own nature. There is no possible way to avoid this absurdity, but by saying, that out of things in their own nature absolutely indifferent, those are chosen by wise governors to be made obligatory by law, the practice of which they judge will tend to the public benefit of the community. But this is an express contradiction in the very terms. For if the practice of certain things tends to the public benefit of the world, and the contrary would tend to the public disadvantage; then those things are not in their own nature indifferent, but were good and reasonable to be practised before any law was made, and can only for that very reason be wisely enforced by the authority of laws. Only here it is to be observed, that by the public benefit must not be understood the interest of any one particular nation, to the plain injury or prejudice of the rest of mankind; any more than the interest of one city or family, in opposition to their neighbours of the same country: but those things only are truly good in their own nature, which either tend to the universal benefit and welfare of *all men*, or at least are not destructive of it. The true state therefore of this case, is plainly this. Some things are in their own nature good and reasonable and fit to be done; such as keeping faith, and performing equitable compacts, and the like; and these receive not their obligatory power, from any law or authority; but are only declared, confirmed and enforced by penalties, upon such as would not perhaps be governed by right reason only. Other things are in their own nature absolutely evil; such as breaking faith, refusing to perform equitable compacts, cruelly destroying those who have neither directly nor indirectly given any occasion for any such treatment, and the like; and these cannot by any law or authority whatsoever, be made fit and reasonable, or excusable to be practised. Lastly, other things are in their own nature indifferent; that is, (not absolutely and strictly so; as such trivial actions, which have no way any tendency at all either to the public welfare or damage; for concerning such things, it would be childish and trifling to suppose any laws to be made at all; but they are) such things, whose tendency to the public benefit or disadvantage, is either so small or so remote, or so obscure and involved, that the generality of people are not able of themselves to discern on which side they ought to act: and these things are made obligatory by the authority of laws; though perhaps every one cannot distinctly perceive the reason and fitness of their being enjoined: of which sort are many particular penal laws, in several countries and nations. But to proceed.

The principal thing that can, with any colour of reason, seem to **229** countenance the opinion of those who deny the natural and eternal difference of good and evil; (for Mr Hobbes's false reasonings I shall hereafter consider by themselves;) is the difficulty there may sometimes be, to define exactly the bounds of right and wrong: the variety of opinions, that have obtained even among understanding and learned men concerning certain questions of just and unjust, especially in political matters: and the many contrary laws that have been made in divers ages and in different countries, concerning these matters. But as, in painting, two very different colours, by diluting each other very slowly and gradually, may from the highest intenseness in either extreme, terminate in the midst insensibly, and so run one into the other, that it shall not be possible even for a skilful eye to determine exactly where the one ends, and the other begins; and yet the colours may really differ as much as can be, not in degree only but entirely in kind, as red and blue, or white and black: so, though it may perhaps be very difficult in some nice and perplexed cases (which yet are very far from occurring frequently,) to define exactly the bounds of right and wrong, just and unjust; and there may be some latitude in the judgement of different men, and the laws of divers nations; yet right and wrong are nevertheless in themselves totally and essentially different; even altogether as much, as white and black, light and darkness. The Spartan law perhaps, which permitted their youth to steal; may, as absurd as it was, bear much dispute whether it was absolutely unjust or no; because every man having an absolute right in his own goods, it may seem that the members of any society may agree to transfer or alter their own properties upon what conditions they shall think fit. But if it could be supposed that a law had been made at Sparta; or at Rome, or in India, or in any other part of the world; whereby it had been commanded or allowed, that every man might rob by violence, and murder whomsoever he met with; or that no faith should be kept with any man, nor any equitable compacts performed; no man, with any tolerable use of his reason, whatever diversity of judgement might be among them in other matters, would have thought that such a law could have authorized or excused, much less have justified such actions, and have made them become good: because it is plainly not in men's power to make falsehood be truth, though they may alter the property of their goods as they please. Now if in flagrant cases, the natural and essential difference between good and evil, right and wrong, cannot but be confessed to be plainly and undeniably evident; the difference between them must be also essential and unalterable in all even the smallest and nicest and most intricate cases, though it be not so easy to be discerned and accurately distinguished. For if from the difficulty of determining exactly the bounds of right and wrong in many perplexed cases, it could truly be concluded that just and unjust were not essentially different by nature, but only by positive constitution and custom; it would follow equally, that they were not really, essentially, and unalterably different, even in the most flagrant cases that can be supposed. Which is an assertion so very absurd, that Mr Hobbes himself could hardly vent it without blushing, and discovering plainly, by his shifting expressions, his secret self-condemnation. There *are* therefore certain necessary and eternal differences of things; and certain consequent fitnesses or unfitnesses of the application of different things or different relations one to another; not depending on any positive constitutions, but founded unchangeably in the nature and reason of things, and unavoidably arising from the differences of the things themselves. Which is the first branch of the general proposition I proposed to prove.

230   2. Now what these eternal and unalterable relations, respects, or proportions of things, with their consequent agreements or disagreements, fitnesses or unfitnesses, absolutely and necessarily *are* in themselves; *that* also they *appear to be*, to the *understandings* of all intelligent beings; except those only, who understand things to be what they are not, that is, whose understandings are either very imperfect, or very much depraved. And by this understanding or knowledge of the natural and necessary relations, fitnesses, and proportions of things, the *wills* likewise of all intelligent beings are constantly directed, and must needs be determined to act accordingly; excepting those only, who will things to be what they are not and cannot be; that is, whose wills are corrupted by particular interest or affection, or swayed by some unreasonable and prevailing passion. Wherefore since the *natural* attributes of God, his infinite knowledge, wisdom and power, set him infinitely above all possibility of being deceived by any error, or of being influenced by any wrong affection; it is manifest his divine will cannot but always and necessarily determine itself to choose to do what in the whole is absolutely best and fittest to be done; that is, to act constantly according to the eternal rules of infinite goodness, justice and truth. As I have endeavoured to show distinctly in my former discourse, in deducing severally the *moral* attributes of God.

3. And now, that the same reason of things, with regard to which **231** the will of God always and necessarily *does* determine itself to act in constant conformity to the eternal rules of justice, equity, goodness and truth; *ought* also constantly to determine the wills of all subordinate rational beings, to govern all *their* actions by the same rules; is very evident. For, as it is absolutely impossible in nature, that God should be deceived by any error, or influenced by any wrong affection: so it is very unreasonable and blame-worthy in practice, that any intelligent creatures, whom God has made so far like unto himself, as to endue them with those excellent faculties of reason and will, whereby they are enabled to distinguish good from evil, and to choose the one and refuse the other; should either negligently suffer themselves to be imposed upon and deceived in matters of good and evil, right and wrong; or wilfully and perversely allow themselves to be over-ruled by absurd passions, and corrupt or partial affections, to act contrary to what they know is fit to be done. Which two things, viz. negligent misunderstanding and wilful passions or lusts, are, as I said, the only causes which can make a reasonable creature act contrary to reason, that is, contrary to the eternal rules of justice, equity, righteousness and truth. For, was it not for these inexcusable corruptions and depravations; it is impossible but the same proportions and fitnesses of things, which have so much weight and so much excellency and beauty in them, that the all-powerful creator and governor of the universe, (who has the absolute and uncontrollable dominion of all things in his own hands, and is accountable to none for what he does, yet) thinks it no

diminution of his power to make this reason of things the unalterable rule and law of his own actions in the government of the world, and does nothing by mere will and arbitrariness; it is impossible (I say,) if it was not for inexcusable corruption and depravation, but the same eternal reason of things must much more have weight enough to determine constantly the wills and actions of all sub-
232 ordinate, finite, dependent and accountable beings. For originally and in reality, it is as natural and (morally speaking) necessary, that the will should be determined in every action by the reason of the thing, and the right of the case; as it is natural and (absolutely speaking) necessary, that the understanding should submit to a demonstrated truth. And it is as absurd and blame-worthy, to mistake negligently plain right and wrong, that is, to understand the proportions of things in morality to be what they are not; or wilfully to act contrary to known justice and equity, that is, to will things to be what they are not and cannot be; as it would be absurd and ridiculous for a man in arithmetical matters, ignorantly to believe that twice two is not equal to four; or wilfully and obstinately to contend, against his own clear knowledge, that the whole is not equal to all its parts. The only difference is, that *assent* to a plain speculative truth, is not in a man's power to withhold; but to *act* according to the plain right and reason of things, this he may, by the natural liberty of his will, forbear. But the one he *ought* to do; and it is as much his plain and indispensable *duty*; as the other he *cannot but do*, and it is the *necessity* of his nature to do it. He that wilfully refuses to honour and obey God, from whom he received his being, and to whom he continually owes his preservation; is really guilty of an equal absurdity and inconsistency in practice; as he that in speculation denies the effect to owe any thing to its cause, or the whole to be bigger than its part. He that refuses to deal with all men equitably, and with every man as he desires they should deal with him: is guilty of the very same unreasonableness and contradiction in one case; as he that in another case should affirm one number or quantity to be equal to another, and yet that other at the same time not to be equal to the first. Lastly, he that acknowledges himself obliged to the practice of certain *duties* both towards God and towards men, and yet takes no care either to preserve his own being, or at least not to preserve himself in such a state and temper of mind and body, as may best enable him to perform those duties; is altogether as inexcusable and

ridiculous, as he that in any other matter should *affirm* one thing at the same time that he *denies* another, without which the former could not possibly be *true*; or *undertake* one thing, at the same time that he obstinately *omits* another, without which the former is by no means *practicable*. Wherefore all rational creatures, whose wills are not constantly and regularly determined, and their actions governed, by right reason and the necessary differences of good and evil, according to the eternal and invariable rules of justice, equity, goodness and truth; but suffer themselves to be swayed by unaccountable arbitrary humours, and rash passions, by lusts, vanity and pride; by private interest, or present sensual pleasures: these, setting up their own un-reasonable self-will in opposition to the nature and reason of things, endeavour (as much as in them lies) to make things be what they are not, and cannot be. Which is the highest presumption and greatest insolence, as well as the greatest absurdity, imaginable. It is acting contrary to that understanding, reason and judgement, which God has implanted in their natures on purpose to enable them to discern the difference between good and evil. It is attempting to destroy that order, by which the universe subsists. It is offering the highest affront imaginable to the creator of all things, who made things to be what they are, and governs every thing himself according to the laws of their several natures. In a word; all wilful wickedness and perversion of right, is the very same insolence and absurdity in *moral matters*; as it would be in *natural things*, for a man to pretend to alter the certain proportions of numbers, to take away the demonstrable relations and properties of mathematical figures; to make light darkness, and darkness light; or to call sweet bitter, and bitter sweet.

Further: as it appears thus from the abstract and absolute reason **233** and nature of things, that all rational creatures ought, that is, are obliged to take care that their wills and actions be constantly deter-mined and governed by the eternal rule of right and equity: so the certainty and universality of that obligation is plainly confirmed, and the force of it particularly discovered and applied to every man, by this; that in like manner as no one, who is instructed in mathematics, can forbear giving his assent to every geometrical demonstration, of which he understands the terms, either by his own study, or by having had them explained to him by others; so no man, who either has patience and opportunities to examine and consider things himself, or has the means of being taught and instructed in any tolerable manner by others, concerning the necessary relations and dependencies of things; can avoid giving his assent to the fitness and reasonableness of his governing all his actions by the law or rule before mentioned, even though his practice, through the prevalence of brutish lusts, be most absurdly contradictory to that assent. That is to say: by the reason of his mind, he cannot but be compelled to own and acknowledge, that there is really such an obligation indispensably incumbent upon him; even at the same time that in the actions of his life he is endeavouring to throw it off and despise it. For the judgement and conscience of a man's own mind, concerning the reasonableness and fitness of the thing, that his actions should be conformed to such or such a rule or law; is the truest and formallest *obligation*; even more properly and strictly so, than any opinion whatsoever of the authority of the giver of a law, or any regard he may have to its sanction by rewards and punishments. For whoever acts contrary to this sense and conscience of his own mind, is necessarily self-condemned; and the greatest and strongest of all obligations is that, which a man cannot break through without condemning himself. The dread of superior power and authority, and the sanction of rewards and punishments; however indeed absolutely necessary to the government of frail and fallible creatures, and truly the most effectual means of keeping them in their duty; is yet really in itself, only a *secondary* and *additional* obligation, or *enforcement* of the first.[1] The original *obligation* of all, (the ambiguous use of which word as a term of art, has caused some perplexity and confusion in this matter,) is the eternal reason of things; that reason, which God himself, who has no superior to direct him, and to whose happiness nothing can be added nor any thing diminished from it, yet constantly obliges himself to govern the world by: and the more excellent and perfect any creatures are, the more cheerfully and steadily are their wills always determined by this supreme obligation, in conformity to the nature, and in imitation of the most perfect will of God. So far therefore as men are conscious of what is right and wrong, so far they *are* under an *obligation* to act accordingly; and consequently that eternal rule of right, which I have been hitherto describing, it is evident *ought* as indispensably to govern men's actions, as it *cannot but* necessarily determine their assent.

234　　Now that the case is truly thus; that the eternal differences of good

[1 Cf. Hobbes, § 100.]

and evil, the unalterable rule of right and equity, do necessarily and unavoidably determine the judgement, and force the assent of all men that use any consideration; is undeniably manifest from the universal experience of mankind. For no man willingly and deliberately transgresses this rule, in any great and considerable instance; but he acts contrary to the judgement and reason of his own mind, and secretly reproaches himself for so doing. And no man observes and obeys it steadily, especially in cases of difficulty and temptation, when it interferes with any present interest, pleasure or passion; but his own mind commends and applauds him for his resolution, in executing what his conscience could not forbear giving its assent to, as just and right. And this is what St Paul means, when he says, (*Rom.* ii; 14, 15.) that when the Gentiles which have not the law, do by nature the things contained in the law, these having not the law, are a law unto themselves; which show the work of the law written in their hearts, their conscience also bearing witness, and their thoughts the mean while *accusing*, or else *excusing* one another.

It was a very wise observation of Plato, which he received from **235** Socrates; that if you take a young man, impartial and unprejudiced, one that never had any learning, nor any experience in the world; and examine him about the *natural relations and proportions* of things, [or the *moral differences* of *good and evil*;] you may, only by asking him questions, without teaching him any thing at all directly, cause him to express in his answers just and adequate notions of *geometrical truths*, [and true and exact determinations concerning *matters of right and wrong*.] From whence *he* thought it was to be concluded, that all knowledge and learning is nothing but memory, or only a recollecting upon every new occasion, what had been before known in a state of pre-existence. And some others both ancient and moderns, have concluded that the *ideas* of all first and simple truths, either natural or moral, are *innate* and originally impressed or stamped upon the mind. In their inference from the observation, the authors of both these opinions seem to be mistaken. But thus much it proves unavoidably; that the differences, relations, and proportions of things both natural and moral, in which all unprejudiced minds thus naturally agree, are certain, unalterable, and real in the things themselves; and do not at all depend on the variable opinions, fancies, or imaginations of men prejudiced by education, laws, customs, or evil practices: and also that the mind of man naturally and unavoidably gives its assent, as to natural and geometrical truth, so also to the moral differences of things, and to the fitness and reasonableness of the obligation of the everlasting law of righteousness, whenever fairly and plainly proposed.

236   Some men indeed, who, by means of a very evil and vicious education, or through a long habit of wickedness and debauchery, have extremely corrupted the principles of their nature, and have long accustomed themselves to bear down their own reason, by the force of prejudice, lust and passion; that they may not be forced to confess themselves self-condemned, will confidently and absolutely contend that they do not really see any natural and necessary difference between what we call right and wrong, just and unjust; that the reason and judgement of their own mind, does not tell them they are under any such indispensable obligations, as we would endeavour to persuade them; and that they are not sensible they ought to be governed by any other rule, than their own will and pleasure. But even these men, the most abandoned of all mankind; however industriously they endeavour to conceal and deny their self-condemnation; yet they cannot avoid making a discovery of it sometimes when they are not aware of it. For example: there is no man so vile and desperate, who commits at any time a murder and robbery, with the most unrelenting mind; but would choose, if such a thing could be proposed to him, to obtain all the same profit or advantage, whatsoever it be that he aims at, *without* committing the crime, rather than *with* it; even though he was sure to go unpunished for committing the crime. Nay, I believe, there is no man, even in Mr Hobbes's state of nature, and of Mr Hobbes's own principles; but if he was equally assured of securing his main end, his self-preservation, by either way; would choose to preserve himself rather *without* destroying all his fellow-creatures, than *with* it; even supposing all impunity, and all other future conveniencies of life, equal in either case. Mr Hobbes's own scheme, of men's agreeing by compact to preserve one another, can hardly be supposed without this. And this plainly evinces, that the mind of man unavoidably acknowledges a natural and necessary difference between good and evil, antecedent to all arbitrary and positive constitution whatsoever.

237   But the truth of this, that the mind of man naturally and necessarily assents to the eternal law of righteousness; may still better and more clearly and more universally appear, from the judgement that

men pass upon each *other's* actions, than from what we can discern concerning their consciousness of their *own*. For men may dissemble and conceal from the world, the judgement of their own conscience; nay, by a strange partiality, they may even impose upon and deceive *themselves*; (for who is there, that does not sometimes allow himself, nay, and even justify himself in that, wherein he condemns another?) But men's judgements concerning the actions of *others*, especially where they have no relation to themselves, or repugnance to their interest, are commonly impartial; and from this we may judge, what sense men naturally have of the unalterable difference of right and wrong. Now the observation which every one cannot but make in this matter, is this; that virtue and true goodness, righteousness and equity, are things so truly noble and excellent, so lovely and venerable in themselves, and do so necessarily approve themselves to the reason and consciences of men; that even those very persons, who, by the prevailing power of some interest or lust, are themselves drawn aside out of the paths of virtue, can yet hardly ever forbear to give it its true character and commendation in *others*. And this observation holds true, not only in the generality of vicious men, but very frequently even in the worst sort of them, viz. those who persecute others for being better than themselves. . . . At least, there is hardly any wicked man, but when his own case is represented to him under the person of another, will freely enough pass sentence against he wickedness he himself is guilty of; and, with sufficient severity, exclaim against all iniquity. This shows abundantly, that all variation from the eternal rule of right, is absolutely and in the nature of the thing itself to be abhorred and detested; and that the unprejudiced mind of man, as naturally disapproves injustice in moral matters, as in natural things it cannot but dissent from falsehood, or dislike incongruities. Even in reading the histories of past and far distant ages, where it is plain we can have no concern for the events of things, nor prejudices concerning the characters of persons; who is there, that does not praise and admire, nay highly esteem and in his imagination love (as it were) the equity, justice, truth and fidelity of some persons; and with the greatest indignation and hatred, detest the barbarity, injustice, and treachery of others? Nay further; when the prejudices of corrupt minds lie all on the side of injustice; as when we have obtained some very great profit or advantage through another man's treachery or breach of faith; yet who is there, that upon that very occasion does not (even to a proverb) dislike the person and the action, how much soever he may rejoice at the event? But when we come *ourselves* to *suffer* by iniquity, *then* where are all the arguments and sophistries, by which unjust men, while they are oppressing others, would persuade themselves that they are not sensible of any natural difference between good and evil? When it comes to be these men's *own* case, to be oppressed by violence, or over-reached by fraud; where *then* are all their pleas against the eternal distinction of right and wrong? How, on the contrary, do they *then* cry out for equity, and exclaim against injustice! How do they *then* challenge and object against Providence, and think neither God nor man severe enough, in punishing the violators of right and truth! Whereas, if there was no natural and eternal difference between just and unjust; no man could have any reason to complain of injury, any other than what laws and compacts made so; which in innumerable cases will be always to be evaded.

238   There is but one thing, that I am sensible of, which can here with any colour be objected against what has been hitherto said concerning the necessity of the mind's giving its assent to the eternal law of righteousness; and that is, the total ignorance, which some whole nations are reported to lie under, of the nature and force of these moral obligations. The matter of fact, is not very true: but if it was, it is certain there are more nations and people totally ignorant of the plainest mathematical truths; as, of the proportion, for example, of a square to a triangle of the same base and height: and yet these truths are such, to which the mind cannot but give its assent necessarily and unavoidably, as soon as they are distinctly proposed to it. All that this objection proves therefore, supposing the matter of it to be true, is only this; not, that the mind of man can ever dissent from the rule of right; much less, that there is no necessary difference in nature, between moral good and evil; any more than it proves, that there are no certain and necessary proportions of numbers, lines, or figures: but this it proves only, that men have great need to be taught and instructed in some very plain and easy, as well as certain truths; and, if they be important truths, that then men have need also to have them frequently inculcated, and strongly enforced upon them. Which is very true: and is (as shall hereafter be particularly made to appear) one good argument for the reasonableness of expecting a revelation.

4. Thus it appears *in general*, that the mind of man cannot avoid **239** giving its assent to the eternal law of righteousness; that is, cannot but acknowledge the reasonableness and fitness of men's governing all their actions by the rule of right or equity: and also that this assent is a formal obligation upon every man, actually and constantly to conform himself to that rule. I might now from hence deduce *in particular*, all the several duties of morality or natural religion. But because this would take up too large a portion of my intended discourse, and may easily be supplied abundantly out of several late excellent writers; I shall only mention the three great and principal branches, from which all the other and smaller instances of duty do naturally flow, or may without difficulty be derived.

First then, in respect of *God*, the rule of righteousness is; that we **240** keep up constantly in our minds, the highest possible honour, esteem, and veneration for him; which must express itself in proper and respective influences upon all our passions, and in the suitable direction of all our actions: that we worship and adore him, and him alone, as the only supreme author, preserver and governor of all things: that we employ our whole beings, and all our powers and faculties, in his service, and for his glory; that is, in encouraging the practice of universal righteousness, and promoting the designs of his divine goodness amongst men, in such way and manner as shall at any time appear to be his will we should do it: and finally, that, to enable us to do this continually, we pray unto him constantly for whatever we stand in need of, and return him continual and hearty thanks for whatever good things we at any time receive.

*   *   *   *

Secondly. In respect of our *fellow-creatures*, the rule of righteousness **241** is; that *in particular* we so deal with every man, as in like circumstances we could reasonably expect he should deal with us; and that *in general* we endeavour, by an universal benevolence, to promote the welfare and happiness of all men. The former branch of this rule, is *equity*; the latter, is *love*.

As to the former, viz. *equity*: the reason which *obliges* every man **242** in *practice*, so to deal always with another, as he would reasonably expect that others should in like circumstances deal with him; is the very same, as that which *forces* him in *speculation* to affirm, that if one line or number be equal to another, that other is reciprocally equal to it. *Iniquity* is the very same in *action*, as *falsity* or *contra-diction* in *theory*; and the same cause which makes the one *absurd*, makes the other *unreasonable*. Whatever relation or proportion one man in any case bears to another; the same that other, when put in like circumstances, bears to him. Whatever I judge reasonable or unreasonable for another to do for me; that, by the same judgement, I declare reasonable or unreasonable, that I in the like case should do for him. And to deny this either in word or action, is as if a man should contend, that, though two and three are equal to five, yet five are not equal to two and three. Wherefore, were not men strangely and most unnaturally corrupted, by perverse and unaccountably false opinions, and monstrous evil customs and habits, prevailing against the clearest and plainest reason in the world: it would be impossible, that universal equity should not be practised by all man-kind; and especially among *equals*, where the proportion of equity is simple and obvious, and every man's own case is already the same with all others, without any nice comparing or transposing of cir-cumstances. It would be as impossible, that a man, contrary to the eternal reason of things, should desire to gain some small profit to himself, by doing violence and damage to his neighbour; as that he should be willing to be deprived of necessaries himself, to satisfy the unreasonable covetousness or ambition of another. In a word; it would be impossible for men not to be as much ashamed of *doing iniquity*, as they are of *believing contradictions*. In considering indeed the duties of *superiors* and *inferiors* in various relations, the proportion of equity is somewhat more complex; but still it may always be deduced from the same rule of doing as we would be done by, if careful regard be had at the same time to the difference of relation: that is, if in considering what is fit for you to do to another, you always take into the account, not only every circumstance of the *action*, but also every circumstance wherein the *person* differs from you; and in judging what you would desire that another, if your circumstances were transposed, should do to you; you always con-sider, not what any unreasonable passion or private interest would prompt you, but what impartial reason would dictate to you to desire. For example: a magistrate, in order to deal equitably with a criminal, is not to consider what *fear* or *self-love* would cause him, in the criminal's case, to *desire*; but what *reason* and the *public good* would oblige him to *acknowledge* was fit and just for him to *expect*.

And the same proportion is to be observed, in deducing the duties of parents and children, of masters and servants, of governors and subjects, of citizens and foreigners; in what manner every person is obliged by the rule of equity, to behave himself in each of these and all other relations. In the regular and uniform practice of all which duties among all mankind, in their several and respective relations, through the whole earth; consists that *universal justice*, which is the top and perfection of all virtues.

*   *   *   *

The second branch of the rule of righteousness with respect to our **243** fellow-creatures, I said, was *universal love or benevolence*; that is, not only the doing barely what is just and right, in our dealings with every man; but also a constant endeavouring to promote in general, to the utmost of our power, the welfare and happiness of all men. The obligation to which duty also, may easily be deduced from what has been already laid down. For if (as has been before proved) there be a natural and necessary difference between good and evil; and that which is good is fit and reasonable, and that which is evil is unreasonable to be done; and that which is the greatest good, is always the *most* fit and reasonable to be chosen: then, as the goodness of God extends itself universally over all his works through the whole creation, by doing always what is absolutely best in the whole; so every rational creature *ought* in its sphere and station, according to its respective powers and faculties, to do all the good it can to all its fellow-creatures. To which end, universal love and benevolence is as plainly the most direct, certain, and effectual means; as in mathematics the flowing of a point, is, to produce a line; or in arithmetic, the addition of numbers, to produce a sum; or in physics, certain kinds of motions, to preserve certain bodies, which other kinds of motions tend to corrupt. Of all which, the mind of man is so naturally sensible, that, except in such men whose affections are prodigiously corrupted by most unnatural and habitual vicious practices, there is no duty whatsoever, the performance whereof affords a man so ample pleasure and satisfaction, and fills his mind with so comfortable a sense, of his having done the greatest good he was capable to do, of his having best answered the ends of his creation, and nearliest imitated the perfections of his creator, and consequently of his having fully complied with the highest and principal obligations of his nature; as the performance of this one duty, of universal love and **244** benevolence, naturally affords. But further: the obligation to this great duty, may also otherwise be deduced from the *nature of man*, in the following manner. Next to that natural *self-love*, or care of his own preservation, which every one necessarily has in the first place for himself; there is in all men a certain natural affection for their children and posterity, who have a dependence upon them; and for their near relations and friends, who have an intimacy with them. And because the nature of man is such, that they cannot live comfortably in independent families, without still further society and commerce with each other; therefore they naturally desire to increase their dependencies, by multiplying affinities; and to enlarge their friendships, by mutual good offices; and to establish societies, by a communication of arts and labour: till by degrees the affection of single persons, becomes a friendship of families; and this enlarges itself to society of towns and cities and nations; and terminates in the agreeing community of all mankind. The foundation, preservation, and perfection of which universal friendship or society, is *mutual love and benevolence*. And nothing hinders the world from being actually put into so happy a state, but perverse iniquity and unreasonable want of mutual charity. Wherefore since men are plainly so constituted by nature, that they stand in need of each other's assistance to make themselves easy in the world; and are fitted to live in communities; and society is absolutely necessary for them; and mutual love and benevolence is the only possible means to establish this society in any tolerable and durable manner; and in this respect all men stand upon the same level, and have the same natural wants and desires, and are in the same need of each other's help, and are equally capable of enjoying the benefit and advantage of society: it is evident every man is bound by the law of his nature, as he is also prompted by the inclination of his uncorrupted affections, to look upon himself as a part and member of that one universal body or community, which is made up of all mankind; to think himself born to promote the public good and welfare of all his fellow-creatures; and consequently obliged, as the necessary and only effectual means to that end, to embrace them all with universal love and benevolence: so that he cannot, without acting contrary to the reason of his own mind, and transgressing the plain and known law of his being, do willingly any hurt and mischief to any man; no, not even to those who have first injured him; but ought, for the public benefit, to endeavour to appease with gentleness, rather than exasperate with retaliations; and finally, to comprehend all in one word, (which is the top and complete perfection of this great duty,) ought to *love all others as himself*. This is the argumentation of that great master, Cicero: whose knowledge and understanding of the true state of things, and of the original obligations of human nature, was as much greater than Mr Hobbes's; as his helps and advantages to attain that knowledge, were less.

Thirdly, with respect to *ourselves*, the rule of righteousness is; that **245** every man preserve his own being, as long as he is able; and take care to keep himself at all times in such temper and disposition both of body and mind, as may best fit and enable him to perform his duty in all other instances. That is: he ought to bridle his appetites, with temperance; to govern his passions, with moderation; and to apply himself to the business of his present station in the world, whatsoever it be, with attention and contentment. That every man ought to preserve his own being as long as he is able, is evident; because what he is not himself the author and giver of, he can never of himself have just power or authority to take away. He that sent us into the world, and alone knows for how long time he appointed us our station here, and when we have finished all the business he intended we should do; can alone judge when it is fit for us to be taken hence, and has alone authority to dismiss and discharge us. . . . For the same reason, that a man is obliged to preserve his own *being* at all; he is bound likewise to preserve himself, as far as he is able, in the right use of all his *faculties*: that is, to keep himself constantly in such temper both of body and mind, by regulating his appetites and passions, as may best fit and enable him to perform his duty in all other instances. For, as it matters not whether a soldier deserts his post, or by drunkenness renders himself incapable of performing his duty in it: so for a man to disable himself by any intemperance or passion, from performing the necessary duties of life; is, at least for that time, the same thing as depriving himself of life. And neither is this all. For great intemperance and ungoverned passions, not only incapacitate a man to perform his duty; but also expose him to run headlong into the commission of the greatest enormities: there being no violence or injustice whatsoever, which a man who has deprived himself of his reason by intemperance or passion, is not capable of being tempted to commit. So that all the additional obligations which a man is any way under, to forbear committing the most flagrant crimes; lie equally upon him to govern his passions and restrain his appetites: without doing which, he can never secure himself effectually, from being betrayed into the commission of all iniquity. This is indeed the great difficulty of life, to subdue and conquer our unreasonable appetites and passions. But it is absolutely necessary to be done: and it is moreover the bravest and most glorious conquest in the world. Lastly: for the same reason that a man is obliged not to depart wilfully out of this life, which is the *general station* that God has appointed him; he is obliged likewise to attend the duties of that *particular station* or condition of life, whatsoever it be, wherein Providence has at present placed him; with diligence, and contentment: without being either uneasy and discontented, that others are placed by Providence in different and superior stations in the world; or so extremely and unreasonably solicitous to change his state for the future, as thereby to neglect his present duty.

From these three great and general branches, all the smaller and more particular instances of moral obligations, may (as I said) easily be deduced.

246   5. And now this, (this eternal rule of equity, which I have been hitherto describing,) is that *right reason*, which makes the principal distinction between man and beasts. This is the *law of nature*, which (as Cicero excellently expresses it) is of universal extent, and everlasting duration; which can neither be wholly abrogated, nor repealed in any part of it, nor have any law made contrary to it, nor be dispensed with by any authority: which was in force, before ever any law was written, or the foundation of any city or commonwealth was laid: which was not invented by the wit of man, nor established by the authority of any people; but its obligation was from eternity, and the force of it reaches throughout the universe: which being founded in the nature and reason of things, did not then begin to be a law, when it was first written and enacted by men; but is of the same original with the eternal reasons or proportions of things, and the perfections or attributes of God himself.

★   ★   ★   ★

247   6. Further yet: as this law of nature is infinitely superior to all authority of *men*, and independent upon it; so its obligation,

primarily and originally, is antecedent also even to *this* consideration, of its being the positive will or command of *God* himself. For, as the addition of certain numbers, necessarily produces a certain sum; and certain geometrical or mechanical operations, give a constant and unalterable solution of certain problems or propositions: so in moral matters, there are certain necessary and unalterable respects or relations of things, which have not their original from arbitrary and positive constitution, but are of eternal necessity in their own nature. ... The *existence* indeed of the *things themselves*, whose proportions and relations we consider, depend entirely on the mere arbitrary will and good pleasure of God; who can create things when he pleases, and destroy them again whenever he thinks fit. But when things are created, and so long as it pleases God to continue them in being; their *proportions*, which are *abstractly* of eternal necessity, are also in the *things themselves* absolutely unalterable. Hence God himself, though he has no superior, from whose will to receive any law of his actions; yet disdains not to observe the rule of equity and goodness, as the law of all his actions in the government of the world; and condescends to appeal even to men, for the equity and righteousness of his judgements. To this law, the infinite perfections of his divine nature make it necessary for him (as has been before proved,) to have constant regard: and (as a learned prelate of our own* has excellently shown,) not barely his infinite power, but the rules of this eternal law, are the true foundation and the measure of his dominion over his creatures. (For if *infinite power* was the rule and measure of right, it is evident that *goodness* and *mercy* and all other divine perfections, would be *empty words* without *any signification* at all.) Now for the same reason that God who hath no superior to determine him, yet constantly directs all his own actions by the eternal rule of justice and goodness; it is evident all intelligent creatures in their several spheres and proportions, *ought* to obey the same rule according to the law of their nature; even though it could be supposed separate from that additional obligation, of its being the positive will and command of God. And doubtless there have been many men in all ages in many parts of the heathen world, who not having philosophy enough to collect from mere nature any tolerably just and explicit apprehensions concerning the attributes of God; much less having been able to deduce from thence, any clear and certain knowledge

* Cumberland, *de Leg. Naturae.*

of his will; have yet had a very great sense of right and truth, and been fully persuaded in their own minds, of many unalterable obligations of morality. But this speculation, though necessary to be taken notice of in the distinct order and method of discourse, is in itself too dry, and not of great use to *us*, who are abundantly assured that all moral obligations are moreover the plain and declared will of God; as shall be shown particularly, in its proper place.

248   7. Lastly, this law of nature has its full obligatory power, antecedent to all consideration of any particular private and personal *reward* or *punishment*, annexed either by natural consequence, or by positive appointment, to the observance or neglect of it. This also is very evident: because, if good and evil, right and wrong, fitness and unfitness of being practised, be (as has been shown) originally, eternally, and necessarily, in the nature of the things themselves; it is plain that the view of particular rewards or punishments, which is only an after-consideration, and does not at all alter the nature of things, cannot be the original cause of the obligation of the law, but is only an additional weight to enforce the practice of what men were before obliged to by right reason. There is no man, who has any just sense of the difference between good and evil, but must needs acknowledge, that virtue and goodness are truly amiable, and to be chosen for their own sakes and intrinsic worth; though a man had no prospect of gaining any particular advantage to himself, by the practice of them: and that, on the contrary, cruelty, violence and oppression, fraud, injustice, and all manner of wickedness, are of themselves hateful, and by all means to be avoided; even though a man had absolute assurance, that he should bring no manner of inconvenience upon himself by the commission of any or all of these crimes.

⋆   ⋆   ⋆   ⋆

249   Thus far is clear. But now from hence it does not at all follow, either that a good man ought to have no respect to rewards and punishments, or that rewards and punishments are not absolutely necessary to maintain the practice of virtue and righteousness in this present world. It is certain indeed, that virtue and vice are eternally and necessarily different; and that the one truly deserves to be chosen for its own sake, and the other ought by all means to be avoided, though a man was sure for his own particular, neither to gain nor lose any thing by the practice of either. And if this was truly the state of things in the world; certainly that man must have a very corrupt mind indeed, who could in the least doubt, or so much as once deliberate with himself, which he would choose. But the case does not stand thus. The question now in the general practice of the world, supposing all expectation of rewards and punishments set aside, will not be, whether a man would choose virtue for *its own sake*, and avoid vice; but the practice of vice, is accompanied with great temptations and allurements of pleasure and profit; and the practice of virtue is often threatened with great calamities, losses, and sometimes even with death itself. And this alters the question, and destroys the practice of that which appears so reasonable in the whole speculation, and introduces a necessity of rewards and punishments. For though virtue is unquestionably *worthy to be chosen for its own sake*, even without any expectation of reward; yet it does not follow that it is therefore entirely *self-sufficient*, and able to support a man under all kinds of sufferings, and even death itself, for its sake; without any prospect of future recompense. Here therefore began **250** the error of the Stoics; who taught that the bare practice of virtue, was itself the chief good, and able of itself to make a man happy, under all the calamities in the world. Their defence indeed of the cause of virtue, was very brave: they saw well that its excellency was intrinsic, and founded in the nature of things themselves, and could not be altered by any outward circumstances; that therefore virtue must needs be desirable for its own sake, and not merely for the advantage it might bring along with it; and if so, then consequently neither could any external disadvantage, which it might happen to be attended with, change the intrinsic worth of the thing itself, or ever make it cease to be truly desirable. Wherefore, in the case of sufferings and death for the sake of virtue; not having any *certain* knowledge of a future state of reward, (though the wisest of them did indeed hope for it, and think it highly *probable*;) they were forced, that they might be consistent with their own principles, to suppose the practice of virtue a sufficient reward to itself in all cases, and a full compensation for all the sufferings in the world. And accordingly they very bravely indeed taught, that the practice of virtue was not only infinitely to be preferred before all the sinful pleasures in the world; but also that a man ought without scruple to choose, if the case was proposed to him, rather to undergo all possible sufferings with virtue, than to obtain all possible worldly happiness by sin. And the suitable practice of some few of them, as of Regulus for instance, who chose to die the cruellest death that could be invented, rather than break his faith with an enemy; is indeed very wonderful and to be admired. But yet, after all this, it is plain that the general practice of virtue in the world, can never be supported upon this foot. The discourse is admirable, but it seldom goes further than mere words: and the practice of those few who have acted accordingly, has not been imitated by the rest of the world. Men never will generally, and indeed it is not very reasonably to be expected they should, part with all the comforts of life, and even life itself; without expectation of any future recompense. So that, if we suppose no future state of rewards; it will follow, that God has endued men with such faculties, as put them under a necessity of approving and choosing virtue in the judgement of their own minds; and yet has not given them wherewith to support themselves in the suitable and constant practice of it. The consideration of which inexplicable difficulty, ought to have led the philosophers to a firm belief and expectation of a future state of rewards and punishments, without which their whole scheme of morality cannot be supported. And, because a thing of such necessity and importance to mankind, was not more clearly and directly and universally made known; it might naturally have led them to some farther consequences also, which I shall have occasion particularly to deduce hereafter.

251   Thus have I endeavoured to deduce the *original obligations* of morality, from the *necessary and eternal reason* and *proportions of things*. Some have chosen to found all difference of good and evil, in the mere positive will and power of God: but the absurdity of this, I have shown elsewhere. Others have contended, that all difference of good and evil, and all obligations of morality, ought to be founded originally upon considerations of *public utility*. And true indeed it is, in the whole; that the good of the universal creation, does always *coincide* with the necessary truth and reason of things. But otherwise, (and separate from *this* consideration, that God will certainly cause truth and right to terminate in happiness;) *what* is for the good of the whole creation, in very many cases, none but an infinite understanding can possibly judge. Public utility, is one thing to one nation, and the contrary to another: and the governors of every nation, will

and must be judges of the public good: and by public good, they will generally mean the private good of that particular nation. But truth and right (whether public or private) founded in the eternal and necessary reason of things, is what every man can judge of, when laid before him. It is necessarily one and the same, to every man's understanding; just as light is the same, to every man's eyes.

He who thinks it right and just, upon account of public utility, to break faith (suppose) with a robber; let him consider, that it is much more useful to do the same by a multitude of robbers, by tyrants, by a nation of robbers: and then, all faith is evidently at an end. For,—*mutato nomine, de te*—what fidelity and truth are, is understood by every man; but between two nations at war, who shall be judge, which of them are the robbers? Besides: to rob a man of truth and of eternal happiness, is worse than robbing him of his money and of his temporal happiness: and therefore it will be said that heretics may even more justly, and with much greater utility to the public, be deceived and destroyed by breach of truth and faith, than the most cruel robbers. Where does this terminate?

And now, from what has been said upon this head, it is easy to see 252 the falsity and weakness of Mr Hobbes's doctrines; that there is no such thing as just and unjust, right and wrong originally in the nature of things; that men in their natural state, antecedent to all compacts, are not obliged to universal benevolence, nor to any moral duty whatsoever; but are in a state of war, and have every one a right to do whatever he has power to do; and that, in civil societies, it depends wholly upon positive laws or the will of governors, to define what shall be just or unjust. The contrary to all which, having been already fully demonstrated; there is no need of being large, in further disproving and confuting particularly these assertions themselves. I shall therefore only mention a few observations, from which some of the greatest and most obvious absurdities of the chief principles upon which Mr Hobbes builds his whole doctrine in this matter, may most easily appear.

1. First then; the ground and foundation of Mr Hobbes's scheme, 253 is this; that all men, being equal by nature, and naturally desiring the same things, have every one a right to every thing;[1] are every one desirous to have absolute dominion over all others; and may every

[1 Cf. Hobbes, §§ 47-8, 57.]

one justly do whatever at any time is in his power, by violently
taking from others either their possessions or lives, to gain to himself that absolute dominion. Now this is exactly the same thing, as if
a man should affirm, that a part is equal to the whole, or that one
body can be present in a thousand places at once. For, to say that one
man has a *full right* to the same individual things, which another
man at the same time has a *full right* to; is saying that two *rights* may
be contradictory to each other; that is, that a thing may be *right*, at
the same time that it is confessed to be *wrong*. For instance; if every
man has *a right* to preserve his own life, then it is manifest I can have
no *right* to take any man's life away from him, unless he has first
forfeited his *own right*, by attempting to deprive me of mine. For
otherwise, it might be *right* for me to do that, which at the same
time, because it could not be done but in breach of another man's
right, it could not be *right* for me to do: which is the greatest absurdity in the world. The true state of this case therefore, is plainly this.
In Mr Hobbes's state of nature and equality; every man having an
equal right to preserve his own life, it is evident every man has a
right to an equal proportion of all those things, which are either
necessary or useful to life. And consequently so far is it from being
true, that any one has an original right to possess *all*; that, on
the contrary, whoever first attempts, without the *consent* of his
fellows, and except it be for some *public benefit*, to take to himself
more than his *proportion*, is the beginner of iniquity, and the author
of all succeeding mischief.

254   2. To avoid this absurdity therefore, Mr Hobbes is forced to assert
in the next place, that since every man has confessedly a right to
preserve his own life, and consequently to do every thing that is
necessary to preserve it; and since in the state of nature, men will
necessarily have perpetual jealousies and suspicions of each other's
encroaching; therefore just precaution gives every one a right to
endeavour, for his own security, to prevent, oppress, and destroy
all others, either by secret artifice or open violence, as it shall happen
at any time to be in his power; as being the only certain means of
self-preservation. But this is even a plainer absurdity, if possible,
than the former. For (besides that according to Mr Hobbes's principles, men, before positive compacts, may *justly* do what mischief
they please, even *without* the pretence of *self-preservation*;) what can
be more ridiculous, than to imagine *a war of all men against all*, the

directest and certainest means of the *preservation* of all? Yes, says he, because it leads § men to a necessity of entering into *compact* for each other's security. But then to make these *compacts* obligatory, he is forced (as I shall presently observe more particularly) to recur to an antecedent *law of nature*: and this destroys all that he had before said. For the same law of nature which obliges men to *fidelity*, *after* having made a compact; will unavoidably, upon all the same accounts, be found to oblige them, *before* all compacts, to *contentment* and mutual *benevolence*, as the readiest and certainest means to the preservation and happiness of them all. It is true, men by entering into compacts and making laws, agree to compel one another to do what perhaps the mere sense of duty, however really obligatory in the highest degree, would not, without such compacts, have force enough of itself to hold them to in practice: and so, compacts must be acknowledged to be *in fact* a great addition and strengthening of men's security. But this compulsion makes no alteration in the *obligation itself*; and only shows, that that entirely lawless state, which Mr Hobbes calls the *state of nature*, is by no means truly *natural*, or in any sense suitable to the nature and faculties of man; but on the contrary, is a state of extremely *unnatural and intolerable corruption*: as I shall presently prove more fully from some other considerations.

3. Another notorious absurdity and inconsistency in Mr Hobbes's **255** scheme, is this: that he all along supposes some particular branches of the law of nature, (which he thinks necessary for the foundation of some parts of his own doctrine,) to be originally obligatory from the bare reason of things; at the same time that he denies and takes away innumerable others, which have plainly in the nature and reason of things the same foundation of being obligatory as the former, and without which the obligation of the former can never be solidly made out and defended. Thus he supposes that in the state of nature, before any compact be made, every man's own will is his only law; that nothing a man can do, is unjust;[1] and that* whatever mischief one man does to another, is no injury nor injustice; neither has the person, to whom the mischief is done, how great soever it be, any just reason to complain of wrong; (I think it may here reasonably be presumed, that if Mr Hobbes had lived in such a state

---

* *De Cive, c.* 3. § 4.

[¹ Cf. Hobbes, §§ 53, 67.]

of nature, and had happened to be himself the suffering party, he
would in this case have been of another opinion:) and yet at the
same time he supposes, that in the same state of nature, men are by
all means obliged to seek peace, and to enter into compacts to
remedy the fore-mentioned mischiefs.[1] Now if men are obliged by
the original reason and nature of things to seek terms of peace, and
to get out of the pretended natural state of war, as soon as they can;
how come they not to be obliged originally by the same reason and
nature of things, to live from the beginning in universal benevolence,
and avoid entering into the state of war at all? He must needs confess
they would be obliged to do so, did not self-preservation necessitate
them every man to war upon others: but this cannot be true of the
first aggressor; whom yet Mr Hobbes, in the place now cited,[2]
vindicates from being guilty of any injustice: and therefore herein
256 he unavoidably contradicts himself. Thus again; in *most* instances of
morality, he supposes right and wrong, just and unjust to have no
foundation in the nature of things, but to depend entirely on positive
laws; that the rules or distinctions of good and evil, honest and dishonest, are mere civil constitutions; and whatever the chief magistrate commands, is to be accounted good; whatever he forbids, evil:
that it is the law of the land only, which makes robbery to be
robbery; or adultery to be adultery: that the commandments, to
honour our parents, to do no murder, not to commit adultery; and
all the other laws of God and nature; are no further obligatory, than
the civil power shall think fit to make them so: nay, that where the
supreme authority commands men to worship God by an image or
idol, in heathen countries, (for in this instance he cautiously excepts
Christian ones,) it is lawful and their duty to do it: and (agreeably,
as a natural consequence to all this,) that it is men's positive duty to
obey the commands of the civil power in all things, even in things
clearly and directly against their conscience; (that is, that it is their
positive duty to do that, which at the same time they know plainly
it is their duty not to do:) keeping up indeed always in their own
minds, an inward desire to observe the laws of nature and conscience; but not being bound to observe them in their outward
actions, except when it is safe so to do:[3] (he might as well have said,
that human laws and constitutions have power to make light be

[1 Cf. Hobbes, §§ 57-8, 81.]   [2 i.e., *De Cive*, ch. iii, § 4.]
[3 Cf. Hobbes, § 76.]

darkness, and darkness light; to make sweet be bitter, and bitter sweet: and indeed, as one absurdity will naturally lead a man into another, he does say something very like it; namely that the civil authority is to judge of all opinions and doctrines whatsoever; to determine questions philosophical, mathematical; and, because indeed the signification of words is arbitrary, even arithmetical ones also; as, whether a man shall presume to affirm that two and three make five or not:) and yet at the same time, *some particular* things, which it would either have been too flagrantly scandalous for him to have made depending upon human laws; as that God is to be loved, honoured and adored; that a man ought not to murder his parents; and the like: or else, which were of necessity to be supposed for the foundation of his own scheme; as that compacts ought to be faithfully performed,[1] and obedience to be duly paid to civil powers: the obligation of *these things*, he is forced to deduce entirely from the internal reason and fitness of the things themselves; antecedent to, independent upon, and unalterable by all human constitutions whatsoever. In which matter, he is guilty of the grossest absurdity and 257 inconsistency that can be. For if those greatest and strongest of all our obligations; to love and honour God, for instance; or, to perform compacts faithfully; depend not at all on any human constitution, but must of necessity (to avoid making obligations reciprocally depend on each other in a circle) be confessed to arise originally from, and be founded in, the eternal reason and unalterable nature and relations of things themselves; and the nature and force of these obligations be sufficiently clear and evident; so that he who dishonours God, or wilfully breaks his faith, is (according to Mr Hobbes's own reasoning[2]) guilty of as great an absurdity in *practice*, and of as plainly contradicting the right reason of his own mind, as he who in a *dispute* is reduced to a necessity of asserting something inconsistent with itself; and the original obligation to these duties, can from hence only be distinctly deduced: then, for the same reason, all the other duties likewise of natural religion; such as universal benevolence, justice, equity, and the like; (which I have before proved to receive in like manner their power of obliging, from the eternal reason and relations of things;) must needs be obligatory, antecedent to any consideration of positive compact, and unalterably and independently on all human constitutions whatsoever: and

[1 See Hobbes, § 67.]   [2 See Hobbes, §§ 59, 102.]

consequently Mr Hobbes's whole scheme, (both of a state of nature at first, wherein there was no such thing as right or wrong, just or unjust, at all; and of these things depending afterwards, by virtue of compact, wholly and absolutely on the positive and arbitrary determination of the civil power;) falls this way entirely to the ground, by his having been forced to suppose *some particular* things obligatory, originally, and in their own nature. On the contrary: if the rules of right and wrong, just and unjust, have *none of them* any obligatory force in the state of nature, *antecedent* to positive compact; then, for the same reason, neither will they be of any force *after* the compact, so as to afford men any certain and real security; (excepting only what may arise from the *compulsion of laws*, and *fear of punishment*; which therefore, it may well be supposed, is all that Mr Hobbes really means at the bottom.) For if there be no obligation of just and right antecedent to the *compact*; then *whence* arises the obligation of the *compact itself*, on which he supposes all other obligations to be founded? If, *before* any compact was made, it was no injustice for a man to take away the life of his neighbour, not for his own preservation, but merely to satisfy an arbitrary humour or pleasure, and without any reason or provocation at all; how comes it to be an injustice, *after* he has made a compact, to break and neglect it? Or *what* is it that makes breaking one's word, to be a greater and more unnatural crime, than killing a man merely for no other reason, but because no positive compact has been made to the contrary? So that this way also, Mr Hobbes's whole scheme is entirely destroyed.

258   4. That state, which Mr Hobbes calls the *state of nature*, is not in any sense a natural state; but a state of the greatest, most unnatural, and most intolerable *corruption*, that can be imagined. For *reason*, which is the proper nature of man, can never (as has been before shown) lead men to any thing else than universal love and benevolence: and wars, hatred, and violence, can never arise but from extreme corruption. A man may sometimes, it is true, in his own defence be necessitated, in compliance with the laws of nature and reason, to make war upon his fellows: but the first aggressors, who upon Mr Hobbes's principles, (that all men have a natural will to hurt each other, and that every one in the state of nature has a right to do whatever he has a will to:) the first aggressors, I say, who upon these principles assault and violently spoil as many as they are superior to in strength, without any regard to equity or proportion;

these can never, by any colour whatsoever, be excused from having utterly divested themselves of human nature, and having introduced into the world, contrary to all the laws of nature and reason, the greatest calamities and most unnatural confusion, that mankind by the highest abuse of their natural powers and faculties, are capable of falling under. Mr Hobbes pretends indeed, that one of the first and most natural principles of human life, is a desire necessarily arising in every man's mind, of having power and dominion over others;[1] and that this naturally impels men to use force and violence to obtain it. But neither is it true, that men, following the dictates of reason and uncorrupted nature, desire disproportionate power and dominion over others; neither, if it was natural to desire such power, would it at all follow, that it was agreeable to nature to use violent and hurtful means to obtain it. For since the only natural and good reason to desire power and dominion (more than what is necessary for every man's self-preservation) is, that the possessor of such power may have a larger compass and greater abilities and opportunities of doing good, (as is evident from God's exercise of perfectly absolute power;) it is plain that no man, obeying the uncorrupted dictates of nature and reason, can desire to increase his power by such destructive and pernicious methods, the prevention of which is *the only good reason* that makes the power itself truly desirable. All violence therefore and war are plainly the effects, not of natural desires, but of unnatural and extreme corruption. And this Mr Hobbes himself unwarily proves against himself, by those very arguments, whereby he endeavours to prove that war and contention is more *natural* to men, than to bees or ants.[2] For his arguments on this head, are all drawn from men's using themselves (as the animals he is speaking of, cannot do,) to strive about honours and dignities, till the contention grows up into hatred, seditions and wars; to separate each one his private interest from the public, and value himself highly above others, upon getting and engrossing to himself more than his proportion of the things of life; to find fault with each other's management, and, through self-conceit, bring in continual innovation and distractions; to impose one upon another, by lies, falsifying and deceit, calling good evil, and evil good; to grow envious at the prosperity of others, or proud and domineering when themselves are in ease and plenty; and to keep up tolerable peace and agreement among

[1 Cf. Hobbes, §§ 44, 79.]   [2 See Hobbes, § 80.]

themselves, merely by artificial compacts, and the compulsion of laws. All which things, are so far from being truly the *natural* effects and result of men's *reason* and other faculties; that on the contrary they are evidently some of the grossest abuses and most *unnatural* corruptions thereof, that any one who was arguing on the opposite side of the question, could easily have chosen to have instanced in.

259   5. Lastly: the chief and principal argument, which is one of the main foundations of Mr Hobbes's and his followers' system; namely, that *God's* irresistible power is the *only foundation* of his *dominion*, and the *only measure of his right* over his creatures;[1] and consequently, that every other being has just so much *right*, as it has *natural power*; that is, that it is naturally *right* for every thing to do whatever it has *power* to do:[2] this argument, I say, is of all his others the most notoriously false and absurd. As may sufficiently appear, (besides what has been already said, of God's other perfections being as much the measure of his right, as his power is,) from this single consideration. Suppose the Devil, (for when men run into extreme impious assertions, they must be answered with suitable suppositions;) suppose, I say, such a being as we conceive the Devil to be; of extreme malice, cruelty, and iniquity; was endued with supreme absolute power, and made use of it only to render the world as miserable as was possible, in the most cruel, arbitrary, and unequal manner that can be imagined: would it not follow undeniably, upon Mr Hobbes's scheme; since *dominion* is founded in *power*, and *power* is the measure of *right*, and consequently *absolute power* gives *absolute right*; that such a government as this, would not only be as much of necessity indeed to be submitted to, but also that it would be as *just* and *right*, and with as little reason to be complained of, as is the present government of the world in the hands of the ever-blessed and infinitely good God, whose love and goodness and tender mercy appears every where over all his works?

260   Here Mr Hobbes, as an unanswerable argument in defence of his assertion, urges; that the only reason, why men are bound to obey God, is plainly nothing but *weakness* or *want of power*; because, if they themselves were all-powerful, it is manifest they could not be under any obligation to obey;[3] and consequently *power* would give

[1 Cf. Hobbes, §§ 89, 101.]
[2 Clarke refers here to Spinoza, treating him as a follower of Hobbes.]
[3 Cf. Hobbes, § 101.]

them an undoubted *right* to do what they pleased. That is to say: if men were not created and dependent beings, it is true they could not indeed be obliged to the proper relative duty of created and dependent beings, viz. to obey the will and command of another in things *positive*. But from their obligation to the practice of *moral* virtues, of justice, righteousness, equity, holiness, purity, goodness, beneficence, faithfulness and truth, from which Mr Hobbes fallaciously in this argument, and most impiously in his whole scheme, endeavours to discharge them; from this they could not be discharged by any addition of power whatsoever. Because the obligation to these things, is not, as the obligation to obey in things of *arbitrary and positive* constitution, founded only in the weakness, subjection, and dependency of the *persons* obliged; but also and chiefly in the eternal and unchangeable nature and reason of the *things* themselves. For, these things are the law of *God himself*; not only to his *creatures*, but also to *himself*, as being the rule of all his own actions in the government of the world.

I have been the longer upon this head, because *moral virtue* is the **261** foundation and the sum, the essence and the life of all true religion: for the security whereof, all positive institution was principally designed: for the restoration whereof, all revealed religion was ultimately intended: and inconsistent wherewith, or in opposition to which, all doctrines whatsoever, supported by what pretence of reason or authority soever, are as certainly and necessarily false, as God is true.

★   ★   ★   ★

BERNARD MANDEVILLE

1670–1733

AN ENQUIRY INTO THE ORIGIN OF MORAL VIRTUE

[First printed, as part of *The Fable of the Bees: or, Private Vices, Public Benefits*, 1714. Reprinted here from the fourth edition, 1725, with modified spelling and reduction of initial capital letters and italics]

BERNARD MANDEVILLE

—

An Enquiry into the Origin of Moral Virtue

THE INTRODUCTION

One of the greatest reasons why so few people understand them- **262**
selves, is, that most writers are always teaching men what they
should be, and hardly ever trouble their heads with telling them
what they really are. As for my part, without any compliment to
the courteous reader, or myself, I believe man (besides skin, flesh,
bones, etc. that are obvious to the eye) to be a compound of various
passions, that all of them, as they are provoked and come uppermost,
govern him by turns, whether he will or no. To show, that these
qualifications, which we all pretend to be ashamed of, are the great
support of a flourishing society, has been the subject of the foregoing
poem. But there being some passages in it seemingly paradoxical, I
have in the Preface promised some explanatory remarks on it; which
to render more useful, I have thought fit to inquire, how man, no
better qualified, might yet by his own imperfections be taught to
distinguish between virtue and vice: and here I must desire the reader
once for all to take notice, that when I say men, I mean neither Jews
nor Christians; but mere man, in the state of nature and ignorance
of the true Deity.

AN ENQUIRY INTO THE ORIGIN OF MORAL VIRTUE

All untaught animals are only solicitous of pleasing themselves, **263**
and naturally follow the bent of their own inclinations, without
considering the good or harm that from their being pleased will
accrue to others. This is the reason, that in the wild state of nature
those creatures are fittest to live peaceably together in great numbers,
that discover the least of understanding, and have the fewest appetites
to gratify; and consequently no species of animals is, without the

curb of government, less capable of agreeing long together in multitudes than that of man; yet such are his qualities, whether good or bad, I shall not determine, that no creature besides himself can ever be made sociable: but being an extraordinary selfish and headstrong, as well as cunning animal, however he may be subdued by superior strength, it is impossible by force alone to make him tractable, and receive the improvements he is capable of.

The chief thing therefore, which lawgivers and other wise men, that have laboured for the establishment of society, have endeavoured, has been to make the people they were to govern, believe, that it was more beneficial for every body to conquer than indulge his appetites, and much better to mind the public than what seemed his private interest. As this has always been a very difficult task, so no wit or eloquence has been left untried to compass it; and the moralists and philosophers of all ages employed their utmost skill to prove the truth of so useful an assertion. But whether mankind would have ever believed it or not, it is not likely that any body could have persuaded them to disapprove of their natural inclinations, or prefer the good of others to their own, if at the same time he had not showed them an equivalent to be enjoyed as a reward for the violence, which by so doing they of necessity must commit upon themselves. Those that have undertaken to civilize mankind, were not ignorant of this; but being unable to give so many real rewards as would satisfy all persons for every individual action, they were forced to contrive an imaginary one, that as a general equivalent for the trouble of self-denial should serve on all occasions, and without costing any thing either to themselves or others, be yet a most acceptable recompense to the receivers.

264 They thoroughly examined all the strength and frailties of our nature, and observing that none were either so savage as not to be charmed with praise, or so despicable as patiently to bear contempt, justly concluded, that flattery must be the most powerful argument that could be used to human creatures. Making use of this bewitching engine, they extolled the excellency of our nature above other animals, and setting forth with unbounded praises the wonders of our sagacity and vastness of understanding, bestowed a thousand encomiums on the rationality of our souls, by the help of which we were capable of performing the most noble achievements. Having by this artful way of flattery insinuated themselves into the hearts of men, they began to instruct them in the notions of honour and shame; representing the one as the worst of all evils, and the other as the highest good to which mortals could aspire: which being done, they laid before them how unbecoming it was the dignity of such sublime creatures to be solicitous about gratifying those appetites, which they had in common with brutes, and at the same time unmindful of those higher qualities that gave them the pre-eminence over all visible beings. They indeed confessed, that those impulses of nature were very pressing; that it was troublesome to resist, and very difficult wholly to subdue them. But this they only used as an argument to demonstrate, how glorious the conquest of them was on the one hand, and how scandalous on the other not to attempt it.

To introduce moreover an emulation amongst men, they divided **265** the whole species in two classes, vastly differing from one another: the one consisted of abject, low-minded people, that always hunting after immediate enjoyment, were wholly incapable of self-denial, and, without regard to the good of others, had no higher aim than their private advantage; such as, being enslaved by voluptuousness, yielded without resistance to every gross desire, and made no use of their rational faculties but to heighten their sensual pleasure. These vile grovelling wretches, they said, were the dross of their kind, and having only the shape of men, differed from brutes in nothing but their outward figure. But the other class was made up of lofty high-spirited creatures, that free from sordid selfishness, esteemed the improvements of the mind to be their fairest possessions; and setting a true value upon themselves, took no delight but in embellishing that part in which their excellency consisted; such as, despising whatever they had in common with irrational creatures, opposed by the help of reason their most violent inclinations; and making a continual war with themselves, to promote the peace of others, aimed at no less than the public welfare and the conquest of their own passion.

> *Fortior est qui se quam qui fortissima vincit*
> *Moenia*— — —

These they called the true representatives of their sublime species, exceeding in worth the first class by more degrees, than that itself was superior to the beasts of the field.

266   As in all animals that are not too imperfect to discover pride, we find, that the finest and such as are the most beautiful and valuable of their kind, have generally the greatest share of it; so in man, the most perfect of animals, it is so inseparable from his very essence (how cunningly soever some may learn to hide or disguise it) that without it the compound he is made of would want one of the chiefest ingredients: which, if we consider, it is hardly to be doubted but lessons and remonstrances, so skilfully adapted to the good opinion man has of himself, as those I have mentioned, must, if scattered amongst a multitude, not only gain the assent of most of them, as to the speculative part, but likewise induce several, especially the fiercest, most resolute, and best among them, to endure a thousand inconveniencies, and undergo as many hardships, that they may have the pleasure of counting themselves men of the second class, and consequently appropriating to themselves all the excellencies they have heard of it.

From what has been said we ought to expect in the first place that the heroes who took such extraordinary pains to master some of their natural appetites, and preferred the good of others to any visible interest of their own, would not recede an inch from the fine notions they had received concerning the dignity of rational creatures; and having ever the authority of the government on their side, with all imaginable vigour assert the esteem that was due to those of the second class, as well as their superiority over the rest of their kind. In the second, that those who wanted a sufficient stock of either pride or resolution to buoy them up in mortifying of what was dearest to them, and followed the sensual dictates of nature, would yet be ashamed of confessing themselves to be those despicable wretches that belonged to the inferior class, and were generally reckoned to be so little removed from brutes; and that therefore in their own defence they would say, as others did, and hiding their own imperfections as well as they could, cry up self-denial and public-spiritedness as much as any: for it is highly probable, that some of them, convinced by the real proofs of fortitude and self-conquest they had seen, would admire in others what they found wanting in themselves; others be afraid of the resolution and prowess of those of the second class, and that all of them were kept in awe by the power of their rulers; wherefore it is reasonable to think, that none of them (whatever they thought in themselves) would dare openly contradict, what by every body else was thought criminal to doubt of.

This was (or at least might have been) the manner after which **267** savage man was broke; from whence it is evident, that the first rudiments of morality, broached by skilful politicians, to render men useful to each other as well as tractable, were chiefly contrived that the ambitious might reap the more benefit from, and govern vast numbers of them with the greatest ease and security. This foundation of politics being once laid, it is impossible that man should long remain uncivilized: for even those who only strove to gratify their appetites, being continually crossed by others of the same stamp, could not but observe, that whenever they checked their inclinations or but followed them with more circumspection, they avoided a world of troubles, and often escaped many of the calamities that generally attended the too eager pursuit after pleasure.

First, they received, as well as others, the benefit of those actions that were done for the good of the whole society, and consequently could not forbear wishing well to those of the superior class that performed them. Secondly, the more intent they were in seeking their own advantage, without regard to others, the more they were hourly convinced, that none stood so much in their way as those that were most like themselves.

It being the interest then of the very worst of them, more than any, to preach up public-spiritedness, that they might reap the fruits of the labour and self-denial of others, and at the same time indulge their own appetites with less disturbance, they agreed with the rest, to call every thing, which, without regard to the public, man should commit to gratify any of his appetites, VICE; if in that action there could be observed the least prospect, that it might either be injurious to any of the society, or even render himself less serviceable to others: and to give the name of VIRTUE to every performance, by which man, contrary to the impulse of nature, should endeavour the benefit of others, or the conquest of his own passions out of a rational ambition of being good.

It shall be objected, that no society was ever any ways civilized **268** before the major part had agreed upon some worship or other of an over-ruling power, and consequently that the notions of good and evil, and the distinction between *virtue* and *vice*, were never the contrivance of politicians, but the pure effect of religion. Before I answer this objection. I must repeat what I have said already, that in this *Enquiry into the Origin of Moral Virtue*, I speak neither of Jews or Christians, but man in his state of nature and ignorance of the true Deity; and then I affirm, that the idolatrous superstitions of all other nations, and the pitiful notions they had of the supreme being, were incapable of exciting man to virtue, and good for nothing but to awe and amuse a rude and unthinking multitude. It is evident from history, that in all considerable societies, how stupid or ridiculous soever people's received notions have been, as to the deities they worshipped, human nature has ever exerted itself in all its branches, and that there is no earthly wisdom or moral virtue, but at one time or other men have excelled in it in all monarchies and commonwealths, that for riches and power have been any ways remarkable.

*   *   *   *

269   It is visible then that it was not any heathen religion or other idolatrous superstition, that first put man upon crossing his appetites and subduing his dearest inclinations, but the skilful management of wary politicians; and the nearer we search into human nature, the more we shall be convinced, that the moral virtues are the political offspring which flattery begot upon pride.

There is no man of what capacity or penetration soever, that is wholly proof against the witchcraft of flattery, if artfully performed, and suited to his abilities. Children and fools will swallow personal praise, but those that are more cunning, must be managed with greater circumspection; and the more general the flattery is, the less it is suspected by those it is levelled at. What you say in commendation of a whole town is received with pleasure by all the inhabitants: speak in commendation of letters in general, and every man of learning will think himself in particular obliged to you. You may safely praise the employment a man is of, or the country he was born in; because you give him an opportunity of screening the joy he feels upon his own account, under the esteem which he pretends to have for others.

It is common among cunning men, that understand the power which flattery has upon pride, when they are afraid they shall be imposed upon, to enlarge, though much against their conscience, upon the honour, fair dealing and integrity of the family, country, or sometimes the profession of him they suspect; because they know that men often will change their resolution, and act against their inclination, that they may have the pleasure of continuing to appear in the opinion of some, what they are conscious not to be in reality. Thus sagacious moralists draw men like angels, in hopes that the pride at least of some will put them upon copying after the beautiful originals which they are represented to be.

★   ★   ★   ★

But here I shall be told, that besides the noisy toils of war and **270** public bustle of the ambitious, there are noble and generous actions that are performed in silence; that virtue being its own reward, those who are really good have a satisfaction in their consciousness of being so, which is all the recompense they expect from the most worthy performances; that among the heathens there have been men, who, when they did good to others, were so far from coveting thanks and applause, that they took all imaginable care to be for ever concealed from those on whom they bestowed their benefits, and consequently that pride has no hand in spurring man on to the highest pitch of self-denial.

In answer to this I say, that it is impossible to judge of a man's performance, unless we are thoroughly acquainted with the principle and motive from which he acts. Pity, though it is the most gentle and the least mischievous of all our passions, is yet as much a frailty of our nature, as anger, pride, or fear. The weakest minds have generally the greatest share of it, for which reason none are more compassionate than women and children. It must be owned, that of all our weaknesses it is the most amiable, and bears the greatest resemblance to virtue; nay, without a considerable mixture of it the society could hardly subsist: but as it is an impulse of nature, that consults neither the public interest nor our own reason, it may produce evil as well as good. It has helped to destroy the honour of virgins, and corrupted the integrity of judges; and whoever acts from it as a principle, what good soever he may bring to the society, has nothing to boast of but that he has indulged a passion that has happened to be beneficial to the public. There is no merit in saving an innocent babe ready to drop into the fire: the action is neither good nor bad, and what benefit soever the infant received, we only obliged ourselves; for to have seen it fall, and not strove to hinder it, would have caused a pain, which self-preservation compelled us to prevent: nor has a rich prodigal, that happens to be of a commiserating temper, and loves to gratify his passions, greater virtue to boast of when he relieves an object of compassion with what to himself is a trifle.

271   But such men, as without complying with any weakness of their own, can part from what they value themselves, and, from no other motive but their love to goodness, perform a worthy action in silence; such men, I confess, have acquired more refined notions of virtue than those I have hitherto spoke of; yet even in these (with which the world has yet never swarmed) we may discover no small symptoms of pride, and the humblest man alive must confess, that the reward of a virtuous action, which is the satisfaction that ensues upon it, consists in a certain pleasure he procures to himself by contemplating on his own worth: which pleasure, together with the occasion of it, are as certain signs of pride, as looking pale and trembling at any imminent danger, are the symptoms of fear.

If the too scrupulous reader should at first view condemn these notions concerning the origin of moral virtue, and think them perhaps offensive to Christianity, I hope he'll forbear his censures, when he shall consider, that nothing can render the unsearchable depth of the divine wisdom more conspicuous, than that *man*, whom Providence had designed for society, should not only by his own frailties and imperfections be led into the road to temporal happiness, but likewise receive, from a seeming necessity of natural causes, a tincture of that knowledge, in which he was afterwards to be made perfect by the true religion, to his eternal welfare.

WILLIAM WOLLASTON

1659–1724

THE RELIGION OF NATURE
DELINEATED

[Privately printed, 1722. First public edition, corrected,
1724. Reprinted here from the edition of 1724, with
modified spelling, some reduction of italics and initial
capital letters, and omission of nearly all footnotes]

WILLIAM WOLLASTON

———

The Religion of Nature delineated

SECTION I—OF MORAL GOOD AND EVIL

The foundation of religion lies in that difference between the acts 272
of men, which distinguishes them into *good, evil, indifferent*. For if
there is such a difference, there must be religion; and *contra*. Upon
this account it is that such a long and laborious inquiry hath been
made after some general *idea*, or some *rule*, by comparing the fore-
said acts with which it might appear, to which kind they respectively
belong. And though men have not yet agreed upon any one, yet one
certainly there must be. That, which I am going to propose, has
always seemed to me not only evidently true, but withal so obvious
and plain, that perhaps for this very reason it hath not merited the
notice of authors: and the use and application of it is so easy, that if
things are but fairly permitted to speak for themselves their own
natural language, they will, with a moderate attention, be found
themselves to proclaim their own rectitude or obliquity; that is,
whether they are disagreeable to it, or not. I shall endeavour by
degrees to explain my meaning.

I. *That act, which may be denominated morally good or evil, must be the* 273
act of a being capable of distinguishing, choosing, and acting for himself: or
more briefly, *of an intelligent and free agent*. Because in proper speaking no act at all can be ascribed to that, which is not endued with
these capacities. For that, which cannot distinguish, cannot choose:
and that, which has not the opportunity, or liberty of choosing for
itself, and acting accordingly, from an internal principle, acts, if it
acts at all, under a necessity incumbent *ab extra*. But that, which acts
thus, is in reality only *an instrument* in the hand of something which
imposes the necessity; and cannot properly be said *to act*, but *to be
acted*. The act must be the act of an agent: therefore not of his
instrument.

A being under the above mentioned inabilities is, as to the morality of its acts, in the state of inert and passive matter, and can be but a *machine*: to which no language or philosophy ever ascribed ἤθη or *mores*.

274 II. *Those propositions are true, which express things as they are: or, truth is the conformity of those words or signs, by which things are expressed, to the things themselves,* Defin.

275 III. *A true proposition may be denied, or things may be denied to be what they are, by deeds, as well as by express words or another proposition.* It is certain there is a meaning in many acts and gestures. Every body understands weeping, laughing, shrugs, frowns, etc.; these are a sort of universal language. Applications are many times made, and a kind of dialogue maintained only by casts of the eye and motions of the adjacent muscles. And we read of feet, that *speak*;[1] of a philosopher, who *answered* an argument by only getting up and walking; and of one, who pretended to *express* the same sentence as many ways by gesticulation, as even Cicero himself could by all his *copia* of words and eloquence. But these instances do not come up to my meaning. There are many acts of *other* kinds, such as constitute the character of a man's conduct in life, which have *in nature*, and would be taken by any indifferent judge *to have a signification*, and *to imply some proposition*, as plainly to be understood as if it was declared in words: and therefore if what such acts declare to be, is not, they must *contradict truth*, as much as any false proposition or assertion can.

276 If a body of soldiers, seeing another body approach, should fire upon them, would not this action declare that they were enemies; and if they were *not* enemies, would not this military language declare what was *false*? No, perhaps it may be said; this can only be called a mistake, like that which happened to the Athenians in the attack of Epipolae, or to the Carthaginians in their last encampment against Agathocles in Africa. Suppose then, instead of this firing, some officer to have *said* they were enemies, when indeed they were friends: would not that sentence affirming them to be enemies be false, notwithstanding he who spoke it was mistaken? The truth or falsehood of this affirmation doth not depend upon the affirmer's knowledge or ignorance: because there is a *certain* sense affixed to the

[1 Wollaston's footnote here quotes a Hebrew phrase from the Book of Proverbs.]

words, which must either agree or disagree to that, concerning which the affirmation is made. The thing is the very same still, if into the place of *words* be substituted *actions*. The salute here was in *nature* the salute of an enemy, but should have been the salute of a friend: therefore it implied a falsity. Any *spectator* would have understood this action as I do; for a declaration, that the other were enemies. Now what is to be understood, has a meaning: and what has a meaning, may be either *true* or *false*: which is as much as can be said of any verbal sentence.

★   ★   ★   ★

A pertinacious objector may perhaps still say, it is the business of soldiers to defend themselves and their country from enemies, and to annoy them as opportunity permits; and self-preservation requires all men not only barely to defend themselves against aggressors, but many times also to prosecute such, and only such, as are wicked and dangerous: therefore it is *natural* to conclude, that they are enemies against whom we see soldiers defending themselves, and those men wicked and dangerous, whom we see prosecuted with zeal and ardour. Not that those acts of defending and prosecuting *speak* or signify so much: but conjectures are raised upon the *common sense*, which mankind has of such proceedings. *Ans.* If it be *natural* to conclude any thing from them, do they not *naturally* convey the notice of something to be concluded? And what is conveying the *notice* of any thing but *notifying* or signifying that thing? And then again, if this signification is *natural* and founded in the *common* principles and sense of mankind, is not this more than to have a meaning which results only from the use of some *particular* place or country, as that of language doth?

If *A* should enter into a compact with *B*, by which he *promises* and **277** engages never to do some certain thing, and after this he does that thing: in this case it must be granted, that his act *interferes* with his promise, and is *contrary* to it. Now it cannot interfere with his promise, but it must also interfere with the truth of that *proposition*, which says there was such a promise made, or that there is such a compact subsisting. If this proposition be true, *A made such a certain agreement with B*, it would be denied by this, *A never made any agreement with B*. Why? Because the truth of this latter is *inconsistent* with the agreement asserted in the former. The formality of the denial, or that, which makes it to be a denial, is this *inconsistence*. If then the behaviour of *A* be *inconsistent* with the agreement mentioned in the former proposition, that proposition is as much denied by *A*'s *behaviour*, as it can be by the latter, or any other *proposition*. Or thus, if one proposition imports or contains that which is *contrary* to what is contained in another, it is said to *contradict* this other, and denies the existence of what is contained in it. Just so if one act imports that which is *contrary* to the import of another, it *contradicts* this other, and *denies its existence*. In a word, if *A* by his actions denies the engagements, to which he hath subjected himself, his actions deny them; just as we say, Ptolemy by his writings denies the motion of the earth, or his writings deny it.

278 When the question was asked, *Whose sheep are these?* the answer was, *Aegon's: for he committed them to my care*[a] (he uses and disposes of them as his). By this act Damoetas understood them to be *his*; and if they had *not* been his, but Alphondas's or Meliboeus's, Aegon, by an *act* very intelligible to Damoetas, had expressed what was not true. What is said here is the stronger, because he, who has the *use* and *disposal* of any thing, has *all* he can have of it; and *vice versa* he who has the *all* (or property) of any thing, must have all the *use* and *disposal* of it. So that a man cannot more fully proclaim any thing to be *his*, than by *using* it, etc. But of this something more hereafter.

*   *   *   *

When a man lives, as if he had the estate which he has not, or was in other regards (all fairly cast up) what he is not, what judgement is to be passed upon him? Doth not his whole conduct breathe untruth? May we not say (if the propriety of language permits), that he *lives a lie*?

279 In common speech we say some actions are *insignificant*, which would not be sense, if there were not some that are *significant*, that have a tendency and meaning. And this is as much as can be said of articulate sounds, that they are either *significant* or *insignificant*.

It may not be improper by the way to observe, that the *significancy* here attributed to men's acts, proceeds not always from nature, but sometimes from custom and agreement among people, as that of words and sounds mostly doth. Acts of the latter kind may in different times and places have different, or even contrary

[a] Virgil and Theocritus.

significations. The generality of Christians, when they pray, take off their hats: the Jews, when they pray or say any of their *berakoth*,[1] put them on. The same thing which among Christians denotes reverence, imports irreverence among the Jews. The reason is, because covering the head with a hat (if it has no influence upon one's health) is in itself an *indifferent* thing, and people by usage or consent may *make* it interpretable either way. Such acts seem to be adopted into their language, and may be reckoned part of it. But acts of the former kind, such as I chiefly here intend, have an *unalterable* signification, and can by no agreement or force ever be made to express the contrary to it. Aegon's treating the flock, and disposing of it as if it was his, can by no torture be brought to signify, that it was not his. From whence it appears, that *facts* express more strongly, even than *words* themselves; or to contradict any proposition by facts is a fuller and more effectual contradiction, than can possibly be made by words only. *Words* are but *arbitrary signs* of our ideas, or indications of our thoughts (that word, which in one language denotes *poverty*, in another denotes *riches*): but *facts* may be taken as the effects of them, or rather as the *thoughts themselves produced into act*; as the very conceptions of the mind brought forth and grown to maturity; and therefore as the most natural and express representations of them. And, beside this, they bear certain *respects* to things, which are not arbitrary, but as determinate and immutable as any *ratios* are in mathematics. For the facts and the things they respect are just what they are, as much as any two given quantities are; and therefore the respects interceding between those must be as *fixed*, as the ratio is which one of these bears to the other: that is, they must remain the same, and always speak the same language, till things cease to be what they are.

I lay this down then as a fundamental maxim, *that whoever acts as if things were so, or not so, doth by his acts declare, that they are so, or not so*; as plainly as he could by words, and with more reality. And if the things are otherwise, his acts contradict *those propositions*, which assert them to be as they are.

IV. *No act* (whether word or deed) *of any being, to whom moral* **280** *good and evil are imputable, that interferes with any true proposition, or denies any thing to be as it is, can be right.* For,

[1 Benedictions.]

1. If that proposition, which is false, be wrong, that act which *implies* such a proposition, or is founded in it, cannot be right: because it is the very proposition itself in practice.

2. Those propositions, which are true, and express things as they are, express the *relation* between the subject and the attribute as it is: that is, this is either affirmed or denied of that according to the nature of *that relation*. And further, this relation (or, if you will, the nature of this relation) is determined and fixed by the natures of the things themselves. Therefore nothing can interfere with any proposition that is true, but it must likewise interfere with nature (the nature of the relation, and the natures of the things themselves too), and consequently be *unnatural*, or *wrong in nature*. So very much are those gentlemen mistaken, who by *following nature* mean only complying with their bodily inclinations, though in opposition to truth, or at least without any regard to it. Truth is but a conformity to nature: and to follow nature cannot be to combat truth.

281　　3. If there is a supreme being, upon whom the existence of the world depends; and nothing can be in it but what he either causes, or permits to be; then to own things *to be as they are* is to own what he causes, or at least permits, *to be thus caused or permitted*: and this is to take things as he gives them, to go into his constitution of the world, and to submit to his will, revealed in the books of nature. To do this therefore must be agreeable to *his will*. And if so, the contrary must be disagreeable to it; and, since (as we shall find in due time) there is a perfect rectitude in his will, certainly *wrong*.

I desire that I may not be misunderstood in respect to the actings of wicked men. I do not say, it is agreeable to the will of God, that what is *ill* done by them, should be *so* done; i.e. that they should use their liberty ill: but I say, when they *have* done this and committed some evil, it is agreeable to his will, that we should allow it to *have been* committed; or, it would be disagreeable to his will, that we should *deny* it to have been committed.

As the owning of things, in all our conduct, *to be as they are*, is direct obedience: so the contrary, not to own things *to be* or *to have been* that are or have been, or not *to be what they are*,[1] is direct rebellion against him, who is the Author of nature. For it is as much as to say, 'God indeed causes such a thing to be, or at least permits it, and it is; or the relation, that lies between this and that, is of such a nature,

[1 Cf. Clarke, §§ 230, 232.]

that one may be affirmed of the other, etc.; this is true: but yet *to me* it shall *not* be so: I will not endure it, or act as if it were so: the laws of nature are ill framed, nor will I *mind* them, or what follows from them: even existence shall be non-existence, when my pleasures require.' Such an impious declaration as this attends every *voluntary* infraction of truth.

4. Things cannot be denied to be what they are, in any instance **282** or manner whatsoever, without contradicting axioms and truths eternal. For such are these: *every thing is what it is*; *that which is done, cannot be undone*; and the like. And then if those truths be considered as having always subsisted in the divine mind, to which they have always been true, and which differs not from the Deity himself, to do this is to act not only in opposition to his *government* or *sovereignty*, but to his *nature* also: which, if he be perfect, and there be nothing in him but what is most right, must also upon this account be most *wrong*.

Pardon these inadequate ways of speaking of God. You will apprehend my meaning: which perhaps may be better represented thus. If there are such things as *axioms*, which are and always have been immutably true, and consequently have been always known to God to be so, the truth of them cannot be denied any way, either directly or indirectly, but the truth of the divine knowledge must be denied too.

5. Designedly to treat things as being what they are not is the **283** greatest possible absurdity. It is to put bitter for sweet, darkness for light, crooked for straight, etc.[1] It is to subvert all science, to renounce all sense of truth, and flatly to deny the existence of any thing. For nothing can be true, nothing does exist, if things are not what they are.

To talk to a post, or otherwise treat it as if it was a man, would surely be reckoned an absurdity, if not distraction. Why? because this is to treat it as being what it is not. And why should not the converse be reckoned as bad; that is, to treat a man as a post; as if he had no sense, and felt not injuries, which he doth feel; as if to him pain and sorrow were not pain; happiness not happiness? This is what the cruel and unjust often do.

Lastly, to deny things to be as they are is a transgression of the great *law of our nature*, the law of reason. For truth cannot be

[1 Cf. Clarke, § 232.]

opposed, but reason must be violated. But of this more in the proper place.

Much might be added here concerning the *amiable* nature, and great *force* of truth. If I may judge by what I feel within myself, the least truth cannot be contradicted without much reluctance: even to see other men disregard it does something more than displease; it is shocking.

284   V. *What has been said of acts inconsistent with truth, may also be said of many omissions, or neglects to act: that is, by these also true propositions may be denied to be true; and then those omissions, by which this is done, must be wrong for the same reasons with those assigned under the former proposition.*

Nothing can be asserted or denied by any act with regard to those things, to which it bears no relation: and here no truth can be affected. And when acts *do* bear such relations to other things, as to be declaratory of something concerning them, this commonly is visible; and it is not difficult to determine, whether truth suffers by them, or not. Some things cannot possibly be done, but truth must be directly and positively denied; and the thing will be clear. But the cases arising from omissions are not always so well determined, and plain: it is not always easy to know *when* or *how far* truth is violated by omitting. Here therefore more latitude must be allowed, and much must be left to every one's own judgement and ingenuity.

This may be said in general, that when any truth would be denied by acting, the omitting to act can deny no truth. For no truth can be contrary to truth. And there may be omissions in other cases, that are silent as to truth. But yet there are some neglects or refusals to act, which are manifestly inconsistent with it (or, with some true propositions).

285   We before supposed *A* to have engaged *not to do* some certain thing, etc. If now, on the other side, he should by some solemn promise, oath, or other act undertake *to do* some certain thing before such a time, and he *voluntarily* omits to do it, he would behave himself as if there had been no such promise or engagement; which is equal to denying there was any: and truth is as much contradicted in this as in the former instance.

Again, there are some ends, which the nature of things and truth require us to aim at, and at which therefore if we do not aim, *nature* and *truth* are denied. If a man does not desire to prevent evils, and to be happy, he denies both his *own* nature and the nature and definition of *happiness* to be what they are. And then further, willingly to neglect the *means*, leading to any such end, is the same as not to propose that end, and must fall under the same censure. As retreating from any end commonly attends the not advancing towards it, and that may be considered as an act, many omissions of this kind may be turned over to the other side, and brought under the foregoing proposition.

It must be confessed there is a difficulty as to the means, by which we are to consult our own preservation and happiness; to know what those are, and what they are with respect to us. For our abilities and opportunities are not equal: some labour under disadvantages invincible: and our ignorance of the true natures of things, of their operations and effects in such an irregular distempered world, and of those many incidents, that may happen either to further or break our measures, deprive us of certainty in these matters. But still we may judge as well as we can, and do what we can; and the neglect *to do this* will be an omission within the reach of the proposition.

There are omissions of other kinds, which will deserve to be **286** annumerated to these by being either total, or notorious, or upon the score of some other circumstance. It is certain I should not deny the *Phoenissae* of Euripides to be an excellent drama by not reading it: nor do I deny Chihil-menâr to be a rare piece of antiquity by not going to see it. But should I, having leisure, health, and proper opportunities, read nothing, nor make any inquiries in order to improve my *mind*, and attain such knowledge as may be *useful* to me, I should then deny my mind to be what it is, and that knowledge to be what it is. And if it doth not appear precisely, into what kind of studies this respect to truth will carry a man preferably to all others, how far it will oblige him to continue his pursuit after knowledge, and where the discontinuance begins to be no offence against truth, he must consult his own opportunities and genius, and judge for himself *as well as he can*. This is one of those cases which I said before were not so well determined.

If I give nothing to this or that poor body, to whom I am under no particular obligation, I do not by this deny them to be *poor*, any more than I should deny a man to have a squalid beard by not shaving him, to be nasty by not washing him, or to be lame by not taking him on my back.

Many things are here to be taken into consideration (according to the next proposition): perhaps I might entrench upon truth by *doing* this; and then I cannot by *not doing* it. But if I, being in circumstances to afford now and then something in charity to the poor, should yet *never* give them any thing at all, I should *then* certainly deny the condition of the poor to be what it is, and my own to be what it is: and thus truth would be injured. So, again,

If I should not say my prayers at such a certain hour, or in such a certain place and manner, this would not imply a denial of the existence of God, his providence, or my dependence upon him: nay, there may be reasons perhaps against that particular time, place, manner. But if I should *never* pray to him, or worship him at all, such a *total* omission would be equivalent to this assertion, *There is no God, who governs the world, to be adored*: which, if there is such a being, must be contrary to truth. Also *generally* and *notoriously* to neglect this duty (permit me to call it so), though not quite always, will *favour*, if not directly proclaim the same untruth. For certainly to worship God after this manner is only to worship him *accidentally*, which is to declare it a great accident that he is worshipped at all, and this approaches as near as it is possible to a *total* neglect. Beside, such a sparing and infrequent worship of the Deity betrays such an habitual disregard of him, as will render every religious act insignificant and null.

Should I, in the last place, find a man grievously hurt by some accident, fallen down, alone, and without present help like to perish; or see his house on fire, no body being near to help, or call out: in this extremity if I do not give him my assistance immediately, I do not do it at all: and by this refusing to do it according to my ability, I deny his case to be what it is; human nature to be what it is; and even those desires and expectations, which I am conscious to myself I should have under the like misfortune, to be what they are.

287 VI. *In order to judge rightly what any thing is, it must be considered not only what it is in itself or in one respect, but also what it may be in any other respect, which is capable of being denied by facts or practice: and the whole description of the thing ought to be taken in.*

If a man steals a horse, and rides away upon him, he may be said indeed by riding him to use him as a *horse*, but not as *the horse of another man*, who gave him no licence to do this. He does not therefore consider him as being what he is, unless he takes in the respect he bears to his true owner. But it is not necessary perhaps to consider what he is in respect to his colour, shape, or age: because the thief's riding away with him may neither affirm nor deny him to be of any particular colour, etc. I say therefore, that those, and *all* those properties, respects, and circumstances, which may be contradicted by practice, are to be taken into consideration. For otherwise the thing to be considered is but imperfectly surveyed; and the whole compass of it being not taken in, it is taken not as being what it is, but as what it is *in part* only, and in other respects perhaps as being what it is not.

If a rich man, being upon a journey, should be robbed and stripped, it would be a second robbery and injustice committed upon him to take from him part of his then character, and to consider him only as a rich man. His character completed is a *rich man robbed and abused*, and indeed at that time a *poor* man and distressed, though able to repay afterwards the assistance lent him.

Moreover a man in giving assistance of any kind to another **288** should consider what his own circumstances are, as well as what the other's are. If they do not permit him to give it, he does not by his forbearance deny the other to want it: but if he should give it, and by that deny his own or his family's circumstances to be what they are, he would actually contradict truth. And since (as I have observed already) all truths are consistent, nor can any thing be true any further than it is compatible with other things that are true; when both parties are placed in a *right* light, and the case *fairly* stated for a judgement, the latter may indeed be truly said to want assistance, but not the assistance of the former: any more than a man, who wants a guide, may be said to want a blind or a lame guide. By putting things thus may be *truly* known what the latter is with respect to the former.

The case becomes more difficult, when a man (A) is under some *promise* or *compact* to assist another (B), and at the same time bound to consult his own happiness, provide for his family, etc., and he cannot do these, if he does that, *effectually*. For what must A do? Here are not indeed opposite *truths*, but there are truths on opposite *sides*. I answer: though there cannot be two incompatible duties, or though two inconsistent acts cannot be both A's duty at the same time (for then his duty would be an impossibility); yet an obligation, which I will call *mixed*, may arise out of those *differing* considerations. A should assist B; but so, as not to neglect himself and family, etc., and so to take care of himself and family, as not to forget the other engagement, *as well and honestly as he can*. Here the *importance* of the truths on the one and the other side should be diligently compared: and there must in such cases be always some *exception* or *limitation* understood. It is not in man's power to promise *absolutely*. He can only promise as one, who may be *disabled* by the weight and incumbency of truths not then existing.

★   ★   ★   ★

289   VII. *When any act would be wrong, the forbearing that act must be right: likewise when the omission of any thing would be wrong, the doing of it* (i.e. not omitting it) *must be right.* Because *contrariorum contraria est ratio.*

VIII. *Moral good and evil are coincident with right and wrong.* For that cannot be good, which is wrong; nor that evil, which is right.

290   IX. *Every act* therefore *of such a being, as is before described, and all those omissions, which interfere with truth* (i.e. deny any proposition to be true, which is true; or suppose any thing not to be what it is, in any regard) *are morally evil, in some degree or other: the forbearing such acts, and the acting in opposition to such omissions are morally good: and when any thing may be either done, or not done, equally without the violation of truth, that thing is indifferent.*

I would have it to be noted well, that when I speak of acts inconsistent with truth, I mean any truth; any true proposition whatsoever, whether containing matter of speculation, or plain fact. I would have every thing taken to be what in fact and truth it is.

It may be of use also to remember, that I have added those words *in some degree or other*. For neither all evil, nor all good actions are equal. Those truths which they respect, though they are equally true, may comprise matters of very different importance; or more truths may be violated one way than another: and then the crimes committed by the violation of them may be equally (one as well as the other) said to be crimes, but not *equal crimes*. If A steals a *book* from B which was pleasing and useful to him, it is true A is guilty of a crime in not treating the book as being what it is, the book of B, who is the proprietor of it, and one whose happiness partly depends upon it: but still if A should deprive B of a *good estate*, of which he was the true owner, he would be guilty of a much greater crime. For if we suppose the book to be worth to him one pound, and the estate 10000*l.*, that truth, which is violated by depriving B of his book, is in effect violated 10000 times by robbing him of his estate. It is the same as to repeat the theft of one pound 10000 times over: and therefore if 10000 thefts (or crimes) are more, and all together greater than one, one equal to 10000 must be greater too: greater than that, which is but the 10000th part of it, sure. Then, though the convenience and innocent pleasure, that B found in the use of the book, was a degree of happiness: yet the happiness accruing to him from the estate, by which he was supplied not only with necessaries, but also with many other comforts and harmless enjoyments, vastly exceeded it. And therefore the truth violated in the former case was, *B had a property in that, which gave him such a degree of happiness*: that violated in the latter, *B had a property in that, which gave him a happiness vastly superior to the other*. The violation therefore in the latter case is upon this account a vastly greater violation than in the former. Lastly, the truths violated in the former case might end in B, those in the latter may perhaps be repeated in them of his family, who subsist also by the estate, and are to be provided for out of it. And these truths are very many in respect of every one of them, and all their descendants. Thus the degrees of evil or guilt are as the *importance* and *number* of truths violated. I shall only add, on the other side, that the value of good actions will rise at least in proportion to the degrees of evil in the omission of them: and that therefore they cannot be *equal*, any more than the opposite evil omissions.

But let us return to that, which is our main subject, the *distinction* **291** between moral good and evil. Some have been so wild as to deny there is any such thing: but from what has been said here, it is manifest, that there is as certainly moral *good* and *evil* as there is *true* and *false*; and that there is as natural and immutable a difference between those as between these, the difference at the bottom being indeed the same. Others acknowledge, that there is indeed moral good and evil; but they want some criterion, or mark, by the help of which they might know them asunder. And others there are, who pretend to have found that rule, by which our actions ought to be squared, and may be discriminated; or that ultimate end, to which they ought all to be referred: but what they have advanced is either false, or not sufficiently guarded, or not comprehensive enough, or not clear and firm, or (so far as it is just) reducible to my rule. For

They, who reckon nothing to be good but what they call *honestum*, may denominate actions according as that is, or is not the end of them: but then what is *honestum*? Something is still wanting to measure things by, and to separate the *honesta* from the *inhonesta*.

They who place all in *following nature*, if they mean by that phrase acting according to the natures of things (that is, treating things as being what they in nature are, or according to truth) say what is right. But this does not seem to be their meaning. And if it is only that a man must follow his own nature, since his nature is not purely rational, but there is a part of him, which he has in common with brutes, they appoint him a guide which I fear will mislead him, this being commonly more likely to prevail, than the rational part. At best this talk is loose.

292　　They who make *right reason* to be the law, by which our acts are to be judged, and according to their conformity to this or deflexion from it call them lawful or unlawful, good or bad, say something more particular and precise. And indeed it is true, that whatever will bear to be tried by right reason, is right; and that which is condemned by it, wrong. And moreover, if by right reason is meant that, which is found by the right use of our rational faculties, this is the same with truth: and what is said by them, will be comprehended in what I have said. But the manner in which they have delivered themselves, is not yet explicit *enough*. It leaves room for so many *disputes* and *opposite right-reasons*, that nothing can be settled, while every one pretends that *his* reason is right. And beside, what I have said, extends further: for we are not only to respect those truths, which we discover by reasoning, but even such *matters of fact*, as are fairly discovered to us by our senses. We ought to regard things as being what they are, which way soever we come to the knowledge of them.

They, who contenting themselves with superficial and transient views deduce the difference between good and evil from the *common sense* of mankind, and certain *principles* that are born with us, put the matter upon a very infirm foot. For it is much to be suspected there are no such *innate* maxims as they pretend, but that the impressions of education are mistaken for them: and beside that, the sentiments of mankind are not so *uniform* and *constant*, as that we may safely trust such an important distinction upon them.

They, who own nothing to be good but *pleasure*, or what they 293 call *jucundum*, nothing evil but *pain*, and distinguish things by their tendencies to this or that, do not agree in what this pleasure is to be placed, or by what methods and actings the most of it may be obtained. These are left to be questions still. As men have different tastes, different degrees of sense and philosophy, the same thing cannot be pleasant to *all*: and if particular actions are to be proved by this test, the morality of them will be very uncertain; the same act may be of one nature to one man and of another to another. Beside, unless there be some strong *limitation* added as a fence for virtue, men will be apt to sink into gross voluptuousness, as in fact the generality of Epicurus's herd have done (notwithstanding all his talk of temperance, virtue, tranquillity of mind, etc.); and the bridle will be usurped by those appetites, which it is a principal part of all religion, *natural* as well as any other, to curb and restrain. So these men say what is intelligible indeed: but what they say is false. For not all pleasures, but only such pleasure as is *true*, or happiness (of which afterwards), may be reckoned among the *fines* or *ultima bonorum*.

★   ★   ★   ★

Whether any of those other *foundations*, upon which morality has been built, will hold better than these mentioned, I much question. But if the *formal ratio* of moral good and evil be made to consist in a conformity of men's acts to the *truth of the case* or the contrary, as I have here explained it, the distinction seems to be settled in a manner undeniable, intelligible, practicable. For as what is meant by *a true proposition* and *matter of fact* is perfectly understood by every body; so will it be easy for any one, so far as he knows any such propositions and facts, to compare not only *words*, but also *actions* with them. A very little skill and attention will serve to interpret even these, and discover whether they *speak truth*, or not.

X. *If there be moral good and evil, distinguished as before, there is* 294 *religion; and such as may most properly be styled natural.* By *religion* I mean nothing else but an obligation to do (under which word I comprehend acts both of body and mind. I say, *to do*) what ought not to be omitted, and to *forbear* what ought not to be done. So that there must be religion, if there are things, of which some ought not to be done, some not to be omitted. But that there are such, appears from what has been said concerning moral good and evil: because that, which to omit would be evil, and which therefore being done would be good or well done, ought certainly by the terms *to be done*; and so that, which being done would be evil, and implies such absurdities and rebellion against the supreme being, as are mentioned under proposition the IVth, ought most undoubtedly *not to be done*. And then since there is *religion*, which follows from the distinction between moral good and evil; since this distinction is founded in the respect, which men's acts bear to truth; and since no proposition can be true, which expresses things otherwise than as they are in nature: since things are so, there must be religion, which is founded in nature, and may upon that account be most properly and truly called the *religion of nature* or *natural religion*; the great *law* of which religion, the law of nature, or rather (as we shall afterwards find reason to call it) of the Author of nature is,

XI. *That every intelligent, active, and free being should so behave himself, as by no act to contradict truth*; or, *that he should treat every thing as being what it is.*

★   ★   ★   ★

SECTION II—OF HAPPINESS

295   That, which demands to be next considered, is *happiness*; as being in itself most considerable; as abetting the cause of truth; and as being indeed so nearly allied to it, that they cannot well be parted. We cannot pay the respects due to one, unless we regard the other. Happiness must not be denied to be what it is: and it is by the practice of truth that we aim at happiness, which is true.

★   ★   ★   ★

I. *Pleasure is a consciousness of something agreeable, pain of the contrary*: and vice versa *the consciousness of any thing agreeable is pleasure, of the contrary pain.*

★   ★   ★   ★

II. *Pain considered in itself is a real evil, pleasure a real good.* I take this as a *postulatum*, that will without difficulty be granted. Therefore,

III. *By the general idea of good and evil the one* [pleasure] *is in itself desirable, the other* [pain] *to be avoided.* What is here said, respects mere pleasure and pain, abstracted from all circumstances, consequences, etc. But because there are some of these generally adhering to them, and such as enter so deep into their nature, that unless these be taken in, the full and true character of the other cannot be had, nor can it therefore be known what *happiness* is, I must proceed to some other propositions relating to this subject.

IV. *Pleasure compared with pain may either be equal, or more, or less:* **296** *also pleasures may be compared with other pleasures, and pains with pains.* Because all the moments of the pleasure must bear some respect or be in some ratio to all the moments of pain: as also all the degrees of one to all the degrees of the other: and so must those of one pleasure, or one pain, be to those of another. And if the degrees of intenseness be multiplied by the moments of duration, there must still be some ratio of the one product to the other.

★   ★   ★   ★

V. *When pleasures and pains are equal, they mutually destroy each other: when the one exceeds, the excess gives the true quantity of pleasure or pain.* For nine degrees of pleasure, less by nine degrees of pain, are equal to nothing: but nine degrees of one, less by three degrees of the other, give six of the former *net* and *true*.

VI. *As therefore there may be true pleasure and pain: so there may be* **297** *some pleasures, which compared with what attends or follows them, not only may vanish into nothing, but may even degenerate into pain, and ought to be reckoned as pains; and* vice versa *some pains, that may be annumerated to pleasures.* For the *true quantity of pleasure* differs not from that *quantity of true pleasure*; or it is so much of that kind of pleasure, which is *true* (clear of all discounts and future payments): nor can the *true quantity of pain* not be the same with that *quantity of true* or mere *pain*. Then, the man who enjoys three degrees of such pleasure as will bring upon him nine degrees of pain, when three degrees of pain are set off to balance and sink the three of pleasure, can have remaining to him only six degrees of pain: and into these therefore is his pleasure finally resolved. And so the three degrees of pain, which any one endures to obtain nine of pleasure, end in six of the latter. By the same manner of computing, some pleasures will be found to be the loss of pleasure, compared with greater: and some pains the alleviation of pain; because by undergoing them greater are evaded. Thus the natures of pleasures and pains are varied, and sometimes transmuted: which ought never to be forgot.

Nor this moreover. As in the sense of most men, I believe, a *little* pain will weigh against a *great deal* of pleasure: so perhaps there may be some pains, which exceed all pleasures; that is, such pains as no man would choose to suffer for any pleasure whatever, or at least any that we know of in this world. So that it is possible the difference, or excess of pain, may rise so high as to become immense: and then the pleasure to be set against that pain will be but a point, or cipher; a quantity of no value.

298 VII. *Happiness differs not from the true quantity of pleasure, unhappiness of pain.* Or, *any being may be said to be so far happy, as his pleasures are true,* etc. That cannot be the happiness of any being, which is bad for him: nor can happiness be disagreeable. It must be something therefore, that is both *agreeable* and *good* for the possessor. Now present pleasure is for the present indeed agreeable; but if it be not true, and he who enjoys it must pay more for it than it is worth, it cannot be for his good, or good for him. This therefore cannot be his *happiness.* Nor, again, can that pleasure be reckoned happiness, for which one pays the full price in pain: because these are quantities, which mutually destroy each other. But yet since happiness is something, which, by the general idea of it, must be desirable, and therefore agreeable, it must be some kind of pleasure: and this, from what has been said, can only be such pleasure as is true. That only can be both agreeable and good for him. And thus every one's happiness will be as his true quantity of pleasure.

*　　*　　*　　*

VIII. *That being may be said to be ultimately happy, in some degree or other, the sum total of whose pleasures exceeds the sum of all his pains:* or, *ultimate happiness is the sum of happiness, or true pleasure, at the foot of the account.* And so on the other side, *that being may be said to be ultimately unhappy, the sum of all whose pains exceeds that of all his pleasures.*

IX. *To make itself happy is a duty, which every being, in proportion to* **299** *its capacity, owes to itself; and that, which every intelligent being may be supposed to aim at, in general.* For happiness is some quantity of true pleasure: and that pleasure, which I call true, may be considered by itself, and so will be justly desirable (according to prop. II, and III). On the contrary, unhappiness is certainly to be avoided: because being a quantity of mere pain, it may be considered by itself, as a real, mere evil, etc.; and because if I am obliged to pursue happiness, I am at the same time obliged to recede, as far as I can, from its contrary. All this is self-evident. And hence it follows, that,

X. *We cannot act with respect to either ourselves, or other men, as being* **300** *what we and they are, unless both are considered as beings susceptive of happiness and unhappiness, and naturally desirous of the one and averse to the other.* Other animals may be considered after the same manner in proportion to their several degrees of apprehension.

But that the nature of happiness, and the road to it, which is so very apt to be mistaken, may be better understood; and true pleasures more certainly distinguished from false; the following propositions must still be added.

XI. *As the true and ultimate happiness of no being can be produced by* **301** *any thing, that interferes with truth, and denies the natures of things: so neither can the practice of truth make any being ultimately unhappy.* For that, which contradicts nature and truth, opposes the will of the Author of nature (whose existence, etc. I shall prove afterwards); and to suppose, that an inferior being may in opposition to his will *break through* the constitution of things, and by so doing make himself happy, is to suppose that being more potent than the Author of nature, and consequently more potent than the author of the nature and power of that very being himself, which is absurd. And as to the other part of the proposition, it is also absurd to think, that, by the constitution of nature and will of its author, any being should be finally miserable only for conforming himself to truth, and owning things and the relations lying between them to be what they are. It is much the same as to say, God has made it natural to contradict nature; or unnatural, and therefore punishable, to act according to nature and reality. If such a blunder (excuse the boldness of the word) could be, it must come either through a defect of *power* in him to cause a better and more equitable scheme, or from some *delight*, which he finds in the misery of his dependants. The former cannot be ascribed to the first cause, who is the fountain of power: nor the latter to him, who gives so many proofs of his goodness and beneficence.

★   ★   ★   ★

302 XIV. To conclude this section, *the way to happiness and the practice of truth incur the one into the other*. For no being can be styled happy, that is not ultimately so: because if all his pains exceed all his pleasures, he is so far from being happy, that he is a being unhappy, or miserable, in proportion to that excess. Now by prop. XI. nothing can produce the ultimate happiness of any being, which interferes with truth: and therefore that, which doth produce it, must be something that is consistent and *coincident* with it.

Two things then (but such as are met together, and embrace each other), which are to be religiously regarded in all our conduct, are *truth* (of which in the preceding sect.) and *happiness* (that is, such pleasures, as accompany, or follow the practice of truth, or are not inconsistent with it: of which I have been treating in this). And as that religion, which arises from the distinction between moral good and evil, was called *natural*, because grounded upon truth and the natures of things: so perhaps may that too, which proposes happiness for its end, in as much as it proceeds upon that difference, which there is between true pleasure and pain, which are physical (or *natural*) good and evil. And since both these unite so amicably, and are at last the same, here is *one* religion which may be called natural upon *two* accounts.

★   ★   ★   ★

FRANCIS HUTCHESON

1694–1746

I. *AN INQUIRY CONCERNING THE ORIGINAL OF OUR IDEAS OF VIRTUE OR MORAL GOOD*

[Treatise II of a volume entitled *An Inquiry into the Original of our Ideas of Beauty and Virtue*, first printed, 1725. Reprinted here from the revised fourth edition, 1738, with misprints corrected, spelling modified, reduction of italics and initial capital letters, and some footnotes omitted]

II. *AN ESSAY ON THE NATURE AND CONDUCT OF THE PASSIONS AND AFFECTIONS. WITH ILLUSTRATIONS ON THE MORAL SENSE*

[First printed, 1728. Reprinted here from the third edition, 1742, with spelling modified and reduction of italics and initial capital letters. The two parts of this work are referred to by Hutcheson as Treatises III and IV]

FRANCIS HUTCHESON

An Inquiry concerning Moral Good and Evil

INTRODUCTION

The word MORAL GOODNESS, in this treatise, denotes our idea of **303** some quality apprehended in actions, which procures approbation, attended with desire of the agent's happiness. MORAL EVIL denotes our idea of a contrary quality, which excites condemnation or dislike. Approbation and condemnation are probably simple ideas, which cannot be farther explained. We must be contented with these imperfect descriptions, until we discover whether we really have such ideas, and what general foundation there is in nature for this difference of actions, as morally good or evil.

These descriptions seem to contain an universally acknowledged difference of *moral good* and *evil*, from *natural*. All men who speak of moral good, acknowledge that it procures approbation and good-will toward those we apprehend possessed of it; whereas natural good does not. In this matter men must consult their own breasts. How differently are they affected toward these they suppose possessed of honesty, faith, generosity, kindness; and those who are possessed of the natural goods, such as houses, lands, gardens, vineyards, health, strength, sagacity? We shall find that we necessarily love and approve the possessors of the former; but the possession of the latter procures no approbation or good-will at all toward the possessor, but often contrary affections of envy and hatred. In the same manner, whatever quality we apprehend to be morally evil, raises our dislike toward the person in whom we observe it, such as treachery, cruelty, ingratitude; whereas we heartily love, esteem, and pity many who are exposed to natural evils, such as pain, poverty, hunger, sickness, death.

Now the first question on this subject is, 'Whence arise these **304** different ideas of actions?'

Because we shall afterwards frequently use the words *interest, advantage, natural good,* it is necessary here to fix their ideas. The pleasure in our sensible perceptions of any kind, gives us our first idea of *natural good* or *happiness*; and then all objects which are apt to excite this pleasure are called *immediately good.* Those objects which may procure others immediately pleasant, are called *advantageous*: and we pursue both kinds from a view of *interest,* or from *self-love.*

Our *sense* of pleasure is antecedent to advantage or interest, and is the foundation of it. We do not perceive pleasure in objects, because it is our interest to do so; but objects or actions are advantageous, and are pursued or undertaken from interest, because we receive pleasure from them. Our perception of pleasure is necessary, and nothing is advantageous or naturally good to us, but what is apt to raise pleasure mediately, or immediately. Such objects as we know either from experience of sense, or reason, to be immediately or mediately advantageous, or apt to minister pleasure, we are said to pursue from *self-interest,* when our intention is only to enjoy this pleasure, which they have the power of exciting. Thus meats, drink, harmony, fine prospects, painting, statues, are perceived by our senses to be immediately good; and our reason shows riches and power to be mediately so, that is, apt to furnish us with objects of immediate pleasure: and both kinds of these natural goods are pursued from interest, or self-love.

305   Now the greatest part of our latter moralists establish it as undeniable, 'that all moral qualities have necessarily some relation to the *law* of a *superior,* of sufficient power to make us happy or miserable;' and since all laws operate only by sanctions of rewards, or punishments, which determine us to obedience by motives of *self-interest,* they suppose, 'that it is thus that laws do constitute some actions *mediately good,* or *advantageous,* and others the same way *disadvantageous.*' They say indeed, 'that a benevolent legislator constitutes no actions advantageous to the agent by law, but such as in their own nature tend to the natural good of the *whole,* or, at least, are not inconsistent with it; and that therefore we approve the virtue of others, because it has some small tendency to our happiness, either from its own nature, or from this general consideration, that obedience to a benevolent legislator is in general advantageous to the whole, and to us in particular; and that for the contrary reasons alone, we disapprove the vice of others, that is, the prohibited action,

as tending to our particular detriment in some degree.' And then they maintain, 'that we are determined to obedience to laws, or deterred from disobedience, merely by motives of self-interest, to obtain either the natural good arising from the commanded action, or the rewards promised by the sanction; or to avoid the natural evil consequences of disobedience, or at least the penalties of the law.'

Some other moralists suppose 'an *immediate natural good* in the actions called virtuous; that is, that we are determined to perceive some *beauty* in the actions of others, and to love the agent, even without reflecting upon any advantage which can any way redound to us from the action; that we have also a secret sense of pleasure arising from reflection upon such of our own actions as we call virtuous, even when we expect no other advantage from them.' But they allege at the same time, 'that we are excited to perform these actions, even as we pursue, or purchase pictures, statues, landscapes, from *self-interest*, to obtain this pleasure which arises from reflection upon the action, or some other future advantage.' The design of the following sections is to inquire into this matter; and perhaps the reasons to be offered may prove,

I. 'That some actions have to men an *immediate goodness*; or, that **306** by a *superior sense*, which I call a *moral one*, we *approve* the actions of others, and perceive them to be their perfection and dignity, and are determined to love the agent; a like perception we have in reflecting on such actions of our own, without any view of natural advantage from them.'

II. It may perhaps also appear, 'that the *affection, desire,* or *intention,* which gains approbation to the actions flowing from it, is not an intention to obtain even this pleasant self-approbation; much less the future rewards from sanctions of laws, or any other natural good, which may be the consequence of the virtuous action; but an entirely different principle of action from self-love, or desire of private good.'

SECT. I—OF THE MORAL SENSE BY WHICH WE PERCEIVE VIRTUE AND VICE, AND APPROVE OR DISAPPROVE THEM IN OTHERS

I. That the perceptions of *moral good* and *evil*, are perfectly differ- **307** ent from those of *natural good* or *advantage*, every one must convince himself, by reflecting upon the different manner in which he finds himself affected when these objects occur to him. Had we no sense of good distinct from the advantage or interest arising from the external senses, and the perceptions of beauty and harmony; the sensations and affections toward a fruitful field, or commodious habitation, would be much the same with what we have toward a generous friend, or any noble character; for both are or may be advantageous to us: and we should no more admire any action, or love any person in a distant country, or age, whose influence could not extend to us, than we love the mountains of Peru, while we are unconcerned in the Spanish trade. We should have the same sentiments and affections toward inanimate beings, which we have toward rational agents, which yet every one knows to be false. Upon comparison, we say, 'Why should we approve or love inanimate beings? They have no intention of good to us, or to any other person; their nature makes them fit for our uses, which they neither know nor study to serve. But it is not so with rational agents: they study the interest, and desire the happiness of other beings with whom they converse.'

We are all then conscious of the difference between that *approbation* or perception of *moral excellence*, which *benevolence* excites toward the person in whom we observe it, and that opinion of *natural goodness*, which only raises *desire* of possession toward the good object. Now 'what should make this difference, if all approbation, or sense of good be from prospect of advantage? Do not inanimate objects promote our advantage as well as benevolent persons, who do us offices of kindness and friendship? should we not then have the same endearing approbation of both? or only the same cold opinion of advantage in both?' The reason why it is not so, must be this, 'that we have a distinct perception of *beauty* or *excellence* in the kind affections of rational agents; whence we are determined to admire and love such characters and persons.'

Suppose we reap the same advantage from two men, one of whom serves us from an ultimate desire of our happiness, or good-will toward us; the other from views of self-interest, or by constraint: both are in this case equally beneficial or advantageous to us, and yet we shall have quite different sentiments of them. We must then certainly have other perceptions of moral actions, than those of advantage: and that power of receiving these perceptions may be called a MORAL SENSE, since the definition agrees to it, viz. a

determination of the mind, to receive any idea from the presence
of an object which occurs to us, independent on our will*.

This perhaps will be equally evident from our ideas of evil, done **308**
to us designedly by a rational agent. Our senses of natural good and
evil would make us receive, with equal serenity and composure, an
assault, a buffet, an affront from a neighbour, a cheat from a partner,
or trustee, as we would an equal damage from the fall of a beam, a
tile, or a tempest; and we should have the same affections and sentiments on both occasions. Villainy, treachery, cruelty, would be as
meekly resented as a blast, or mildew, or an overflowing stream.
But I fancy every one is very differently affected on these occasions,
though there may be equal natural evil in both. Nay, actions no way
detrimental may occasion the strongest anger and indignation, if
they evidence only impotent hatred or contempt. And, on the other
hand, the intervention of moral ideas may prevent our condemnation of the agent, or bad moral apprehension of that action, which
causes to us the greatest natural evil. Thus the opinion of justice in
any sentence, will prevent all ideas of moral evil in the execution, or
hatred toward the magistrate, who is the immediate cause of our
greatest sufferings.

II. In our sentiments of actions which affect ourselves, there is **309**
indeed a mixture of the ideas of natural and moral good, which
require some attention to separate them. But when we reflect upon
the actions which affect other persons only, we may observe the
moral ideas unmixed with those of natural good or evil. For let it be
here observed, that those senses by which we perceive pleasure in
natural objects, whence they are constituted advantageous, could
never raise in us any desire of *public good*, but only of what was good
to ourselves in particular. Nor could they ever make us approve an
action merely because of its promoting the happiness of others. And
yet, as soon as any action is represented to us as flowing from love,
humanity, gratitude, compassion, a study of the good of others, and
an ultimate desire of their happiness, although it were in the most
distant part of the world, or in some past age, we feel joy within us,
admire the lovely action, and praise its author. And on the contrary,
every action represented as flowing from ill-will, desire of the misery
of others without view to any prevalent good to the public, or ingratitude, raises abhorrence and aversion.

* See the Preface. [Cf. § 356, below.]

It is true indeed, that the actions we approve in others, are generally imagined to tend to the natural good of mankind, or of some parts of it. But whence this secret chain between each person and mankind? How is my interest connected with the most distant parts of it? And yet I must admire actions which show good-will toward them, and love the author. Whence this love, compassion, indignation and hatred toward even feigned characters, in the most distant ages, and nations, according as they appear kind, faithful, compassionate, or of the opposite dispositions, toward their imaginary contemporaries? If there is no moral sense, which makes benevolent actions appear beautiful; if all approbation be from the interest of the approver,

What's Hecuba to us, or we to Hecuba?★

310 III. Some refined explainers of self-love may tell us, 'that we approve or condemn characters, according as we apprehend we should have been supported, or injured by them, had we lived in their days.' But how obvious is the answer, if we only observe, that had we no sense of moral good in humanity, mercy, faithfulness, why should not self-love, and our sense of natural good engage us always to the victorious side, and make us admire and love the successful tyrant, or traitor? Why do not we love Sinon or Pyrrhus, in the Aeneid? for, had we been Greeks, these two would have been very advantageous characters. Why are we affected with the fortunes of Priamus, Polites, Choroebus or Aeneas? Would not the parsimony of a miser be as advantageous to his heir, as the generosity of a worthy man is to his friend? And cannot we as easily imagine ourselves heirs to misers, as the favourites of heroes? Why don't we then approve both alike? It is plain we have some secret sense which determines our approbation without regard to self-interest; otherwise we should always favour the fortunate side without regard to virtue, and suppose ourselves engaged with that party.

As Mr. Hobbes explains all the sensations of pity by our fear of the like evils, when by imagination we place ourselves in the case of the sufferers;[1] so others explain all approbation and condemnation of actions in distant ages or nations, by a like effort of imagination:

★ *Tragedy of Hamlet.*

[1 Cf. Hobbes, §§ 10, 32.]

we place ourselves in the case of others, and then discern an imaginary private advantage or disadvantage in these actions. But as his account of pity will never explain how the sensation increases, according to the apprehended worth of the sufferer, or according to the affection we formerly had to him;[1] since the sufferings of any stranger may suggest the same possibility of our suffering the like: so this explication will never account for our high approbation of brave unsuccessful attempts, which we see prove detrimental both to the agent, and to those for whose service they were intended; here there is no private advantage to be imagined. Nor will it account for our abhorrence of such injuries as we are incapable of suffering. Sure, when a man abhors the attempt of the young Tarquin, he does not imagine that he has changed his sex like Caeneus. And then, when one corrects his imagination, by remembering his own situation, and circumstances, we find the moral approbation and condemnation continues as lively as it was before, though the imagination of advantage is gone.

★   ★   ★   ★

VI. A late witty author★ says, 'that the leaders of mankind do not **311** really admire such actions as those of Regulus, or Decius, but only observe, that men of such dispositions are very useful for the defence of any State; and therefore by panegyrics, and statues, they encourage such tempers in others, as the most tractable and useful.' Here first let us consider, if a traitor, who would sell his own country to us, may not often be as advantageous to us, as an hero who defends us: and yet we can love the treason, and hate the traitor. We can at the same time praise a gallant enemy, who is very pernicious to us. Is there nothing in all this but an opinion of advantage?

Again, upon this scheme what could a statue or panegyric effect? —Men love praise.[2]—They will do the actions which they observe to be praised.—Praise, with men who have no other idea of good but self-interest, is the opinion which a nation or party have of a man as useful to them.—Regulus, or Cato, or Decius, had no advantage by the actions which profited their country, and therefore they themselves could not admire them, however the persons who reaped the

---

★ See the Fable of the Bees, page 34, 36. 3d. edition [cf. Mandeville, § 267].

[1 But see Hobbes, § 10.]   [2 Cf. Mandeville, § 264.]

advantage might praise such actions.—Regulus or Cato could not possibly praise or love another hero for a virtuous action; for this would not gain them the advantage of honour; and their own actions they must have looked upon as the hard terms on which honour was to be purchased, without any thing amiable in them, which they could contemplate or reflect upon with pleasure. Nay, what should excite a Cato or a Decius to desire praise, if it is only the cold opinion of others that they were useful to the State, without any perception of excellence in such conduct?—Now how unlike is this to what the least observation would teach a man concerning such characters?

But says* he, 'These wondrous cunning governors made men believe, by their statues and panegyrics, that there was public spirit, and that this was in itself excellent; and hence men are led to admire it in others, and to imitate it in themselves, forgetting the pursuit of their own advantage.' So easy a matter it seems to him, to quit judging of others by what we feel in ourselves!—for a person who is wholly selfish, to imagine others to be public-spirited!—for one who has no ideas of good but in his own advantage, to be led by the persuasions of others, into a conception of goodness in what is avowedly detrimental to himself, and profitable to others; nay, so entirely, as not to approve the action thoroughly, but so far as he was conscious that it proceeded from a disinterested study of the good of others!—Yet this it seems statues and panegyrics can accomplish!

Nil intra est oleam, nil extra est in nuce duri!†

*   *   *   *

312   VII. If what is said makes it appear, that we have some other amiable idea of actions than that of advantageous to ourselves, we may conclude, 'that this perception of moral good is not derived from custom, education, example, or study.' These give us no new ideas: they might make us see private advantage in actions whose usefulness did not at first appear; or give us opinions of some tendency of actions to our detriment, by some nice deductions of reason, or by a rash prejudice, when upon the first view of the action

---

* See the same author in the same place [cf. Mandeville, §§ 265–6].
† Hor. Ep. 1. Lib. 2. v. 31.

we should have observed no such thing: but they never could have made us apprehend actions as amiable or odious, without any consideration of our own advantage.

VIII. It remains then, 'that as the Author of nature has determined **313** us to receive, by our external senses, pleasant or disagreeable ideas of objects, according as they are useful or hurtful to our bodies; and to receive from uniform objects the pleasures of beauty and harmony, to excite us to the pursuit of knowledge, and to reward us for it; or to be an argument to us of his goodness, as the uniformity itself proves his existence, whether we had a sense of beauty in uniformity or not; in the same manner he has given us a MORAL SENSE, to direct our actions, and to give us still nobler pleasures: so that while we are only intending the good of others, we undesignedly promote our own greatest private good.'

We are not to imagine, that this moral sense, more than the other senses, supposes any innate ideas, knowledge, or practical proposition: we mean by it only a determination of our minds to receive the simple ideas of approbation or condemnation, from actions observed, antecedent to any opinions of advantage or loss to redound to ourselves from them; even as we are pleased with a regular form, or an harmonious composition, without having any knowledge of mathematics, or seeing any advantage in that form or composition, different from the immediate pleasure.

That we may discern more distinctly the difference between moral **314** perceptions and others, let us consider, when we taste a pleasant fruit, we are conscious of pleasure; when another tastes it, we only conclude or form an opinion that he enjoys pleasure; and, abstracting from some previous good-will or anger, his enjoying this pleasure is to us a matter wholly indifferent, raising no new sentiment or affection. But when we are under the influence of a virtuous temper, and thereby engaged in virtuous actions, we are not always conscious of any pleasure, nor are we only pursuing private pleasures, as will appear hereafter: it is only by *reflex acts*[1] upon our temper and conduct, that virtue never fails to give pleasure. When also we judge the temper of another to be virtuous, we do not necessarily imagine him *then* to enjoy pleasure, though we know *reflection* will give it to him: and farther, our apprehension of his virtuous temper raises sentiments of approbation, esteem or admiration, and the affection

[1 Cf. Shaftesbury, §§ 200, 204.]

of good-will toward him. The quality approved by our moral sense is conceived to reside in the person approved, and to be a perfection and dignity in him: approbation of another's virtue is not conceived as making the approver happy, or virtuous, or worthy, though it is attended with some small pleasure. Virtue is then called *amiable* or *lovely*, from its raising good-will or love in spectators toward the agent; and not from the agent's perceiving the virtuous temper to be advantageous to him, or desiring to obtain it under that view. A virtuous temper is called *good* or *beatific*, not that it is always attended with pleasure in the agent; much less that some small pleasure attends the contemplation of it in the approver: but from this, that every spectator is persuaded that the reflex acts of the virtuous agent upon his own temper will give him the highest pleasures. The admired quality is conceived as the perfection of the agent, and such a one as is distinct from the pleasure either in the agent or the approver; though it is a sure source of pleasure to the agent. The perception of the approver, though attended with pleasure, plainly represents something quite distinct from this pleasure; even as the perception of external forms is attended with pleasure, and yet represents something distinct from this pleasure. This may prevent many cavils upon this subject.

SECT. II—CONCERNING THE IMMEDIATE MOTIVE TO VIRTUOUS ACTIONS

315 The *motives* of human actions, or their immediate causes, would be best understood after considering the passions and affections; but here we shall only consider the springs of the actions which we call *virtuous*, as far as it is necessary to settle the general foundation of the moral sense.

I. Every action, which we apprehend as either *morally good* or *evil*, is always supposed to flow from some *affection* toward sensitive natures; and whatever we call *virtue* or *vice*, is either some such *affection*, or some *action* consequent upon it. Or it may perhaps be enough to make an action or omission, appear vicious, if it argues the want of such affection toward rational agents, as we expect in characters counted morally good. All the actions counted *religious* in any country, are supposed, by those who count them so, to flow from some affections toward the Deity; and whatever we call *social virtue*, we still suppose to flow from affections toward our fellow-creatures: for in this all seem to agree, 'that external motions, when accompanied with no affections toward God or man, or evidencing no want of the *expected* affections toward either, can have no moral good or evil in them.'

Ask, for instance, the most abstemious hermit, if *temperance* of itself would be morally good, supposing it showed no obedience toward the Deity, made us no fitter for devotion, or the service of mankind, or the search after truth, than *luxury*; and he will easily grant, that it would be no moral good, though still it might be naturally good or advantageous to health: and mere *courage*, or contempt of danger, if we conceive it to have no regard to the defence of the innocent, or repairing of wrongs or self-interest, would only entitle its possessor to bedlam. When such sort of courage is sometimes admired, it is upon some secret apprehension of a good intention in the use of it, or as a natural ability capable of an useful application. *Prudence*, if it was only employed in promoting private interest, is never imagined to be a *virtue*: and *justice*, or observing a strict equality, if it has no regard to the good of mankind, the preservation of rights, and securing peace, is a quality properer for its ordinary *gestamen*, a beam and scales, than for a rational agent. So that these four qualities, commonly called *cardinal virtues*, obtain that name, because they are dispositions universally necessary to promote *public good*, and denote *affections* toward *rational agents*; otherwise there would appear no *virtue* in them.

II. Now, if it can be made appear, that none of these affections **316** which we approve as virtuous, are either self-love, or desire of private interest; since all virtue is either some such affections, or actions consequent upon them; it must necessarily follow, 'that virtue springs from some other affection than self-love, or desire of private advantage. And where self-interest excites to the same action, the approbation is given only to the disinterested principle.'

The affections which are of most importance in morals, are commonly included under the names LOVE and HATRED. Now in discoursing of *love*, we need not be cautioned not to include that love between the sexes, which, when no other affections accompany it, is only desire of pleasure, and is never counted a virtue. *Love* toward rational agents, is subdivided into love of *complacence* or *esteem*, and love of *benevolence*: and *hatred* is subdivided into hatred of *displicence* or *contempt*, and hatred of *malice*. *Complacence* denotes approbation of any person by our moral sense; and is rather a perception than an affection; though the affection of good-will is ordinarily subsequent to it. *Benevolence* is the desire of the happiness of another. Their opposites are called *dislike* and *malice*. Concerning each of these separately we shall consider, 'whether they can be influenced by motives of self-interest.'

317   *Complacence*, esteem, or good-liking, at first view appears to be disinterested, and so *displicence* or dislike; and are entirely excited by some moral qualities, good or evil, apprehended to be in the objects; which qualities the very frame of our nature determines us to approve or disapprove, according to the moral sense *above explained. Propose to a man all the rewards in the world, or threaten all the punishments, to engage him to esteem and complacence toward a person entirely unknown, or if known, apprehended to be cruel, treacherous, ungrateful; you may procure external obsequiousness, or good offices, or dissimulation; but real esteem no price can purchase. And the same is obvious as to contempt, which no motive of advantage can prevent. On the contrary, represent a character as generous, kind, faithful, humane, though in the most distant parts of the world, and we cannot avoid esteem and complacence. A bribe may possibly make us attempt to ruin such a man, or some strong motive of advantage may excite us to oppose his interest; but it can never make us disapprove him, while we retain the same opinion of his temper and intentions. Nay, when we consult our own hearts, we shall find, that we can scarce ever persuade ourselves to attempt any mischief against such persons, from any motive of advantage; nor execute it without the strongest reluctance and remorse, until we have blinded ourselves into a false opinion about his temper.

318   III. As to the love of *benevolence*, the very name excludes self-interest. We never call that man *benevolent*, who is in fact useful to others, but at the same time only intends his own interest, without any ultimate desire of the good of others. If there be any real good-will or kindness at all, it must be disinterested; for the most useful action imaginable loses all appearance of benevolence, as soon as we discern that it only flowed from self-love, or interest. Thus, never were any human actions more advantageous, than the inventions of fire, and iron; but if these were casual, or if the inventor only

---

* See Sect. i.

intended his own interest in them, there is nothing which can be called *benevolent* in them. Wherever then benevolence is supposed, there it is imagined disinterested, and designed for the good of others. To raise benevolence, no more is required than calmly to consider any sensitive nature not pernicious to others. Gratitude arises from benefits conferred from good-will on ourselves, or those we love; complacence is a perception of the moral sense. Gratitude includes some complacence, and complacence still raises a stronger good-will than that we have toward indifferent characters, where there is no opposition of interests.

But it must be here observed, that as all men have *self-love*, as well **319** as *benevolence*, these two principles may jointly excite a man to the same action; and then they are to be considered as two forces impelling the same body to motion; sometimes they conspire, sometimes are indifferent to each other, and sometimes are in some degree opposite. Thus, if a man have such strong benevolence, as would have produced an action without any views of self-interest; that such a man has also in view private advantage, along with public good, as the effect of his action, does no way diminish the benevolence of the action. When he would not have produced so much public good, had it not been for prospect of self-interest, then the effect of self-love is to be deducted, and his benevolence is proportioned to the remainder of good, which pure benevolence would have produced. When a man's benevolence is hurtful to himself, then self-love is opposite to benevolence, and the benevolence is proportioned to the sum of the good produced, added to the resistance of self-love surmounted by it. In most cases it is impossible for men to know how far their fellows are influenced by the one or other of these principles; but yet the general truth is sufficiently certain, that this is the way in which the benevolence of actions is to be computed.

IV. There are two ways in which some may deduce benevolence **320** from self-love, the one supposing that 'we voluntarily bring this affection upon ourselves, whenever we have an opinion that it will be for our interest to have this affection, either as it may be immediately pleasant, or may afford pleasant reflection afterwards by our moral sense, or as it may tend to procure some external reward from God or man.' The other scheme alleges no such power in us of raising desire or affection of any kind by our choice or volition; but 'supposes our minds determined by the frame of their nature to desire whatever is apprehended as the means of any private happiness; and that the observation of the happiness of other persons, in many cases is made the necessary occasion of pleasure to the observer, as their misery is the occasion of his uneasiness: and in consequence of this connection, as soon as we have observed it, we begin to desire the happiness of others as the means of obtaining this happiness to ourselves, which we expect from the contemplation of others in a happy state. They allege it to be impossible to desire either the happiness of another, or any event whatsoever, without conceiving it as the means of some happiness or pleasure to ourselves; but own at the same time, that desire is not raised in us directly by any volition, but arises necessarily upon our apprehending any object or event to be conducive to our happiness.'

321　　That the former scheme is not just, may appear from this general consideration, that 'neither benevolence nor any other affection or desire can be directly raised by volition.' If they could, then we could be bribed into any affection whatsoever toward any object, even the most improper: we might raise jealousy, fear, anger, love, toward any sort of persons indifferently by an hire, even as we engage men to external actions, or to the dissimulation of passions; but this every person will by his own reflection find to be impossible. The prospect of any advantage to arise to us from having any affection, may indeed turn our attention to those qualities in the object, which are naturally constituted the necessary causes or occasions of the advantageous affection; and if we find such qualities in the object, the affection will certainly arise. Thus indirectly the prospect of advantage may tend to raise any affection; but if these qualities be not found or apprehended in the object, no volition of ours, nor desire, will ever raise any affection in us.

322　　But more particularly, that desire of the good of others, which we approve as virtuous, cannot be alleged to be voluntarily raised from prospect of any pleasure accompanying the affection itself: for it is plain that our benevolence is not always accompanied with pleasure; nay, it is often attended with pain, when the object is in distress. Desire in general is rather uneasy than pleasant. It is true, indeed, all the passions and affections justify themselves; while they continue, (as Malebranche expresses it) we generally approve our being thus affected on this occasion, as an innocent disposition, or a just one, and condemn a person who would be otherwise affected on the like occasion. So the sorrowful, the angry, the jealous, the compassionate, approve their several passions on the apprehended occasion; but we should not therefore conclude, that sorrow, anger, jealousy or pity are pleasant, or chosen for their concomitant pleasure. The case is plainly thus: the frame of our nature on the occasions which move these passions, determines us to be thus affected, and to approve our affection at least as innocent. Uneasiness generally attends our desires of any kind; and this sensation tends to fix our attention, and to continue the desire. But the desire does not terminate upon the removal of the pain accompanying the desire, but upon some other event: the concomitant pain is what we seldom reflect upon, unless when it is very violent. Nor does any desire or affection terminate upon the pleasure which may accompany the affection; much less is it raised by an act of our will, with a view to obtain this pleasure.

The same reflection will show, that we do not by an act of our will raise in ourselves that benevolence which we approve as virtuous, with a view to obtain future pleasures of self-approbation by our moral sense. Could we raise affections in this manner, we should be engaged to any affection by the prospect of an interest equivalent to this of self-approbation, such as wealth or sensual pleasure, which with many tempers are more powerful; and yet we universally own, that *that* disposition to do good offices to others, which is raised by these motives, is not virtuous: how can we then imagine, that the virtuous benevolence is brought upon us by a motive equally *selfish*?

*   *   *   *

V. The other scheme is more plausible: that benevolence is not 323 raised by any volition upon prospect of advantage; but that we desire the happiness of others, as conceiving it necessary to procure some pleasant sensations which we expect to feel upon seeing others happy; and that for like reason we have aversion to their misery. This connection between the happiness of others and our pleasure, say they, is chiefly felt among friends, parents and children, and eminently virtuous characters. But this benevolence flows as directly from self-love as any other desire.

To show that this scheme is not true in fact, let us consider, that if in our benevolence we only desired the happiness of others as the means of this pleasure to ourselves, whence is it that no man approves the desire of the happiness of others as a means of procuring wealth or sensual pleasure to ourselves? If a person had wagered concerning the future happiness of a man of such veracity, that he would sincerely confess whether he were happy or not; would this wagerer's desire of the happiness of another, in order to win the wager, be approved as virtuous? If not, wherein does this desire differ from the former? except that in one case there is one pleasant sensation expected, and in the other case other sensations: for by increasing or diminishing the sum wagered, the interest in this case may be made either greater or less than that in the other.

324   Reflecting on our own minds again will best discover the truth. Many have never thought upon this connection: nor do we ordinarily intend the obtaining of any such pleasure when we do generous offices. We all often feel delight upon seeing others happy, but during our pursuit of their happiness we have no intention of obtaining this delight. We often feel the pain of compassion; but were our sole ultimate intention or desire the freeing ourselves from this pain, would the Deity offer to us either wholly to blot out all memory of the person in distress, to take away this connection, so that we should be easy during the misery of our friend on the one hand, or on the other would relieve him from his misery, we should be as ready to choose the former way as the latter; since either of them would free us from our pain, which upon this scheme is the sole end proposed by the compassionate person.—Don't we find in ourselves that our desire does not terminate upon the removal of our own pain? Were this our sole intention, we would run away, shut our eyes, or divert our thoughts from the miserable object, as the readiest way of removing our pain: this we seldom do, nay, we crowd about such objects, and voluntarily expose ourselves to this pain, unless calm reflection upon our inability to relieve the miserable, countermand our inclination, or some selfish affection, as fear of danger, overpower it.

To make this yet clearer, suppose that the Deity should declare to a good man that he should be suddenly annihilated, but at the instant of his exit it should be left to his choice whether his friend, his children, or his country should be made happy or miserable for the future, when he himself could have no sense of either pleasure or pain from their state. Pray would he be any more indifferent about their state now, that he neither hoped or feared any thing to himself from it, than he was in any prior period of his life? Nay, is it not a pretty common opinion among us, that after our decease we know nothing of what befalls those who survive us? How comes it then that we do not lose, at the approach of death, all concern for our families, friends, or country? Can there be any instance given of our desiring any thing only as the means of private good, as violently when we know that we shall not enjoy this good many minutes, as if we expected the possession of this good for many years? Is this the way we compute the value of annuities?

How the disinterested desire of the good of others should seem 325 inconceivable, it is hard to account: perhaps it is owing to the attempts of some great men to give definitions of simple ideas.— *Desire*, say they, is uneasiness, or uneasy sensation upon the absence of any good.[1]—Whereas desire is as distinct from uneasiness, as volition is from sensation. Don't they themselves often speak of our desiring to remove uneasiness? Desire then is different from uneasiness, however a sense of uneasiness accompanies it, as extension does the idea of colour, which yet is a very distinct idea. Now wherein lies the impossibility of desiring the happiness of another without conceiving it as the means of obtaining any thing farther, even as we desire our own happiness without farther view? If any allege, that we desire our own happiness as the means of removing the uneasiness we feel in the absence of happiness, then at least the desire of removing our own uneasiness is an ultimate desire: and why may we not have other ultimate desires?

'But can any being be concerned about the absence of an event which gives it no uneasiness?' Perhaps superior natures desire without uneasy sensation. But what if we cannot? We may be uneasy while a desired event is in suspense, and yet not desire this event only as the means of removing this uneasiness: nay, if we did not desire the event without view to this uneasiness, we should never have brought the uneasiness upon ourselves by desiring it. So likewise we may feel delight upon the existence of a desired event, when yet we did not desire the event only as the means of obtaining this delight; even as we often receive delight from events which we had an aversion to.

★   ★   ★   ★

[1 Cf. Locke, §§ 161, 174.]

326 VII. As to malice, *human nature* seems scarce capable of malicious disinterested hatred,[1] or a sedate ultimate desire of the misery of others, when we imagine them no way pernicious to us, or opposite to our interest: and for that hatred which makes us oppose those whose interests are opposite to ours, it is only the effect of self-love, and not of disinterested malice. A sudden passion may give us wrong representations of our fellow-creatures, and for a little time represent them as absolutely evil; and during this imagination perhaps we may give some evidences of disinterested malice: but as soon as we reflect upon human nature, and form just conceptions, this unnatural passion is allayed, and only self-love remains, which may make us, from self-interest, oppose our adversaries.

$$\star \qquad \star \qquad \star \qquad \star$$

327 X. Having removed these false springs of virtuous actions, let us next establish the true one, viz. some determination of our nature to study the good of others; or some instinct, antecedent to all reason from interest, which influences us to the love of others; even as the moral sense, *above explained, determines us to approve the actions which flow from this love in ourselves or others. This *disinterested affection*, may appear strange to men impressed with notions of *self-love*, as the *sole* spring of action, from the pulpit, the schools, the systems, and conversations regulated by them: but let us consider it in its strongest and simplest kinds; and when we see the possibility of it in these instances, we may easily discover its universal extent.

An honest *farmer* will tell you, that he studies the preservation and happiness of his children, and loves them without any design of good to himself. But say some of our *philosophers*, 'The happiness of their children gives parents pleasure, and their misery gives them pain; and therefore to obtain the former, and avoid the latter, they study, from *self-love*, the good of their children.' Suppose several merchants joined in partnership of their whole effects; one of them is employed abroad in managing the stock of the company; his prosperity occasions gain to all, and his losses give them pain for their share in the loss: is this then the same kind of affection with that of parents to

* See Sect. i.

[1 Cf. Hobbes on cruelty, § 32.]

their children? Is there the same tender, personal regard? I fancy no parent will say so. In this case of merchants there is a plain conjunction of interest; but whence the conjunction of interest between the parent and child? Do the child's sensations give pleasure or pain to the parent? Is the parent hungry, thirsty, sick, when his children are so? No; but *his* naturally implanted desire of their good, and aversion to their misery, makes him be affected with joy or sorrow from their pleasures or pains. This desire then is antecedent to the conjunction of interest, and the cause of it, not the effect: it then must be *disinterested*. 'No; say others, children are parts of ourselves, and in loving them we but love ourselves in them.' A very good answer! Let us carry it as far as it will go. How are they parts of ourselves? Not as a leg or an arm: we are not conscious of their sensations. 'But their bodies were formed from parts of ours.' So is a fly, or a maggot, which may breed in any discharged blood or humour: very dear insects surely! there must be something else then which makes children parts of ourselves; and what is this but that affection, which NATURE determines us to have toward them? This love makes them parts of ourselves, and therefore does not flow from their being so before. This is indeed a good metaphor; and wherever we find a determination among several rational agents to mutual love, let each individual be looked upon as a part of a great whole, or system,[1] and concern himself in the public good of it.

Another author thinks all this easily deducible from self-love. 'Children are not only made of our bodies, but resemble us in body and mind; they are rational agents as we are, and we only love our own likeness in them.' Very good all this. What is *likeness*? It is not *individual sameness*; it is only being included under one general or specifical idea. Thus there is likeness between us and other men's children, thus any man is like any other, in some respects; a man is also like an angel, and in some respects like a brute. Is there then a natural disposition in every man to *love his like*, to wish well not only to his individual self, but to any other like rational or sensitive being? and this disposition strongest, where there is the greatest likeness in the more noble qualities? If all this is called by the name *self-love*; be it so: the highest mystic needs no more disinterested principle; it is not confined to the individual, but terminates ultimately on the good of others, and may extend to all; since each one

[1 Cf. Shaftesbury, §§ 197, 206.]

some way resembles each other. Nothing can be better than this self-love, nothing more generous.

★ ★ ★ ★

SECT. III—THE SENSE OF VIRTUE, AND THE VARIOUS OPINIONS ABOUT IT, REDUCIBLE TO ONE GENERAL FOUNDATION. THE MANNER OF COMPUTING THE MORALITY OF ACTIONS

328 I. If we examine all the actions which are counted *amiable* anywhere, and inquire into the grounds upon which they are *approved*, we shall find that in the opinion of the person who approves them, they generally appear as BENEVOLENT, or flowing from *good-will to others*, and a study of their happiness, whether the approver be one of the persons beloved, or profited, or not; so that all those kind affections which incline us to make others happy, and all actions supposed to flow from such affections, appear *morally good*, if, while they are benevolent towards some persons, they be not pernicious to others. Nor shall we find any thing amiable in any action whatsoever, where there is no benevolence imagined; nor in any disposition, or capacity, which is not supposed applicable to, and designed for, benevolent purposes. Nay, as was before observed★, the actions which in fact are exceedingly useful, shall appear void of moral beauty, if we know they proceeded from no kind intentions towards others; and yet an unsuccessful attempt of kindness, or of promoting public good, shall appear as amiable as the most successful, if it flowed from as strong benevolence.

★ ★ ★ ★

329 IV. Contraries may illustrate each other; let us therefore observe the general foundation of our sense of *moral evil* more particularly. *Disinterested malice*, or ultimate desire of the misery of others, is the highest pitch of what we count vicious; and every action appears evil, which is imagined to flow from any degree of this affection. Perhaps a violent passion may hurry men into it for a few moments, and our rash angry sentiments of our enemies, may represent them as having such odious dispositions; but it is very probable, from the reasons offered above†, that there is no such degree of wickedness in

★ See Sect. ii. Art. 3. par. 1 [§ 318]. Art. 9. par. 2.
† See Sect. ii. Art. 7 [§ 326].

human nature, as, in cold blood, to desire the misery of others, when it is conceived no way useful to our interests.

★   ★   ★   ★

The ordinary spring of vice then among men, must be a mistaken self-love, made so violent, as to overcome benevolence; or such strong appetites, or passions either selfish, or toward some narrow systems, as overcome our regard to public good; or affections arising from false, and rashly-formed opinions of mankind; which we run into through the weakness of our benevolence. When men, who had good opinions of each other, happen to have contrary interests, they are apt to have their good opinions of each other abated, by imagining a designed opposition from malice; without this, they can scarcely hate one another. Thus two candidates for the same office wish each other dead, because that is an ordinary way by which men make room for each other; but if there remains any reflection on each other's virtue, as there sometimes may in benevolent tempers, then their opposition may be without hatred; and if another better post, where there is no competition, were bestowed on one of them, the other shall rejoice at it.

V. Actions which flow solely from self-love, and yet evidence no **330** want of benevolence, having no hurtful effects upon others, seem of a middle nature, neither virtuous nor vicious, and neither raise the love or hatred of the observer. Our reason can indeed discover certain bounds, within which we may not only act from self-love, consistently with the good of the whole; but every mortal's acting thus within these bounds for his own good, is absolutely necessary for the good of the whole; and the want of such self-love would be universally pernicious. Hence, he who pursues his own private good, with an intention also to concur with that constitution which tends to the good of the whole; and much more he who promotes his own good, with a direct view of making himself more capable of serving God, or doing good to mankind; acts not only innocently, but also honourably, and virtuously: for in both these cases, benevolence concurs with self-love to excite him to the action. And thus *a neglect* of our own good may be morally evil, and argue a want of benevolence toward the whole. But when self-love breaks over the bounds above-mentioned, and leads us into actions detrimental to others, and to the whole; or makes us insensible of the generous kind affections; then it appears vicious, and is disapproved. So also, when upon any small injuries, or sudden resentment, or any weak superstitious suggestions, our benevolence becomes so faint, as to let us entertain odious conceptions of men, or any part of them, without just ground, as if they were wholly evil, or malicious, or as if they were a worse sort of beings than they really are; these conceptions must lead us into malevolent affections, or at least weaken our good ones, and make us really vicious.

331   VI. *Benevolence* is a word fit enough in general, to denote the internal spring of virtue, as Bishop Cumberland always uses it.[1] But to understand this more distinctly, it is highly necessary to observe, that under this name are included very different dispositions of the soul. Sometimes it denotes a calm, extensive affection, or good-will toward all beings capable of happiness or misery: sometimes, 2. a calm deliberate affection of the soul toward the happiness of certain smaller systems or individuals; such as patriotism, or love of a country, friendship, parental affection, as it is in persons of wisdom and self-government: or, 3. the several kind particular passions of love, pity, sympathy, congratulation. This distinction between the calm motions of the will, affections, dispositions, or instincts of the soul, and the several turbulent passions, is elsewhere more fully considered*.

Now though all these different dispositions come under the general character of benevolent, yet as they are in nature different, so they have very different degrees of moral beauty. The first sort is above all amiable and excellent: it is perhaps the sole moral perfection of some superior natures; and the more this prevails and rules in any human mind, the more amiable the person appears, even when it not only checks and limits our lower appetites, but when it controls our kind particular passions, or counteracts them. The second sort of benevolence is more amiable than the third, when it is sufficiently strong to influence our conduct: and the third sort, though of a lesser moral dignity, is also beautiful, when it is no way opposite to these more noble principles. And when it is opposite, though it does not justify such actions as are really detrimental to greater systems, yet it is a strong extenuating circumstance, and

---

* See Treatise III. Sect. ii. Art. 2 [§ 357]. and Treatise IV. Sect. vi. Art. 4.

[1 Cf. Cumberland, § 107.]

much alleviates the moral deformity. We are all sensible of this, when any person from friendship, parental affection, or pity, has done something hurtful to larger societies.

VII. Here we must also observe, that every moral agent justly **332** considers himself as a *part* of this rational system, which may be useful to the *whole*; so that he may be, in part, an object of his own universal *benevolence*. Nay farther, as was hinted above, he may see, that the preservation of the system requires every one to be innocently solicitous about himself. Hence he may conclude, that an action which brings *greater evil* to the agent, than *good* to others, however it may evidence the strength of some particular kind attachment, or of a virtuous disposition in the agent, yet it must be founded upon a mistaken opinion of its tendency to public good; so that a man who reasoned justly, and considered the whole, would not be led into it, by the calm extensive benevolence, how strong soever it were; nor would he recommend it to the practice of others; however he might acknowledge, that the detriment arising to the agent from a kind action, did evidence a strong virtuous disposition. Nay farther, if any good was proposed to the pursuit of an agent, and he had a competitor in every respect *only equal* to himself; the *highest* universal *benevolence* possible would not lead a wise man to prefer another to himself, were there no ties of gratitude, or some other external circumstance, to move him to yield to his competitor. A man surely of the *strongest benevolence*, may justly treat himself as he would do a third person, who was a competitor of *equal merit* with the other; and as his preferring one to another, in such a case, would argue no weakness of *benevolence*; so no more would he evidence it by preferring himself to a man of only *equal abilities*.

*   *   *   *

VIII. . . . In comparing the moral qualities of actions, in order to **333** regulate our election among various actions proposed, or to find which of them has the greatest moral excellency, we are led by our moral sense of virtue to judge thus; that in *equal degrees* of happiness, expected to proceed from the action, the virtue is in proportion to the *number* of persons to whom the happiness shall extend (and here the *dignity*,[1] or *moral importance* of persons, may compensate numbers); and in equal *numbers*, the virtue is as the *quantity* of the

[1 See §§ 306, 314, 331, 335.]

happiness, or natural good; or that the virtue is in a compound ratio of the *quantity* of good, and *number* of enjoyers. In the same manner, the moral evil, or vice, is as the degree of misery, and number of sufferers; so that *that action* is *best*, which procures the *greatest happiness* for the *greatest numbers*;[1] and *that worst*, which, in *like manner*, occasions *misery*.

Again, when the consequences of actions are of a mixed nature, partly advantageous, and partly pernicious; *that action* is *good*, whose *good* effects preponderate the *evil* by being useful to many, and pernicious to few; and *that evil*, which is otherwise. Here also the moral importance of characters, or dignity of persons may compensate numbers; as may also the degrees of happiness or misery: for to procure an inconsiderable good to many, but an immense evil to few, may be evil; and an immense good to few, may preponderate a small evil to many.

334   But the consequences which affect the morality of actions, are not only the direct and natural effects of the actions themselves; but also all those events which otherwise would not have happened. For many actions which have no immediate or natural evil effects, nay, which actually produce good effects, may be evil; if a man foresees, that the evil consequences, which will probably flow from the folly of others, upon his doing of such actions, are so great as to overbalance all the good produced by those actions, or all the evils which would flow from the omission of them: and in such cases the *probability* is to be computed on both sides. Thus, if an action of mine will probably, through the mistake or corruption of others, be made a precedent in unlike cases, to very evil actions; or when my action, though good in itself, will probably provoke men to very evil actions, upon some mistaken notion of their right; any of these considerations foreseen by me, may make such an action of mine evil, whenever the evils which will probably be occasioned by the action, are greater than the evils occasioned by the omission.

And this is the reason, that many laws prohibit actions in general, even when some particular instances of those actions would be very useful; because an universal allowance of them, considering the mistakes men would probably fall into, would be more pernicious than an universal prohibition; nor could there be any more special

---

[1 Hutcheson appears to be the first to use this explicit formulation of the Utilitarian doctrine.]

boundaries fixed between the right and wrong cases. In such cases, it is the duty of persons to comply with the generally useful constitution; or if in some very important instances, the violation of the law would be of less evil consequence, than obedience to it, they must patiently resolve to undergo those penalties, which the State has, for valuable ends to the whole, appointed: and this disobedience will have nothing criminal in it.

*   *   *   *

XI. To find a *universal rule* to compute the morality of any actions, **335** with all their circumstances, when we judge of the actions done by ourselves, or by others, we must observe the following propositions or axioms.

1. The moral *importance*[1] of any agent, or the quantity of public good he produces, is in a compound proportion of his *benevolence* and *abilities*. For it is plain that his good offices depend upon these two jointly. In like manner, the quantity of private good which any agent obtains for himself, is in a like compound proportion of his *selfish principles*, and his *abilities*. We speak here only of the external goods of this world, which one pursues from some selfish principles. For as to internal goods of the mind, these are most effectually obtained by the exercise of other affections than those called *selfish*, even those which carry the agent beyond himself toward the good of others.

2. In comparing the virtues of different agents, when the abilities are equal, the *moments* of public good are proportioned to the goodness of the temper, or the *benevolence*; and when the *tempers* are equal, the quantities of good are as the *abilities*.

3. The virtue then or goodness of temper is directly as the *moment of good*, when other circumstances are equal, and inversely as the abilities. That is to say, where the abilities are greatest, there is less virtue evidenced in any given moment of good produced.

4. But as the natural consequences of our actions are various, some **336** good to ourselves, and evil to the public; and others evil to ourselves, and good to the public; or either useful both to ourselves and others, or pernicious to both; the entire spring of good actions is not always *benevolence alone*; or of evil, *malice alone* (nay, sedate malice is rarely found); but in most actions we must look upon *self-love* as another

[1 Cf. § 333.]

force, sometimes conspiring with benevolence, and assisting it, when we are excited by views of private interest, as well as public good; and sometimes opposing benevolence, when the good action is any way difficult or painful in the performance, or detrimental in its consequences to the agent.

These selfish motives shall be *hereafter more fully explained; here we may in general denote them by the word *interest*: which when it concurs with benevolence, in any action capable of increase or diminution, must produce a greater quantity of good, than benevolence alone in the same abilities; and therefore when the moment of good, in an action partly intended for the good of the agent, is but equal to the moment of good in the action of another agent, influenced only by benevolence, the former is less virtuous; and in this case the interest must be deducted to find the true effect of the benevolence or virtue. In the same manner, when interest is opposite to benevolence, and yet is surmounted by it; this interest must be added to the moment, to increase the virtue of the action, or the strength of the benevolence. By *interest*, in this last case, is understood all the advantage which the agent might have obtained by omitting the action, which is a negative motive to it; and this, when subtracted, becomes positive.

But here we must observe, that no advantage, not *intended*, although casually, or naturally, redounding to us from the action, does at all affect its morality to make it less amiable: nor does any difficulty or evil unforeseen, or not resolved upon, make a kind action more virtuous; since in such cases self-love neither assists nor opposes benevolence. Nay, self-interest then only diminishes the benevolence, when without this view of interest the action would not have been undertaken, or so much good would not have been produced by the agent; and it extenuates the vice of an evil action, only when without this interest the action would not have been done by the agent, or so much evil have been produced by him.

The fourth axiom only explains the external marks by which men must judge, who do not see into each other's hearts; for it may really happen in many cases, that men may have benevolence sufficient to surmount any difficulty, and yet they may meet with none at all: and in that case, it is certain there is as much virtue in the agent, though he does not give such proof of it to his fellow-creatures,

* *Vide* Sect. v.

as if he had surmounted difficulties in his kind actions. And this too must be the case with the Deity, to whom nothing is difficult.

Since then, in judging of the goodness of temper in any agent, the **337** abilities must come into computation, as is above-mentioned, and none can act beyond their natural abilities; that must be the perfection of virtue, where the moment of good produced equals the ability, or when the being acts to the utmost of his power for the public good; and hence the perfection of virtue, in this case, is as unity. And this may show us the only foundation for the boasting of the Stoics, 'that a creature supposed innocent, by pursuing virtue with his utmost power, may in virtue equal the gods.' For in their case, if the ability be *infinite*, unless the good to be produced in the whole, be so too, the virtue is not *absolutely perfect*; and the quotient can never surmount unity.

XII. In the same manner we may compute the degree of depravity **338** of any temper, directly as the moment of evil effected, and inversely as the abilities. The springs of vicious actions however are seldom any real ultimate intention of mischief, and never ultimate deliberate malice; but only sudden anger, self-love, some selfish passion or appetite, some kind attachments to parties, or particular kind passions.

The motives of interest may sometimes strongly co-operate with a depraved temper, or may oppose it, in the same manner that they co-operate with or oppose a good temper. When they co-operate, they diminish the moral evil; when they oppose, they may argue the depravity of temper to be greater, which is able to surmount such motives of interest.

But we must observe, that not only *innocence* is expected from all **339** mortals, but they are presumed, from their *nature*, in some measure inclined to *public good**; so that a bare absence of this desire is enough to make an agent be reputed evil: nor is a direct intention of *public evil* necessary to make an action evil; it is enough that it flows from *self-love*, with a plain neglect of the good of others, or an insensibility of their misery, which we either *actually* foresee, or have a probable *presumption* of.

It is true indeed, that that public evil which I neither certainly foresee, nor have actual presumptions of, as the consequence of my action, does not make my *present action* criminal or odious; even although I might have foreseen this evil by a serious examination of

* See Treatise IV. Sect. 6.

my own actions; because such actions do not, at present, evidence either malice, or want of benevolence. But then it is also certain, that my *prior negligence*, in not examining the tendency of my actions, is a plain evidence of the want of that degree of good affections which is necessary to a virtuous character; and consequently the guilt properly lies in this neglect, rather than in an action which really flows from a good intention. *Human laws* however, which cannot examine the intentions, or secret knowledge of the agent, must judge in gross of the action itself; presupposing all that knowledge as actually attained, which we are obliged to attain.

In like manner, no good effect, which I did not actually foresee and intend, makes my action *morally good*; however *human laws* or *governors*, who cannot search into men's intentions, or know their secret designs, justly reward actions which tend to the public good, although the agent was engaged to those actions only by selfish views; and consequently had no virtuous disposition influencing him to them.

The difference in degree of guilt between *crimes of ignorance*, when the ignorance is vincible, and faulty, as to the natural tendency of the action; and *crimes of malice*, or direct evil intention; consists in this, that the former, by a *prior neglect*, argues a want of the due degree of *benevolence*, or *right affection*; the latter evidences direct *evil affections*, which are vastly more odious.

340   XIII. From the former reasonings we may form almost a demonstrative conclusion, 'that we have a *sense* of *goodness* and *moral beauty* in actions, distinct from *advantage*;' for had we no other foundation of approbation of actions, but the *advantage* which might arise to us from them, if they were done toward ourselves, we should make no account of the *abilities* of the agent, but would barely esteem them according to their *moment*. The abilities come in only to show the degree of *benevolence*, which supposes benevolence necessarily amiable. Who was ever the better pleased with a barren rocky farm, or an inconvenient house, by being told that the poor farm gave as great increase as it could; or that the house accommodated its possessor as well as it could? And yet in our sentiments of actions, whose *moment* is very inconsiderable, it shall wonderfully increase the *beauty* to allege, 'that it was all the poor agent could do for the public, or his friend.'

★   ★   ★   ★

SECT. V—A FARTHER CONFIRMATION, THAT WE HAVE PRACTICAL DISPOSITIONS TO VIRTUE IMPLANTED IN OUR NATURE; WITH A FARTHER EXPLICATION OF OUR BENEVOLENT INSTINCTS OF VARIOUS KINDS, WITH THE ADDITIONAL MOTIVES OF INTEREST, VIZ. HONOUR, SHAME AND PITY

I. We have already endeavoured to prove, 'that there is a *universal* **341** *determination* to *benevolence* in mankind, even toward the most distant parts of the species:' but we are not to imagine, that all benevolent affections are of one kind, or alike strong. There are nearer and stronger kinds of benevolence, when the objects stand in some nearer relations to ourselves, which have obtained distinct names; such as *natural affection, gratitude, esteem.*

One species of *natural affection*, viz. that in parents towards their children, has been considered already★; we shall only observe farther, that there is the same kind of affection among collateral relations, though in a weaker degree; which is universally observable, where no opposition of interest produces contrary actions, or counterbalances the power of this natural affection.

★   ★   ★   ★

II. But nothing will give us a juster idea of the wise order in which **342** human nature is formed for universal love, and mutual good offices, than considering that strong attraction of benevolence, which we call *gratitude.* Every one knows that beneficence toward ourselves makes a much deeper impression upon us, and raises gratitude, or a stronger love toward the benefactor, than equal beneficence toward a third person. Now because of the great numbers of mankind, their distant habitations, and the incapacity of any one to be remarkably useful to great multitudes; that our benevolence might not be quite distracted with a multiplicity of objects, whose equal virtues would equally recommend them to our regard; or become useless, by being equally extended to multitudes, whose interests we could not understand, nor be capable of promoting, having no intercourse of offices with them; NATURE has so well ordered it, that as our attention is more raised by those good offices which are done to ourselves or our friends, so they cause a stronger sense of approbation in us, and produce a stronger benevolence toward the authors of them.

★ See above, Sect. ii. Art. 10. par. 2, 3 [§ 327].

This we call *gratitude*. And thus a foundation is laid for joyful associations in all kinds of business, and virtuous friendships.

By this constitution also the benefactor is more encouraged in his beneficence, and better secured of an increase of happiness by grateful returns, than if his virtue were only to be honoured by the colder general sentiments of persons unconcerned, who could not know his necessities, nor how to be profitable to him; especially, when they would all be equally determined to love innumerable multitudes, whose equal virtues would have the same pretensions to their love.

343   The *universal benevolence* toward all men, we may compare to that principle of *gravitation*, which perhaps extends to all bodies in the universe; but increases as the distance is diminished, and is strongest when bodies come to touch each other. Now this increase, upon nearer approach, is as necessary as that there should be any attraction at all. For a general attraction, equal in all distances, would by the contrariety of such multitudes of equal forces, put an end to all regularity of motion, and perhaps stop it altogether. Beside this general attraction, the learned in these subjects show us a great many other attractions among several sorts of bodies, answering to some particular sorts of passions, from some special causes. And that attraction or force by which the parts of each body cohere, may represent the self-love of each individual.

These different sorts of love to persons according to their nearer approaches to ourselves by their benefits, is observable in the high degree of love, which heroes and lawgivers universally obtain in their own countries, above what they find abroad, even among those who are not insensible of their virtues; and in all the strong ties of friendship, acquaintance, neighbourhood, partnership; which are exceedingly necessary to the order and happiness of human society.

344   III. From considering that natural gratitude, and love toward our benefactors, which was already shown to be disinterested*; we are easily led to consider another determination of our minds, equally natural with the former, which is to desire and delight in the good opinion and love of others, even when we expect no other advantage from them, except what flows from this constitution, whereby HONOUR is made an *immediate good*. This desire of honour I would call AMBITION, had not custom joined some evil ideas to that word, making it denote such a violent desire of honour, and of power also,

---

* See above, Sect. ii. Art. 9.

as will make us stop at no base means to obtain them. On the other hand, we are by NATURE subjected to a grievous sensation of misery, from the unfavourable opinions of others concerning us, even when we dread no other evil from them. This we call SHAME; which in the same manner is constituted an *immediate evil*, as we said *honour* was an *immediate good*.

Now, were there no moral sense, or had we no other idea of actions but as advantageous or hurtful, I see no reason why we should be delighted with honour, or subjected to the uneasiness of shame; or how it could ever happen, that a man, who is secure from punishment for any action, should ever be uneasy at its being known to all the world. The world may have an opinion of him as pernicious to his neighbours; but what subjects his ease to this opinion of the world? Why, perhaps, he shall not be so much trusted henceforward in business, and so suffer loss. If this be the only reason of shame, and it has no immediate evil or pain in it, distinct from fear of loss, then, wherever we expose ourselves to loss, we should be ashamed, and endeavour to conceal the action: and yet it is quite otherwise.

A merchant, for instance, lest it should impair his credit, conceals a shipwreck, or a very bad market, which he has sent his goods to. But is this the same with the passion of SHAME? Has he that anguish, that dejection of mind, and self-condemnation, which one shall have whose *treachery* is detected? Nay, how will men sometimes glory in their losses, when in a cause imagined morally good, though they really weaken their credit in the merchant's sense; that is, the opinion of their wealth, or fitness for business? Was any man ever *ashamed* of impoverishing himself to serve his country, or his friend?

* * * *

VIII. Let us next consider another determination of our mind, **345** which strongly proves benevolence to be *natural* to us, and that is COMPASSION; by which we are disposed to study the interest of others, without any views of private advantage. This needs little illustration. Every mortal is made uneasy by any grievous misery he sees another involved in, unless the person be imagined morally evil: nay, it is almost impossible for us to be unmoved, even in that case. Advantage may make us do a cruel action, or may overcome pity; but it scarce ever extinguishes it. A sudden passion of hatred or anger may represent a person as absolutely evil, and so extinguish pity; but when the passion is over, it often returns. Another *disinterested* view may even in cold blood overcome pity; such as love to our country, or zeal for religion. Persecution is generally occasioned by love of virtue, and a desire of the eternal happiness of mankind, although our folly makes us choose absurd means to promote it; and is often accompanied with pity enough to make the persecutor uneasy, in what, for prepollent reasons, he chooses; unless his opinion leads him to look upon the heretic as absolutely and entirely evil.

★　　★　　★　　★

How independent this disposition to compassion is on custom, education, or instruction, will appear from the prevalence of it in women and children, who are less influenced by these. That children delight in some actions which are cruel and tormenting to animals which they have in their power, flows not from malice, or want of compassion, but from their ignorance of those signs of pain which many creatures make; together with a curiosity to see the various contortions of their bodies. For when they are more acquainted with these creatures, or come by any means to know their sufferings, their compassion often becomes too strong for their reason; as it generally does in beholding executions, where as soon as they observe the evidences of distress, or pain in the malefactor, they are apt to condemn this necessary method of self-defence in the State. Some have alleged, that 'however the sight of another's misery some way or other gives us pain, yet the very feeling of compassion is also attended with pleasure: this pleasure is superior to the pain of sympathy, and hence we desire to raise compassion in ourselves, and incline to indulge it.' Were this truly the case, the *continuation of the suffering* would be the natural desire of the compassionate, in order to continue this state, not of pure pleasure indeed, but of pleasure superior to all pains.

SECT. VII—A DEDUCTION OF SOME COMPLEX MORAL IDEAS;
VIZ. OF OBLIGATION, AND RIGHT, PERFECT, IMPERFECT,
AND EXTERNAL, ALIENABLE, AND UNALIENABLE, FROM
THIS MORAL SENSE

346　　I. To conclude this subject, we may, from what has been said, see the true original of moral ideas, viz. *this moral sense of excellence in every appearance, or evidence of benevolence.* It remains to be explained, how we acquire more particular ideas of virtue and vice, abstracting from any *law*, human, or divine.

If any one ask, can we have any sense of OBLIGATION, abstracting from the *laws* of a *superior*? we must answer according to the various senses of the word *obligation*. If by *obligation* we understand a determination, without regard to our own interest, to approve actions, and to perform them; which determination shall also make us displeased with ourselves, and uneasy upon having acted contrary to it: in this meaning of the word *obligation*, there is *naturally* an obligation upon all men to *benevolence*; and they are still under its influence, even when by false, or partial opinions of the natural tendency of their actions, this moral sense leads them to evil; unless by long inveterate habits it be exceedingly weakened; for it scarce seems possible wholly to extinguish it. Or, which is to the same purpose, this internal sense, and instinct of benevolence, will either influence our actions, or make us very uneasy and dissatisfied; and we shall be conscious, that we are in a base unhappy state, even without considering any *law* whatsoever, or any external advantages lost, or disadvantages impending from its sanctions. And farther, there are still such indications given us of what is in the whole beneficent, and what not, as may probably discover to us the true tendency of every action; and let us see, some time or other, the evil tendency of what upon a partial view appeared good: or if we have no friends so faithful as to admonish us, the persons injured will not fail to upbraid us. So that no mortal can secure to himself a perpetual serenity, satisfaction, and self-approbation, but by a serious inquiry into the tendency of his actions, and a perpetual study of universal good, according to the justest notions of it.

But if, by *obligation*, we understand a motive from self-interest, 347 sufficient to determine all those who duly consider it, and pursue their own advantage wisely, to a certain course of actions; we may have a sense of such an obligation, by reflecting on this *determination* of our *nature* to approve *virtue*, to be pleased and happy when we reflect upon our having done virtuous actions, and to be uneasy when we are conscious of having acted otherwise; and also by considering how much superior we esteem the happiness of virtue to any other enjoyment*. We may likewise have a sense of this sort of obligation, by considering those reasons which prove a constant

---

* See above, Sect. vi. Art. 1, 2.

course of *benevolent* and *social actions*, to be the most probable means of promoting the *natural good* of every *individual*; as Cumberland and Pufendorf have proved: and all this without relation to a *law*.

But farther, if our moral sense be supposed exceedingly weakened, and the selfish passions grown strong, either through some general corruption of nature, or inveterate habits; if our understanding be weak, and we be often in danger of being hurried by our passions into precipitate and rash judgements, that malicious actions shall promote our advantage more than beneficence; in such a case, if it be inquired what is necessary to engage men to beneficent actions, or induce a steady sense of an obligation to act for the public good; then, no doubt, 'a law with sanctions, given by a superior being, of sufficient power to make us happy or miserable, must be necessary to counterbalance those apparent motives of interest, to calm our passions, and give room for the recovery of our moral sense, or at least for a just view of our interest.'

*   *   *   *

348   III. We are often told, 'that there is no need of supposing such a *sense* of *morality* given to men, since *reflection* and *instruction* would recommend the same actions from arguments of *self-interest*, and engage us, from the acknowledged principle of *self-love*, to the practice of them, without this unintelligible determination to benevolence, or the occult quality of a moral sense.'

It is perhaps true, that reflection, and reason might lead us to approve the same actions as *advantageous*. But would not the same reflection and reason likewise generally recommend the same meats to us, which our *taste* represents as pleasant? And shall we thence conclude, that we have no *sense* of tasting, or that such a sense is useless? No: the use is plain in both cases. Notwithstanding the mighty *reason* we boast of above other animals, its processes are too slow, too full of doubt and hesitation, to serve us in every exigency, either for our own preservation, without the *external senses*, or to influence our actions for the good of the whole, without this *moral sense*. Nor could we be so strongly determined at all times to what is most conducive to either of these ends, without these expeditious monitors, and importunate solicitors; nor so nobly rewarded, when we act vigorously in pursuit of these ends, by the calm dull reflections of self-interest, as by those delightful sensations.

This *natural determination* to approve and admire, or hate and dislike actions, is, no doubt, an occult quality. But is it any way more mysterious, that the idea of an action should raise esteem or contempt, than that the motion or tearing of flesh should give pleasure or pain; or the act of volition should move flesh and bones? In the latter case, we have got the brain, and elastic fibres, and animal spirits, and elastic fluids, like the Indian's elephant, and tortoise, to bear the burden of the difficulty: but go one step farther, and you find the whole as difficult as at first, and equally a mystery with this determination to love and approve, or condemn and despise actions and agents, without any views of *interest*, as they appear *benevolent*, or the contrary.

Some also object, that according to this account, brutes may be **349** capable of virtue; and this is thought a great absurdity. But it is manifest, that, 1. brutes are not capable of that, in which this scheme places the highest virtue, to wit, the *calm motions of the will* toward the good of others; if our common accounts of brutes are true, that they are merely led by particular passions toward present objects of sense. Again, it is plain there is something in certain tempers of brutes, which engages our liking, and some lower good-will and esteem, though we do not usually call it virtue, nor do we call the sweeter dispositions of children virtue; and yet they are so very like the lower kinds of virtue, that I see no harm in calling them virtues. What if there are low virtues in creatures void of reflection, incapable of knowing laws, or of being moved by their sanctions, or by example of rewards or punishments? Such creatures cannot be brought to a proper trial or judgement: laws, rewards, or punishments won't have these effects upon them, which they may have upon rational agents. Perhaps they are no farther rewarded or punished than by the immediate pleasure or pain of their actions, or what men immediately inflict upon them. Where is the harm of all this, that there are lower virtues, and lower vices, the rewarding or punishing of which, in creatures void of reason and reflection, can answer no wise end of government?

*   *   *   *

IV. The writers upon opposite schemes, who deduce all ideas of **350** good and evil from the private advantage of the actor, or from relation to a law, and its sanctions, either known from reason or revelation, are perpetually recurring to this moral sense which they deny; not only in calling the laws of the Deity *just* and *good*, and alleging *justice* and *right* in the Deity to govern us; but by using a set of words which import something different from what they will allow to be their only meaning. *Obligation*, with them, is only such a constitution, either of nature, or some governing power, as makes it advantageous for the agent to act in a certain manner. Let this definition be substituted, wherever we meet with the words, *ought, should, must*, in a moral sense, and many of their sentences would seem very strange; as that the Deity *must* act rationally, *must* not, or *ought* not to punish the innocent, *must* make the state of the virtuous better than that of the wicked, *must* observe promises; substituting the definition of the words, *must, ought, should*, would make these sentences either ridiculous, or very disputable.

351   V. But that our first ideas of moral good depend not on *laws*, may plainly appear from our constant inquiries into the *justice* of *laws themselves*; and that not only of human laws, but of the divine. What else can be the meaning of that universal opinion, 'that the *laws* of God are *just*, and *holy*, and *good*?' Human laws may be called *good*, because of their conformity to the divine. But to call the laws of the supreme Deity *good*, or *holy*, or *just*, if all goodness, holiness, and justice be constituted by *laws*, or the *will* of a *superior* any way revealed, must be an insignificant tautology, amounting to no more than this, 'that God *wills* what he *wills*. Or that his *will* is conformable to his *will*.'

It must then first be supposed, that there is something in actions which is apprehended *absolutely good*; and this is *benevolence*, or desire of the *public natural happiness* of *rational agents*; and that our *moral sense* perceives this *excellence*: and then we call the *laws* of the Deity *good*, when we imagine that they are contrived to promote the *public good* in the most effectual and impartial manner. And the Deity is called *morally good*, when we apprehend that his *whole providence* tends to the universal happiness of his *creatures*; whence we conclude his *benevolence*, and *desire* in their happiness.

Some tell us, 'that the goodness of the divine laws consists in their conformity to some essential rectitude of his nature.' But they must excuse us from assenting to this, till they make us understand the meaning of this metaphor, *essential rectitude*; and till we discern whether any thing more is meant by it than a perfectly wise, uniform, impartial benevolence.

Hence we may see the difference between *constraint* and *obligation*.   **352**
There is indeed no difference between *constraint*, and the second sense
of the word *obligation*, viz. a constitution which makes an action
eligible from self-interest, if we only mean *external interest*, distinct
from the delightful consciousness which arises from the moral sense.
The reader need scarcely be told, that by *constraint*, we do not understand an *external force* moving our limbs without our consent; for in
that case we are not *agents* at all; but that *constraint* which arises from
the threatening and presenting some *evil*, in order to make us act in
a certain manner. And yet there seems an universally acknowledged
difference between even this sort of *constraint* and *obligation*. We
never say, we are *obliged* to do an action which we count base, but we
may be *constrained* to it: we never say, that the divine laws, by their
sanctions, *constrain* us, but *oblige* us; nor do we call obedience to the
Deity *constraint*, unless by a metaphor, though many own they are
influenced by fear of punishments. And yet supposing an almighty
evil being should require, under grievous penalties, treachery,
cruelty, ingratitude, we would call this *constraint*. The difference is
plainly this: when any sanctions co-operate with our moral sense,
in exciting us to actions which we count morally good, we say we
are *obliged*; but when sanctions of rewards or punishments oppose
our moral sense, then we say we are *bribed* or *constrained*. In the
former case we call the lawgiver *good*, as designing the public happiness; in the latter we call him *evil*, or *unjust*, for the supposed contrary
intention. But were all our ideas of moral good or evil derived solely
from opinions of private advantage or loss in actions, I see no
possible difference which could be made in the meaning of these
words.

VI. From this sense too we derive our ideas of RIGHTS. Whenever it   **353**
appears to us, that a faculty of doing, demanding, or possessing any
thing, universally allowed in certain circumstances, would in the
whole tend to the general good, we say, that one in such circumstances has a right to do, possess, or demand that thing. And according as this tendency to the public good is greater or less, the right is
greater or less.

The *rights* called *perfect*, are of such necessity to the public good,
that the universal violation of them would make human life intolerable; and it actually makes those miserable, whose rights are thus
violated. On the contrary, to fulfil these rights in every instance,

tends to the public good, either directly, or by promoting the innocent advantage of a part. . . . Instances of perfect rights are those to
our lives; to the fruits of our labours; to demand performance of
contracts upon valuable considerations, from men capable of performing them; to direct our own actions either for public, or
innocent private good, before we have submitted them to the
direction of others in any measure: and many others of like nature.

Imperfect rights are such as, when universally violated, would not
necessarily make men miserable. These rights tend to the improvement and increase of positive good in any society, but are not absolutely necessary to prevent universal misery. The violation of them
only disappoints men of the happiness expected from the humanity
or gratitude of others; but does not deprive men of any good which
they had before. . . . Instances of imperfect rights are those which the
poor have to the charity of the wealthy; which all men have to
offices of no trouble or expense to the performer; which benefactors
have to returns of gratitude, and such-like.

The violation of imperfect rights only argues a man to have such
weak benevolence, as not to study advancing the positive good of
others, when in the least opposite to his own: but the violation of
perfect rights argues the injurious person to be positively evil or
cruel; or at least so immoderately selfish, as to be indifferent about
the positive misery and ruin of others, when he imagines he can find
his interest in it. In violating the former, we show a weak desire of
public happiness, which every small view of private interest over-
balances; but in violating the latter, we show ourselves so entirely
negligent of the misery of others, that views of increasing our own
good overcome all our compassion toward their sufferings. Now as
the absence of good is more easily borne than the presence of misery;
so our good wishes toward the positive good of others, are weaker
than our compassion toward their misery. He then who violates
imperfect rights, shows that his self-love overcomes only the desire
of positive good to others; but he who violates perfect rights,
betrays such a selfish desire of advancing his own positive good, as
overcomes all compassion toward the misery of others.

★　　★　　★　　★

354　XIII. It has often been taken for granted in these papers, 'that the
Deity is morally good;' though the reasoning is not at all built upon

this supposition. If we inquire into the reason of the great agreement of mankind in this opinion, we shall perhaps find no demonstrative arguments *a priori*, from the idea of an *independent being*, to prove his *goodness*. But there is abundant probability, deduced from the whole frame of nature, which seems, as far as we know, plainly contrived for the good of the whole; and the casual evils seem the necessary concomitants of some mechanism designed for prepollent good. Nay, this very moral sense, implanted in rational agents, to approve and admire whatever actions flow from a study of the good of others, is one of the strongest evidences of goodness in the Author of nature.

But these reflections are not so universal as the opinion, nor are they often inculcated. What then more probably leads mankind into that opinion, is this: the obvious frame of the world gives us ideas of *boundless wisdom* and *power* in its Author. Such a being we cannot conceive indigent, and must conclude *happy*, and in the *best state* possible, since he can still gratify himself. The best state of rational agents, and their greatest and most worthy happiness, we are necessarily led to imagine must consist in *universal efficacious benevolence*: and hence we conclude the Deity *benevolent* in the most *universal impartial manner*. Nor can we well imagine what else deserves the name of *perfection* more than *benevolence*, and those capacities or abilities which are necessary to make it *effectual*; such as *wisdom* and *power*: at least we can have no more lovely conception of it.

An Essay on the Nature and Conduct of the Passions and Affections

★   ★   ★   ★

355   Some strange love of simplicity in the structure of human nature, or attachment to some favourite hypothesis, has engaged many writers to pass over a great many *simple perceptions*, which we may find in ourselves. We have got the number five fixed for our external senses, though a larger number might perhaps as easily be defended. We have multitudes of perceptions which have no relation to any external sensation; if by it we mean perceptions immediately occasioned by motions or impressions made on our bodies, such as the ideas of number, duration, proportion, virtue, vice, pleasures of honour, of congratulation; the pains of remorse, shame, sympathy, and many others. It were to be wished, that those who are at such pains to prove a beloved maxim, that 'all ideas arise from *sensation* and *reflection*,' had so explained themselves, that none should take their meaning to be, that all our ideas are either *external sensations*, or *reflex acts* upon *external sensations*: or if by *reflection* they mean an inward power of perception, as Mr. Locke declares expressly, calling it *internal sensation*, that they had as carefully examined into the several kinds of internal perceptions, as they have done into the external sensations: that we might have seen whether the former be not as natural and necessary and ultimate, without reference to any other, as the latter. Had they in like manner considered our *affections* without a previous notion, that they were all from *self-love*, they might have felt an *ultimate desire* of the happiness of others as easily conceivable, and as certainly implanted in the human breast, though perhaps not so strong as self-love.

★   ★   ★   ★

SECT. I—A GENERAL ACCOUNT OF OUR SEVERAL SENSES
AND DESIRES, SELFISH OR PUBLIC

*   *   *   *

Art. I. 'Objects, actions, or events obtain the name of *good*, or *evil*, **356**
according as they are the causes, or occasions, mediately, or immediately, of a grateful, or ungrateful *perception* to some sensitive
nature.' To understand therefore the several kinds of good, or evil,
we must apprehend the several powers of perception or *senses*
natural to us.

*   *   *   *

If we may call 'every determination of our minds to receive ideas
independently on our will, and to have perceptions of pleasure and
pain, A SENSE,'[1] we shall find many other *senses* beside those commonly explained. Though it is not easy to assign accurate divisions
on such subjects, yet we may reduce them to the following classes,
leaving it to others to arrange them as they think convenient. A little
reflection will show that there are such *natural powers* in the human
mind, in whatever order we place them. In the 1st class are the
external senses, universally known. In the 2d, the pleasant perceptions
arising from regular, harmonious, uniform objects; as also from
grandeur and novelty. These we may call, after Mr. Addison, the
pleasures of the *imagination*; or we may call the power of receiving
them, an *internal sense*. Whoever dislikes this name may substitute
another. 3. The next class of perceptions we may call a *public sense*,
viz. 'our determination to be pleased with the happiness of others,
and to be uneasy at their misery.' This is found in some degree in all
men, and was sometimes called κοινονοημοσύνη, or *sensus communis*
by some of the ancients. This inward pain of compassion cannot be
called a sensation of sight. It solely arises from an opinion of misery
felt by another, and not immediately from a visible form. The same
form presented to the eye by the exactest painting, or the action of a
player, gives no pain to those who remember that there is no misery
felt. When men by imagination conceive real pain felt by an actor,
without recollecting that it is merely feigned, or when they think of
the real story represented, then, as there is a confused opinion of real
misery, there is also pain in compassion. 4. The fourth class we may

[¹ Cf. § 307.]

call the *moral sense*, by which 'we perceive virtue or vice, in ourselves, or others.' This is plainly distinct from the former class of perceptions, since many are strongly affected with the fortunes of others, who seldom reflect[1] upon virtue or vice, in themselves, or others, as an object: as we may find in natural affection, compassion, friendship, or even general benevolence to mankind, which connect our happiness or pleasure with that of others, even when we are not reflecting upon our own temper, nor delighted with the perception of our own virtue. 5. The fifth class is a *sense of honour*, which makes the approbation, or gratitude of others, for any good actions we have done, the necessary occasion of pleasure; and their dislike, condemnation, or resentment of injuries done by us, the occasion of that uneasy sensation called *shame*, even when we fear no further evil from them.

There are perhaps other perceptions distinct from all these classes, such as some ideas 'of decency, dignity, suitableness to human nature in certain actions and circumstances; and of an indecency, meanness, and unworthiness, in the contrary actions or circumstances, even without any conception of *moral* good, or evil.' Thus the pleasures of sight, and hearing, are more esteemed than those of taste or touch: the pursuits of the pleasures of the imagination, are more approved than those of simple external sensations. Plato makes one of his dialogists* account for this difference from a constant opinion of innocence in this sort of pleasures, which would reduce this perception to the moral sense. Others may imagine that the difference is not owing to any such reflection upon their innocence, but that there is a different sort of perceptions in these cases, to be reckoned another class of sensations.

*　　*　　*　　*

SECT. II—OF THE AFFECTIONS AND PASSIONS: THE NATURAL LAWS OF PURE AFFECTION: THE CONFUSED SENSATIONS OF THE PASSIONS, WITH THEIR FINAL CAUSES

*　　*　　*　　*

357　II. . . . There is a distinction to be observed on this subject, between 'the *calm desire* of good, and aversion to evil, either selfish or

* Hippias Major. See also Treat. II. Sect. 5. Art. 7.

[1 Cf. § 314; Shaftesbury, §§ 200, 204.]

public, as they appear to our reason or reflection; and the *particular passions* towards objects immediately presented to some sense.'[1] Thus nothing can be more distinct than the *general calm desire* of private good of any kind, which alone would incline us to pursue whatever objects were apprehended as the means of good, and the particular *selfish passions*, such as ambition, covetousness, hunger, lust, revenge, anger, as they arise upon particular occasions. In like manner our public desires may be distinguished into the *general calm desire* of the happiness of others, or aversion to their misery upon reflection; and the *particular affections* or *passions* of love, congratulation, compassion, natural affection. These particular affections are found in many tempers, where, through want of reflection, the general calm desires are not found: nay, the former may be opposite to the latter, where they are found in the same temper. Sometimes the calm motion of the will conquers the passion, and sometimes is conquered by it. Thus lust or revenge may conquer the calm affection toward private good, and sometimes are conquered by it. Compassion will prevent the necessary correction of a child, or the use of a severe cure, while the calm parental affection is exciting to it. Sometimes the latter prevails over the former. All this is beautifully represented in the 9th book of Plato's *Republic*. We obtain command over the particular passions, principally by strengthening the general desires through frequent reflection, and making them habitual, so as to obtain strength superior to the particular passions.*

Again, the *calm public desires* may be considered as 'they either regard the good of particular persons or societies presented to our senses; or that of some more abstracted or general community, such as a species or system.' This latter sort we may call *universal calm*

---

* The Schoolmen express this distinction by the *appetitus rationalis*, and the *appetitus sensitivus*. All animals have in common the external senses suggesting notions of things as pleasant or painful; and have also the *appetitus sensitivus*, or some instinctive desires and aversions. Rational agents have, superadded to these, two higher analogous powers; viz. the understanding, or reason, presenting farther notions, and attended with an higher sort of sensations; and the *appetitus rationalis*. This latter is a 'constant natural disposition of soul to desire what the understanding, or these sublimer sensations, represent as good, and to shun what they represent as evil, and this either when it respects ourselves or others.' This many call the *will* as distinct from the passions. Some later writers seem to have forgot it, by ascribing to the understanding not only ideas, notions, knowledge; but action, inclinations, desires, prosecution, and their contraries.

[1 Cf. § 331; Butler, §§ 382-3, 414-16.]

benevolence. Now it is plain, that not only *particular kind passions*, but even *calm particular benevolence* do not always arise from, or necessarily presuppose, the *universal benevolence*; both the former may be found in persons of little reflection, where the latter is wanting: and the former two may be opposite to the other, where they meet together in one temper. So the *universal benevolence* might be where there was neither of the former; as in any superior nature or angel, who had no particular intercourse with any part of mankind.

Our moral sense, though it approves all particular kind affection or passion, as well as calm particular benevolence abstractedly considered; yet it also approves the restraint or limitation of all particular affections or passions, by the calm universal benevolence. To make this desire prevalent above all particular affections, is the only sure way to obtain constant self-approbation.

★   ★   ★   ★

Illustrations upon the Moral Sense

The differences of actions from which some are constituted *morally*
good, and others *morally evil*, have always been accounted a very
important subject of inquiry: and therefore, every attempt to free
this subject from the usual causes of error and dispute, the *confusion
of ambiguous words*, must be excusable.

In the following discourse, *happiness* denotes pleasant sensation of
any kind, or a continued state of such sensations; and *misery* denotes
the contrary sensations.

Such actions as tend to procure happiness to the agent, are called
for shortness, *privately useful*: and such actions as procure misery to
the agent, *privately hurtful*.

Actions procuring happiness to others may be called *publicly useful*,
and the contrary actions *publicly hurtful*. Some actions may be both
publicly and privately useful, and others both publicly and privately
hurtful.

These different natural tendencies of actions are universally acknowledged; and in proportion to our reflection upon human affairs,
we shall enlarge our knowledge of these differences.

When these natural differences are known, it remains to be inquired into; 1st, 'What quality in any action determines our *election*
of it rather than the contrary?' Or, if the mind determines itself,
'What motives or desires excite to an action, rather than the contrary, or rather than to the omission?' 2dly, 'What quality determines
our *approbation* of one action, rather than of the contrary action?'

The words *election* and *approbation* seem to denote simple ideas
known by consciousness; which can only be explained by synonymous words, or by concomitant or consequent circumstances.
Election is purposing to do an action rather than its contrary, or than
being inactive. *Approbation* of our own action denotes, or is attended
with, a pleasure in the contemplation of it, and in reflection upon
the affections which inclined us to it. *Approbation* of the action of
another has some little pleasure attending it in the observer, and
raises love toward the agent, in whom the quality approved is

deemed to reside, and not in the observer, who has a satisfaction in the act of approving.*

The qualities moving to *election*, or *exciting to action*, are different from those moving to *approbation*: we often do actions which we do not *approve*, and *approve* actions which we omit: we often *desire* that an agent had omitted an action which we *approve*; and *wish* he would do an action which we *condemn*. Approbation is employed about the

359 actions of *others*, where there is no room for our election.

Now in our search into the qualities exciting either our election or approbation, let us consider the several notions advanced of moral good and evil in both these respects; and what senses, instincts, or affections, must be necessarily supposed to account for our approbation or election.

There are two opinions on this subject entirely opposite: the one that of the old Epicureans, as it is beautifully explained in the first book of Cicero, *De finibus*; which is revived by Hobbes, Rochefoucauld, and others of the last century,[1] and followed by many better writers: 'that all the desires of the human mind, nay of all thinking natures, are reducible to *self-love*, or *desire of private happiness*: that from this desire all actions of any agent do flow.' Our Christian moralists of this scheme introduce other sorts of happiness to be desired, but still it is the '*prospect of private happiness*, which, with some of them, is the sole *motive of election*. And that, in like manner, what determines any agent to *approve* his own action, is its *tendency to his private happiness* in the whole, though it may bring present pain along with it: that the *approbation* of the action of another, is from an opinion of its tendency to the happiness of the *approver*, either immediately or more remotely: that each agent may discover it to be the surest way to promote his private happiness, to do publicly useful actions, and to abstain from those which are publicly hurtful: that the neglecting to observe this, and doing publicly hurtful actions, does mischief to the whole of mankind, by hurting any one part; that every one has some little damage by this action: such an inadvertent person might possibly be pernicious to any one, were he in his neighbourhood; and the very example of such actions may extend over the whole world, and produce some pernicious effects

---

* See Treat. II. Sect. 1. parag. ult. [§ 314].

[1 Cf. Butler, § 382.]

upon any observer. That therefore every one may look upon such actions as hurtful to himself, and in this view does disapprove them, and hates the agent. In the like manner, a publicly useful action may diffuse some small advantage to every observer, whence he may approve it, and love the agent.'

★   ★   ★   ★

The other opinion is this, 'that we have not only *self-love*, but *benevolent affections* also toward others, in various degrees, making us desire their happiness as an *ultimate end*, without any view to private happiness: that we have a *moral sense* or determination of our mind, to *approve* every *kind affection* either in ourselves or others, and all publicly useful actions which we imagine flow from such affection, without our having a view to our *private happiness*, in our approbation of these actions.'

These two opinions seem both intelligible, each consistent with itself. The former seems not to represent human nature as it is; the other seems to do it.

There have been many *ways of speaking* introduced, which seem to signify something different from both the former opinions. Such as these, that 'morality of actions consists in *conformity to reason, or difformity from it*:' that 'virtue is acting according to the *absolute fitness and unfitness of things*, or agreeably to the *natures* or *relations* of things,' and many others in different authors. To examine these is the design of the following sections; and to explain more fully how the *moral sense* alleged to be in mankind, must be presupposed even in these schemes.

SECT. I—CONCERNING THE CHARACTER OF VIRTUE, AGREEABLE TO TRUTH OR REASON

Since reason is understood to denote our *power of finding out true propositions*, reasonableness must denote the same thing, with *conformity to true propositions, or to truth*. **360**

Reasonableness in an action is a very common expression, but yet upon inquiry, it will appear very confused, whether we suppose it the motive to *election*, or the quality determining *approbation*.

There is one sort of *conformity to truth* which neither determines to the one or the other; viz. that conformity which is between every true proposition and its object.[1] This sort of conformity can never

[1 Cf. Wollaston, § 274.]

make us choose or approve one action more than its contrary, for it is found in all actions alike: whatever attribute can be ascribed to a generous kind action, the contrary attribute may as *truly* be ascribed to a selfish cruel action: both propositions are equally *true*, and the two contrary actions, the objects of the two *truths*, are equally *conformable* to their several truths, with that sort of conformity which is between a truth and its object. This conformity then cannot make a difference among actions, or recommend one more than another either to election or approbation, since any man may make as many truths about villainy, as about heroism, by ascribing to it contrary attributes.

★   ★   ★   ★

361 If *reasonableness*, the character of virtue, denote some other sort of conformity to truth, it were to be wished that these gentlemen, who make it the original idea of moral good, antecedent to any sense or affections, would explain it, and show how it determines us antecedently to a sense, either to election or approbation.

They tell us, 'we must have some *standard* antecedently to all sense or affections, since we judge even of our senses and affections themselves, and approve or disapprove them: this standard must be our *reason*, conformity to which must be the original idea of moral good.'

But what is this *conformity of actions to reason*? When we ask the reason of an action, we sometimes mean, 'What truth shows a quality in the action, exciting the agent to do it?' Thus, why does a luxurious man pursue wealth? The reason is given by this truth, 'Wealth is useful to purchase pleasures.' Sometimes for a reason of actions we show the truth expressing a quality, engaging our approbation. Thus the reason of hazarding life in just war, is, that 'it tends to preserve our honest countrymen, or evidences public spirit:' the reason for temperance, and against luxury is given thus, 'Luxury evidences a selfish base temper.' The former sort of reasons we will call *exciting*, and the latter *justifying*.★ Now we shall find that all *exciting reasons* presuppose *instincts* and *affections*; and the *justifying* presuppose a *moral sense*.

362 As to *exciting reasons*, in every calm rational action some *end* is desired or intended; no end can be intended or desired previously to

★ Thus Grotius distinguishes the reasons of war, into the *justificae*, and *suasoriae*, or these, *sub ratione utilis*.

some one of these classes of affections, *self-love*, *self-hatred*, or desire of private misery (if this be possible), *benevolence* toward others, or *malice*: all affections are included under these: no *end* can be previous to them all; there can therefore be no *exciting reason* previous to *affection*.

*   *   *   *

But are there not also exciting reasons, even previous to any end, moving us to propose one end rather than another? To this Aristotle long ago answered, 'that there are *ultimate ends* desired without a view to any thing else, and *subordinate ends* or objects desired with a view to something else.' To *subordinate ends* those *reasons* or *truths* excite, which show them to be conducive to the *ultimate end*, and show one object to be more effectual than another: thus *subordinate ends* may be called *reasonable*. But as to the *ultimate ends*, to suppose exciting reasons for them, would infer, that there is no ultimate end,[1] but that we desire one thing for another in an infinite series.

*   *   *   *

Should any one ask even concerning these two *ultimate ends*, *private good* and *public*, is not the latter more *reasonable* than the former?—what means the word *reasonable* in this question? If we are allowed to presuppose *instincts* and *affections*, then the truth just now supposed to be discoverable concerning our state, is an exciting reason to serve the public interest, since this conduct is the most effectual means to obtain both ends. But I doubt if any truth can be assigned which excites in us either the desire of private happiness or public. For the former none ever alleged any exciting reason: and a benevolent temper finds as little reason exciting him to the latter; which he desires without any view to private good. If the meaning of the question be this, 'does not every *spectator approve* the pursuit of public good more than private?' the answer is obvious, that he does: but not for any *reason* or *truth*, but from a *moral sense* in the constitution of the soul.

This leads to consider *approbation* of actions, whether it be for **363** *conformity to any truth*, or *reasonableness*, that actions are ultimately approved, independently of any *moral sense*? Or if all *justifying reasons* do not presuppose it?

[1 Cf. Hobbes, §§ 4, 44.]

If *conformity to truth*, or *reasonable*, denote nothing else but that 'an action is the object of a true proposition,' it is plain, that all actions should be approved equally, since as many truths may be made about the worst, as can be made about the best. See what was said above about exciting reasons.

But let the *truths* commonly assigned as justifying be examined. Here it is plain, 'a truth showing an action to be fit to attain an end,' does not justify it; nor do we approve a subordinate end for any truth, which only shows it to be fit to promote the ultimate end; for the worst actions may be conducive to their ends, and *reasonable* in that sense. The justifying reasons then must be about the ends themselves, especially the ultimate ends. The question then is, 'Does a conformity to any truth make us approve an ultimate end, previously to any moral sense?' For example, we approve pursuing the public good. For what *reason*? Or what is the *truth* for conformity to which we call it a *reasonable end*? I fancy we can find none in these cases, more than we could give for our liking any pleasant fruit.*

The reasons assigned are such as these; 'It is the end proposed by the Deity.' But why do we approve concurring with the divine ends? This reason is given, 'He is our benefactor:' but then, for what *reason* do we approve concurrence with a benefactor? Here we must recur to a *sense*. Is this the reason moving to approbation, 'Study of public good tends to the advantage of the approver?' Then the quality moving us to approve an action, is its being advantageous to us, and not conformity to a truth. This scheme is intelligible, but not true in fact. Men approve without perception of private advantage; and often do not condemn or disapprove what is plainly pernicious; as in the execution of a just sentence, which even the sufferer may approve.

If any allege, that this is the justifying reason of the pursuit of public good, 'that it is best all be happy,' then we approve actions for their tendency to that state which is best, and not for conformity to reason. But here again, what means *best*? morally best, or naturally best? If the former, they explain the same word by itself in a circle: if they mean the latter, that 'it is the most happy state where all are happy;' then, most happy, for whom? the system, or the individual? If for the former, what reason makes us approve the happiness of a

---

* This is what Aristotle so often asserts that the προαιρετόν or βουλευτόν is not the end, but the means.

system? Here we must recur to a sense or kind affections. Is it most happy for the individual? Then the quality moving approbation is again tendency to private happiness, not reasonableness.

*   *   *   *

Two arguments are brought in defence of this epithet, as ante- **364** cedent to any sense, viz. 'that we judge even of our affections and senses themselves, whether they are morally good or evil.'

The second argument is, that 'if all moral ideas depend upon the constitution of our sense, then all constitutions would have been alike reasonable and good to the Deity, which is absurd.'

As to the first argument, it is plain we judge of our own *affections*, or those of others by our *moral sense*, by which we approve kind affections, and disapprove the contrary. But none can apply moral attributes to the very *faculty* of perceiving moral qualities; or call his moral sense morally good or evil, any more than he calls the power of tasting, sweet or bitter; or of seeing, straight or crooked, white or black.

Every one judges the *affections* of others by his own *sense*; so that it seems not impossible that in these senses men might differ as they do in taste. A sense approving benevolence would disapprove that temper, which a sense approving malice would delight in. The former would judge of the latter by his own sense, so would the latter of the former. Each one would at first view think the sense of the other perverted. But then, is there no difference? Are both senses equally *good*? No certainly, any *man* who observed them would think the sense of the former more desirable than of the latter; but this is, because the *moral sense* of every *man* is constituted in the former manner. But were there any nature with no *moral sense* at all observing these two persons, would he not think the state of the former preferable to that of the latter? Yes, he might: but not from any perception of *moral goodness* in the one *sense* more than in the other. Any rational nature observing two men thus constituted, with opposite senses, might by reasoning see, not *moral goodness* in one *sense* more than in the contrary, but a *tendency to the happiness of the person himself*, who had the former sense in the one constitution, and a *contrary tendency* in the opposite constitution: nay, the persons themselves might observe this; since the former sense would make these actions grateful to the agent which were useful to others; who, if they had a like sense, would *love* him, and return *good offices*; whereas the latter sense would make all such actions as are useful to others, and apt to engage their good offices, ungrateful to the agent; and would lead him into *publicly hurtful actions*, which would not only procure the hatred of others, if they had a contrary sense, but engage them out of their self-love to study his destruction, though their senses agreed. Thus any observer, or the agent himself with this latter sense, might perceive that the *pains* to be feared, as the consequence of *malicious actions*, did overbalance the *pleasures* of this *sense*; so that it would be to the agent's *interest* to counteract it. Thus one constitution of the moral sense might appear to be more *advantageous* to those who had it, than the contrary; as we may call that sense of tasting healthful, which made wholesome meat pleasant; and we would call a contrary taste pernicious. And yet we should no more call the moral sense morally good or evil, than we call the sense of tasting savoury or unsavoury, sweet or bitter.

365 But must we not own, that we judge of all our *senses* by our *reason*, and often correct their reports of the magnitude, figure, colour, taste of objects, and pronounce them *right* or *wrong*, as they agree or disagree with *reason*? This is true. But does it then follow, that extension, figure, colour, taste, are not *sensible ideas*, but only denote *reasonableness*, or *agreement with reason*? Or that these qualities are perceivable antecedently to any *sense*, by our *power of finding out truth*? Just so a compassionate temper may rashly imagine the correction of a child, or the execution of a criminal, to be cruel and inhuman: but by *reasoning* may discover the *superior good* arising from them in the whole; and then the same *moral sense* may determine the observer to approve them. But we must not hence conclude, that it is any *reasoning* antecedent to a *moral sense*, which determines us to *approve* the study of public good, any more than we can in the former case conclude, that we perceive extension, figure, colour, taste, antecedently to a sense. All these sensations are often corrected by reasoning, as well as our approbations of actions as good or evil:* and yet no body ever placed the original idea of extension, figure, colour, or taste, in conformity to reason.

*   *   *   *

366 As to the second argument, what means [*alike reasonable or good*

* See Sect. 4. of this Treatise [§ 371].

to the Deity?] Does it mean, 'that the Deity could have had no reasons exciting him to make one constitution rather than another?' It is plain, if the Deity had nothing essential to his nature, resembling or analogous to our sweetest and most kind affections, we can scarce suppose he could have any reason exciting him to any thing he has done: but grant such a disposition in the Deity, and then the manifest tendency of the present constitution to the happiness of his creatures was an exciting reason for choosing it before the contrary. Each sort of constitution might have given men an equal immediate pleasure in present self-approbation for any sort of action; but the actions approved by the present sense, procure all pleasures of the other senses; and the actions which would have been approved by a contrary moral sense, would have been productive of all torments of the other senses.

If it be meant, that 'upon this supposition, that all our approbation presupposes in us a moral sense, the Deity could not have approved one constitution more than another:' where is the consequence? Why may not the Deity have something of a superior kind, analogous to our moral sense, essential to him? How does any constitution of the senses of men hinder the Deity to reflect and judge of his own actions? How does it affect the divine apprehension, which way soever moral ideas arise with men?

If it means 'that we cannot approve one constitution more than another, or approve the Deity for making the present constitution:' this consequence is also false. The present constitution of our moral sense determines us to approve all *kind affections*: this constitution the Deity must have foreseen as *tending* to the *happiness* of his creatures; it does therefore evidence *kind affection* or *benevolence* in the Deity, this therefore we must *approve*.

*   *   *   *

SECT. II—CONCERNING THAT CHARACTER OF VIRTUE AND VICE, THE FITNESS OR UNFITNESS OF ACTIONS

We come next to examine some other explications of morality, **367** which have been much insisted on of late. *We are told, 'that there

---

* See Dr. Samuel Clarke's Boyle's lectures [§§ 225 ff.]; and many late authors.

are *eternal and immutable differences* of things, absolutely and antecedently: that there are also *eternal and unalterable relations* in the
natures of the things themselves, from which arise *agreements* and
disagreements, *congruities* and *incongruities*, *fitness* and *unfitness* of the
application of circumstances, to the qualifications of persons; that
actions agreeable to these relations are morally good, and that the
contrary actions are morally evil.' These expressions are sometimes
made of the same import with those more common ones: 'acting
agreeably to the eternal reason and truth of things.' It is asserted,
that 'God who knows all these *relations*, etc. does guide his actions by
them, since he has no wrong affection' (the word [wrong] should
have been first explained): 'and that in like manner these *relations*,
etc. *ought*' (another unlucky word in morals) 'to determine the choice
of all rationals, abstractly from any views of interest. If they do not,
these creatures are insolently *counteracting their Creator*, and as far as
they can, *making things to be what they are not*,[1] which is the greatest
impiety.'

That things are now *different* is certain. That *ideas*, to which there
is no *object* yet existing conformable, are also *different*, is certain.
That upon comparing two *ideas* there arises a *relative idea*, generally
when the two ideas compared have in them any modes of the same
simple idea, is also obvious. Thus every extended being may be
compared to any other of the same kinds of dimensions; and *relative
ideas* be formed of greater, less, equal, double, triple, subduple, etc.
with infinite variety. This may let us see that relations are not *real
qualities* inherent in external natures, but only *ideas* necessarily accompanying our *perception* of two objects at once, and comparing
them. *Relative ideas* continue, when the external objects do not exist,
provided we retain the *two ideas*. But what the *eternal relations*, in
the natures of things do mean, is not so easy perhaps to be conceived.

*   *   *   *

There is certainly, independently of fancy or custom, a natural
tendency in some actions to give pleasure, either to the agent or
others; and a contrary tendency in other actions to give pain, either
to the agent or others. This sort of *relation* of actions to the agents
or objects is indisputable. If we call these relations *fitnesses*, then the
most contrary actions have *equal fitnesses* for contrary ends; and each

[1 Cf. Clarke, §§ 230, 232.]

one is *unfit* for the end of the *other*. Thus compassion is *fit* to make others happy, and *unfit* to make others miserable. Violation of property is *fit* to make men miserable, and *unfit* to make them happy. Each of these is both *fit* and *unfit*, with respect to different ends. The bare *fitness then to an end*, is not the idea of moral goodness.

Perhaps the *virtuous fitness* is that of *ends*. The fitness of a *subordinate end* to the ultimate, cannot constitute the action *good*, unless the *ultimate end* be good. To keep a conspiracy secret is not a good end, though it be fit for obtaining a farther end, the success of the conspiracy. The *moral fitness* must be that of the *ultimate end* itself: the *public good* alone is a *fit end*, therefore the means fit for this end alone are good.

What means the *fitness of an ultimate end*? For what is it fit? Why, it is an *ultimate end*, not fit for any thing farther, but *absolutely fit*. What means that word *fit*? If it notes a *simple idea* it must be the *perception of some sense*: thus we must recur, upon this scheme too, to a *moral sense*.

★   ★   ★   ★

SECT. III—MR. WOLLASTON'S SIGNIFICANCY OF TRUTH,
AS THE IDEA OF VIRTUE, CONSIDERED

Mr. Wollaston★ has introduced a new explication of moral **368** virtue, viz. *significancy of truth in actions*, supposing that in every[1] action there is some *significancy*, like that which moralists and civilians speak of in their *tacit conventions*, and *quasi contractus*!

★   ★   ★   ★

To do actions from which the observer will form *false opinions*, while yet the agent is not understood to possess any intention of communicating to him his opinions or designs, is never of itself imagined *evil*, let the signs be natural or instituted;[2] provided there be no *malicious intention*, or *neglect of public good*. It is never called a crime in a teacher, to pronounce an absurd sentence for an instance; in a nobleman, to travel without coronets; or a clergyman in lay-habit, for private conveniency, or to avoid troublesome ceremony;

★ In his *Religion of Nature delineated*.

[1 Contrast Wollaston, §§ 275, 279.]   [2 See Wollaston, § 279.]

to leave lights in a lodge, to make people conclude there is a watch kept. This *significancy* may be in any action which is observed; but as *true conclusions* argue no *virtue* in the agent, so *false ones* argue no *vice*.

$$\star \qquad \star \qquad \star \qquad \star$$

Mr. Wollaston acknowledges that there may be very little evil in some actions signifying falsehood; such as throwing away that which is of but little use or value. It is objected to him, that there is equal *contrariety to truth* in such actions, as in the greatest villainy: he, in answer to it, really unawares gives up his whole cause. He must own, that there may be the strictest truth and certainty about trifles; so there may be the most obvious falsehood signified by trifling actions. If then significancy of falsehood be the very same with moral evil, all crimes must be equal. He answers, that *crimes* increase according to the *importance* of the truth denied; and so the *virtue* increases, as the *importance* of the truths affirmed.[1] Then

Virtue and *vice* increase, as the *importance* of propositions affirmed or denied;

But *signification of truth and falsehood* does not so increase:

Therefore *signification of truth or falsehood*, are not the same with *virtue* and *vice*.

But what is this *importance of truth*? Nothing else but the *moment* or *quantity* of good or evil, either private or public, which should be produced by actions, concerning which these true judgements are made. But it is plain, the *signification* of truth or falsehood is not varied by this *importance*; therefore virtue or vice denote something different from this *signification*.

But farther, the *importance* of actions toward public good or evil, is not the *idea of virtue* or *vice*: nor does the one prove *virtue* in an action, any farther than it evidences *kind affections*; or the other *vice*, farther than it evidences either *malice* or *want* of kind affections: otherwise a casual invention, an action wholly from views of private interest, might be as virtuous as the most kind and generous offices: and chance-medley, or kindly intended, but unsuccessful attempts would be as vicious as murder or treason.

$$\star \qquad \star \qquad \star \qquad \star$$

[1 Cf. Wollaston, § 290.]

SECT. IV—SHOWING THE USE OF REASON CONCERNING
VIRTUE AND VICE, UPON SUPPOSITION THAT WE RECEIVE
THESE IDEAS BY A MORAL SENSE

★   ★   ★   ★

Perhaps what has brought the epithet *reasonable*, or *flowing from*   **369**
reason, in opposition to what flows from *instinct*, *affection*, or *passion*,
so much into use, is this, 'that it is often observed, that the very best
of our particular affections or desires, when they are grown violent
and passionate, through the confused sensations and propensities
which attend them, make us incapable of considering calmly the
whole tendency of our actions, and lead us often into what is absolutely pernicious, under some appearance of relative or particular
good.' This indeed may give some ground for distinguishing between *passionate actions*, and those from *calm desire* or *affection*[1] which
employs our *reason* freely: but can never set *rational actions* in opposition to those from *instinct, desire* or *affection*. And it must be owned,
that the most perfect virtue consists in the *calm, unpassionate bene-*
volence, rather than in particular affections.

If one asks 'How do we know that our affections are right when   **370**
they are kind?' what does the word [right] mean? Does it mean what
we approve? This we know by consciousness of our sense. Again,
how do we know that our sense is right, or that we approve our
approbation? This can only be answered by another question, viz.
'How do we know we are pleased when we are pleased?'—Or does
it mean, 'How do we know that we shall *always* approve what we
now approve?' To answer this, we must first know that the same
constitution of our sense shall always remain: and again, that we
have applied ourselves carefully to consider the natural tendency of
our actions. Of the *continuance* of the same constitution of our sense,
we are as sure as of the continuance of gravitation, or any other law
of nature: the *tendency* of our own actions we cannot always know;
but we may know certainly that we *heartily* and *sincerely* study to
act according to what, by all the evidence now in our power to
obtain, appears as most *probably tending to public good*. When we are
conscious of this *sincere endeavour*, the evil consequences which we
could not have foreseen, never will make us *condemn* our conduct.

[1 Cf. §§ 331, 357.]

But without this *sincere endeavour*, we may often approve at present what we shall afterwards condemn.

If the question means, 'How are we sure that what *we* approve, *all others* shall also approve?' of this we can be sure upon no scheme; but it is highly probable that the *senses* of all men are pretty *uniform*: that the Deity also approves *kind affections*, otherwise he would not have implanted them in us, nor determined us by a *moral sense* to approve them. Now since the probability that men shall judge truly, abstracting from any presupposed prejudice, is greater than that they shall judge falsely; it is more probable, when our actions are really *kind* and *publicly useful*, that all observers shall judge truly of our intentions, and of the tendency of our actions, and consequently approve what we approve ourselves, than that they shall judge falsely and condemn them.

If the meaning of the question be, 'Will the doing what our *moral sense* approves tend to *our happiness*, and to the avoiding misery?' it is thus we call a taste wrong, when it makes that food at present grateful, which shall occasion future pains, or death. This question concerning our *self-interest* must be answered by such *reasoning* as was mentioned above, to be well managed by our moralists both ancient and modern.

Thus there seems no part of that *reasoning* which was ever used by moralists, to be superseded by supposing a *moral sense*. And yet without a moral sense there is no explication can be given of our *ideas* of *morality*; nor of that *reasonableness* supposed antecedent to all instincts, affections, or sense.

371 'But may there not be a *right* or *wrong state* of our *moral sense*, as there is in our other *senses*, according as they represent their objects to be as they really are, or represent them otherwise?' So may not our moral sense approve that which is vicious, and disapprove virtue, as a sickly palate may dislike grateful food, or a vitiated sight misrepresent colours or dimensions? Must we not know therefore antecedently what is morally good or evil by our *reason*, before we can know that our *moral sense* is *right*?

To answer this, we must remember that of the sensible ideas, some are allowed to be only perceptions in our minds, and not images of any like external quality, as colours, sounds, tastes, smells, pleasure, pain. Other ideas are images of something external, as duration, number, extension, motion, rest: these latter, for distinction, we may call *concomitant ideas of sensation*, and the former *purely sensible*. As to the purely sensible ideas, we know they are altered by any disorder in our organs, and made different from what arise in us from the same objects at other times. We do not denominate objects from our perceptions during the disorder, but according to our ordinary perceptions, or those of others in good health: yet no body imagines that therefore colours, sounds, tastes, are not sensible ideas. In like manner many circumstances diversify the concomitant ideas: but we denominate objects from the appearances they make to us in an uniform medium, when our organs are in no disorder, and the object not very distant from them. But none therefore imagines that it is reason and not sense which discovers these concomitant ideas, or primary qualities.

Just so in our ideas of actions. These three things are to be distinguished, 1. The idea of the external motion, known first by sense, and its tendency to the happiness or misery of some sensitive nature, often inferred by argument or reason, which on these subjects, suggests as invariable eternal or necessary truths as any whatsoever. 2. Apprehension or opinion of the affections in the agent, inferred by our reason: so far the idea of an action represents something external to the observer, really existing whether he had perceived it or not, and having a real tendency to certain ends. 3. The perception of approbation or disapprobation arising in the observer, according as the affections of the agent are apprehended kind in their just degree, or deficient, or malicious. This approbation cannot be supposed an image of any thing external, more than the pleasures of harmony, of taste, of smell. But let none imagine, that calling the ideas of virtue and vice perceptions of a sense, upon apprehending the actions and affections of another does diminish their reality, more than the like assertions concerning all pleasure and pain, happiness or misery. Our reason often corrects the report of our senses, about the natural tendency of the external action, and corrects rash conclusions about the affections of the agent. But whether our moral sense be subject to such a disorder, as to have different perceptions, from the same apprehended affections in an agent, at different times, as the eye may have of the colours of an unaltered object, it is not easy to determine: perhaps it will be hard to find any instances of such a change. What reason could correct, if it fell into such a disorder, I know not; except suggesting to its remembrance its former approbations, and representing the general sense of mankind. But this does not prove ideas of virtue and vice to be previous to a sense, more than a like correction of the ideas of colour in a person under the jaundice, proves that colours are perceived by reason, previously to sense.

372   If any say, 'this moral sense is not a *rule*:' what means that word? It is not a straight rigid body: it is not a general proposition, showing what means are fit to obtain an end: it is not a proposition, asserting, that a superior will make those happy who act one way, and miserable who act the contrary way. If these be the meanings of *rule*, it is no rule; yet by reflecting upon it our understanding may find out a rule. But what rule of actions can be formed, without relation to some end proposed? Or what end can be proposed, without presupposing instincts, desires, affections, or a moral sense, it will not be easy to explain.

SECT. V—SHOWING THAT VIRTUE MAY HAVE WHATEVER IS MEANT BY MERIT; AND BE REWARDABLE, UPON THE SUPPOSITION, THAT IT IS PERCEIVED BY A SENSE, AND ELECTED FROM AFFECTION OR INSTINCT

373   Some will not allow any *merit* in actions flowing from kind instincts: '*merit*, say they, attends actions to which we are excited by *reason* alone, or to which we *freely* determine ourselves. The operation of instincts or affections is *necessary*, and not *voluntary*; nor is there more merit in them than in the shining of the sun, the fruitfulness of a tree, or the overflowing of a stream, which are all publicly useful.'

But what does *merit* mean? or *praise-worthiness*? Do these words denote the 'quality in actions, which gains approbation from the observer, according to the present constitution of the human mind?' Or, 2dly, are these actions called meritorious, 'which, when any observer does approve, all other observers approve him for his approbation of it; and would condemn any observer who did not approve these actions?' These are the only meanings of *meritorious*, which I can conceive as distinct from *rewardable*, which is considered hereafter separately. Let those who are not satisfied with either of these explications of *merit*, endeavour to give a definition of it reducing it to its simple ideas: and not, as a late author has done, quarrelling these descriptions, tell us only that it is *deserving or being worthy of approbation*,[1] which is defining by giving a synonymous term.

★　　　★　　　★　　　★

Perhaps by meritorious is meant the same thing with another word used in like manner, viz. *rewardable*. Then indeed the quality in which merit or rewardableness is founded, is different from that which is denoted by merit in the former meanings.

Rewardable, or *deserving reward*, denotes either that quality which would incline a superior nature to make an agent happy: or, 2dly, that quality of actions which would make a spectator approve a superior nature, when he conferred happiness on the agent, and disapprove that superior, who inflicted misery on the agent, or punished him. Let any one try to give a meaning to the word *rewardable* distinct from these, and not satisfy himself with the words *worthy of*, or *deserving*, which are of very complex and ambiguous signification.

★　　　★　　　★　　　★

[1 Cf. Balguy, § 442.]

JOSEPH BUTLER
BISHOP OF DURHAM

1692–1752

I. *FIFTEEN SERMONS*
preached at the Rolls Chapel

[First printed, 1726. Reprinted here from the fourth
edition, 1749, with misprints corrected, spelling modified, and reduction of initial capital letters]

II. *DISSERTATION OF THE NATURE*
OF VIRTUE

[First printed, as an appendix to *The Analogy of Religion*,
1736. Reprinted here from the third edition, 1740, with
misprints corrected, spelling modified, and reduction
of initial capital letters]

BISHOP BUTLER

Fifteen Sermons

★   ★   ★   ★

There are two ways in which the subject of morals may be treated. **374**
One begins from inquiring into the abstract relations of things: the
other from a matter of fact, namely, what the particular nature of
man is, its several parts, their economy or constitution; from whence
it proceeds to determine what course of life it is, which is correspondent to this whole nature. In the former method the conclusion
is expressed thus, that vice is contrary to the nature and reason of
things: in the latter, that it is a violation or breaking in upon our
own nature. Thus they both lead us to the same thing, our obligations to the practice of virtue; and thus they exceedingly strengthen
and enforce each other. The first seems the most direct formal proof,
and in some respects the least liable to cavil and dispute: the latter
is in a peculiar manner adapted to satisfy a fair mind; and is more
easily applicable to the several particular relations and circumstances
in life.

The following discourses proceed chiefly in this latter method. **375**
The three first wholly. They were intended to explain what is meant
by the nature of man, when it is said that virtue consists in following,
and vice in deviating from it; and by explaining to show that the
assertion is true. That the ancient moralists had some inward feeling
or other, which they chose to express in this manner, that man is
born to virtue, that it consists in following nature, and that vice is
more contrary to this nature than tortures or death, their works in
our hands are instances. Now a person who found no mystery in
this way of speaking of the ancients; who, without being very explicit with himself, kept to his natural feeling, went along with them,
and found within himself a full conviction that what they laid down

was just and true; such an one would probably wonder to see a point, in which he never perceived any difficulty, so laboured as this is, in the second and third sermons; insomuch perhaps as to be at a loss for the occasion, scope and drift of them. But it need not be thought strange that this manner of expression, though familiar with them, and, if not usually carried so far, yet not uncommon amongst ourselves, should want explaining; since there are several perceptions daily felt and spoken of, which yet it may not be very easy at first view to explicate, to distinguish from all others, and ascertain exactly what the idea or perception is. The many treatises upon the passions are a proof of this; since so many would never have undertaken to unfold their several complications, and trace and resolve them into their principles, if they had thought, what they were endeavouring to show, was obvious to every one, who felt and talked of those passions. Thus, though there seems no ground to doubt, but that the generality of mankind have the inward perception expressed so commonly in that manner by the ancient moralists, more than to doubt whether they have those passions; yet it appeared of use to unfold that inward conviction, and lay it open in a more explicit manner, than I had seen done; especially when there were not wanting persons, who manifestly mistook the whole thing, and so had great reason to express themselves dissatisfied with it. A late author of great and deserved reputation says, that to place virtue in following nature, is at best a loose way of talk. And he has reason to say this, if what I think he intends to express, though with great decency, be true, that scarce any other sense can be put upon those words, but acting as any of the several parts without distinction, of a man's nature happened most to incline him*.

376   Whoever thinks it worth while to consider this matter thoroughly, should begin with stating to himself exactly the idea of a system, economy or constitution of any particular nature, or particular any thing: and he will, I suppose, find, that it is an one or a whole, made up of several parts; but yet, that the several parts even considered as a whole, do not complete the idea, unless in the notion of a whole, you include the relations and respects, which those parts have to each other. Every work both of nature and of art is a system: and as every particular thing both natural and artificial is for some use or purpose out of and beyond itself, one may add, to what has

---

* Rel. of Nature delin. Ed. 1724. P. 22, 23 [i.e. Wollaston, § 291].

been already brought into the idea of a system, its conduciveness to this one or more ends. Let us instance in a watch.—Suppose the several parts of it taken to pieces, and placed apart from each other: let a man have ever so exact a notion of these several parts, unless he considers the respects and relations which they have to each other, he will not have any thing like the idea of a watch. Suppose these several parts brought together and any how united: neither will he yet, be the union ever so close, have an idea which will bear any resemblance to that of a watch. But let him view those several parts put together, or consider them as to be put together in the manner of a watch; let him form a notion of the relations which those several parts have to each other—all conducive in their respective ways, to this purpose, showing the hour of the day; and then he has the idea of a watch. Thus it is with regard to the inward frame of man. Appetites, passions, affections, and the principle of reflection, considered merely as the several parts of our inward nature, do not at all give us an idea of the system or constitution of this nature: because the constitution is formed by somewhat not yet taken into consideration, namely by the relations, which these several parts have to each other; the chief of which is the authority of reflection or conscience. It is from considering the relations which the several appetites and passions in the inward frame have to each other, and above all the supremacy of reflection or conscience, that we get the idea of the system or constitution of human nature. And from the idea itself it will as fully appear, that this our nature, i.e. constitution, is adapted to virtue, as from the idea of a watch it appears, that its nature, i.e. constitution or system, is adapted to measure time. What in fact or event commonly happens, is nothing to this question. Every work of art is apt to be out of order: but this is so far from being according to its system, that let the disorder increase, and it will totally destroy it. This is merely by way of explanation, what an economy, system or constitution is. And thus far the cases are perfectly parallel. If we go further, there is indeed a difference, nothing to the present purpose, but too important an one ever to be omitted. A machine is inanimate and passive: but we are agents. Our constitution is put in our own power. We are charged with it: and therefore are accountable for any disorder or violation of it.

Thus nothing can possibly be more contrary to nature than vice; **377** meaning by nature, not only the *several parts* of our internal frame, but also the *constitution* of it. Poverty and disgrace, tortures and death are not so contrary to it. Misery and injustice are indeed equally contrary to some different parts of our nature taken singly: but injustice is moreover contrary to the whole constitution of the nature.

If it be asked whether this constitution be really what those philosophers meant, and whether they would have explained themselves in this manner: the answer is the same, as if it should be asked, whether a person, who had often used the word resentment and felt the thing, would have explained this passion exactly in the same manner, in which it is done in one of these discourses. As I have no doubt, but that this is a true account of that passion, which he referred to and intended to express by the word, resentment; so I have no doubt, but that this is the true account of the ground of that conviction, which they referred to, when they said, vice was contrary to nature. And though it should be thought that they meant no more than, that vice was contrary to the higher and better part of our nature; even this implies such a constitution as I have endeavoured to explain. For the very terms, higher and better, imply a relation or respect of parts to each other; and these relative parts, being in one and the same nature, form a constitution and are the very idea of it. They had a perception that injustice was contrary to their nature, and that pain was so also. They observed these two perceptions totally different, not in degree, but in kind: and the reflecting upon each of them as they thus stood in their nature, wrought a full intuitive conviction, that more was due and of right belonged to one of these inward perceptions, than to the other; that it demanded in all cases to govern such a creature as man. So that upon the whole, this is a fair and true account of what was the ground of their conviction; of what they intended to refer to when they said, virtue consisted in following nature: a manner of speaking not loose and undeterminate, but clear and distinct, strictly just and true.

378   Though I am persuaded the force of this conviction is felt by almost every one; yet since, considered as an argument and put in words, it appears somewhat abstruse, and since the connection of it is broken in the three first sermons, it may not be amiss to give the reader the whole argument here in one view.

Mankind has various instincts and principles of action, as brute creatures have; some leading most directly and immediately to the good of the community, and some most directly to private good.

Man has several which brutes have not; particularly reflection or conscience, an approbation of some principles or actions, and disapprobation of others.

Brutes obey their instincts or principles of action, according to certain rules; suppose the constitution of their body, and the objects around them.

The generality of mankind also obey their instincts and principles, all of them; those propensions we call good, as well as the bad, according to the same rules; namely the constitution of their body, and the external circumstances which they are in. [Therefore it is not a true representation of mankind, to affirm that they are wholly governed by self-love, the love of power and sensual appetites: since, as on the one hand, they are often actuated by these, without any regard to right or wrong; so on the other, it is manifest fact, that the same persons, the generality, are frequently influenced by friendship, compassion, gratitude; and even a general abhorrence of what is base, and liking of what is fair and just, takes its turn amongst the other motives of action. This is the partial inadequate notion of human nature treated of in the first discourse: and it is by this nature, if one may speak so, that the world is in fact influenced, and kept in that tolerable order, in which it is.]

Brutes in acting according to the rules before-mentioned, their **379** bodily constitution and circumstances, act suitably to their whole nature. [It is however to be distinctly noted, that the reason why we affirm this, is not merely that brutes in fact act so; for this alone, however universal, does not at all determine, whether such course of action be correspondent to their whole nature: but the reason of the assertion is, that as in acting thus, they plainly act conformably to somewhat in their nature, so from all observations we are able to make upon them, there does not appear the least ground to imagine them to have any thing else in their nature, which requires a different rule or course of action.]

Mankind also in acting thus would act suitably to their whole nature, if no more were to be said of man's nature, than what has been now said; if that, as it is a true, were also a complete, adequate account of our nature.

But that is not a complete account of man's nature. Somewhat further must be brought in to give us an adequate notion of it; namely, that one of those principles of action, conscience or reflection, compared with the rest as they all stand together in the nature of man, plainly bears upon it marks of authority over all the rest, and claims the absolute direction of them all, to allow or forbid their gratification: a disapprobation of reflection being in itself a principle manifestly superior to a mere propension. And the conclusion is, that to allow no more to this superior principle or part of our nature, than to other parts; to let it govern and guide only occasionally in common with the rest, as its turn happens to come, from the temper and circumstances one happens to be in; this is not to act conformably to the constitution of man: neither can any human creature be said to act conformably to his constitution of nature, unless he allows to that superior principle the absolute authority which is due to it. And this conclusion is abundantly confirmed from hence, that one may determine what course of action the economy of man's nature requires, without so much as knowing in what degree of *strength* the several principles prevail, or which of them have actually the greatest influence.

The practical reason of insisting so much upon this natural authority of the principle of reflection or conscience is, that it seems in great measure overlooked by many, who are by no means the worse sort of men. It is thought sufficient to abstain from gross wickedness, and to be humane and kind to such as happen to come in their way. Whereas in reality the very constitution of our nature requires, that we bring our whole conduct before this superior faculty; wait its determination; enforce upon ourselves its authority, and make it the business of our lives, as it is absolutely the whole business of a moral agent, to conform ourselves to it. This is the true meaning of that ancient precept, *Reverence thyself.*

380   The not taking into consideration this authority, which is implied in the idea of reflex approbation[1] or disapprobation, seems a material deficiency or omission in Lord Shaftesbury's *Inquiry concerning Virtue.* He has shown beyond all contradiction, that virtue is naturally the interest or happiness, and vice the misery of such a creature as man, placed in the circumstances which we are in this world. But suppose there are particular exceptions; a case which this author was

[1 Cf. Shaftesbury, §§ 200, 204; Hutcheson, § 314.]

unwilling to put, and yet surely it is to be put: or suppose a case which he has put and determined, that of a sceptic not convinced of this happy tendency of virtue, or being of a contrary opinion. His determination is, that it would be *without remedy**. One may say more explicitly, that leaving out the authority of reflex approbation or disapprobation, such an one would be under an obligation to act viciously; since interest, one's own happiness, is a manifest obligation, and there is not supposed to be any other obligation in the case. 'But does it much mend the matter, to take in that natural authority of reflection? There indeed would be an obligation to virtue; but would not the obligation from supposed interest on the side of vice remain?' If it should, yet to be under two contrary obligations, i.e. under none at all, would not be exactly the same, as to be under a formal obligation to be vicious, or to be in circumstances in which the constitution of man's nature plainly required, that vice should be preferred. But the obligation on the side of interest really does not remain. For the natural authority of the principle of reflection, is an obligation the most near and intimate, the most certain and known: whereas the contrary obligation can at the utmost appear no more than probable; since no man can be *certain* in any circumstances, that vice is his interest in the present world, much less can he be certain against another: and thus the certain obligation would entirely supersede and destroy the uncertain one; which yet would have been of real force without the former.

In truth the taking in this consideration, totally changes the whole **381** state of the case; and shows, what this author does not seem to have been aware of, that the greatest degree of scepticism which he thought possible, will still leave men under the strictest moral obligations, whatever their opinion be concerning the happiness of virtue. For that mankind upon reflection felt an approbation of what was good, and disapprobation of the contrary, he thought a plain matter of fact, as it undoubtedly is, which none could deny, but from mere affectation. Take in then that authority and obligation, which is a constituent part of this reflex approbation, and it will undeniably follow, though a man should doubt of every thing else, yet, that he would still remain under the nearest and most certain obligation to the practice of virtue; an obligation implied in the very idea of virtue, in the very idea of reflex approbation.

* Characteristics, V. II. p. 69.

And how little influence soever this obligation alone, can be expected to have in fact upon mankind, yet one may appeal even to interest and self-love, and ask, since from man's nature, condition, and the shortness of life, so little, so very little indeed, can possibly in any case be gained by vice; whether it be so prodigious a thing to sacrifice that little, to the most intimate of all obligations; and which a man cannot transgress without being self-condemned, and, unless he has corrupted his nature, without real self-dislike: this question I say may be asked, even upon supposition that the prospect of a future life were ever so uncertain.

The observation that man is thus by his very nature a law to himself, pursued to its just consequences, is of the utmost importance; because from it it will follow, that though men should, through stupidity or speculative scepticism, be ignorant of or disbelieve any authority in the universe to punish the violation of this law; yet, if there should be such authority, they would be as really liable to punishment, as though they had been beforehand convinced, that such punishment would follow. For in whatever sense we understand justice, even supposing, what I think would be very presumptuous to assert, that the end of divine punishment is no other than that of civil punishment, namely, to prevent future mischief; upon this bold supposition, ignorance or disbelief of the sanction would by no means exempt even from this justice: because it is not foreknowledge of the punishment, which renders obnoxious to it; but merely violating a known obligation.

*   *   *   *

382   The chief design of the eleventh discourse is to state the notion of self-love and disinterestedness, in order to show that benevolence is not more unfriendly to self-love, than any other particular affection whatever. There is a strange affectation in many people of explaining away all particular affections, and representing the whole of life as nothing but one continued exercise of self-love. Hence arises that surprising confusion and perplexity in the Epicureans* of

---

* One need only look into Torquatus's account of the Epicurean system, in Cicero's first book *De Finibus*, to see, in what a surprising manner this was done by them. Thus the desire of praise, and of being beloved, he explains to be no other than desire of safety: regard to our country, even in the most virtuous character, to be nothing but regard to ourselves. The author[1] of *Reflexions etc. Morales* says, curiosity proceeds from

[1 La Rochefoucauld.]

old, Hobbes, the author[1] of *Reflexions, Sentences et Maximes Morales*, and this whole set of writers; the confusion of calling actions interested which are done in contradiction to the most manifest known interest, merely for the gratification of a present passion. Now all this confusion might easily be avoided, by stating to ourselves wherein the idea of self-love in general consists, as distinguished from all particular movements towards particular external objects; the appetites of sense, resentment, compassion, curiosity, ambition, and the rest*. When this is done, if the words *selfish* and *interested* cannot be parted with, but must be applied to every thing; yet, to avoid such total confusion of all language, let the distinction be made by epithets: and the first may be called cool or settled selfishness, and the other passionate or sensual selfishness. But the most natural way of speaking plainly is, to call the first only, self-love, and the actions proceeding from it, interested: and to say of the latter, that they are not love to ourselves, but movements towards somewhat external: honour, power, the harm or good of another: and that the pursuit of these external objects, so far as it proceeds from these movements (for it may proceed from self-love†) is no otherwise interested, than as every action of every creature must, from the nature of the thing, be; for no one can act but from a desire, or choice, or preference of his own.

Self-love and any particular passion may be joined together; and **383** from this complication, it becomes impossible in numberless instances to determine precisely, how far an action, perhaps even of one's own, has for its principle general self-love, or some particular passion. But this need create no confusion in the ideas themselves of self-love and particular passions. We distinctly discern what one is, and what the other are: though we may be uncertain how far one or the other influences us. And though from this uncertainty, it cannot but be, that there will be different opinions concerning mankind, as more or less governed by interest; and some will ascribe actions to self-love, which others will ascribe to particular passions: yet it

---

interest or pride; which pride also would doubtless have been explained to be self-love. Pag. 85. Ed. 1725. As if there were no such passions in mankind, as desire of esteem, or of being beloved, or of knowledge. Hobbes's account of the affections of good-will and pity, are instances of the same kind.

* § 414, etc.   † See the [first] Note, § 389.

[1 La Rochefoucauld.]

is absurd to say that mankind are wholly actuated by either; since it is manifest that both have their influence. For as on the one hand, men form a general notion of interest, some placing it in one thing, and some in another, and have a considerable regard to it throughout the course of their life, which is owing to self-love; so on the other hand, they are often set on work by the particular passions themselves, and a considerable part of life is spent in the actual gratification of them, i.e. is employed, not by self-love, but by the passions.

Besides, the very idea of an interested pursuit, necessarily presupposes particular passions or appetites; since the very idea of interest or happiness consists in this, that an appetite or affection enjoys its object. It is not because we love ourselves that we find delight in such and such objects, but because we have particular affections towards them. Take away these affections, and you leave self-love absolutely nothing at all to employ itself about*; no end or object for it to pursue, excepting only that of avoiding pain. Indeed the Epicureans, who maintained that absence of pain, was the highest happiness, might, consistently with themselves, deny all affection, and, if they had so pleased, every sensual appetite too: but the very idea of interest or happiness other than absence of pain, implies particular appetites or passions; these being necessary to constitute that interest or happiness.

384   The observation that benevolence is no more disinterested than any of the common particular passions†, seems in itself worth being taken notice of; but is insisted upon to obviate that scorn, which one sees rising upon the faces of people who are said to know the world, when mention is made of a disinterested, generous or public-spirited action. The truth of that observation might be made appear, in a more formal manner of proof: for whoever will consider all the possible respects and relations which any particular affection can have to self-love and private interest, will, I think, see demonstrably, that benevolence is not in any respect more at variance with self-love, than any other particular affection whatever, but that it is in every respect, at least, as friendly to it.

If the observation be true, it follows, that self-love and benevolence, virtue and interest, are not to be opposed, but only to be distinguished from each other; in the same way as virtue and any other particular affection, love of arts, suppose, are to be distinguished.

* § 417.   † § 419, etc.

Every thing is what it is, and not another thing. The goodness or badness of actions does not arise from hence, that the epithet, interested or disinterested, may be applied to them, any more than that any other indifferent epithet, suppose inquisitive or jealous, may or may not be applied to them; not from their being attended with present or future pleasure or pain; but from their being what they are: namely, what becomes such creatures as we are, what the state of the case requires, or the contrary. Or in other words, we may judge and determine, that an action is morally good or evil, before we so much as consider, whether it be interested or disinterested. This consideration no more comes in to determine whether an action be virtuous, than to determine whether it be resentful. Self-love in its due degree is as just and morally good, as any affection whatever. Benevolence towards particular persons may be to a degree of weakness, and so be blameable: and disinterestedness is so far from being in itself commendable, that the utmost possible depravity, which we can in imagination conceive, is that of disinterested cruelty.[1]

Neither does there appear any reason to wish self-love were **385** weaker in the generality of the world, than it is. The influence which it has, seems plainly owing to its being constant and habitual, which it cannot but be, and not to the degree or strength of it. Every caprice of the imagination, every curiosity of the understanding, every affection of the heart, is perpetually showing its weakness, by prevailing over it. Men daily, hourly sacrifice the greatest known interest, to fancy, inquisitiveness, love or hatred, any vagrant inclination. The thing to be lamented is, not that men have so great regard to their own good or interest in the present world, for they have not enough*; but that they have so little to the good of others. And this seems plainly owing to their being so much engaged in the gratification of particular passions unfriendly to benevolence, and which happen to be most prevalent in them, much more than to self-love. As a proof of this may be observed, that there is no character more void of friendship, gratitude, natural affection, love to their country, common justice, or more equally and uniformly hard-hearted, than the *abandoned* in, what is called, the way of

* § 393 [and cf. Shaftesbury, § 212].

[[1] Cf. Hutcheson, § 329.]

pleasure—hard-hearted and totally without feeling in behalf of others; except when they cannot escape the sight of distress, and so are interrupted by it in their pleasures. And yet it is ridiculous to call such an abandoned course of pleasure interested, when the person engaged in it knows beforehand, and goes on under the feeling and apprehension, that it will be as ruinous to himself, as to those who depend upon him.

Upon the whole, if the generality of mankind were to cultivate within themselves the principle of self-love; if they were to accustom themselves often to set down and consider, what was the greatest happiness they were capable of attaining for themselves in this life, and if self-love were so strong and prevalent, as that they would uniformly pursue this their supposed chief temporal good, without being diverted from it by any particular passion; it would manifestly prevent numberless follies and vices. This was in a great measure the Epicurean system of philosophy. It is indeed by no means the religious, or even moral institution of life. Yet, with all the mistakes men would fall into about interest, it would be less mischievous, than the extravagancies of mere appetite, will and pleasure: for certainly self-love, though confined to the interest of this life, is, of the two, a much better guide than passion*, which has absolutely no bound nor measure, but what is set to it by this self-love, or moral considerations.

386   From the distinction above made between self-love, and the several particular principles or affections in our nature, we may see how good ground there was for that assertion, maintained by the several ancient schools of philosophy, against the Epicureans, namely, that virtue is to be pursued as an end, eligible in and for itself. For, if there be any principles or affections in the mind of man distinct from self-love, that the things those principles tend towards, or that the objects of those affections are, each of them, in themselves eligible, to be pursued upon its own account, and to be rested in as an end, is implied in the very idea of such principle or affection. They indeed asserted much higher things of virtue, and with very good reason; but to say thus much of it, that it is to be pursued for itself, is to say no more of it, than may truly be said of the object of every natural affection whatever.

★   ★   ★   ★

* § 400.

SERMONS I, II, III—UPON HUMAN NATURE, OR MAN CONSIDERED AS A MORAL AGENT

SERMON I—UPON THE SOCIAL NATURE OF MAN

ROM. xii. 4, 5—*For as we have many members in one body, and all members have not the same office: so we being many are one body in Christ, and every one members one of another.*

★　　★　　★　　★

The relation, which the several parts or members of the natural **387** body have to each other and to the whole body, is here compared to the relation which each particular person in society has to other particular persons and to the whole society: and the latter is intended to be illustrated by the former. And if there be a likeness between these two relations, the consequence is obvious: that the latter shows us we were intended to do good to others, as the former shows us that the several members of the natural body were intended to be instruments of good to each other and to the whole body. But as there is scarce any ground for a comparison between society and the mere material body, this without the mind being a dead unactive thing; much less can the comparison be carried to any length. And since the Apostle speaks of the several members as having distinct offices, which implies the mind; it cannot be thought an unallowable liberty; instead of the *body* and *its members,* to substitute the *whole nature of man,* and *all the variety of internal principles which belong to it.* And then the comparison will be between the nature of man as respecting self, and tending to private good, his own preservation and happiness; and the nature of man as having respect to society, and tending to promote public good, the happiness of that society. These ends do indeed perfectly coincide; and to aim at public and private good are so far from being inconsistent, that they mutually promote each other: yet in the following discourse they must be considered as entirely distinct; otherwise the nature of man as tending to one, or as tending to the other, cannot be compared. There can no comparison be made, without considering the things compared as distinct and different.

From this review and comparison of the nature of man as respecting self, and as respecting society, it will plainly appear, that *there are as real and the same kind of indications in human nature, that we were made for society and to do good to our fellow-creatures; as that we were intended to take care of our own life and health and private good: and that the same objections lie against one of these assertions, as against the other.* For

388   *First,* there is a natural principle of *benevolence** in man; which is

* Suppose a man of learning to be writing a grave book upon *Human Nature,* and to show in several parts of it that he had an insight into the subject he was considering: amongst other things, the following one would require to be accounted for; the appearance of benevolence or good-will in men towards each other in the instances of natural relation, and in others†. Cautious of being deceived with outward show, he retires within himself to see exactly, what that is in the mind of man from whence this appearance proceeds; and, upon deep reflection, asserts the principle in the mind to be only the love of power,[1] and delight in the exercise of it. Would not every body think here was a mistake of one word for another? That the philosopher was contemplating and accounting for some other *human actions,* some other behaviour of man to man? And could any one be thoroughly satisfied, that what is commonly called benevolence or good-will was really the affection meant, but only by being made to understand that this learned person had a general hypothesis, to which the appearance of good-will could no otherwise be reconciled? That what has this appearance is often nothing but ambition; that delight in superiority often (suppose always) mixes itself with benevolence, only makes it more specious to call it ambition than hunger, of the two: but in reality that passion does no more account for the whole appearances of good-will, than this appetite does. Is there not often the appearance of one man's wishing that good to another, which he knows himself unable to procure him; and rejoicing in it, though bestowed by a third person? And can love of power any way possibly come in to account for this desire or delight? Is there not often the appearance of men's distinguishing between two or more persons, preferring one before another to do good to, in cases where love of power cannot in the least account for the distinction and preference? For this principle can no otherwise distinguish between objects, than as it is a greater instance and exertion of power to do good to one rather than to another. Again, suppose good-will in the mind of man to be nothing but delight in the exercise of power: men might indeed be restrained by distant and accidental considerations; but these restraints being removed, they would have a disposition to, and delight in mischief as an exercise and proof of power: and this disposition and delight would arise from or be the same principle in the mind, as a disposition to and delight in charity. Thus cruelty, as distinct from envy and resentment, would be exactly the same in the mind of man as good-will: that one tends to the happiness, the other to the misery of our fellow-creatures, is, it seems, merely an accidental circumstance, which the mind has not the least regard to. These are the absurdities which even men of capacity run into, when they have occasion to belie their nature, and will perversely disclaim that image of God which was originally stamped upon it; the traces of which, however faint, are plainly discernible upon the mind of man.

If any person can in earnest doubt, whether there be such a thing as good-will in one man towards another; (for the question is not concerning either the degree or exten-

† Hobbes, of Human Nature, c. 9. § 17 [i.e. Hobbes, § 13].

[1 But contrast what Hobbes actually says in § 13, and cf. § 29.]

in some degree to *society*, what *self-love* is to the *individual*. And if there be in mankind any disposition to friendship; if there be any such thing as compassion, for compassion is momentary love; if there be any such thing as the paternal or filial affections; if there be any affection in human nature, the object and end of which is the good of another; this is itself benevolence, or the love of another. Be it ever so short, be it in ever so low a degree, or ever so unhappily confined; it proves the assertion, and points out what we were designed for, as really as though it were in a higher degree and more extensive. I must however remind you, that though benevolence and self-love are different; though the former tends most directly to public good, and the latter to private: yet they are so perfectly coincident, that the greatest satisfactions to ourselves depend upon our having benevolence in a due degree; and that self-love is one chief security of our right behaviour towards society. It may be added, that their mutual coinciding, so that we can scarce promote one without the other, is equally a proof that we were made for both.

Secondly, this will further appear from observing that the *several* **389** *passions* and *affections*, which are distinct* both from benevolence[1]

siveness of it, but concerning the affection itself;) let it be observed, that *whether man be thus, or otherwise constituted, what is the inward frame in this particular*, is a mere question of fact or natural history, not provable immediately by reason. It is therefore to be judged of and determined in the same way other facts or matters of natural history are: by appealing to the external senses, or inward perceptions, respectively, as the matter under consideration is cognizable by one or the other: by arguing from acknowledged facts and actions; for a great number of actions of the same kind, in different circumstances, and respecting different objects, will prove, to a certainty, what principles they do not, and, to the greatest probability, what principles they do proceed from: and lastly, by the testimony of mankind. Now that there is some degree of benevolence amongst men, may be as strongly and plainly proved in all these ways, as it could possibly be proved, supposing there was this affection in our nature. And should any one think fit to assert, that resentment in the mind of man was absolutely nothing but reasonable concern for our own safety; the falsity of this, and what is the real nature of that passion, could be shown in no other ways than those in which it may be shown, that there is such a thing in *some degree* as *real* good-will in man towards man. It is sufficient that the seeds of it be implanted in our nature by God. There is, it is owned, much left for us to do upon our own heart and temper; to cultivate, to improve, to call it forth, to exercise it in a steady, uniform manner. This is our work: this is virtue and religion.

* Every body makes a distinction between self-love, and the several particular passions, appetites, and affections; and yet they are often confounded again. That they are totally different will be seen by any one who will distinguish between the passions and appetites *themselves*, and *endeavouring* after the means of their gratification.

[1 Cf. Hutcheson, § 331.]

and self-love, do in general contribute and lead us to *public* good, as really as to *private*. It might be thought too minute and particular, and would carry us too great a length, to distinguish between and compare together the several passions or appetites distinct from benevolence, whose primary use and intention is the security and good of society; and the passions distinct from self-love, whose primary intention and design is the security and good of the individual★. It is enough to the present argument, that desire of esteem from others, contempt and esteem of them, love of society as distinct from affection to the good of it, indignation against successful vice, that these are public affections or passions; have an immediate respect to others, naturally lead us to regulate our behaviour in such a manner as will be of service to our fellow-creatures. If any or all of these may be considered likewise as private affections, as tending to private good;

Consider the appetite of hunger, and the desire of esteem: these being the occasion both of pleasure and pain, the coolest *self-love*, as well as the appetites and passions themselves, may put us upon making use of the *proper methods of obtaining* that pleasure, and avoiding that pain; but the *feelings themselves*, the pain of hunger and shame, and the delight from esteem, are no more self-love than they are any thing in the world. Though a man hated himself, he would as much feel the pain of hunger as he would that of the gout: and it is plainly supposable there may be creatures with self-love in them to the highest degree, who may be quite insensible and indifferent (as men in some cases are) to the contempt and esteem of those, upon whom their happiness does not in some further respects depend. And as self-love and the several particular passions and appetites are in themselves totally different; so, that some actions proceed from one, and some from the other, will be manifest to any who will observe the two following very supposable cases. One man rushes upon certain ruin for the gratification of a present desire: no body will call the principle of this action self-love. Suppose another man to go through some laborious work upon promise of a great reward, without any distinct knowledge what the reward will be: this course of action cannot be ascribed to any particular passion. The former of these actions is plainly to be imputed to some particular passion or affection, the latter as plainly to the general affection or principle of self-love. That there are some particular pursuits or actions concerning which we cannot determine how far they are owing to one, and how far to the other, proceeds from this, that the two principles are frequently mixed together, and run up into each other. This distinction is further explained in the eleventh sermon.

★ If any desire to see this distinction and comparison made in a particular instance, the appetite and passion now mentioned may serve for one. Hunger is to be considered as a private appetite; because the end for which it was given us is the preservation of the individual. Desire of esteem is a public passion; because the end for which it was given us is to regulate our behaviour towards society. The respect which this has to private good is as remote, as the respect that has to public good: and the appetite is no more self-love, than the passion is benevolence. The object and end of the former is merely food; the object and end of the latter is merely esteem: but the latter can no more be gratified, without contributing to the good of society; than the former can be gratified, without contributing to the preservation of the individual.

this does not hinder them from being public affections too, or destroy the good influence of them upon society, and their tendency to public good. It may be added, that as persons without any conviction from reason of the desirableness of life, would yet of course preserve it merely from the appetite of hunger; so by acting merely from regard (suppose) to reputation, without any consideration of the good of others, men often contribute to public good. In both these instances they are plainly instruments in the hands of another, in the hands of Providence, to carry on ends, the preservation of the individual and good of society, which they themselves have not in their view or intention. The sum is, men have various appetites, passions, and particular affections, quite distinct both from self-love, and from benevolence: all of these have a tendency to promote both public and private good, and may be considered as respecting others and ourselves equally and in common: but some of them seem most immediately to respect others, or tend to public good; others of them most immediately to respect self, or tend to private good: as the former are not benevolence, so the latter are not self-love: neither sort are instances of our love either to ourselves or others; but only instances of our Maker's care and love both of the individual and the species, and proofs that he intended we should be instruments of good to each other, as well as that we should be so to ourselves.

Thirdly, there is a principle of reflection in men, by which they **390** distinguish between, approve and disapprove their own actions. We are plainly constituted such sort of creatures as to reflect upon our own nature.[1] The mind can take a view of what passes within itself, its propensions, aversions, passions, affections, as respecting such objects, and in such degrees; and of the several actions consequent thereupon. In this survey it approves of one, disapproves of another, and towards a third is affected in neither of these ways, but is quite indifferent. This principle in man, by which he approves or disapproves his heart, temper, and actions, is conscience; for this is the strict sense of the word, though sometimes it is used so as to take in more. And that this faculty tends to restrain men from doing mischief to each other, and leads them to do good, is too manifest to need being insisted upon. Thus a parent has the affection of love to his children: this leads him to take care of, to educate, to make due provision for them; the natural affection leads to this: but the

[1 Cf. Shaftesbury, §§ 200, 204, 220; Hutcheson, § 314.]

reflection that it is his proper business, what belongs to him, that it is right and commendable so to do; this added to the affection, becomes a much more settled principle, and carries him on through more labour and difficulties for the sake of his children, than he would undergo from that affection, alone; if he thought it, and the course of action it led to, either indifferent or criminal. This indeed is impossible, to do that which is good and not to approve of it; for which reason they are frequently not considered as distinct, though they really are: for men often approve of the actions of others, which they will not imitate, and likewise do that which they approve not. It cannot possibly be denied that there is this principle of reflection or conscience in human nature. Suppose a man to relieve an innocent person in great distress; suppose the same man afterwards, in the fury of anger, to do the greatest mischief to a person who had given no just cause of offence; to aggravate the injury, add the circumstances of former friendship, and obligation from the injured person; let the man who is supposed to have done these two different actions, coolly reflect upon them afterwards, without regard to their consequences to himself: to assert that any common man would be affected in the same way towards these different actions, that he would make no distinction between them, but approve or disapprove them equally, is too glaring a falsity to need being confuted. There is therefore this principle of reflection or conscience in mankind. It is needless to compare the respect it has to private good, with the respect it has to public; since it plainly tends as much to the latter as to the former, and is commonly thought to tend chiefly to the latter. This faculty is now mentioned merely as another part in the inward frame of man, pointing out to us in some degree what we are intended for, and as what will naturally and of course have some influence. The particular place assigned to it by nature, what authority it has, and how great influence it ought to have, shall be hereafter considered.

391　　From this comparison of benevolence and self-love, of our public and private affections, of the courses of life they lead to, and of the principle of reflection or conscience as respecting each of them, it is as manifest, that *we were made for society, and to promote the happiness of it; as that we were intended to take care of our own life, and health, and private good.*

And from this whole review must be given a different draught of human nature from what we are often presented with. Mankind are by nature so closely united, there is such a correspondence between the inward sensations of one man and those of another, that disgrace is as much avoided as bodily pain, and to be the object of esteem and love as much desired as any external goods: and in many particular cases, persons are carried on to do good to others, as the end their affection tends to and rests in; and manifest that they find real satisfaction and enjoyment in this course of behaviour. There is such a natural principle of attraction[1] in man towards man, that having trod the same tract of land, having breathed in the same climate, barely having been born in the same artificial district or division, becomes the occasion of contracting acquaintances and familiarities many years after: for any thing may serve the purpose. Thus relations merely nominal are sought and invented, not by governors,[2] but by the lowest of the people; which are found sufficient to hold mankind together in little fraternities and copartnerships: weak ties indeed, and what may afford fund enough for ridicule, if they are absurdly considered as the real principles of that union: but they are in truth merely the occasions, as any thing may be of any thing, upon which our nature carries us on according to its own previous bent and bias; which occasions therefore would be nothing at all, were there not this prior disposition and bias of nature. Men are so much one body, that in a peculiar manner they feel for each other, shame, sudden danger, resentment, honour, prosperity, distress; one or another, or all of these, from the social nature in general, from benevolence, upon the occasion of natural relation, acquaintance, protection, dependence; each of these being distinct cements of society. And therefore to have no restraint from, no regard to others in our behaviour, is the speculative absurdity of considering ourselves as single and independent, as having nothing in our nature which has respect to our fellow-creatures, reduced to action and practice. And this is the same absurdity, as to suppose a hand, or any part to have no natural respect to any other, or to the whole body.

But allowing all this, it may be asked, 'Has not man dispositions **392** and principles within, which lead him to do evil to others, as well as to do good? Whence come the many miseries else, which men are the authors and instruments of to each other?' These questions, so far as they relate to the foregoing discourse, may be answered by

[1 Cf. Hutcheson, § 343.]　　　　[2 Contrast Mandeville, §§ 263, 267-8.]

asking, Has not man also dispositions and principles within, which lead him to do evil to himself, as well as good? Whence come the many miseries else, sickness, pain and death, which men are the instruments and authors of to themselves?

It may be thought more easy to answer one of these questions than the other, but the answer to both is really the same; that mankind have ungoverned passions which they will gratify at any rate, as well to the injury of others, as in contradiction to known private interest: but that as there is no such thing as self-hatred, so neither is there any such thing as ill-will in one man towards another,[1] emulation and resentment being away; whereas there is plainly benevolence or good-will: there is no such thing as love of injustice, oppression, treachery, ingratitude; but only eager desires after such and such external goods; which, according to a very ancient observation, the most abandoned would choose to obtain by innocent means, if they were as easy, and as effectual to their end: that even emulation and resentment, by any one who will consider what these passions really are in nature*, will be found nothing to the purpose of this objection: and that the principles and passions in the mind of man, which are distinct both from self-love and benevolence, primarily and most directly lead to right behaviour with regard to others as well as himself, and only secondarily and accidentally to what is evil. Thus, though men, to avoid the shame of one villainy, are sometimes guilty of a greater, yet it is easy to see, that the original tendency of shame is to prevent the doing of shameful actions; and its leading men to conceal such actions when done, is only in consequence of their being done; i.e. of the passion's not having answered its first end.

393   If it be said, that there are persons in the world, who are in great

* Emulation is merely the desire and hope of equality with or superiority over others, with whom we compare ourselves. There does not appear to be any *other grief* in the natural passion, but only *that want* which is implied in desire. However this may be so strong as to be the occasion of great *grief*. To desire the attainment of this equality or superiority by the *particular means* of others, being brought down to our own level, or below it, is, I think, the distinct notion of envy. From whence it is easy to see, that the real end, which the natural passion emulation, and which the unlawful one envy aims at, is exactly the same; namely, that equality or superiority: and consequently, that to do mischief is not the end of envy, but merely the means it makes use of to attain its end. As to resentment, see the eighth sermon.

[1 Cf. Hobbes on cruelty, § 32, and Hutcheson on disinterested malice, §§ 326, 329, 336, 338.]

measure without the natural affections towards their fellow-creatures: there are likewise instances of persons without the common natural affections to themselves: but the nature of man is not to be judged of by either of these, but by what appears in the common world, in the bulk of mankind.

I am afraid it would be thought very strange, if to confirm the truth of this account of human nature, and make out the justness of the foregoing comparison, it should be added, that from what appears, men in fact as much and as often contradict that *part* of their nature which respects *self*, and which leads them to their *own private* good and happiness; as they contradict that *part* of it which respects *society*, and tends to *public* good: that there are as few persons, who attain the greatest satisfaction and enjoyment which they might attain in the present world; as who do the greatest good to others which they might do: nay, that there are as few who can be said really and in earnest to aim at one, as at the other. Take a survey of mankind: the world in general, the good and bad, almost without exception, equally are agreed, that were religion out of the case, the happiness of the present life would consist in a manner wholly in riches, honours, sensual gratifications; insomuch that one scarce hears a reflection made upon prudence, life, conduct, but upon this supposition. Yet on the contrary, that persons in the greatest affluence of fortune are no happier than such as have only a competency; that the cares and disappointments of ambition for the most part far exceed the satisfactions of it; as also the miserable intervals of intemperance and excess, and the many untimely deaths occasioned by a dissolute course of life: these things are all seen, acknowledged, by every one acknowledged; but are thought no objections against, though they expressly contradict, this universal principle, that the happiness of the present life consists in one or other of them. Whence is all this absurdity and contradiction? Is not the middle way obvious? Can any thing be more manifest, than that the happiness of life consists in these possessed and enjoyed only to a certain degree; that to pursue them beyond this degree, is always attended with more inconvenience than advantage to a man's self, and often with extreme misery and unhappiness. Whence then, I say, is all this absurdity and contradiction? Is it really the result of consideration in mankind, how they may become most easy to themselves, most free from care, and enjoy the chief happiness attainable in this world?

Or is it not manifestly owing either to this, that they have not cool and reasonable concern enough for themselves, to consider wherein their chief happiness in the present life consists; or else, if they do consider it, that they will not act conformably to what is the result of that consideration: i.e. reasonable concern for themselves, or cool self-love is prevailed over by passion and appetite. So that from what appears, there is no ground to assert that those principles in the nature of man, which most directly lead to promote the good of our fellow-creatures, are more generally or in a greater degree violated, than those, which most directly lead us to promote our own private good and happiness.

394   The sum of the whole is plainly this. The nature of man considered in his single capacity, and with respect only to the present world, is adapted and leads him to attain the greatest happiness he can for himself in the present world. The nature of man considered in his public or social capacity leads him to a right behaviour in society, to that course of life which we call virtue. Men follow or obey their nature in both these capacities and respects to a certain degree, but not entirely: their actions do not come up to the whole of what their nature leads them to in either of these capacities or respects: and they often violate their nature in both. I.e., as they neglect the duties they owe to their fellow-creatures, to which their nature leads them; and are injurious, to which their nature is abhorrent: so there is a manifest negligence in men of their real happiness or interest in the present world, when that interest is inconsistent with a present gratification; for the sake of which they negligently, nay, even knowingly are the authors and instruments of their own misery and ruin. Thus they are as often unjust to themselves as to others, and for the most part are equally so to both by the same actions.

SERMON II, III—UPON THE NATURAL SUPREMACY OF CONSCIENCE

ROM. ii. 14—*For when the Gentiles which have not the law, do by nature the things contained in the law, these having not the law, are a law unto themselves.*[1]

395   As speculative truth admits of different kinds of proof, so likewise moral obligations may be shown by different methods. If the real

[1 Cf. Clarke, § 234.]

nature of any creature leads him and is adapted to such and such purposes only, or more than to any other; this is a reason to believe the Author of that nature intended it for those purposes. Thus there is no doubt the eye was intended for us to see with. And the more complex any constitution is, and the greater variety of parts there are which thus tend to some one end, the stronger is the proof that such end was designed. However, when the inward frame of man is considered as any guide in morals, the utmost caution must be used that none make peculiarities in their own temper, or any thing which is the effect of particular customs, though observable in several, the standard of what is common to the species; and above all, that the highest principle be not forgot or excluded, that to which belongs the adjustment and correction of all other inward movements and affections: which principle will of course have some influence, but which being in nature supreme, as shall now be shown, ought to preside over and govern all the rest. The difficulty of rightly observing the two former cautions; the appearance there is of some small diversity amongst mankind with respect to this faculty, with respect to their natural sense of moral good and evil; and the attention necessary to survey with any exactness what passes within, have occasioned that it is not so much agreed what is the standard of the internal nature of man, as of his external form. Neither is this last exactly settled. Yet we understand one another when we speak of the shape of a human body: so likewise we do when we speak of the heart and inward principles, how far soever the standard is from being exact or precisely fixed. There is therefore ground for an attempt of showing men to themselves, of showing them what course of life and behaviour their real nature points out and would lead them to. Now obligations of virtue shown, and motives to the practice of it enforced, from a review of the nature of man, are to be considered as an appeal to each particular person's heart and natural conscience: as the external senses are appealed to for the proof of things cognizable by them. Since then our inward feelings, and the perceptions we receive from our external senses, are equally real; to argue from the former to life and conduct, is as little liable to exception, as to argue from the latter to absolute speculative truth. A man can as little doubt whether his eyes were given him to see with, as he can doubt of the truth of the science of *optics*, deduced from ocular experiments. And allowing the inward feeling, shame;

a man can as little doubt whether it was given him to prevent his doing shameful actions, as he can doubt whether his eyes were given him to guide his steps. And as to these inward feelings themselves; that they are real, that man has in his nature passions and affections, can no more be questioned, than that he has external senses. Neither can the former be wholly mistaken; though to a certain degree liable to greater mistakes than the latter.

396   There can be no doubt but that several propensions or instincts, several principles in the heart of man, carry him to society, and to contribute to the happiness of it, in a sense and a manner in which no inward principle leads him to evil. These principles, propensions or instincts which lead him to do good, are approved of by a certain faculty within, quite distinct from these propensions themselves. All this hath been fully made out in the foregoing discourse.

But it may be said, 'What is all this, though true, to the purpose of virtue and religion? These require, not only that we do good to others when we are led this way, by benevolence or reflection, happening to be stronger than other principles, passions, or appetites; but likewise that the *whole* character be formed upon thought and reflection; that *every* action be directed by some determinate rule, some other rule than the strength and prevalency of any principle or passion. What sign is there in our nature (for the inquiry is only about what is to be collected from thence) that this was intended by its Author? Or how does so various and fickle a temper as that of man appear adapted thereto? It may indeed be absurd and unnatural for men to act without any reflection; nay, without regard to that particular kind of reflection which you call conscience; because this does belong to our nature. For as there never was a man but who approved one place, prospect, building, before another: so it does not appear that there ever was a man who would not have approved an action of humanity rather than of cruelty; interest and passion being quite out of the case. But interest and passion do come in, and are often too strong for and prevail over reflection and conscience. Now as brutes have various instincts, by which they are carried on to the end the Author of their nature intended them for: is not man in the same condition; with this difference only, that to his instincts (i.e. appetites and passions) is added the principle of reflection or conscience? And as brutes act agreeably to their nature, in following that principle or particular instinct which for the present is strongest in them: does not man likewise act agreeably to his nature, or obey the law of his creation, by following that principle, be it passion or conscience, which for the present happens to be strongest in him? Thus different men are by their particular nature hurried on to pursue honour, or riches, or pleasure: there are also persons whose temper leads them in an uncommon degree to kindness, compassion, doing good to their fellow-creatures: as there are others who are given to suspend their judgement, to weigh and consider things, and to act upon thought and reflection. Let every one then quietly follow his nature; as passion, reflection, appetite, the several parts of it, happen to be strongest: but let not the man of virtue take upon him to blame the ambitious, the covetous, the dissolute; since these equally with him obey and follow their nature. Thus, as in some cases we follow our nature in doing the works *contained in the law*, so in other cases we follow nature in doing contrary.'

Now all this licentious talk entirely goes upon a supposition, that **397** men follow their nature in the same sense, in violating the known rules of justice and honesty for the sake of a present gratification, as they do in following those rules when they have no temptation to the contrary. And if this were true, that could not be so which St. Paul asserts, that men are *by nature a law to themselves*. If by following nature were meant only acting as we please, it would indeed be ridiculous to speak of nature as any guide in morals: nay the very mention of deviating from nature would be absurd; and the mention of following it, when spoken by way of distinction, would absolutely have no meaning. For did ever any one act otherwise than as he pleased? And yet the ancients speak of deviating from nature as vice; and of following nature so much as a distinction, that according to them the perfection of virtue consists therein. So that language itself should teach people another sense to the words *following nature*, than barely acting as we please. Let it however be observed, that though the words *human nature* are to be explained, yet the real question of this discourse is not concerning the meaning of words, any otherwise than as the explanation of them may be needful to make out and explain the assertion, that *every man is naturally a law to himself*, that *every one may find within himself the rule of right, and obligations to follow it*. This St. Paul affirms in the words of the text, and this the foregoing objection really denies by seeming to allow it. And the objection will be fully answered, and the text before us explained, by observing that *nature* is considered in different views, and the word used in different senses; and by showing in what view it is considered, and in what sense the word is used, when intended to express and signify that which is the guide of life, that by which men are a law to themselves. I say, the explanation of the term will be sufficient, because from thence it will appear, that in some senses of the word, *nature* cannot be, but that in another sense it manifestly is, a law to us.

398   I. By *nature* is often meant no more than some principle in man, without regard either to the kind or degree of it. Thus the passion of anger, and the affection of parents to their children, would be called equally *natural*. And as the same person hath often contrary principles, which at the same time draw contrary ways, he may by the same action both follow and contradict his nature in this sense of the word; he may follow one passion and contradict another.

II. *Nature* is frequently spoken of as consisting in those passions which are strongest, and most influence the actions; which being vicious ones, mankind is in this sense naturally vicious, or vicious by nature. Thus St. Paul says of the Gentiles, *who were dead in trespasses and sins, and walked according to the spirit of disobedience*, that *they were by nature the children of wrath**. They could be no otherwise *children of wrath* by nature, than they were vicious by nature.

Here then are two different senses of the word *nature*, in neither of which men can at all be said to be a law to themselves. They are mentioned only to be excluded; to prevent their being confounded, as the latter is in the objection, with another sense of it, which is now to be inquired after, and explained.

399   III. The Apostle asserts, that *the Gentiles do by* NATURE *the things contained in the law*. Nature is indeed here put by way of distinction from revelation, but yet it is not a mere negative. He intends to express more than that by which they *did not*, that by which they *did* the works of the law; namely, by *nature*. It is plain the meaning of the word is not the same in this passage as in the former, where it is spoken of as evil; for in this latter it is spoken of as good; as that by which they acted, or might have acted virtuously. What that is in man by which he is *naturally a law to himself*, is explained in the following words: *which show the work of the law written in their hearts*,

* Ephes. ii. 3.

*their consciences also bearing witness, and their thoughts the mean while
accusing or else excusing one another.* If there be a distinction to be
made between the *works written in their hearts,* and the *witness of
conscience;* by the former must be meant the natural disposition to
kindness and compassion, to do what is of good report, to which
this Apostle often refers: that part of the nature of man, treated of
in the foregoing discourse, which with very little reflection and of
course leads him to society, and by means of which he naturally
acts a just and good part in it, unless other passions or interest lead
him astray. Yet since other passions, and regards to private interest,
which lead us (though indirectly, yet they lead us) astray, are themselves in a degree equally natural, and often most prevalent; and
since we have no method of seeing the particular degrees in which
one or the other is placed in us by nature; it is plain the former,
considered merely as natural, good and right as they are, can no
more be a law to us than the latter. But there is a superior principle
of reflection or conscience in every man, which distinguishes between the internal principles of his heart, as well as his external
actions: which passes judgement upon himself and them; pronounces
determinately some actions to be in themselves just, right, good;
others to be in themselves evil, wrong, unjust: which, without
being consulted, without being advised with, magisterially exerts
itself, and approves or condemns him the doer of them accordingly:
and which, if not forcibly stopped, naturally and always of course
goes on to anticipate a higher and more effectual sentence, which
shall hereafter second and affirm its own. But this part of the office
of conscience is beyond my present design explicitly to consider. It
is by this faculty, natural to man, that he is a moral agent, that he is
a law to himself: but this faculty, I say, not to be considered merely
as a principle in his heart, which is to have some influence as well
as others; but considered as a faculty in kind and in nature supreme
over all others, and which bears its own authority of being so.

This *prerogative,* this *natural supremacy,* of the faculty which sur-   **400**
veys, approves or disapproves the several affections of our mind,
and actions of our lives, being that by which men *are a law to themselves,* their conformity or disobedience to which law of our nature
renders their actions, in the highest and most proper sense, natural
or unnatural; it is fit it be further explained to you: and I hope it
will be so, if you will attend to the following reflections.

Man may act according to that principle or inclination which for the present happens to be strongest, and yet act in a way disproportionate to, and violate his real proper nature. Suppose a brute creature by any bait to be allured into a snare, by which he is destroyed. He plainly followed the bent of his nature, leading him to gratify his appetite: there is an entire correspondence between his whole nature and such an action: such action therefore is natural. But suppose a man, foreseeing the same danger of certain ruin, should rush into it for the sake of a present gratification. He in this instance would follow his strongest desire, as did the brute creature: but there would be as manifest a disproportion, between the nature of a man and such an action, as between the meanest work of art and the skill of the greatest master in that art: which disproportion arises, not from considering the action singly in *itself*, or in its *consequences*; but from *comparison* of it with the nature of the agent. And since such an action is utterly disproportionate to the nature of man, it is in the strictest and most proper sense unnatural; this word expressing that disproportion. Therefore instead of the words *disproportionate to his nature*, the word, *unnatural*, may now be put; this being more familiar to us: but let it be observed, that it stands for the same thing precisely.

Now what is it which renders such a rash action unnatural? Is it that he went against the principle of reasonable and cool self-love, considered *merely* as a part of his nature? No: for if he had acted the contrary way, he would equally have gone against a principle or part of his nature, namely, passion or appetite. But to deny a present appetite, from foresight that the gratification of it would end in immediate ruin or extreme misery, is by no means an unnatural action: whereas to contradict or go against cool self-love for the sake of such gratification, is so in the instance before us. Such an action then being unnatural; and its being so not arising from a man's going against a principle or desire barely, nor in going against that principle or desire which happens for the present to be strongest; it necessarily follows, that there must be some other difference or distinction to be made between these two principles, passion and cool self-love, than what I have yet taken notice of. And this difference, not being a difference in strength or degree, I call a difference in *nature* and in *kind*. And since, in the instance still before us, if passion prevails over self-love, the consequent action is unnatural; but if self-love prevails over passion, the action is natural: it is manifest that self-love is in human nature a superior principle to passion. This may be contradicted without violating that nature; but the former cannot. So that, if we will act conformably to the economy of man's nature, reasonable self-love must govern. Thus, without particular consideration of conscience, we may have a clear conception of the *superior nature* of one inward principle to another; and see that there really is this natural superiority, quite distinct from degrees of strength and prevalency.

Let us now take a view of the nature of man, as consisting partly **401** of various appetites, passions, affections, and partly of the principle of reflection or conscience; leaving quite out all consideration of the different degrees of strength, in which either of them prevail, and it will further appear that there is this natural superiority of one inward principle to another, and that it is even part of the idea of reflection or conscience.

Passion or appetite implies a direct simple tendency towards such and such objects, without distinction of the means by which they are to be obtained. Consequently it will often happen there will be a desire of particular objects, in cases where they cannot be obtained without manifest injury to others. Reflection or conscience comes in, and disapproves the pursuit of them in these circumstances; but the desire remains. Which is to be obeyed, appetite or reflection? Cannot this question be answered from the economy and constitution of human nature merely, without saying which is strongest? Or need this at all come into consideration? Would not the question be *intelligibly* and fully answered by saying, that the principle of reflection or conscience being compared with the various appetites, passions, and affections in men, the former is manifestly superior and chief, without regard to strength? And how often soever the latter happens to prevail, it is mere *usurpation*: the former remains in nature and in kind its superior; and every instance of such prevalence of the latter is an instance of breaking in upon and violation of the constitution of man.

All this is no more than the distinction, which every body is **402** acquainted with, between *mere power* and *authority*: only, instead of being intended to express the difference between what is possible, and what is lawful in civil government; here it has been shown applicable to the several principles in the mind of man. Thus that principle, by which we survey, and either approve or disapprove our own heart, temper and actions, is not only to be considered as what is in its turn to have some influence; which may be said of every passion, of the lowest appetites: but likewise as being superior; as from its very nature manifestly claiming superiority over all others: insomuch that you cannot form a notion of this faculty, conscience, without taking in judgement, direction, superintendency. This is a constituent part of the idea, that is, of the faculty itself: and, to preside and govern, from the very economy and constitution of man, belongs to it. Had it strength, as it has right; had it power, as it has manifest authority; it would absolutely govern the world.

This gives us a further view of the nature of man; shows us what course of life we were made for: not only that our real nature leads us to be influenced in some degree by reflection and conscience; but likewise in what degree we are to be influenced by it, if we will fall in with, and act agreeably to the constitution of our nature: that this faculty was placed within to be our proper governor; to direct and regulate all under principles, passions, and motives of action. This is its right and office: thus sacred is its authority. And how often soever men violate and rebelliously refuse to submit to it, for supposed interest which they cannot otherwise obtain, or for the sake of passion which they cannot otherwise gratify; this makes no alteration as to the *natural right* and *office* of conscience.

403   Let us now turn this whole matter another way, and suppose there was no such thing at all as this natural supremacy of conscience; that there was no distinction to be made between one inward principle and another, but only that of strength; and see what would be the consequence.

Consider then what is the latitude and compass of the actions of man with regard to himself, his fellow-creatures and the Supreme Being? What are their bounds, besides that of our natural power? With respect to the two first, they are plainly no other than these: no man seeks misery as such for himself; and no one unprovoked does mischief to another for its own sake. For in every degree within these bounds, mankind knowingly from passion or wantonness bring ruin and misery upon themselves and others. And impiety and profaneness, I mean, what every one would call so who believes the being of God, have absolutely no bounds at all. Men blaspheme the Author of nature, formally and in words renounce their allegiance to their Creator. Put an instance then with respect to any one of these three. Though we should suppose profane swearing, and in general that kind of impiety now mentioned, to mean nothing, yet it implies wanton disregard and irreverence towards an Infinite Being, our Creator; and is this as suitable to the nature of man, as reverence and dutiful submission of heart towards that Almighty Being? Or suppose a man guilty of parricide, with all the circumstances of cruelty which such an action can admit of. This action is done in consequence of its principle being for the present strongest: and if there be no difference between inward principles, but only that of strength; the strength being given, you have the whole nature of the man given, so far as it relates to this matter. The action plainly corresponds to the principle, the principle being in that degree of strength it was: it therefore corresponds to the whole nature of the man. Upon comparing the action and the whole nature, there arises no disproportion, there appears no unsuitableness between them. Thus the *murder of a father* and the *nature of man* correspond to each other, as the same nature and an act of filial duty. If there be no difference between inward principles, but only that of strength; we can make no distinction between these two actions, considered as the actions of such a creature; but in our coolest hours must approve or disapprove them equally: than which nothing can be reduced to a greater absurdity.

SERMON III

The natural supremacy of reflection or conscience being thus **404** established; we may from it form a distinct notion of what is meant by *human nature*, when virtue is said to consist in following it, and vice in deviating from it.

As the idea of a civil constitution implies in it united strength, various subordinations, under one direction, that of the supreme authority; the different strength of each particular member of the society not coming into the idea; whereas, if you leave out the subordination, the union and the one direction, you destroy and lose it: so reason, several appetites, passions and affections, prevailing in different degrees of strength, is not *that* idea or notion of *human nature*; but *that nature* consists in these several principles considered as having a natural respect to each other, in the several passions being naturally subordinate to the one superior principle of reflection or conscience. Every bias, instinct, propension within, is a real part of our nature, but not the whole: add to these the superior faculty, whose office it is to adjust, manage and preside over them, and take in this its natural superiority, and you complete the idea of human nature. And as in civil government the constitution is broken in upon and violated by power and strength prevailing over authority; so the constitution of man is broken in upon and violated by the lower faculties or principles within prevailing over that which is in its nature supreme over them all. Thus, when it is said by ancient writers, that tortures and death are not so contrary to human nature as injustice; by this to be sure is not meant, that the aversion to the former in mankind is less strong and prevalent than their aversion to the latter: but that the former is only contrary to our nature considered in a partial view, and which takes in only the lowest part of it, that which we have in common with the brutes; whereas the latter is contrary to our nature, considered in a higher sense, as a system and constitution, contrary to the whole economy of man*.

* Every man in his physical nature is one individual single agent. He has likewise properties and principles, each of which may be considered separately, and without regard to the respects which they have to each other. Neither of these are the nature we are taking a view of. But it is the inward frame of man considered as a *system* or *constitution*: whose several parts are united, not by a physical principle of individuation, but by the respects they have to each other; the chief of which is the subjection which the appetites, passions, and particular affections have to the one supreme principle of reflection or conscience. The system or constitution is formed by and consists in these respects and this subjection. Thus the body is a *system* or *constitution*: so is a tree: so is every machine. Consider all the several parts of a tree without the natural respects they have to each other, and you have not at all the idea of a tree; but add these respects, and this gives you the idea. The body may be impaired by sickness, a tree may decay, a machine be out of order, and yet the system and constitution of them not totally dissolved. There is plainly somewhat which answers to all this in the moral constitution of man. Whoever will consider his own nature, will see that the several appetites, passions, and particular affections, have different respects amongst themselves. They are restraints upon, and are in a proportion to each other. This proportion is just and perfect, when all those under principles are perfectly coincident with conscience, so far as their nature permits, and in all cases under its absolute and entire direction. The least excess or defect, the least alteration of the due proportions amongst themselves, or of their coincidence with conscience, though not proceeding into action, is some degree of disorder in the moral constitution. But perfection, though plainly intelligible and supposable, was never attained by any man. If the higher principle of reflection maintains its place, and as much as it can corrects that disorder, and hinders it from breaking out into action, this is all that can be expected in such a creature as man. And though the appetites and passions have not their exact due proportion to each other;

And from all these things put together, nothing can be more **405**
evident, than that, exclusive of revelation, man cannot be considered
as a creature left by his Maker to act at random, and live at large
up to the extent of his natural power, as passion, humour, wilfulness,
happen to carry him; which is the condition brute creatures are in:
but that *from his make, constitution, or nature, he is in the strictest and
most proper sense a law to himself.* He hath the rule of right within:
what is wanting is only that he honestly attend to it.

The inquiries which have been made by men of leisure after some
general rule, the conformity to, or disagreement from which, should
denominate our actions good or evil, are in many respects of great
service. Yet let any plain honest man, before he engages in any course
of action, ask himself, Is this I am going about right, or is it wrong? Is
it good, or is it evil? I do not in the least doubt but that this question
would be answered agreeably to truth and virtue, by almost any
fair man in almost any circumstance. Neither do there appear any
cases which look like exceptions to this; but those of superstition,
and of partiality to ourselves. Superstition may perhaps be somewhat of an exception: but partiality to ourselves is not; this being
itself dishonesty. For a man to judge that to be the equitable, the
moderate, the right part for him to act, which he would see to be
hard, unjust, oppressive in another; this is plain vice, and can proceed only from great unfairness of mind.

But allowing that mankind hath the rule of right within himself, **406**
yet it may be asked, 'What obligations are we under to attend to and
follow it?' I answer: it has been proved that man by his nature is a
law to himself, without the particular distinct consideration of the
positive sanctions of that law; the rewards and punishments which
we feel, and those which from the light of reason we have ground
to believe, are annexed to it. The question then carries its own answer
along with it. Your obligation to obey this law, is its being the law of
your nature. That your conscience approves of and attests to such a
course of action, is itself alone an obligation. Conscience does not
only offer itself to show us the way we should walk in, but it likewise carries its own authority with it, that it is our natural guide;

though they often strive for mastery with judgement or reflection; yet, since the
superiority of this principle to all others is the chief respect which forms the constitution, so far as this superiority is maintained, the character, the man, is good, worthy,
virtuous.

the guide assigned us by the Author of our nature: it therefore belongs to our condition of being, it is our duty, to walk in that path and follow this guide without looking about to see whether we may not possibly forsake them with impunity.

407 However, let us hear what is to be said against obeying this law of our nature. And the sum is no more than this. 'Why should we be concerned about any thing out of and beyond ourselves? If we do find within ourselves regards to others, and restraints of we know not how many different kinds; yet these being embarrassments, and hindering us from going the nearest way to our own good, why should we not endeavour to suppress and get over them?'

Thus people go on with words, which, when applied to human nature, and the condition in which it is placed in this world, have really no meaning. For does not all this kind of talk go upon supposition, that our happiness in this world consists in somewhat quite distinct from regards to others; and that it is the privilege of vice to be without restraint or confinement? Whereas on the contrary, the enjoyments, in a manner all the common enjoyments of life, even the pleasures of vice, depend upon these regards of one kind or another to our fellow-creatures. Throw off all regards to others, and we should be quite indifferent to infamy and to honour; there could be no such thing at all as ambition; and scarce any such thing as covetousness; for we should likewise be equally indifferent to the disgrace of poverty, the several neglects and kinds of contempt which accompany this state; and to the reputation of riches, the regard and respect they usually procure. Neither is restraint by any means peculiar to one course of life: but our very nature, exclusive of conscience, and our condition, lays us under an absolute necessity of it. We cannot gain any end whatever without being confined to the proper means, which is often the most painful and uneasy confinement. And in numberless instances a present appetite cannot be gratified without such apparent and immediate ruin and misery, that the most dissolute man in the world chooses to forego the pleasure, rather than endure the pain.

408 Is the meaning then, to indulge those regards to our fellow-creatures, and submit to those restraints, which upon the whole are attended with more satisfaction than uneasiness, and get over only those which bring more uneasiness and inconvenience than satisfaction? 'Doubtless this was our meaning.' You have changed sides then. Keep to this; be consistent with yourselves; and you and the men of virtue are *in general* perfectly agreed. But let us take care and avoid mistakes. Let it not be taken for granted that the temper of envy, rage, resentment, yields greater delight than meekness, forgiveness, compassion, and good-will: especially when it is acknowledged that rage, envy, resentment, are in themselves mere misery; and the satisfaction arising from the indulgence of them is little more than relief from that misery; whereas the temper of compassion and benevolence is itself delightful; and the indulgence of it, by doing good, affords new positive delight and enjoyment. Let it not be taken for granted, that the satisfaction arising from the reputation of riches and power however obtained, and from the respect paid to them, is greater than the satisfaction arising from the reputation of justice, honesty, charity, and the esteem which is universally acknowledged to be their due. And if it be doubtful which of these satisfactions is the greatest, as there are persons who think neither of them very considerable, yet there can be no doubt concerning ambition and covetousness, virtue and a good mind, considered in themselves, and as leading to different courses of life; there can, I say, be no doubt, which temper and which course is attended with most peace and tranquillity of mind, which with most perplexity, vexation and inconvenience. And both the virtues and vices which have been now mentioned, do in a manner equally imply in them regards of one kind or another to our fellow-creatures. And with respect to restraint and confinement: whoever will consider the restraints from fear and shame, the dissimulation, mean arts of concealment, servile compliances, one or other of which belong to almost every course of vice; will soon be convinced that the man of virtue is by no means upon a disadvantage in this respect. How many instances are there in which men feel and own and cry aloud under the chains of vice with which they are enthralled, and which yet they will not shake off? How many instances, in which persons manifestly go through more pains and self-denial to gratify a vicious passion, than would have been necessary to the conquest of it? To this is to be added, that when virtue is become habitual, when the temper of it is acquired, what was before confinement ceases to be so, by becoming choice and delight. Whatever restraint and guard upon ourselves may be needful to unlearn any unnatural distortion or odd gesture; yet, in all propriety of speech, natural behaviour must be the most easy and unrestrained. It is manifest that, in the common course of life, there is seldom any inconsistency between our duty and what is *called* interest: it is much seldomer that there is an inconsistency between duty and what is really our present interest; meaning by interest, happiness and satisfaction. Self-love then, though confined to the interest of the present world, does in general perfectly coincide with virtue; and leads us to one and the same course of life. But, whatever exceptions there are to this, which are much fewer than they are commonly thought, all shall be set right at the final distribution of things. It is a manifest absurdity to suppose evil prevailing finally over good, under the conduct and administration of a perfect mind.

409   The whole argument, which I have been now insisting upon, may be thus summed up and given you in one view. The nature of man is adapted to some course of action or other. Upon comparing some actions with this nature, they appear suitable and correspondent to it: from comparison of other actions with the same nature, there arises to our view some unsuitableness or disproportion. The correspondence of actions to the nature of the agent renders them natural: their disproportion to it, unnatural. That an action is correspondent to the nature of the agent, does not arise from its being agreeable to the principle which happens to be the strongest: for it may be so, and yet be quite disproportionate to the nature of the agent. The correspondence therefore, or disproportion, arises from somewhat else. This can be nothing but a difference in nature and kind (altogether distinct from strength) between the inward principles. Some then are in nature and kind superior to others. And the correspondence arises from the action being conformable to the higher principle; and the unsuitableness from its being contrary to it. Reasonable self-love and conscience are the chief or superior principles in the nature of man: because an action may be suitable to this nature, though all other principles be violated; but becomes unsuitable, if either of those are. Conscience and self-love, if we understand our true happiness, always lead us the same way. Duty and interest are perfectly coincident; for the most part in this world, but entirely and in every instance if we take in the future, and the whole; this being implied in the notion of a good and perfect administration of things. Thus they who have been so wise in their generation as to regard only their own supposed interest, at the expense and to the injury of others, shall at last find, that he who has given up all the advantages of the present world, rather than violate his conscience and the relations of life, has infinitely better provided for himself, and secured his own interest and happiness.

SERMON V—UPON COMPASSION

ROM. xii. 15—*Rejoice with them that do rejoice, and weep with them that weep.*

Every man is to be considered in two capacities, the private and **410** public; as designed to pursue his own interest, and likewise to contribute to the good of others. Whoever will consider, may see, that in general there is no contrariety between these; but that from the original constitution of man, and the circumstances he is placed in, they perfectly coincide, and mutually carry on each other. But, amongst the great variety of affections or principles of action in our nature, some in their primary intention and design seem to belong to the single or private, others to the public or social capacity. The affections required in the text are of the latter sort. When we rejoice in the prosperity of others, and compassionate their distresses, we, as it were, substitute them for ourselves, their interest for our own; and have the same kind of pleasure in their prosperity and sorrow in their distress, as we have from reflection upon our own. Now there is nothing strange or unaccountable in our being thus carried out, and affected towards the interests of others. For, if there be any appetite, or any inward principle besides self-love; why may there not be an affection to the good of our fellow-creatures, and delight from that affection's being gratified, and uneasiness from things going contrary to it*?

* There being manifestly this appearance of men's substituting others for themselves, **411** and being carried out and affected towards them as towards themselves; some persons, who have a system which excludes every affection of this sort, have taken a pleasant method to solve it; and tell you it is *not another* you are at all concerned about, but your *self only*, when you feel the affection called compassion. I.e., here is a plain matter of fact, which men cannot reconcile with the general account they think fit to give of things: they therefore, instead of *that* manifest fact, substitute *another*, which is reconcilable to their own scheme. For does not every body by compassion mean, an affection the object of which is another in distress? Instead of this, but designing to have it mistaken for this, they speak of an affection or passion, the object of which is **ourselves**, or danger to ourselves. Hobbes defines *pity, imagination, or fiction of future calamity to ourselves, proceeding from the sense* (he means sight or knowledge) *of another man's calamity*

412   Of these two, delight in the prosperity of others and compassion for their distresses, the last is felt much more generally than the former. Though men do not universally rejoice with all whom they

Thus fear and compassion would be the same idea, and a fearful and a compassionate man the same character, which every one immediately sees are totally different. Further, to those who give any scope to their affections, there is no perception or inward feeling more universal than this: that one who has been merciful and compassionate throughout the course of his behaviour, should himself be treated with kindness, if he happens to fall into circumstances of distress. Is fear then or cowardice so great a recommendation to the favour of the bulk of mankind? Or is it not plain, that mere fearlessness (and therefore not the contrary) is one of the most popular qualifications? This shows that mankind are not affected towards compassion as fear, but as somewhat totally different.

Nothing would more expose such accounts as these of the affections which are favourable and friendly to our fellow-creatures, than to substitute the definitions which this author, and others who follow his steps, give of such affections, instead of the words by which they are commonly expressed.[1] Hobbes, after having laid down that pity or compassion is only fear for ourselves, goes on to explain the reason why we pity our friends in distress more than others. Now substitute the *definition* instead of the word *pity* in this place, and the inquiry will be, why we fear our friends, etc., which words (since he really does not mean why we are afraid of them) make no question or sentence at all. So that common language, the words *to compassionate, to pity*, cannot be accommodated to his account of compassion. The very joining of the words to *pity our friends*, is a direct contradiction to his definition of pity: because those words so joined, necessarily express that our friends are the objects of the passion; whereas his definition of it asserts, that ourselves (or danger to ourselves) are the only objects of it. He might indeed have avoided this absurdity, by plainly saying what he is going to account for; namely, why the sight of the innocent, or of our friends in distress, raises greater fear for ourselves than the sight of other persons in distress. But had he put the thing thus plainly, the fact itself would have been doubted; that *the sight of our friends in distress raises in us greater fear for ourselves, than the sight of others in distress*. And in the next place it would immediately have occurred to every one, that the fact now mentioned, which at least is *doubtful*, whether true or false, was not the same with this fact, which no body ever doubted, that *the sight of our friends in distress raises in us greater compassion than the sight of others in distress*: every one, I say, would have seen that these are not the *same*, but *two different* inquiries; and consequently, that fear and compassion are not the same. Suppose a person to be in real danger, and by some means or other to have forgot it; any trifling accident, any sound might alarm him, recall the danger to his remembrance, and renew his fear: but it is almost too grossly ridiculous (though it is to show an absurdity) to speak of that sound or accident as an object of compassion; and yet according to Mr. Hobbes, our greatest friend in distress is no more to us, no more the object of compassion or of any affection in our heart: neither the one or the other raises any emotion in our mind, but only the thoughts of our liableness to calamity, and the fear of it; and both equally do this. It is fit such sort of accounts of human nature should be shown to be what they really are, because there is raised upon them a general scheme which undermines the whole foundation of common justice and honesty. See Hobbes, *of Hum. Nat.* c. 9. § 10 [i.e. Hobbes, § 10; but cf. the more careful statement in § 32].

[1 Cf. Hutcheson, § 350.]

see rejoice, yet, accidental obstacles removed, they naturally compassionate all in some degree whom they see in distress, so far as
they have any real perception or sense of that distress: insomuch
that words expressing this latter, pity, compassion, frequently occur;
whereas we have scarce any single one, by which the former is
distinctly expressed. Congratulation indeed answers condolence:
but both these words are intended to signify certain forms of civility,
rather than any inward sensation or feeling. This difference or inequality is so remarkable, that we plainly consider compassion as
itself an original, distinct, particular affection in human nature;
whereas to rejoice in the good of others, is only a consequence of
the general affection of love and good-will to them. The reason and
account of which matter is this. When a man has obtained any
particular advantage or felicity, his end is gained; and he does not
in that particular want the assistance of another: there was therefore
no need of a distinct affection towards that felicity of another already
obtained; neither would such affection directly carry him to do good
to that person: whereas men in distress want assistance; and compassion leads us directly to assist them. The object of the former is
the present felicity of another; the object of the latter is the present
misery of another: it is easy to see that the latter wants a particular

There are often three distinct perceptions or inward feelings upon sight of persons
in distress: real sorrow and concern for the misery of our fellow-creatures; some degree
of satisfaction from a consciousness of our freedom from that misery; and, as the mind
passes on from one thing to another, it is not unnatural from such an occasion to reflect
upon our own liableness to the same or other calamities. The two last frequently
accompany the first, but it is the first *only* which is properly compassion, of which the
distressed are the objects, and which directly carries us with calmness and thought to
their assistance. Any one of these, from various and complicated reasons, may in
particular cases prevail over the other two; and there are, I suppose, instances where
the bare *sight* of distress, without our feeling any compassion for it, may be the
occasion of either or both of the two latter perceptions. One might add, that if there
be really any such thing as the fiction or imagination of danger to ourselves from sight
of the miseries of others, which Hobbes speaks of, and which he has absurdly mistaken
for the whole of compassion; if there be any thing of this sort common to mankind,
distinct from the reflection of reason, it would be a most remarkable instance of what
was furthest from his thoughts, namely, of a mutual sympathy between each particular
of the species, a fellow-feeling[1] common to mankind. It would not indeed be an
example of our substituting others for ourselves, but it would be an example of our
substituting ourselves for others. And as it would not be an instance of benevolence,
so neither would it be any instance of self-love: for this phantom of danger to ourselves,
naturally rising to view upon sight of the distresses of others, would be no more an
instance of love to ourselves, than the pain of hunger is.

[1 But cf. Hobbes, § 32.]

affection for its relief, and that the former does not want one, because it does not want assistance. And upon supposition of a distinct affection in both cases, the one must rest in the exercise of itself, having nothing further to gain; the other does not rest in itself, but carries us on to assist the distressed.

★   ★   ★   ★

SERMON XI—UPON THE LOVE OF OUR NEIGHBOUR

ROM. xiii. 9—*And if there be any other commandment, it is briefly comprehended in this saying, namely, Thou shalt love thy neighbour as thyself.*

413   It is commonly observed, that there is a disposition in men to complain of the viciousness and corruption of the age in which they live, as greater than that of former ones; which is usually followed with this further observation, that mankind has been in that respect much the same in all times. Now not to determine whether this last be not contradicted by the accounts of history; thus much can scarce be doubted, that vice and folly takes different turns, and some particular kinds of it are more open and avowed in some ages than in others: and, I suppose, it may be spoken of as very much the distinction of the present, to profess a contracted spirit, and greater regards to self-interest, than appears to have been done formerly. Upon this account it seems worth while to inquire, whether private interest is likely to be promoted in proportion to the degree in which self-love engrosses us, and prevails over all other principles; *or whether the contracted affection may not possibly be so prevalent as to disappoint itself, and even contradict its own end, private good.*

And since further, there is generally thought to be some peculiar kind of contrariety between self-love and the love of our neighbour, between the pursuit of public and of private good; insomuch that when you are recommending one of these, you are supposed to be speaking against the other; and from hence arises a secret prejudice against, and frequently open scorn of all talk of public spirit, and real good-will to our fellow-creatures; it will be necessary to *inquire what respect benevolence hath to self-love, and the pursuit of private interest to the pursuit of public*: or whether there be any thing of that peculiar inconsistence and contrariety between them, over and above what there is between self-love and other passions and particular affections, and their respective pursuits.

These inquiries, it is hoped, may be favourably attended to: for there shall be all possible concessions made to the favourite passion, which hath so much allowed to it, and whose cause is so universally pleaded: it shall be treated with the utmost tenderness, and concern for its interests.

In order to this, as well as to determine the forementioned questions, it will be necessary to *consider the nature, the object and end of that self-love, as distinguished from other principles or affections in the mind, and their respective objects.*

Every man hath a general desire of his own happiness; and likewise a variety of particular affections, passions and appetites to particular external objects. The former proceeds from, or is self-love; and seems inseparable from all sensible creatures, who can reflect upon themselves and their own interest or happiness, so as to have that interest an object to their minds: what is to be said of the latter is, that they proceed from, or together make up that particular nature, according to which man is made. The object the former pursues is somewhat internal, our own happiness, enjoyment, satisfaction; whether we have, or have not, a distinct particular perception what it is, or wherein it consists: the objects of the latter are this or that particular external thing, which the affections tend towards, and of which it hath always a particular idea or perception. The principle we call self-love never seeks any thing external for the sake of the thing, but only as a means of happiness or good: particular affections rest in the external things themselves. One belongs to man as a reasonable creature reflecting upon his own interest or happiness. The other, though quite distinct from reason, are as much a part of human nature.

That all particular appetites and passions are towards *external* **415** *things themselves*, distinct from the *pleasure arising from them*, is manifested from hence; that there could not be this pleasure, were it not for that prior suitableness between the object and the passion: there could be no enjoyment or delight from one thing more than another, from eating food more than from swallowing a stone, if there were not an affection or appetite to one thing more than another.

Every particular affection, even the love of our neighbour, is as really our own affection, as self-love; and the pleasure arising from its gratification is as much my own pleasure, as the pleasure self-love would have, from knowing I myself should be happy some time hence, would be my own pleasure. And if, because every particular affection is a man's own, and the pleasure arising from its gratification his own pleasure, or pleasure to himself, such particular affection must be called self-love; according to this way of speaking, no creature whatever can possibly act but merely from self-love; and every action and every affection whatever is to be resolved up into this one principle. But then this is not the language of mankind: or if it were, we should want words to express the difference, between the principle of an action, proceeding from cool consideration that it will be to my own advantage; and an action, suppose of revenge, or of friendship, by which a man runs upon certain ruin, to do evil or good to another. It is manifest the principles of these actions are totally different, and so want different words to be distinguished by: all that they agree in is, that they both proceed from, and are done to gratify an inclination in a man's self. But the principle or inclination in one case is self-love; in the other, hatred or love of another. There is then a distinction between the cool principle of self-love, or general desire of our own happiness, as one part of our nature, and one principle of action; and the particular affections towards particular external objects, as another part of our nature, and another principle of action. How much soever therefore is to be allowed for self-love, yet it cannot be allowed to be the whole of our inward constitution; because, you see, there are other parts or principles which come into it.

416 Further, private happiness or good is all which self-love can make us desire, or be concerned about: in having this consists its gratification: it is an affection to ourselves; a regard to our own interest, happiness, and private good: and in the proportion a man hath this, he is interested, or a lover of himself. Let this be kept in mind; because there is commonly, as I shall presently have occasion to observe, another sense put upon these words. On the other hand, particular affections tend towards particular external things: these are their objects: having these is their end: in this consists their gratification: no matter whether it be, or be not, upon the whole, our interest or happiness. An action done from the former of these principles is called an interested action. An action proceeding from any of the latter has its denomination of passionate, ambitious, friendly, revengeful, or any other, from the particular appetite or affection from which it proceeds. Thus self-love as one part of human nature, and the several particular principles as the other part, are, themselves, their objects and ends, stated and shown.

From hence it will be easy to see, how far, and in what ways, **417** each of these can contribute and be subservient to the private good of the individual. Happiness does not consist in self-love. The desire of happiness is no more the thing itself, than the desire of riches is the possession or enjoyment of them. People may love themselves with the most entire and unbounded affection, and yet be extremely miserable. Neither can self-love any way help them out, but by setting them on work to get rid of the causes of their misery, to gain or make use of those objects which are by nature adapted to afford satisfaction. Happiness or satisfaction consists only in the enjoyment of those objects, which are by nature suited to our several particular appetites, passions and affections. So that if self-love wholly engrosses us, and leaves no room for any other principle, there can be absolutely no such thing at all as happiness, or enjoyment of any kind whatever; since happiness consists in the gratification of particular passions, which supposes the having of them. Self-love then does not constitute *this* or *that* to be our interest or good; but, our interest or good being constituted by nature and supposed, self-love only puts us upon obtaining and securing it. Therefore, if it be possible, that self-love may prevail and exert itself in a degree or manner which is not subservient to this end; then it will not follow, that our interest will be promoted in proportion to the degree in which that principle engrosses us, and prevails over others. Nay further, the private and contracted affection, when it is not subservient to this end, private good, may, for any thing that appears, have a direct contrary tendency and effect. And if we will consider the matter, we shall see that it often really has. *Disengagement* is absolutely necessary to enjoyment: and a person may have so steady and fixed an eye upon his own interest, whatever he places it in, as may hinder him from *attending* to many gratifications within his reach, which others have their minds *free* and *open* to. Over-fondness for a child is not generally thought to be for its advantage: and, if there be any guess to be made from appearances, surely that character we call selfish is not the most promising for happiness.

Such a temper may plainly be and exert itself in a degree and manner which may give unnecessary and useless solicitude and anxiety, in a degree and manner which may prevent obtaining the means and materials of enjoyment, as well as the making use of them. Immoderate self-love does very ill consult its own interest: and, how much soever a paradox it may appear, it is certainly true, that even from self-love we should endeavour to get over all inordinate regard to, and consideration of ourselves. Every one of our passions and affections hath its natural stint and bound, which may easily be exceeded; whereas our enjoyments can possibly be but in a determinate measure and degree. Therefore such excess of the affection, since it cannot procure any enjoyment, must in all cases be useless; but it is generally attended with inconveniences, and often is downright pain and misery. This holds as much with regard to self-love as to all other affections. The natural degree of it, so far as it sets us on work to gain and make use of the materials of satisfaction, may be to our real advantage; but beyond or besides this, it is in several respects an inconvenience and disadvantage. Thus it appears, that private interest is so far from being likely to be promoted in proportion to the degree in which self-love engrosses us, and prevails over all other principles; that *the contracted affection may be so prevalent as to disappoint itself, and even contradict its own end, private good.*

418 'But who, except the most sordidly covetous, ever thought there was any rivalship between the love of greatness, honour, power, or between sensual appetites, and self-love? No, there is a perfect harmony between them. It is by means of these particular appetites and affections that self-love is gratified in enjoyment, happiness and satisfaction. The competition and rivalship is between self-love, and the love of our neighbour: that affection which leads us out of ourselves, makes us regardless of our own interest, and substitute that of another in its stead.' Whether then there be any peculiar competition and contrariety in this case, shall now be considered.

419 Self-love and interestedness was stated to consist in or be an affection to ourselves, a regard to our own private good: it is therefore distinct from benevolence, which is an affection to the good of our fellow-creatures. But that benevolence is distinct from, that is, not the same thing with self-love, is no reason for its being looked upon with any peculiar suspicion; because every principle whatever, by means of which self-love is gratified, is distinct from it: and all

things which are distinct from each other, are equally so. A man has an affection or aversion to another: that one of these tends to and is gratified by doing good, that the other tends to and is gratified by doing harm, does not in the least alter the respect which either one or the other of these inward feelings has to self-love. We use the word *property* so as to exclude any other persons having an interest in that of which we say a particular man has the property. And we often use the word *selfish* so as to exclude in the same manner all regards to the good of others. But the cases are not parallel: for though that exclusion is really part of the idea of property; yet such positive exclusion, or bringing this peculiar disregard to the good of others into the idea of self-love, is in reality adding to the idea, or changing it from what it was before stated to consist in, namely, in an affection to ourselves*. This being the whole idea of self-love, it can no otherwise exclude good-will or love of others, than merely by not including it, no otherwise, than it excludes love of arts or reputation, or of any thing else. Neither on the other hand does benevolence, any more than love of arts or of reputation, exclude self-love. Love of our neighbour then has just the same respect to, is no more distant from, self-love, than hatred of our neighbour, or than love or hatred of any thing else. Thus the principles, from which men rush upon certain ruin for the destruction of an enemy, and for the preservation of a friend, have the same respect to the private affection, and are equally interested, or equally disinterested: and it is of no avail, whether they are said to be one or the other. Therefore to those who are shocked to hear virtue spoken of as disinterested, it may be allowed that it is indeed absurd to speak thus of it; unless hatred, several particular instances of vice, and all the common affections and aversions in mankind, are acknowledged to be disinterested too. Is there any less inconsistence, between the love of inanimate things, or of creatures merely sensitive, and self-love; than between self-love, and the love of our neighbour? Is desire of and delight in the happiness of another any more a diminution of self-love, than desire of and delight in the esteem of another? They are both equally desire of and delight in somewhat external to ourselves: either both or neither are so. The object of self-love is expressed in the term, self: and every appetite of sense, and every particular affection of the heart, are equally interested or disinterested, because the objects

* § 416.

of them all are equally self or somewhat else. Whatever ridicule
therefore the mention of a disinterested principle or action may be
supposed to lie open to, must, upon the matter being thus stated,
relate to ambition, and every appetite and particular affection, as
much as to benevolence. And indeed all the ridicule, and all the
grave perplexity, of which this subject hath had its full share, is
merely from words. The most intelligible way of speaking of it
seems to be this: that self-love, and the actions done in consequence
of it (for these will presently appear to be the same as to this question)
are interested; that particular affections towards external objects, and
the actions done in consequence of those affections, are not so. But
every one is at liberty to use words as he pleases. All that is here insisted upon is, that ambition, revenge, benevolence, all particular
passions whatever, and the actions they produce, are equally interested or disinterested.

420   Thus it appears that there is no peculiar contrariety between self-
love and benevolence; no greater competition between these, than
between any other particular affections and self-love. This relates to
the affections themselves. Let us now see whether there be any
peculiar contrariety between the respective courses of life which
these affections lead to; whether there be any greater competition
between the pursuit of private and of public good, than between
any other particular pursuits and that of private good.

There seems no other reason to suspect that there is any such
peculiar contrariety, but only that the course of action which benevolence leads to, has a more direct tendency to promote the good
of others, than that course of action which love of reputation, suppose, or any other particular affection leads to. But that any affection
tends to the happiness of another, does not hinder its tending to
one's own happiness too. That others enjoy the benefit of the air
and the light of the sun, does not hinder but that these are as much
one's own private advantage now, as they would be if we had the
property of them exclusive of all others. So a pursuit which tends
to promote the good of another, yet may have as great tendency to
promote private interest, as a pursuit which does not tend to the
good of another at all, or which is mischievous to him. All particular
affections whatever, resentment, benevolence, love of arts, equally
lead to a course of action for their own gratification, i.e. the gratification of ourselves; and the gratification of each gives delight: so far

then it is manifest they have all the same respect to private interest. Now take into consideration further concerning these three pursuits, that the end of the first is the harm, of the second, the good of another, of the last, somewhat indifferent; and is there any necessity, that these additional considerations should alter the respect, which we before saw these three pursuits had to private interest; or render any one of them less conducive to it, than any other? Thus one man's affection is to honour as his end; in order to obtain which, he thinks no pains too great. Suppose another with such a singularity of mind, as to have the same affection to public good as his end, which he endeavours with the same labour to obtain. In case of success, surely the man of benevolence hath as great enjoyment as the man of ambition; they both equally having the end their affections, in the same degree, tended to: but in case of disappointment, the benevolent man has clearly the advantage; since endeavouring to do good considered as a virtuous pursuit, is gratified by its own consciousness, i.e. is in a degree its own reward.

*   *   *   *

The short of the matter is no more than this. Happiness consists **421** in the gratification of certain affections, appetites, passions, with objects which are by nature adapted to them. Self-love may indeed set us on work to gratify these: but happiness or enjoyment has no immediate connection with self-love, but arises from such gratification alone. Love of our neighbour is one of those affections. This, considered as a *virtuous principle*, is gratified by a consciousness of *endeavouring* to promote the good of others; but considered as a natural affection, its gratification consists in the actual accomplishment of this endeavour. Now indulgence or gratification of this affection, whether in that consciousness, or this accomplishment, has the same respect to interest, as indulgence of any other affection; they equally proceed from or do not proceed from self-love, they equally include or equally exclude this principle. Thus it appears, that *benevolence and the pursuit of public good hath at least as great respect to self-love and the pursuit of private good, as any other particular passions, and their respective pursuits.*

*   *   *   *

422 The general mistake, that there is some greater inconsistence between endeavouring to promote the good of another and self-interest, than between self-interest and pursuing any thing else, seems, as hath already been hinted, to arise from our notions of property; and to be carried on by this property's being supposed to be itself our happiness or good. People are so very much taken up with this one subject, that they seem from it to have formed a general way of thinking, which they apply to other things that they have nothing to do with. Hence, in a confused and slight way, it might well be taken for granted, that another's having no interest in an affection (i.e. his good not being the object of it) renders, as one may speak, the proprietor's interest in it greater; and that if another had an interest in it, this would render his less, or occasion that such affection could not be so friendly to self-love, or conducive to private good, as an affection or pursuit which has not a regard to the good of another. This I say might be taken for granted, whilst it was not attended to, that the object of every particular affection is equally somewhat external to ourselves; and whether it be the good of another person, or whether it be any other external thing, makes no alteration with regard to its being one's own affection, and the gratification of it one's own private enjoyment. And so far as it is taken for granted, that barely having the means and materials of enjoyment is what constitutes interest and happiness; that our interest or good consists in possessions themselves, in having the property of riches, houses, lands, gardens, not in the enjoyment of them; so far it will even more strongly be taken for granted, in the way already explained, that an affection's conducing to the good of another, must even necessarily occasion it to conduce less to private good, if not to be positively detrimental to it. For, if property and happiness are one and the same thing, as by increasing the property of another you lessen your own property, so by promoting the happiness of another you must lessen your own happiness. But whatever occasioned the mistake, I hope it has been fully proved to be one; as it has been proved, that there is no peculiar rivalship or competition between self-love and benevolence; that as there may be a competition between these two, so there may also between any particular affection whatever and self-love; that every particular affection, benevolence among the rest, is subservient to self-love by being the instrument of private enjoyment; and that in one respect benevolence contributes more to private interest, i.e. enjoyment or satisfaction, than any other of the particular common affections, as it is in a degree its own gratification.

And to all these things may be added, that religion, from whence **423** arises our strongest obligation to benevolence, is so far from disowning the principle of self-love, that it often addresses itself to that very principle, and always to the mind in that state when reason presides; and there can no access be had to the understanding, but by convincing men, that the course of life we would persuade them to is not contrary to their interest. It may be allowed, without any prejudice to the cause of virtue and religion, that our ideas of happiness and misery are of all our ideas the nearest and most important to us; that they will, nay, if you please, that they ought to prevail over those of order, and beauty, and harmony, and proportion, if there should ever be, as it is impossible there ever should be, any inconsistence between them: though these last too, as expressing the fitness of actions, are real as truth itself. Let it be allowed, though virtue or moral rectitude does indeed consist in affection to and pursuit of what is right and good, as such; yet, that when we sit down in a cool hour, we can neither justify to ourselves this or any other pursuit, till we are convinced that it will be for our happiness, or at least not contrary to it.

Common reason and humanity will have some influence upon mankind, whatever becomes of speculations: but, so far as the interests of virtue depend upon the theory of it being secured from open scorn, so far its very being in the world depends upon its appearing to have no contrariety to private interest and self-love. The foregoing observations therefore, it is hoped, may have gained a little ground in favour of the precept before us; the particular explanation of which, shall be the subject of the next discourse.

*   *   *   *

SERMON XII—UPON THE LOVE OF OUR NEIGHBOUR

ROM. xiii. 9—*And if there be any other commandment, it is briefly comprehended in this saying, namely, Thou shalt love thy neighbour as thyself.*

Having already removed the prejudices against public spirit, or **424** the love of our neighbour, on the side of private interest and self-love; I proceed to the particular explanation of the precept before us, by showing, *who is our neighbour: in what sense we are required to love him as ourselves: the influence such love would have upon our behaviour in life*: and lastly, *how this commandment comprehends in it all others*.

★   ★   ★   ★

425   IV. I proceed to consider lastly, what is affirmed of the precept now explained, that it comprehends in it all others; i.e. that to love our neighbour as ourselves includes in it all virtues.

Now the way in which every maxim of conduct, or general speculative assertion, when it is to be explained at large, should be treated, is, to show what are the particular truths which were designed to be comprehended under such a general observation, how far it is strictly true; and then the limitations, restrictions, and exceptions, if there be exceptions, with which it is to be understood. But it is only the former of these, namely, how far the assertion in the text holds, and the ground of the pre-eminence assigned to the precept of it, which in strictness comes into our present consideration.

However, in almost every thing that is said, there is somewhat to to be understood beyond what is explicitly laid down, and which we of course supply; somewhat, I mean, which would not be commonly called a restriction or limitation. Thus, when benevolence is said to be the sum of virtue, it is not spoken of as a blind propension, but as a principle in reasonable creatures, and so to be directed by their reason: for reason and reflection comes into our notion of a moral agent. And that will lead us to consider distant consequences, as well as the immediate tendency of an action: it will teach us, that the care of some persons, suppose children and families, is particularly committed to our charge by nature and Providence; as also that there are other circumstances, suppose friendship or former obligations, which require that we do good to some, preferably to others. Reason, considered merely as subservient to benevolence, as assisting to produce the greatest good, will teach us to have particular regard to these relations and circumstances; because it is plainly for the good of the world that they should be regarded. And as there are numberless cases, in which, notwithstanding appearances, we are not competent judges, whether a particular action will upon the whole do good or harm; reason in the same way will teach us to be cautious how we act in these cases of uncertainty. It will suggest

to our consideration, which is the safer side; how liable we are to be
led wrong by passion and private interest; and what regard is due
to laws, and the judgement of mankind. All these things must come
into consideration, were it only in order to determine which way of
acting is likely to produce the greatest good. Thus, upon supposition
that it were in the strictest sense true, without limitation, that benevolence includes in it all virtues; yet reason must come in as its
guide and director, in order to attain its own end, the end of benevolence, the greatest public good. Reason then being thus included,
let us now consider the truth of the assertion itself.

First, it is manifest that nothing can be of consequence to man- **426**
kind or any creature, but happiness. This then is all which any person
can, in strictness of speaking, be said to have a right to. We can
therefore *owe no man any thing*, but only to further and promote his
happiness, according to our abilities. And therefore a disposition and
endeavour to do good to all with whom we have to do, in the degree
and manner which the different relations we stand in to them require, is a discharge of all the obligations we are under to them.

As human nature is not one simple uniform thing, but a composition of various parts; body, spirit, appetites, particular passions and
affections; for each of which reasonable self-love would lead men to
have due regard, and make suitable provision: so society consists of
various parts, to which we stand in different respects and relations;
and just benevolence would as surely lead us to have due regard to
each of these, and behave as the respective relations require. Reasonable good-will, and right behaviour towards our fellow-creatures,
are in a manner the same: only that the former expresseth the principle as it is in the mind; the latter, the principle as it were become
external, i.e. exerted in actions.

And so far as temperance, sobriety, and moderation in sensual
pleasures, and the contrary vices, have any respect to our fellow-
creatures, any influence upon their quiet, welfare, and happiness;
as they always have a real, and often a near influence upon it; so far
it is manifest those virtues may be produced by the love of our
neighbour, and that the contrary vices would be prevented by it.
Indeed, if men's regard to themselves will not restrain them from
excess; it may be thought little probable, that their love to others
will be sufficient: but the reason is, that their love to others is not,
any more than their regard to themselves, just, and in its due degree.

There are however manifest instances of persons kept sober and temperate from regard to their affairs, and the welfare of those who depend upon them. And it is obvious to every one, that habitual excess, a dissolute course of life, implies a general neglect of the duties we owe towards our friends, our families and our country.

427   From hence it is manifest that the common virtues, and the common vices of mankind, may be traced up to benevolence, or the want of it. And this entitles the precept, *Thou shalt love thy neighbour as thyself*, to the pre-eminence given to it; and is a justification of the Apostle's assertion, that all other commandments are comprehended in it; whatever cautions and restrictions* there are, which might require to be considered, if we were to state particularly and at length, what is virtue and right behaviour in mankind. But,

428   *Secondly*, it might be added, that in a higher and more general way of consideration, leaving out the particular nature of creatures, and the particular circumstances in which they are placed, benevolence seems in the strictest sense to include in it all that is good and

---

* For instance: as we are not competent judges, what is upon the whole for the good of the world; there may be other immediate ends appointed us to pursue, besides that one of doing good, or producing happiness. Though the good of the creation be the only end of the Author of it, yet he may have laid us under particular obligations, which we may discern and feel ourselves under, quite distinct from a perception, that the observance or violation of them is for the happiness or misery of our fellow-creatures. And this is in fact the case. For there are certain dispositions of mind, and certain actions, which are in themselves approved or disapproved by mankind, abstracted from the consideration of their tendency to the happiness or misery of the world; approved or disapproved by reflection, by that principle within, which is the guide of life, the judge of right and wrong. Numberless instances of this kind might be mentioned. There are pieces of treachery, which in themselves appear base and detestable to every one. There are actions, which perhaps can scarce have any other general name given them than indecencies, which yet are odious and shocking to human nature. There is such a thing as meanness, a little mind; which, as it is quite distinct from incapacity, so it raises a dislike and disapprobation quite different from that contempt, which men are too apt to have, of mere folly. On the other hand; what we call greatness of mind, is the object of another sort of approbation, than superior understanding. Fidelity, honour, strict justice, are themselves approved in the highest degree, abstracted from the consideration of their tendency. Now, whether it be thought that each of these are connected with benevolence in our nature, and so may be considered as the same thing with it; or whether some of them be thought an inferior kind of virtues and vices, somewhat like natural beauties and deformities; or lastly, plain exceptions to the general rule; thus much however is certain, that the things now instanced in, and numberless others, are approved or disapproved by mankind in general, in quite another view than as conducive to the happiness or misery of the world.

worthy; all that is good, which we have any distinct particular notion of. We have no clear conception of any positive moral attribute in the supreme Being, but what may be resolved up into goodness. And, if we consider a reasonable creature or moral agent, without regard to the particular relations and circumstances in which he is placed; we cannot conceive any thing else to come in towards determining whether he is to be ranked in an higher or lower class of virtuous beings, but the higher or lower degree in which that principle, and what is manifestly connected with it, prevail in him.

That which we more strictly call piety, or the love of God, and which is an essential part of a right temper, some may perhaps imagine no way connected with benevolence: yet surely they must be connected, if there be indeed in being an object infinitely good. Human nature is so constituted, that every good affection implies the love of itself; i.e. becomes the object of a new affection in the same person. Thus, to be righteous implies in it the love of righteousness; to be benevolent the love of benevolence; to be good the love of goodness; whether this righteousness, benevolence, or goodness, be viewed as in our own mind, or in another's: and the love of God as a Being perfectly good, is the love of perfect goodness contemplated in a Being or Person. Thus morality and religion, virtue and piety, will at last necessarily coincide, run up into one and the same point, and *love* will be in all senses *the end of the commandment*.

*   *   *   *

DISSERTATION II

OF THE NATURE OF VIRTUE

That which renders beings capable of moral government, is their having a moral nature, and moral faculties of perception and of action. Brute creatures are impressed and actuated by various instincts and propensions: so also are we. But additional to this, we have a capacity of reflecting upon actions and characters, and making them an object to our thought: and on doing this, we naturally and unavoidably approve some actions, under the peculiar view of their being virtuous and of good-desert; and disapprove others, as vicious and of ill-desert. That we have this moral approving and disapproving[a] faculty, is certain from our experiencing it in ourselves, and recognizing it in each other. It appears from our exercising it unavoidably, in the approbation and disapprobation even of feigned characters: from the words, right and wrong, odious and amiable, base and worthy, with many others of like signification in all languages, applied to actions and characters: from the many written systems of morals which suppose it; since it cannot be imagined, that all these authors, throughout all these treatises, had absolutely no meaning at all to their words, or a meaning merely chimerical: from our natural sense of gratitude, which implies a distinction between merely being the instrument of good, and intending it: from the like distinction, every one makes, between injury and mere harm, which, Hobbes says, is peculiar to mankind; and between injury and just punishment, a distinction plainly natural,

---

[a] This way of speaking is taken from Epictetus*, and is made use of as seeming the most full, and least liable to cavil. And the moral faculty may be understood to have these two epithets, δοκιμαστική and ἀποδοκιμαστική, upon a double account: because, upon a survey of actions, whether before or after they are done, it determines them to be good or evil; and also because it determines itself to be the guide of action and of life, in contradistinction from all other faculties, or natural principles of action: in the very same manner, as speculative reason *directly* and naturally judges of speculative truth and falsehood; and, at the same time, is attended with a consciousness upon *reflection*, that the natural right to judge of them belongs to it.

---

* Arr. Epict. L. I. c. I.

prior to the consideration of human laws. It is manifest great part of common language, and of common behaviour over the world, is formed upon supposition of such a moral faculty; whether called conscience, moral reason, moral sense, or divine reason; whether considered as a sentiment of the understanding, or as a perception of the heart, or, which seems the truth, as including both. Nor is it at all doubtful in the general, what course of action this faculty, or practical discerning power within us, approves, and what it disapproves. For, as much as it has been disputed wherein virtue consists, or whatever ground for doubt there may be about particulars; yet, in general, there is in reality an universally acknowledged standard of it. It is that, which all ages and all countries have made profession of in public: it is that, which every man you meet, puts on the show of: it is that, which the primary and fundamental laws of all civil constitutions, over the face of the earth, make it their business and endeavour to enforce the practice of upon mankind: namely, justice, veracity, and regard to common good. It being manifest then, in general, that we have such a faculty or discernment as this; it may be of use to remark some things, more distinctly, concerning it.

First, it ought to be observed, that the object of this faculty is **430** actions[b], comprehending under that name active or practical principles: those principles from which men would act, if occasions and circumstances gave them power; and which, when fixed and habitual in any person, we call, his character. It does not appear, that brutes have the least reflex sense[1] of actions, as distinguished from events: or that will and design, which constitute the very nature of actions as such, are at all an object to their perception. But to ours they are: and they are the object, and the only one, of the approving and disapproving faculty. Acting, conduct, behaviour, abstracted from all regard to what is, in fact and event, the consequence of it, is itself the natural object of the moral discernment; as speculative truth and falsehood is, of speculative reason. Intention of such and such consequences, indeed, is always included; for it is part of the action itself: but though the intended good or bad consequences do

---

[b] Οὐδὲ ἡ ἀρετὴ καὶ κακία—ἐν πείσει, ἀλλὰ ἐνεργείᾳ. M. Anton. L. 9. 16. Virtutis laus omnis in actione consistit. Cic. Off. l. i. c. 6.

[1 Cf. Shaftesbury, § 200.]

not follow, we have exactly the same sense of the action as if they did. In like manner we think well or ill of characters, abstracted from all consideration of the good or the evil, which persons of such characters have it actually in their power to do. We never, in the moral way, applaud or blame either ourselves or others, for what we enjoy or what we suffer, or for having impressions made upon us which we consider as altogether out of our power: but only for what we do, or would have done, had it been in our power; or for what we leave undone which we might have done, or would have left undone though we could have done it.

431   *Secondly*, our sense or discernment of actions as morally good or evil, implies in it a sense or discernment of them as of good or ill desert. It may be difficult to explain this perception, so as to answer all the questions which may be asked concerning it: but every one speaks of such and such actions as deserving punishment; and it is not, I suppose, pretended that they have absolutely no meaning at all to the expression. Now the meaning plainly is not, that we conceive it for the good of society, that the doer of such actions should be made to suffer. For if unhappily it were resolved, that a man who, by some innocent action, was infected with the plague, should be left to perish, lest, by other people's coming near him, the infection should spread: no one would say, he deserved this treatment. Innocence and ill-desert are inconsistent ideas. Ill-desert always supposes guilt: and if one be not part of the other, yet they are evidently and naturally connected in our mind. The sight of a man in misery raises our compassion towards him; and, if this misery be inflicted on him by another, our indignation against the author of it. But when we are informed, that the sufferer is a villain, and is punished only for his treachery or cruelty; our compassion exceedingly lessens, and, in many instances, our indignation wholly subsides. Now what produces this effect, is the conception of that in the sufferer, which we call ill-desert. Upon considering then, or viewing together, our notion of vice and that of misery, there results a third, that of ill-desert. And thus there is in human creatures an association of the two ideas, natural and moral evil, wickedness and punishment. If this association were merely artificial or accidental, it were nothing: but being most unquestionably natural, it greatly concerns us to attend to it, instead of endeavouring to explain it away.

It may be observed farther, concerning our perception of good and of ill desert, that the former is very weak with respect to common instances of virtue. One reason of which may be, that it does not appear to a spectator, how far such instances of virtue proceed from a virtuous principle, or in what degree this principle is prevalent: since a very weak regard to virtue may be sufficient to make men act well in many common instances. And on the other hand, our perception of ill-desert in vicious actions lessens, in proportion to the temptations men are thought to have had to such vices. For, vice in human creatures consisting chiefly in the absence or want of the virtuous principle; though a man be overcome, suppose, by tortures, it does not from thence appear, to what degree the virtuous principle was wanting. All that appears is, that he had it not in such a degree, as to prevail over the temptation: but possibly he had it in a degree, which would have rendered him proof against common temptations.

Thirdly, our perception of vice and ill-desert arises from, and is **432** the result of, a comparison of actions with the nature and capacities of the agent. For, the mere neglect of doing what we ought to do, would, in many cases, be determined by all men to be in the highest degree vicious. And this determination must arise from such comparison, and be the result of it; because such neglect would not be vicious in creatures of other natures and capacities, as brutes. And it is the same also with respect to positive vices, or such as consist in doing what we ought not. For, every one has a different sense of harm done by an idiot, madman or child, and by one of mature and common understanding; though the action of both, including the intention which is part of the action, be the same: as it may be, since idiots and madmen, as well as children, are capable not only of doing mischief, but also of intending it. Now this difference must arise from somewhat discerned in the nature or capacities of one, which renders the action vicious; and the want of which in the other, renders the same action innocent or less vicious: and this plainly supposes a comparison, whether reflected upon or not, between the action and capacities of the agent, previous to our determining an action to be vicious. And hence arises a proper application of the epithets, incongruous, unsuitable, disproportionate, unfit, to actions which our moral faculty determines to be vicious.

Fourthly, it deserves to be considered, whether men are more at **433** liberty, in point of morals, to make themselves miserable without reason, than to make other people so: or dissolutely to neglect their own greater good, for the sake of a present lesser gratification, than they are to neglect the good of others, whom nature has committed to their care. It should seem, that a due concern about our own interest or happiness, and a reasonable endeavour to secure and promote it, which is, I think, very much the meaning of the word, prudence, in our language; it should seem, that this is virtue,[1] and the contrary behaviour faulty and blameable: since, in the calmest way of reflection, we approve of the first, and condemn the other conduct, both in ourselves and others. This approbation and disapprobation are altogether different from mere desire of our own or of their happiness, and from sorrow upon missing it. For the object or occasion of this last kind of perception, is satisfaction, or uneasiness: whereas the object of the first is active behaviour. In one case, what our thoughts fix upon, is our condition: in the other, our conduct. It is true indeed, that nature has not given us so sensible a disapprobation of imprudence and folly, either in *ourselves* or *others*, as of falsehood, injustice and cruelty: I suppose, because that constant habitual sense of private interest and good, which we always carry about with us, renders such sensible disapprobation less necessary, less wanting, to keep us from imprudently neglecting our own happiness, and foolishly injuring ourselves, than it is necessary and wanting to keep us from injuring others, to whose good we cannot have so strong and constant a regard: and also because imprudence and folly, appearing to bring its own punishment more immediately and constantly than injurious behaviour, it less needs the additional punishment, which would be inflicted upon it by others, had they the same sensible indignation against it, as against injustice and fraud and cruelty. Besides, unhappiness being in itself the natural object of compassion; the unhappiness which people bring upon themselves, though it be wilfully, excites in us some pity for them: and this of course lessens our displeasure against them. But still it is matter of experience, that we are formed so, as to reflect very severely upon the greater instances of imprudent neglects and foolish rashness, both in ourselves and others. In instances of this kind, men often say of themselves with remorse, and of others with some indignation, that they deserved to suffer such calamities, because they

[1 Contrast Hutcheson, § 315.]

brought them upon themselves, and would not take warning. Particularly when persons come to poverty and distress by a long course of extravagance, and after frequent admonitions, though without falsehood or injustice; we plainly do not regard such people as alike objects of compassion with those, who are brought into the same condition by unavoidable accidents. From these things it appears, that prudence is a species of virtue, and folly of vice: meaning by *folly*, somewhat quite different from mere incapacity; a thoughtless want of that regard and attention to our own happiness, which we had capacity for. And this the word properly includes; and, as it seems, in its usual acceptation: for we scarce apply it to brute creatures.

However, if any person be disposed to dispute the matter, I shall very willingly give him up the words virtue and vice, as not applicable to prudence and folly: but must beg leave to insist, that the faculty within us, which is the judge of actions, approves of prudent actions, and disapproves imprudent ones; I say prudent and imprudent *actions* as such, and considered distinctly from the happiness or misery which they occasion. And by the way, this observation may help to determine, what justness there is in that objection against religion, that it teaches us to be interested and selfish.

Fifthly, without inquiring how far, and in what sense, virtue is **434** resolvable into benevolence, and vice into the want of it;[1] it may be proper to observe, that benevolence and the want of it, singly considered, are in no sort the whole of virtue and vice. For if this were the case, in the review of one's own character or that of others, our moral understanding and moral sense would be indifferent to every thing, but the degrees in which benevolence prevailed, and the degrees in which it was wanting. That is, we should neither approve of benevolence to some persons rather than to others, nor disapprove injustice and falsehood upon any other account, than merely as an overbalance of happiness was foreseen likely to be produced by the first, and of misery by the second. But now on the contrary, suppose two men competitors for any thing whatever, which would be of equal advantage to each of them: though nothing indeed would be more impertinent, than for a stranger to busy himself to get one of them preferred to the other; yet such endeavour would be virtue, in behalf of a friend or benefactor, abstracted from

[1 See §§ 425–8.]

all consideration of distant consequences: as that examples of gratitude, and the cultivation of friendship, would be of general good to the world. Again, suppose one man should, by fraud or violence, take from another the fruit of his labour, with intent to give it to a third, who, he thought, would have as much pleasure from it, as would balance the pleasure which the first possessor would have had in the enjoyment, and his vexation in the loss of it; suppose also that no bad consequences would follow: yet such an action would surely be vicious. Nay farther, were treachery, violence and injustice, no otherwise vicious, than as foreseen likely to produce an overbalance of misery to society; then, if in any case a man could procure to himself as great advantage by an act of injustice, as the whole foreseen inconvenience, likely to be brought upon others by it, would amount to; such a piece of injustice would not be faulty or vicious at all: because it would be no more than, in any other case, for a man to prefer his own satisfaction to another's in equal degrees. The fact then appears to be, that we are constituted so as to condemn falsehood, unprovoked violence, injustice, and to approve of benevolence to some preferably to others, abstracted from all consideration, which conduct is likeliest to produce an overbalance of happiness or misery. And therefore, were the Author of nature to propose nothing to himself as an end but the production of happiness, were his moral character merely that of benevolence; yet ours is not so.[1] Upon that supposition indeed, the only reason of his giving us the above-mentioned approbation of benevolence to some persons rather than others, and disapprobation of falsehood, unprovoked violence, and injustice, must be, that he foresaw, this constitution of our nature would produce more happiness, than forming us with a temper of mere general benevolence. But still, since this is our constitution; falsehood, violence, injustice, must be vice in us, and benevolence to some preferably to others, virtue; abstracted from all consideration of the overbalance of evil or good, which they may appear likely to produce.

Now if human creatures are endued with such a moral nature as we have been explaining, or with a moral faculty, the natural object of which is actions: moral government must consist, in rendering them happy and unhappy, in rewarding and punishing them, as they follow, neglect, or depart from, the moral rule of action interwoven

[1 Cf. § 427, footnote.]

in their nature, or suggested and enforced by this moral faculty; in rewarding and punishing them upon account of their so doing.

I am not sensible, that I have, in this fifth observation, contradicted **435** what any author designed to assert. But some[1] of great and distinguished merit, have, I think, expressed themselves in a manner, which may occasion some danger, to careless readers, of imagining the whole of virtue to consist in singly aiming, according to the best of their judgement, at promoting the happiness of mankind in the present state; and the whole of vice, in doing what they foresee, or might foresee, is likely to produce an overbalance of unhappiness in it: than which mistakes, none can be conceived more terrible. For it is certain, that some of the most shocking instances of injustice, adultery, murder, perjury, and even of persecution, may, in many supposable cases, not have the appearance of being likely to produce an overbalance of misery in the present state: perhaps sometimes may have the contrary appearance. For this reflection might easily be carried on, but I forbear.—The happiness of the world is the concern of him, who is the Lord and the Proprietor of it: nor do we know what we are about, when we endeavour to promote the good of mankind in any ways, but those which he has directed; that is indeed in all ways, not contrary to veracity and justice. I speak thus upon supposition of persons really endeavouring, in some sort, to do good without regard to these. But the truth seems to be, that such supposed endeavours proceed, almost always, from ambition, the spirit of party, or some indirect principle, concealed perhaps in great measure from persons themselves. And though it is our business and our duty to endeavour, within the bounds of veracity and justice, to contribute to the ease, convenience, and even cheerfulness and diversion of our fellow-creatures: yet from our short views, it is greatly uncertain, whether this endeavour will, in particular instances, produce an overbalance of happiness upon the whole; since so many and distant things must come into the account. And that which makes it our duty, is, that there is some appearance that it will, and no positive appearance sufficient to balance this, on the contrary side; and also, that such benevolent endeavour is a cultivation of that most excellent of all virtuous principles, the active principle of benevolence.

However, though veracity, as well as justice, is to be our rule of

[1 Butler is thinking chiefly of Hutcheson.]

life; it must be added, otherwise a snare will be laid in the way of some plain men, that the use of common forms of speech generally understood, cannot be falsehood; and, in general, that there can be no designed falsehood without designing to deceive. It must likewise be observed, that in numberless cases, a man may be under the strictest obligations to what he foresees will deceive, without his intending it. For it is impossible not to foresee, that the words and actions of men in different ranks and employments, and of different educations, will perpetually be mistaken by each other: and it cannot but be so, whilst they will judge with the utmost carelessness, as they daily do, of what they are not, perhaps, enough informed to be competent judges of, even though they considered it with great attention.

JOHN BALGUY

1686–1748

THE FOUNDATION OF MORAL GOODNESS

[Part I first printed, 1728. Part II first printed, 1729. Both reprinted here from *A Collection of Tracts Moral and Theological*, 1734, containing the fourth edition of Part I and the third edition of Part II. Misprints have been corrected, spelling modified, some footnotes (mainly quotations from classical authors) omitted, and italics and initial capital letters reduced]

JOHN BALGUY

The Foundation of Moral Goodness

PART I

The ingenious author of the *Inquiry into the Original of our Ideas* **436**
of Beauty and Virtue, has written both his books with so good a
design, is every where so instructive or entertaining, and discovers
upon all occasions such a fund of good nature, as well as good sense,
that I find myself much more inclined to join with the public in
his just praise, than offer any objections against his performance.
And indeed it is not without pain, that I attempt to point out some
particulars, wherein I apprehend he has erred. I should scarce content
myself with the old excuse of *magis amica veritas*, if the mistakes
which I think he has committed, did not appear to be of the utmost
consequence; if they did not lie at the foundations of morality, and,
like failures in ground-work, affect the whole building.

★   ★   ★   ★

That the Author of nature has planted in our minds *benevolent* **437**
affections towards others, cannot be denied without contradicting
experience, and falsifying our own perceptions. Whoever carefully
reflects on what passes within his own breast, may soon be convinced
of this truth, and even feel the evidences of it. Nor can it be doubted
but these affections were given us in order to engage, assist and
quicken us in a course of virtuous actions. They may be looked
upon as auxiliaries, aiding us in our duty, and supporting and second-
ing our reason and reflection.—But from the passages I have produced, and others of the like nature, it plainly appears that our author
does not consider this *natural affection* or *instinct*, merely as a help or
incentive to virtue, but as the true ground and foundation of it.
He makes virtue entirely to consist in it, or flow from it.[1]

★   ★   ★   ★

[1 See Hutcheson, §§ 327, 331, and the reservation in § 336.]

438   In the *first* place, it seems an insuperable difficulty in our author's scheme, that virtue appears in it to be of an arbitrary and positive nature, as entirely depending upon *instincts*, that might originally have been otherwise, or even contrary to what they now are, and may at any time be altered or inverted, if the Creator pleases. If our affections constitute the *honestum* of a morality, and do not presuppose it, it is natural to ask, what it was that determined the Deity to plant in us these affections rather than any other? This our author answers by supposing a certain *disposition essential to the Deity, corresponding to the affections he has given us. As he also supposes something analogous in the Deity to our moral sense. By such a *disposition* he imagines the Deity would naturally be inclined to give us the *kind affections* in preference to any other. I ask then further, is such a disposition a perfection in the Deity, or is it not? Is it better than a contrary, or than any other disposition would have been; more worthy of his nature, and more agreeable to his other perfections? If it be not, let us not presume to ascribe it to him. Whatever is in the Deity must be absolutely good, and *sui generis* the very best. On the other hand, if this disposition be absolutely good, and really better than any other, then the question will be, why, and upon what account it is so? Whatever shall be assigned as the ground or reason of that goodness or betterness, that we may securely pitch upon, as a proper foundation for virtue. If no reason can be given why the Deity should be benevolently disposed, and yet we suppose him to be so; will it not follow, that he is influenced and acted by a blind unaccountable impulse?

★   ★   ★   ★

439   2. Another objection to our author's account of moral good, is, that according thereto, if God had not framed our natures with such a propensity, and given us this benevolent instinct, we should have been altogether incapable of virtue; and notwithstanding intelligence, reason, and liberty, it would have been out of our power to perform one action in any degree morally good. It is evident that this is a direct consequence of his notion; and how a notion should be true, that labours under such a consequence as this, I cannot understand. Let it be supposed, that we had been formed destitute of *natural affection*; and more particularly, that we found in our hearts

---

★ *Illustrations*, p. 239 [i.e. Hutcheson, § 366], and elsewhere.

no kind instinct towards our benefactors: would *gratitude*, upon this supposition, have been absolutely out of our power? Might we not nevertheless, by the help of reason and reflection, discover ourselves to be under obligations, and that we ought to return good offices or thanks, according to our abilities? If we did not, certainly it would be owing to great inadvertency and absence of thought.—Or, supposing us void of *natural compassion*, as well as *benevolence*; might we not possibly be induced to attempt the relief of a person in distress, merely from the *reason* of the thing, and the *rectitude* of the action? Might we not, by considering the nature of the case, and the circumstances of the sufferer, perceive some fitness, some reasonableness in an act of succour? Might not some such maxim as that of doing as we would be done unto, offer itself to our minds, and prevail with us to stretch out a helping hand upon such an occasion? In short, if we made any use of our understandings, they would not fail, I think, to discover our duty in such a case. Nay, they would prompt us to undertake it, and condemn us if we omitted it.

★   ★   ★   ★

3. Another difficulty in our author's scheme is, that it seems to 440 expose him to the necessity of allowing some degree of virtue to *brutes*.[1] When, in describing a moral action, he directs and confines our affections to *rational* objects; this limitation, as I before took notice, appears to have been only casual; for as much as in other places, he takes in all *sensitive* beings.[2] And indeed, there is no reason to doubt, but brutes, as they are capable of being treated by us either mercifully or cruelly, may be the *objects* either of virtue or vice. But the present question is, whether, according to our author's account of moral good, they are not also in some measure *subjects* of virtue? For if virtue be only kind instincts, or affections, or actions consequent upon them, how shall we be able to disprove or deny the virtue of brutes? They pursue the instincts and impulses of nature, more steadily and regularly than men; they show affection to their respective kinds, and a strong degree of love and tenderness towards their offspring. And if a perception, or a consciousness of the reasonableness of actions, be not required to constitute those

[1 Cf. Hutcheson, § 349.]
[2 Cf. Hutcheson, § 315, which speaks first of 'affection toward sensitive natures', then of 'affection toward rational agents'.]

actions virtuous, what is there wanting to render many of theirs truly such?

*   *   *   *

441   4. Another argument against our author's origin of virtue, is, that if virtue consist in kind affections, then the stronger those affections, the greater the virtue. I presume this consequence is very clear, and yet, if I mistake not, it is both contrary to fact, and to our author's own declarations. He tells us, *that in equal moments of good produced by two agents, when one acts from a general benevolence, the other from a nearer tie, there is greater virtue in the agent who produces greater good from the weaker attachment.—Thus in co-operating with gratitude, natural affection, or friendship, we evidence less virtue in any given moment of good produced, than in equally important actions of general benevolence. From hence I think it follows, that if *equal good* were supposed to be produced by an agent, without any affection or *attachment* at all, his *virtue* would still be *greater* in the same proportion. How then should that be the true ground or principle of virtue, by the total absence of which virtue is mightily increased, and which lessens it when present, in proportion to the degree of its own strength and influence? How to reconcile the foregoing passage with the author's idea of virtue, I must confess myself at a loss.

*   *   *   *

442   5. *Lastly*, it may deserve to be considered (though I have touched upon it already) how much virtue is depreciated and dishonoured by so ignoble an original. In our author's scheme it is resolved ultimately into mere *instinct*,[1] and made to consist in it; and even that universal approbation which it meets with from intelligent creatures, is ascribed to a certain *sense*, and made to depend wholly on it. Now if *virtue* and the *approbation* of virtue, be merely *instinctive*, we must certainly think less highly and less honourably of it, than we should do if we looked upon it as *rational*; for I suppose it will readily be allowed, that *reason* is the nobler principle: it is therefore to be wished that it may be found to have the first and chief place in the original idea of virtue, and the exclusion of it must, I think, be a

---

* Vol. I. p. 292 [i.e. *Inquiry concerning Virtue*, Sect. vii, Art. 9].

[1 Cf. Hutcheson, §§ 327, 361–2.]

disparagement to both.—Some will not allow, our author tells us,* any merit in actions flowing from kind instincts, the operation of which, they say, is not voluntary but necessary. Has our author any where denied their operating in this manner? Or has he attempted to show that they may produce meritorious actions, notwithstanding such a manner of operation? I cannot find that he has done either; and indeed it seems utterly impossible to reconcile *virtue* with any kind of *necessity*. As far as any actions spring from a necessary principle, so far they must be, in a moral sense, worthless. If it be said that instincts do not *force* the mind, but only *incline* it; I answer, that as much room as they leave for the use of liberty and the exercise of reason, so much room they leave for virtue; but then this virtue consists in a *rational determination*, and not in a blind pursuit of the *instinct*. What he objects to this will be considered in its proper place; in the mean time, to his query concerning the meaning of the words *merit* or *praise-worthiness*; I answer, that they denote the quality in actions which not only *gains the approbation of the observer*, but which also *deserves* or is *worthy* of it.[1] *Approbation* does not constitute *merit*, but is produced by it; is not the cause of it, but the effect. An agent might be meritorious, though it were in the power of all other beings to withhold their approbation, he might deserve their praise, though we suppose him at the same time under an universal censure. Notwithstanding all that our author has alleged in behalf of *instincts*, I think it appears, even from what has been already said, that they are so far from constituting *virtue* or moral goodness, that, other things being equal, we always account those actions most virtuous which have the least dependence upon instincts; and though in some sense we approve of those actions which flow from instincts, yet there are others which we approve much more, as flowing from a superior principle, and meriting our approbation in themselves, and upon their own account.

I shall now proceed to consider the other of the two instincts **443** which our author has offered for the support of morality, viz. the *moral sense*, the object of which seems to me not sufficiently specified. —*Virtue*, or moral goodness, may be considered either under the notion of *pulchrum* or *honestum*. As to the *pulchrum* or *beauty* of virtue,

* *Illustrat.* Sect. 5 [i.e. Hutcheson, § 373].

[1 But see Hutcheson's reply in § 373.]

it seems to me somewhat doubtful and difficult to determine, whether the *understanding* alone be sufficient for the perception of it, or whether it be not necessary to suppose some distinct power super-added for that purpose. It should seem indeed, as an ingenious writer has observed,⋆ that our faculty of understanding is of itself sufficient for such a perception, that the *beauty* of virtue inseparably and necessarily adheres to the *ideas* themselves, which whenever presented to the mind, appear invariably the same, always amiable and always beautiful. But when I consider, what perhaps is the case in fact, that perceptions of the *pulchrum* and of the *honestum*, seem not equally universal, or if universal, yet in very different degrees; that while every rational creature clearly and uniformly perceives, in all ordinary cases, what is *fit*, and *just*, and *right*; many men have little or no perception of that *beauty* in actions, with which others are wonderfully charmed: and when I further consider, that some actions appear to all men more *beautiful* than others, though equally *right* and *fit*; as in the case of *social* and *self-duties*; I find myself obliged to suspend, and to wait for further evidence.†—Especially in respect of the *pleasure* resulting from such perceptions. For however *ideas, beautiful* in themselves, may be *seen* by the understanding, yet pleasure is not seen, but *felt*; and therefore seems to be an object of some other faculty than that which we are used to consider as merely *visive*. If the purest pleasures be *sensations*, of some kind or other; the mind in receiving them, must be looked upon, not as *intelligent*, but *sensible*. And indeed, sensibility seems to be as distinct from the understanding, as the understanding is from the will. We should not therefore confound them in our conceptions.

444   But this is a speculation somewhat foreign to my present purpose. It was not the *beauty of virtue*, or the *pleasure* arising from the perception of it, that I proposed to inquire into. My intention was only to consider the nature, and search for the origin of *moral rectitude*. For the perception of this, I presume it will appear, that the faculty

⋆ Letter in the *London Journal*, Numb. 450.

† Since the first publication of these papers, I have been convinced, that all beauty, whether moral or natural, is to be reckoned and reputed as a species of absolute truth; as resulting from, or consisting in, the necessary relations and unchangeable congruities of ideas: and, by consequence, that in order to the perception of beauty, no other power need to be supposed, than what is merely intellectual. And as to the diversity of perceptions above-mentioned, the natural or accidental differences of men's understandings seem now to me sufficient to account for it.

of understanding is altogether sufficient, without the intervention of our author's *moral sense*. But before I enter into this matter, it may be proper to consider how improbable it is, that our perceptions of *right* and *wrong*, and the *approbation* or *disapprobation* consequent thereupon, should depend on such a *sense*, or *instinct*, as he has advanced for that purpose. And here I shall only need to observe, that this opinion is liable to the very same objections, and labours under the same difficulties with the former.—Thus, as deriving virtue merely from natural *affection*, implies it to be of an arbitrary and changeable nature; our judging and approving of it by a *moral sense* implies the same: forasmuch as this sense, as well as that affection, might possibly have been quite contrary to what it is at present; or may be altered at any time hereafter. Accordingly our author grants, *there is nothing in this surpassing the natural power of the Deity. But I humbly apprehend he is mistaken; and that it is no more in the power of the Deity to make rational beings approve of ingratitude, perfidiousness, etc. than it is in his power to make them conclude, that a part of any thing is equal to the whole.—In like manner, as according to our author's scheme, we should have been utterly incapable of *virtue* without *natural affection*; so without a *moral sense*, we could never have *approved* of it; nor ever have had any idea at all of moral goodness; so that in this respect, our understandings would have been entirely useless. As if intelligent creatures could not, as such, perceive the most obvious relations, and judge of a plain *action*, as well as a plain *truth*!—Again, as it seems to follow from our author's idea of virtue, that brutes may be in some degree capable of practising it; so upon the same supposition of a *moral sense*, why may they not, in some measure, *approve* of such a practice? It is not to be doubted but they are sensible of pleasure, in the exercise of their natural affections. Supposing them then endued with a *moral* sense, or something corresponding thereto, why might they not see with complacency others of their own species exercising and exerting the same affections? And indeed, if the reasons and relations of things are out of the question, and this moral sense means no more than a natural determination to receive agreeable or disagreeable ideas of certain actions; I think it will be very difficult to prove brutes incapable of such sense.—Thus again, as I think it **445** follows from our author's notion, that the stronger men's *affections*

* Vol. I. p. 302 [i.e. *Inquiry concerning Virtue*, Sect. vii, Art. 12], and elsewhere.

are, the greater must be their *virtue*; so it may be concluded, that the stronger and quicker their *moral sense* is, the higher must their *approbation* of virtuous actions rise. Let the perceptions of *beauty*, and the *pleasure* which attends them, be supposed as different and various as the author thinks fit. But to make the *rectitude* of moral actions dependent upon *instinct*, and in proportion to the warmth and strength of the *moral sense*, rise and fall like spirits in a thermometer, is depreciating the most sacred thing in the world, and almost exposing it to ridicule. I believe no man living is further from such an intention than our author: but I am obliged to examine his opinion as if it was not his. If what I have now observed be not a real consequence from it, I must be answerable for the mistake: but if it be, as I presume it is, it seems heavy enough to sink any opinion in the world. It might as well be said, that eternal and necessary truths may be altered and diversified, increased or lessened by the difference of men's understandings; as that virtue or moral rectitude should be capable of such a variation. It can receive no change, no alteration any way, much less in consequence of a *sense* or an *instinct*.—Lastly, as I took notice how virtue was dishonoured by so ignoble an original as that of instinct, so the same observation may be applied to the notion of a moral sense, with this addition, that at the same time that it depreciates virtue, it also debases the faculty of reason: the former it does by ascribing to a blind impulse that approbation which virtue eternally claims in its own right; the latter by representing our understandings as incapable, and as insufficient of themselves, to judge and approve of it. And what can be more disparaging to reason, than to deny it a power of distinguishing, in the most ordinary cases, between right and wrong, good and evil? Suppose a man deprived of what our author calls the *moral sense*; and according to his hypothesis, whatever reason and philosophy the man may be possessed of, the characters of Antoninus and Caligula, of Socrates and Apicius, shall appear to him in the same light, and their conduct equally praise-worthy, or rather equally indifferent: than which I cannot easily imagine a more shocking absurdity.

446   Thus I think it appears that our author's opinions concerning the two instincts of *affection* and *moral sense*, stand equally exposed to the same objections. From whence we may observe how nicely they are matched, and how exactly they tally to each other.—Let us then seek out for some other original of our ideas, and inquire whether *virtue* or *moral goodness* do not stand on a surer and nobler foundation. Perhaps we may find it independent of all *instincts*, necessarily fixed, and immovably rooted in the nature of things. And perhaps also we may find *reason* or *intelligence* a proper faculty to perceive and judge of it, without the assistance of any adventitious power; only let it be remembered, that it is not the *beauty* or *pleasure*, but only the *rectitude* of moral actions that we are inquiring after.

Our author observes, as I before took notice, that other ways of 447 speaking have been introduced, which seem to signify something different from the two opposite opinions before mentioned. And he concludes, that to render these intelligible, the moral sense must be presupposed. These *ways of speaking*, as he calls them, are, *that morality of actions consists in conformity to reason, and difformity from it. That virtue is acting according to the absolute fitness of things, or agreeably to the natures and relations of things. That there are eternal and immutable differences of things, absolutely and antecedently; that there are also eternal and unalterable relations in the natures of the things themselves; from which arise agreements and disagreements, congruities and incongruities, fitness and unfitness of the application of circumstances to the qualifications of persons, etc. And here the author refers us to that excellent, that inestimable book, Dr. S. Clarke's *Boyle's Lectures*; from which, how it happened that a person of his discernment and penetration rose dissatisfied, in relation to the points before us, I am not able to imagine, unless I may have leave to attribute it to too close an attachment to the celebrated author of the *Characteristics*.

To these ways of speaking might be added some others; as, that virtue consists in the conformity of our wills to our understandings. That it is a rational endeavour of producing happiness in capable subjects. But since both these and the former appear to me coincident, and to centre in the same idea, I shall not examine them severally, but content myself with laying down the notion contained in them in the following *definitions* and explications. And this method I therefore pitch upon, because our author has complained of the darkness or ambiguity of several of the terms.[1]

---

* *Illustrat.* p. 207, 211 [i.e. Hutcheson, §§ 359, 367].

[1 Cf. Hutcheson, §§ 358, 360, 367, 372-3.]

448   1. Virtue, or *moral goodness*, is the conformity of our moral actions to the reasons of things.[1] Vice the contrary.

2. Moral actions are such as are knowingly directed toward some object intelligent or sensible.—I do not add their springing from free choice; because without this they could not really be actions.—To treat or use an insensible object conformably to reason, or according to what it is,[2] though it may be a *right* action, yet is indifferent in respect of *morality*; which only concerns our behaviour to such beings as are, at least, sensible. But as I exclude not here, beings merely sensible, so neither do I exclude the agent himself. To promote his own real welfare, in subordination to that of the public, is in its kind true virtue.

449   3. The conformity of such actions to reason, or the rectitude of them, is their agreeableness to the nature and circumstances of the agents and the objects.—A *social* action is then *right*, when it is suitable to the nature and relations of the persons concerned. Thus a person obliged acts *rightly* and *reasonably*, when his actions are answerable to the relation of gratitude between him and his benefactor.

4. Relations between things or persons, are their comparative states or modes of existence, necessarily arising from their different natures or circumstances.—Whether relations be qualities inherent in external natures, or not; or however they may be defined, or conceived, they are certainly real, unalterable, and eternal.[3] That is, supposing those natures always continuing to be what they are, the relations interceding between them are invariable. However, the relations between *ideas* are strictly necessary and unchangeable; the ideas themselves being so in the divine understanding.

450   5. Obligation may be considered as either *external or internal*. Of *external*, which arises from just authority, I have no occasion to speak. —Internal obligation is a state of the mind into which it is brought by the perception of a plain reason for acting, or forbearing to act, arising from the nature, circumstances, or relations of persons or things.—The internal reasons of things are the supreme law, inducing the strongest obligation, and affecting all intelligent beings. Though we are certainly obliged to do whatever appears to be the will of God, merely because it is his will, and in consequence of

[1 Cf. Clarke, § 231.]   [2 Cf. Clarke, §§ 230, 232; Wollaston, § 281.]
[3 Contrast Hutcheson, § 367.]

that right which he has to prescribe laws to us; yet our obligation to act conformably to reason is even superior to this, because the divine will itself is certainly subject to the original law or rule of action.—To suppose reasonable beings unconcerned with the reasons of things, is to suppose them reasonable and unreasonable at the same time. The reasons of things are to men, in respect of practice, what evidence is in speculation. Assent in one case, and approbation in the other, are equally and irresistibly gained; only there is this difference, that the will has power to rebel, and the understanding has not. But whenever the will does rebel, the immediate consequence is an odious perception of wrong, and a consciousness of guilt, which may be looked upon as natural sanctions of the law of nature.

6. REASON, or *intelligence*, is a faculty enabling us to perceive, **451** either immediately or mediately, the agreement or disagreement of ideas, whether natural or moral.—This last clause, otherwise super-fluous, is inserted upon our author's account; who seems to exclude *moral ideas*, and to consider them as objects of another faculty. And indeed, if he had thought our understandings capable of moral per-ceptions, he would have had no occasion for introducing his moral sense, except in relation to the τὸ καλόν, concerning which I have already acknowledged myself undetermined. But it is visible, that he ascribes our perceptions of the *rectitude* of virtuous actions to this moral sense, or rather makes that rectitude entirely consist in their correspondence with it. Whereas if there be a real rectitude in such actions, I cannot doubt but our understandings are capable of per-ceiving it. We have confessedly ideas of actions and agents, and find a manifest difference among them. We find likewise that some actions are agreeable, others disagreeable, to the nature and circum-stances of the agent and the object, and the relations interceding between them. Thus, for instance, we find an agreement between the gratitude of A and the kindness of B; and a disagreement be-tween the ingratitude of C and the bounty of D. These agreements and disagreements are visible to every intelligent observer, who attends to the several ideas. The question then is, whether we per-ceive them by our *understanding*, or by what our author calls a *moral sense*? And might it not as well be asked, how it is that we perceive the agreement between the three angles of a triangle, and two right ones? Will our author say, that we perceive this by an *intellectual sense* superadded to our understanding? I believe he will not. Why

then does he ascribe the other perceptions to a *moral* one? If the agreement or disagreement of one sort of ideas be proper objects of our understandings, why not those of another? Especially since, in many cases, they are perceived with equal clearness and evidence. Let therefore our intelligent faculty either be pronounced insufficient in both cases, or in neither. Nay, since moral perceptions are more useful and important than any other, there is peculiar reason to conclude, that they belong to our supreme faculty. It is not to be imagined, that the wise Author of nature would frame our minds in such a manner, as to allot them only *instincts* for the purposes of morality and virtue, and at the same time grant them *reason* and intelligence for inferior uses. This seems to me neither consistent with the dignity of virtue, nor the supremacy of our rational faculty.

452   7. TRUTH, objectively considered, is either of *words, ideas,* or *things.* By which last I mean external natures. VERBAL *truth,* or the *truth of propositions,* is their conformity to one or both of the other two.[1] IDEAL *truth* is the agreement or disagreement of ideas. *Truth of* THINGS is the relative nature of things themselves, or the agreement or disagreement of one thing with another.—That *ideas* correspond or differ, agree or disagree with each other, will readily be allowed, whether such agreements or disagreements be formed into propositions or no. The differences among them constitute various relations, which are fixed and certain, independently of our observation.—In like manner *external natures,* in virtue of their essential or circumstantial differences, abound in real relations to one another, independently of propositions, and in some sense, even of ideas. The things indeed themselves could never have existed without a mind, and antecedent ideas. But when they are once brought into existence, and constituted in such or such a manner, those agreements or disagreements, wherein truth consists, flow necessarily from their respective constitutions; and by consequence, neither depend on the perceptions of intelligent beings, nor on the will of the Creator himself. A cylindrical body would be bigger than a conical one, of the same base and height, and spherical particles fitter for motion than angular, whether any beings perceived it, or no.—There are also the same real agreements and disagreements between actions, agents, and objects, as any other things. Some actions are very different from and even contrary to others. There is likewise a

[1 A more complex definition than in Wollaston, § 274, and Hutcheson, § 360.]

wide difference between the nature of rational creatures, and that of brutes; and between the nature of brutes, and that of inanimate things. They require therefore respectively a suitable treatment. To treat men in the same way we treat brutes, and to treat brutes in the same way we do stocks and stones, is manifestly as disagreeable and dissonant to the natures of things, as it would be to attempt the forming of an angle with two parallel lines. I would not call such a conduct *acting a lie*,[1] because that is confounding objective and subjective truth, and introducing needless perplexities. I would not call it a *contradiction* to some true *proposition*,[2] because that neither comes up to the case, nor is a way of speaking strictly proper; but I would call it a *counter-action to the truth, or real natures of things.*— From hence it appears, how far, and with what propriety a *morally good* action may be said to be *conformable to truth*, or to *consist in such a conformity*. If by truth be meant the *truth of things*, then I think it may properly be said, that the moral goodness of an action consists in a conformity thereto. It may therefore be called either a *true* or a *right* action; though for distinction sake, and the avoiding of ambiguity and confusion, I should constantly prefer the latter. However, since this *truth of things* is, in *morals*, the standard and measure of *true propositions*, which are no otherwise true, than as they agree with it; it is evidently more proper to represent moral goodness as founded on the former, rather than the latter.

*　　*　　*　　*

But the great difficulty in our author's apprehension, is yet be-　**453**
hind: he wants to be informed what are the motives, inducements, or *exciting reasons* for the *choice* of virtue, and what the *justifying reasons* of our *approbation* of it.[3] He seems to think these questions are not to be answered upon the scheme I am defending: let us then try whether this difficulty be not surmountable without the help of those *instincts* which he has introduced for that purpose.—What is the *reason exciting* a man to the *choice* of a virtuous action? I answer, his very *approbation* of it is itself a *sufficient reason*, wherever it is not overruled by another more powerful. What can be more just, what more natural, than *choosing* of a thing that we *approve*, and even choosing it for that very reason?—But why then do we *approve*? or

[1 Contrast Wollaston, § 278.]　　[2 Contrast Wollaston, §§ 275–7, 279.]
[3 Cf. Hutcheson, § 361.]

what *justifies* our *approbation* of it? I answer in one word, *necessity*. The same necessity which compels men to *assent* to what is *true*, forces them to approve what is *right* and fit. And I cannot but wonder, that our author should demand a reason for the one more than for the other. In both cases the mind necessarily acquiesces, without regarding or considering the effects or tendencies of either.

*   *   *   *

454   But our author tells us, *that in every calm rational action, some END is desired or intended. And accordingly, he expects to hear, what is the *end* which a man proposes in the *choice of virtue*, upon the present scheme. He affirms that under benevolence, self-love, and their opposites, all affections are included; and concludes from thence, that there can be *no exciting reason* but what arises from some or other of them.—Before I examine this objection, I desire to know whether that esteem, admiration, complacency which virtue produces, be no *affection*? and, whatever they may be called, whether they may not *excite to election*? Is virtue no otherwise good or amiable, than as it conduces to public or private advantage? Is there no absolute goodness in it? Are all its perfections *relative* and instrumental? Have we no other idea of the *honestum* and the *pulchrum* but this? Is the *lovely form* to be considered only as a kind of *cornucopia*?

455   But to return: our author's question amounts plainly to this: what does a *reasonable* creature propose in *acting reasonably*? Or what is it that induces his *will* to take counsel of his *understanding*? As if this were not the very essence of a rational action! The question therefore might as well have been put thus: what is it that induces a man to be a rational agent, when he has it in his power to be otherwise? Besides the *internal reasons* which I am speaking of, there are indeed likewise *external reasons*, if considerations of interest may properly be called so. Call them what we will, they must, and will be regarded by such creatures as men. But clamorous and importunate as they are, they leave us at liberty, in most cases, to attend to those *internal reasons* which I have been considering. The still voice of conscience may generally be heard amidst all the bustle and tumult

---

* Vol. II. page 216 [i.e. *Illustrations on the Moral Sense*, Sect. i; Hutcheson, § 362].

of our appetites and passions.—But to come to the point, if by the *end* which our author inquires after, he means nothing but some advantage or *natural good*; my answer is, that we may choose reasonable or virtuous actions, without intention or view of any such *end*. But if I may be allowed to take the word in another signification, then I answer as follows.—The *end* of rational actions and rational agents, considered as such, is *reason* or *moral good*. As this is the proper *object* of our moral capacity, and the affection corresponding thereto, it may properly be said to be our *end* as *moral agents*. This affection, like others, reaches out to its proper *object*, and rests in the possession of it, as its true *end*, whether it be, or be not connected with happiness. The end of the speculatist is *truth*, whether it redound to his advantage, or his disadvantage. The end of the moralist is *rectitude*, whether it conduce to his interest or no. Considered as *moral*, this is precisely the mark that he aims at; his judgement directing, and his affection prompting to this *object* as, in a peculiar sense, self-worthy and self-eligible. In short, *moral good* is an *end*, an *ultimate end* of one kind, as *natural good* is of another. And these ends are so closely united and interwoven, that it is sometimes difficult to separate them even in our conceptions. In the pursuit of *pleasure*, we have often the consent and concurrence of *reason*; and when we pursue *reason* or *virtue*, *pleasure* accompanies and follows. If we propose to make ourselves happy, we have reason on our side; and if we determine to act reasonably, pleasure is the consequence.—Nevertheless, they are in themselves, distinct objects, and distinct ends. However pleasure may be the consequence or appendage of virtue, yet, strictly speaking, it is not the end of a moral agent, nor the object of a moral affection, but virtue alone, antecedent to all considerations, and abstracted from every natural good. As man is a *sensible* creature, as well as *moral*, I deny not but certain circumstances may be supposed, wherein, these ends interfering, the *moral* good would certainly be postponed to the *natural*, and the *external reasons* unavoidably prevail over the *internal*: but such cases can never come into fact, and therefore need not be regarded. As God has framed our natures in such a manner as makes it necessary for us to approve and pursue both these ends, we may infallibly conclude, that he does not intend to suffer them finally to interfere.

*   *   *   *

PART II

(Being an answer to certain remarks communicated by a gentleman
to the author)

★   ★   ★   ★

456   ARTICLE III. The ideas of bounty and gratitude are, if you please,
moral ideas; but no moral proposition can rightly be deduced from
them: or however, no such proposition as includes any sort of obligation. From the mere idea of gratitude, it will no more follow that
men ought to be grateful, than from the idea of ingratitude, that
they ought to be ungrateful, if we suppose no sentiment.

ANSWER. If *moral ideas* had no *relations* belonging to them, or if
these relations were imperceptible to human understandings; then
it might justly be said, that our moral ideas yielded us no *propositions*.
But since some of these ideas agree, and others differ, as much at
least as any other ideas; and since these agreements and differences
are commonly very evident to all who will attend, it follows, that
moral ideas must needs be equally fruitful of propositions.—The
idea of gratitude cannot properly be said to infer any obligation.
But when a man compares the idea of gratitude with that of a bene-
faction received, and examines the relation between them, he cannot
avoid inferring, or concluding that he ought to be grateful. This will
be farther considered under the three following articles.

457   ART. IV. If we had otherwise no idea of obligation, the ideas of
gratitude, ingratitude, and bounty, could never so much as afford us
a general idea of obligation itself; or inform us what is meant by
that term; much less could we be able to deduce the particular obligation to gratitude from these ideas.

ANS. If receiving of benefits be a *good reason*, as it certainly is, why
the receiver should be *grateful*, then it *obliges* him so to be. I observed
in my former *papers, that the perception of such a reason perpetually
binds all rational agents, and is indeed the first and highest of all
moral obligations. The dictates and directions of right reason are the
very rule which the Deity himself inviolably observes, and which
therefore must needs affect all intelligent creatures.—The ideas of

* § 450.

benefits and *obligations* are so closely connected, that to *do a man a kindness*, and to *oblige him*, are used promiscuously, as expressions of the same signification.—Every man who receives a benefit, receives along with it a reason for gratitude: and that reason he must perceive, if he be not quite thoughtless. What *instinct* prompts him to, his *understanding* will immediately second and confirm. His reason will readily suggest to him what behaviour is due to his benefactor, and inform him that no actions but *grateful* ones, can be in any degree *suitable* or *fit*. To be *injuriously*, or even *indifferently* affected towards him, will appear as absurd, as incongruous, as contrary to the nature of things, as it would be for a husbandman, after a full crop, to cover his ground with flints instead of manure. No affections, no actions, and by consequence, no ideas, can possibly be more unsuitable, or mismatched, than kindness and ingratitude.—Moral actions, like other things, agree or disagree, essentially and unalterably. Hence flow those relations and reasons whereon morality is founded, and which derive obligations upon all agents capable of perceiving them.

Art. V. If you will affirm, that by comparing these ideas in your **458** mind, you can perceive any such moral proposition necessarily included, viz. that a man ought to be grateful; I ask, whether you see that necessary consequence immediately upon comparing these ideas, or mediately by the help of some intermediate reasoning or proof? If you see such a connection immediately, or, as it were, intuitively, I wonder every body else cannot see it. If you have any intermediate reasonings or proofs, pray let us have them.

Ans. That a man ought to be grateful to his benefactors, may be looked upon as equivalent to a self-evident proposition. If it need any proofs, they are so obvious and clear, that the mind perceives them in an instant, and immediately allows the truth of the proposition. Between *bounty* and *gratitude* there is a plain congruity of *moral fitness*; and between *bounty* and *ingratitude* a plain incongruity, or *unfitness*.—Therefore gratitude is *reasonable*, and ingratitude *unreasonable*.—Therefore the one ought to be *observed*, and the other *detested*. As these conclusions appear to me incontestable, so I presume the principle from whence they flow is strictly self-evident. Ingratitude is not only shocking to natural affection, but necessarily appears to the understanding irregular, disproportioned, monstrous.—But if this principle, and the connection of those conclusions with it, be so plain and evident, how happens it that they are ever called in question? I answer, that men's understandings, like their eyes, may possibly be sometimes dazzled with too much light. Doubts and scruples have been raised, one time or other, concerning the plainest and most evident truths in the world, even by philosophers and men of letters. But as to the points before us, I may appeal to the general judgement of mankind.—Let any illiterate man be asked these plain questions: Is not ingratitude to a benefactor very unfitting?—Is it not therefore very unreasonable?—Ought it not therefore to be abhorred and avoided by every body? To each of these questions, he will, I doubt not, without any hesitation answer in the affirmative. Should he be further asked, whether he really *understood* these truths? he would not only make the same answer, but be surprised at the question.

459 Art. VI. I know not well what you mean by this expression, viz. *that our understandings are capable of moral perceptions*. I believe every body agrees that in some sense they are; that is, that the mind is capable of receiving or forming moral ideas: but it will not follow from hence, that obligation is deducible merely from our moral ideas, without supposing any sentiment.

Ans. In saying that *our understandings are capable of moral perceptions*, I mean, that they are not only capable of forming ideas of *agents* and *actions*, but of perceiving likewise the *relations* of agreement and disagreement between them. From these relations, *obligation* is plainly deducible in the manner before mentioned. But I shall here lay it down more particularly.—I have already observed, that between such and such *agents*, *actions*, and *objects*, naturally and necessarily intercede certain *relations* of *agreement* or *disagreement*, *fitness* or *unfitness*: conformably whereto, the same relations are observable between their respective *ideas*; which, when just, always correspond to *things* themselves. For the reality of these relations, every man must be referred to his own perceptions, since they admit of no other proof. Such fitnesses or unfitnesses are as manifest to our understandings, as it is visible to our eyes that blue is not green, or scarlet, yellow; or to our imaginations, that a triangle is not a circle, or a cone, a cube.

The next point to be considered, is, whether actions thus *fit*, be not therefore *reasonable*, and actions unfit, therefore unreasonable.

If this *moral fitness* of certain actions be not a reason for the doing of them, I see not how any thing can be a reason for any thing. Moral fitness is conformity to order and truth; and if our reason did not approve of this, we should have cause to conclude it an irregular, disorderly faculty. But it is certain that our reason does approve of it, and that necessarily. The intrinsic goodness of such actions is an irresistible recommendation to our minds and judgements, and by consequence, is a perpetual reason for the concurrence of our wills. Those actions therefore which our reason approves as self-worthy, and which are chosen and done with that view, and upon that account, must not only be *reasonable*, in the strictest sense of the word, but in the highest degree that our actions are capable of. However, we must either allow those actions to be *reasonable*, for the doing of which a good reason may be given, and which our faculty of reason approves of; or it will follow, that none of our actions are or can be reasonable.

What remains, is to deduce from hence the *obligation* that we are **460** now inquiring after. How does it appear that we *ought* to do what is *reasonable*? As moral agents, we are either obliged to this, or nothing. But what is it we mean by *obligation*? Certainly not *compulsion*. Since *obligation* supposes *liberty*, it must be something consistent with liberty. It supposes likewise some *perception* in the mind, since no agent can be obliged to or by any thing while he is ignorant of it. What is it then, which as soon as perceived, produces that state of mind which we call *obligation*? It must be some *motive*, some *inducement*, some *reason*, that is fit to influence and incline the will, and prevail with it to choose and act accordingly.—Is not then *interest* or *pleasure* such an inducement? It is in respect of *sensible agents*, considered as such. And thus it is that men, as *sensible agents*, are *obliged* to pursue *pleasure* or *natural good*; which as soon as they have experienced, they naturally and necessarily approve: but considered as *moral agents*, they have no concern with *natural good*. I took notice in my former papers,[1] that *moral good* is the only object of moral affection, and the only aim or end of moral agents, who are influenced and attracted by it, as sensible agents are by natural good. As the latter therefore are *obliged* to pursue their end, which I call *interest* or *pleasure*; so the former are *obliged* to pursue theirs, which is *moral rectitude, reason*, or *virtue*.—I intend not by this to set natural

[1 § 455.]

and moral obligations on a level, but to show the nature and grounds of obligation in general. In what respects they differ, and how far the one are superior to the other, are points not to be now discussed without too long a digression.

461 I proceed therefore to observe, that the obligation which arises from *authority*, may be looked upon as compounded of the other two. *Laws* affect us in one capacity, and *sanctions* in another. As *sensible agents* we are obliged to aim at rewards, and avoid punishments: as *moral agents*, we may be doubly obliged. It is morally fit and just to pay obedience to a rightful legislator, in all cases not overruled by some higher authority; and if, moreover, his laws be in themselves morally good, our obligations rise in proportion.

It appears, I think, from what has been said, that *moral obligations* are strictly connected with *moral fitness*, and the *reasons* of things. To resolve all obligations into interest, or natural good, seems to me confounding morality with sensibility. It is in effect to say that virtue is not *good in itself*, nor any otherwise good, than as it *does us good*. Whereas it is certainly self-amiable, and self-worthy; and as such, must be exceedingly fit to operate on the wills of moral agents, as it never fails to engage their judgements. And indeed whatever appears worthy of approbation and esteem, as virtue does in the highest degree, must needs appear worthy of choice: and what appears worthy of choice, *ought* to be chosen; or in other words, men are *obliged* to choose it. In short, whatever agent is said to be under an *obligation* to the performance of any action, the true meaning of such an expression, as it appears to me, is, that he perceives some *good reason*, either internal or external, moral or natural, for the performance of it. What falls short of this, can be no obligation; and what goes beyond it, must be coaction.

* * * *

JOHN GAY

1699–1745

CONCERNING THE FUNDAMENTAL PRINCIPLE OF VIRTUE OR MORALITY

[First printed, as a Preliminary Dissertation to the English translation by Edmund Law of William King's *Essay on the Origin of Evil*, 1731. Reprinted here from the third edition of that work, 1739, with misprints corrected, spelling modified, and initial capital letters reduced]

JOHN GAY

Concerning the Fundamental Principle of Virtue or Morality

SECT. I—CONCERNING THE CRITERION OF VIRTUE

*   *   *   *

Virtue is the conformity to a rule of life, directing the actions of all **462** *rational creatures with respect to each other's happiness; to which conformity every one in all cases is obliged: and every one that does so conform, is or ought to be approved of, esteemed and loved for so doing.* What is here expressed, I believe every one, or most, put into their idea of virtue.

For virtue generally does imply some relation to *others*: where *self* is only concerned, a man is called *prudent* (not virtuous), and an action which relates immediately to *God*, is styled *religious*.

I think also that all men, whatever they make virtue to consist in, yet always make it to imply *obligation* and *approbation*.

The idea of virtue being thus fixed, to inquire after the criterion of it, is to inquire what that rule of life is to which we are *obliged* to conform, or how that rule is to be found out which is to direct me in my behaviour towards *others*, which ought *always* to be pursued, and which, if pursued, will or ought to procure me *approbation*, *esteem*, and *love*.

But before I can answer this inquiry: I must first see what I mean by *obligation*.

SECT. II—CONCERNING OBLIGATION

Obligation is the necessity of doing or omitting any action in order to be **463** *happy:* i.e. when there is such a relation between an agent and an action that the agent cannot be happy without doing or omitting that action, then the agent is said to be *obliged* to do or omit that action. So that obligation is evidently founded upon the prospect of *happiness*, and arises from that necessary influence which any action has upon present or future happiness or misery. And no greater obligation can be supposed to be laid upon any *free agent* without an express contradiction.

464 This obligation may be considered four ways, according to the four different manners in which it is induced: First, that obligation which ariseth from perceiving the natural consequences of things, i.e. the consequences of things acting according to the fixed laws of nature, may be called *natural*. Secondly, that arising from merit or demerit, as producing the esteem and favour of our fellow-creatures, or the contrary, is usually styled *virtuous*. Thirdly, that arising from the authority of the civil magistrate, *civil*. Fourthly, that from the authority of God, *religious*.[1]

Now from the consideration of these four sorts of obligation (which are the only ones) it is evident that a full and complete obligation which will extend to all cases, can only be that arising from the authority of *God*; because God only can in all cases make a man happy or miserable: and therefore, since we are *always* obliged to that conformity called virtue, it is evident that the immediate rule or criterion of it is the will of God.[2] But is the *whole* will of God the criterion of virtue? No. For though the whole will of God is equally obligatory; yet, since virtue was defined to be the conformity to a rule directing my behaviour with respect to my *fellow-creatures*, the will of God can be no more farther concerned about virtue, than as it directs me in that behaviour.

465 The next inquiry therefore is, what that will of God in this particular is, or what it directs me to do?

Now it is evident from the nature of God, viz. his being infinitely happy in himself from all eternity, and from his goodness manifested in his works, that he could have no other design in creating mankind than *their* happiness; and therefore he wills their happiness; therefore the means of their happiness: therefore that my behaviour, as far as it may be a means of the happiness of mankind, should be such. Here then we are got one step farther, or to a new criterion: not to a new criterion of virtue *immediately*, but to a criterion of the *will of God*. For it is an answer to the inquiry, how shall I know what the will of God in this particular is? Thus the will of God is the immediate criterion of virtue, and the happiness of mankind the

[1 For the last three, cf. Locke, § 184.]   [2 Cf. Locke, § 185.]

criterion of the will of God; and therefore the happiness of mankind may be said to be the criterion of virtue, but *once removed*.

★   ★   ★   ★

Thus those who either expressly exclude, or do not mention the **466** will of God, making the immediate criterion of virtue to be the good of mankind; must either allow that virtue is not in all cases *obligatory* (contrary to the idea which all or most men have of it) or they must say that the good of mankind is a sufficient obligation. But how can the good of mankind be any obligation to *me*, when perhaps in particular cases, such as laying down my life, or the like, it is contrary to my happiness?

★   ★   ★   ★

SECT. III—CONCERNING APPROBATION AND AFFECTION

Man is not only a *sensible* creature, not only capable of pleasure **467** and pain, but capable also of *foreseeing* this pleasure and pain in the future consequences of things and actions; and as he is capable of knowing, so also of *governing* or directing the causes of them, and thereby in a great measure enabled to avoid the one and procure the other: whence the principle of all action. And therefore, as pleasure and pain are not indifferent to him, nor out of his power, he pursues the former and avoids the latter; and therefore also those things which are *causes* of them are not indifferent, but he pursues or avoids them also, according to their different tendency. That which he pursues for its own sake, which is only pleasure, is called an *end*; that which he apprehends to be apt to produce pleasure, he calls *good*,[1] and approves of, i.e. judges a proper means to attain his end, and therefore looks upon it as an object of choice; and that which is pregnant with misery he disapproves of and styles *evil*. And this good and evil are not only barely approved of, or the contrary, but whenever viewed in imagination (since man considers himself as existing hereafter, and is concerned for his welfare then as well as now) they have a *present pleasure* or pain annexed to them, proportionable to what is apprehended to follow them in real existence; which pleasure or pain arising from the prospect of future pleasure

[1 Cf. Locke, §§ 160, 177, 183.]

or pain is properly called *passion*, and the desire consequent thereupon, *affection*.

And as by reflecting upon pleasure there arises in our minds a *desire* of it; and on pain, an *aversion* from it (which necessarily follows from supposing us to be sensible creatures, and is no more than saying, that all things are not *indifferent* to us); so also by reflecting upon good or evil, the same desires and aversions are excited, and are distinguished into *love* and *hatred*. And from love and hatred variously modified, arise all those other desires and aversions which are promiscuously styled passions or affections; and are generally thought to be implanted in our nature *originally*, like the power of receiving pleasure or pain. And when placed on inanimate objects, are these following, hope, fear, despair and its opposite, for which we want a name.

SECT. IV—APPROBATION AND AFFECTION CONSIDERED WITH REGARD TO MERIT, OR THE LAW OF ESTEEM

468   If a man in the pursuit of pleasure or happiness (by which is meant the sum total of pleasure[1]) had to do only with inanimate creatures, his approbation and affections would be as described in the foregoing section. But, since he is dependent with respect to his happiness, not only on these, but also on rational agents, creatures like himself, which have the power of governing or directing good and evil, and of acting for an end; there will arise different means of happiness, and consequently different pursuits, though tending to the same end, happiness; and therefore different approbations and affections, and the contrary; which deserve particularly to be considered.

That there will arise different means of happiness, is evident from hence, viz. that rational agents, in being subservient to our happiness, are not passive but voluntary. And therefore since we are in pursuit of that to obtain which we apprehend the concurrence of their wills necessary, we cannot but approve of whatever is apt to procure this concurrence. And that can be only the pleasure or pain expected from it by them. And therefore, as I perceive that my happiness is dependent on others, I cannot but judge whatever I apprehend to be proper to excite them to endeavour to promote my happiness, to be a means of happiness, i.e. I cannot but *approve it*.

[1 Cf. Shaftesbury, § 215.]

And since the annexing pleasure to their endeavours to promote my happiness is the only thing in my power to this end, I cannot but approve of the annexing pleasure to such actions of theirs as are undertaken upon my account. Hence to approve of a rational agent as a means of happiness is different from the approbation of any other means, because it implies an approbation also of an endeavour to promote the happiness of that agent, in order to excite him and others to the same concern for my happiness for the future.

And because what we approve of we also desire (as has been shown above) hence also we *desire* the happiness of any agent that has done us good. And therefore *love* or *hatred*, when placed on a rational object, has this difference from the love or hatred of other things, that it implies a desire of, and consequently a pleasure in the happiness of the object beloved; or if hated, the contrary.

The foundation of this approbation and love (which, as we have **469** seen, consists in his voluntary contributing to our happiness) is called the *merit* of the agent so contributing, i.e. that whereby he is entitled (upon supposition that we act like rational, sociable creatures, like creatures, whose happiness is dependent on each other's behaviour) to our approbation and love: *demerit* the contrary.

And this affection or quality of any action which we call *merit* is very consistent with a man's acting *ultimately* for his own private happiness. For any particular action that is undertaken *for the sake of another*, is *meritorious*, i.e. deserves esteem, favour, and approbation from him for whose sake it was undertaken, towards the doer of it. For the presumption of such esteem, etc. was the only motive to that action; and if such esteem, etc. does not follow, or is presumed not to follow it, such a person is reckoned unworthy of any favour, because he shows by his actions that he is incapable of being *obliged* by favours.

The mistake which some have run into, viz. that merit is incon- **470** sistent with acting upon *private happiness*, as an ultimate end, seems to have arisen from hence, viz. that they have not carefully enough distinguished between an inferior, and ultimate end; the end of a particular action, and the end of action in general: which may be explained thus. Though happiness, private happiness, is the proper or ultimate end of all our actions whatever, yet that particular means of happiness which any particular action is chiefly adapted to procure, or the thing chiefly aimed at by that action; the thing which if possessed, we would not undertake that action, may, and generally is called the *end* of that action. As therefore happiness is the general end of all actions, so each particular action may be said to have its proper and peculiar end:[1] thus the end of a beau is to please by his dress; the end of study, knowledge. But neither pleasing by dress, nor knowledge, are ultimate ends, they still tend or ought to tend to something farther as is evident from hence, viz. that a man may ask and expect a reason why either of them are pursued: now to ask the *reason* of any action or pursuit, is only to inquire into the *end* of it: but to expect a reason, i.e. an end, to be assigned for an *ultimate* end, is absurd.[2] To ask why I pursue happiness, will admit of no other answer than an explanation of the terms.

Why *inferior ends*, which in reality are only means, are too often looked upon and acquiesced in as *ultimate*, shall be accounted for hereafter.

471   Whenever therefore the *particular* end of any action is the happiness of another (though the agent designed thereby to procure to himself esteem and favour, and looked upon that esteem and favour as a means of private happiness) that action is meritorious. And the same may be said, though we design to please God by endeavouring to promote the happiness of others. But when an agent has a view in any particular action distinct from my happiness, and that view is his only *motive* to that action, though that action promote my happiness to never so great a degree, yet that agent acquires no *merit*; i.e. he is not thereby entitled to any favour and esteem: because favour and esteem are due from me for any action, no farther than that action was undertaken upon my account. If therefore my happiness is only the pretended end of that action, I am imposed on if I believe it real, and thereby think myself indebted to the agent; and I am discharged from any obligation as soon as I find out the cheat.

But it is far otherwise when my happiness is the sole end of that particular action, i.e. (as I have explained myself above) when the agent endeavours to promote my happiness as a means to procure my favour, i.e. to make me subservient to his happiness as his ultimate end: though I know he aims at my happiness only as a means of his own, yet this lessens not the obligation.

There is one thing, I confess, which makes a great alteration in this case, and that is, whether he aims at my favour *in general*, or only

[1 Cf. Butler, §§ 414–16.]   [2 Cf. Hutcheson, §§ 362–3.]

for some particular end. Because, if he aim at my happiness only to serve himself in some particular thing, the value of my favour will perhaps end with his obtaining that particular thing: and therefore I am under less obligation (*ceteris paribus*) the more *particular* his expectations from me are; but under obligation I am.

Now from the various combinations of this which we call merit,   **472** and its contrary, arise all those various approbations and aversions; all those likings and dislikings which we call *moral*.

As therefore from considering those beings which are the *involuntary* means of our happiness or misery, there were produced in us the passions or affections of love, hatred, hope, fear, despair, and its contrary: so from considering those beings which *voluntarily* contribute to our happiness or misery, there arise the following. Love and hatred (which are different from that love or hatred placed on involuntary beings; that placed on involuntary beings being only a desire to possess or avoid the thing beloved or hated; but this on voluntary agents being a desire to give pleasure or pain to the agent beloved or hated), gratitude, anger (sometimes called by one common name, resentment), generosity, ambition, honour, shame, envy, benevolence: and if there be any other, they are only, as these are, different modifications of love and hatred.

*   *   *   *

Thus having explained what I mean by *obligation* and *approbation*;   **473** and shown that they are founded on and terminate in *happiness*: having also pointed out the difference between our approbations and affections as placed on involuntary and voluntary means of happiness; and farther, that these approbations and affections are not innate or implanted in us by way of *instinct*, but are all *acquired*, being fairly deducible from supposing only sensible and rational creatures dependent on each other for their happiness, as explained above: I shall in the next place endeavour to answer a grand objection to what has here been said concerning approbations and affections arising from a prospect of private happiness.

The objection is this,   **474**
The reason or end of every action is always known to the agent; for nothing can move a man but what is perceived: but the generality of mankind love and hate, approve and disapprove, immediately,

as soon as any moral character either occurs in life, or is proposed to them, without considering whether their private happiness is affected with it, or no: or if they do consider any moral character in relation to their own happiness, and find themselves, as to their private happiness, unconcerned in it, or even find their private happiness lessened by it in some particular instance, yet they still approve the moral character, and love the agent: nay they cannot do otherwise. Whatever reason may be assigned by speculative men why we should be grateful to a benefactor, or pity the distressed; yet if the grateful or compassionate mind never thought of that reason, it is no reason to him. The inquiry is not why he *ought to be* grateful, but why he *is* so. These after-reasons therefore rather show the wisdom and providence of our Maker in implanting the immediate powers of these approbations (i.e. in Mr. Hutcheson's language, *a moral sense*) and these public affections in us, than give any satisfactory account of their origin. And therefore these public affections, and this moral sense, are quite independent on private happiness, and in reality act upon us as mere instincts.

475   *Answer,*

The matter of fact contained in this argument, in my opinion, is not to be contested; and therefore it remains either that we make the matter of fact consistent with what we have before laid down, or give up the cause.

Now, in order to show this consistency, I beg leave to observe, that as in the pursuit of truth we do not always trace every proposition whose truth we are examining, to a first principle or axiom, but acquiesce, as soon as we perceive it deducible from some known or presumed truth; so in our conduct we do not always travel to the ultimate end of our actions, *happiness*: but rest contented, as soon as we perceive any action subservient to a known or presumed *means* of happiness. And these presumed truths and means of happiness whether real or otherwise, always influence us after the same manner as if they were real. The undeniable consequences of prejudices are as firmly adhered to as the consequences of real truths or arguments; and what is subservient to a false (but imagined) means of happiness, is as industriously pursued as what is subservient to a true one.

476   Now every man, both in his pursuit after truth, and in his conduct, has settled and fixed a great many of these in his mind, which he always acts upon, as upon *principles*, without examining. And this is occasioned by the narrowness of our understandings: we can consider but a few things at once; and therefore, to run every thing to the fountain-head would be tedious, through a long series of consequences; to avoid this we choose out certain truths and means of happiness, which we look upon as RESTING PLACES, which we may safely acquiesce in, in the conduct both of our understanding and practice; in relation to the one, regarding them as *axioms*; in the other, as *ends*. And we are more easily inclined to this by imagining that we may safely rely upon what we call *habitual* knowledge, thinking it needless to examine what we are already satisfied in. And hence it is that prejudices, both speculative and practical, are difficult to be rooted out, viz. few will examine them.

And these RESTING PLACES are so often used as principles, that at last, letting that slip out of our minds which first inclined us to embrace them, we are apt to imagine them not as they really are, the *substitutes* of principles, but principles themselves.

And from hence, as some men have imagined *innate ideas*, because forgetting how they came by them; so others have set up almost as many distinct *instincts* as there are *acquired principles* of acting. And I cannot but wonder why the *pecuniary* sense, a sense of *power* and *party*, etc. were not mentioned, as well as the *moral*, that of *honour*, *order*, and some others.[1]

The case is really this. We first perceive or imagine some real **477** good, i.e. fitness to promote our happiness, in those things which we love and approve of. Hence (as was above explained) we annex pleasure to those things. Hence those things and pleasure are so tied together and associated in our minds, that one cannot present itself but the other will also occur. And the *association* remains even after that which at first gave them the connection is quite forgot, or perhaps does not exist, but the contrary. An instance or two may perhaps make this clear. How many men are there in the world who have as strong a taste for *money* as others have for virtue; who count so much money, so much happiness; nay, even sell their happiness for money; or to speak more properly, make the *having* money, without any design or thought of using it, their ultimate end? But was this propensity to money born with them? or rather, did not they at first perceive a great many advantages from being possessed of money,

[1 Cf. Hutcheson, § 356.]

and from thence conceive a pleasure in having it, thence desire it, thence endeavour to obtain it, thence receive an actual pleasure in obtaining it, thence desire to preserve the possession of it? Hence by dropping the intermediate steps between money and happiness, they join money and happiness immediately together, and content themselves with the fantastical pleasure of having it, and make that which was at first pursued only as a *means*, be to them a real *end*, and what their real happiness or misery consists in. Thus the connection between money and happiness remains in the mind; though it has long since ceased between the things themselves.

The same might be observed concerning the thirst after knowledge, fame, etc., the delight in reading, building, planting, and most of the various exercises and entertainments of life. These were at first entered on with a view to some farther end, but at length become habitual amusements; the idea of pleasure is associated with them, and leads us on still in the same eager pursuit of them, when the first reason is quite vanished, or at least out of our minds. Nay, we find this power of *association* so great as not only to transport our passions and affections beyond their proper bounds, both as to intenseness and duration; as is evident from daily instances of avarice, ambition, love, revenge, etc.; but also, that it is able to transfer them to improper objects, and such as are of a quite different nature from those to which our reason had at first directed them. Thus being accustomed to resent an injury done to our body by a retaliation of the like to him that offered it, we are apt to conceive the same kind of resentment, and often express it in the same manner, upon receiving hurt from a stock or a stone, whereby the hatred which we are used to place on voluntary beings, is substituted in the room of that aversion which belongs to involuntary ones. The like may be observed in most of the other passions above-mentioned.

★   ★   ★   ★

478 There is one thing more to be observed in answer to this objection, and that is, that we do not always (and perhaps not for the most part) *make* this association ourselves, but *learn* it from *others*: i.e. that we annex pleasure or pain to certain things or actions because we see others do it, and acquire principles of action by imitating those whom we admire, or whose esteem we would procure: hence the son too often inherits both the vices and the party of his father, as well as his estate: hence *national* virtues and vices, dispositions and opinions: and from hence we may observe how easy it is to account for what is generally called the *prejudice of education*;[1] how soon we catch the temper and affections of those whom we daily converse with; how almost insensibly we are *taught* to love, admire or hate; to be grateful, generous, compassionate or cruel, etc.

What I say then in answer to the objection is this: 'That it is necessary in order to solve the principal actions of human life to suppose a *moral sense* (or what is signified by that name) and also *public affections*; but I deny that this moral sense, or these public affections, are innate, or *implanted* in us. They are acquired either from our own *observation* or the *imitation* of others.'

[1 Cf. Wollaston, § 292; and contrast Hutcheson, § 312.]